KIERON GILLEN   DAN MORA
TAMRA BONVILLAIN

ONCE &
FUTURE™

VOLUME ONE
THE KING IS UNDEAD

BOOM!
STUDIOS

DESIGNER
SCOTT NEWMAN

ASSOCIATE EDITOR
AMANDA LaFRANCO

EDITOR
MATT GAGNON

ONCE & FUTURE Volume One, March 2020.
Published by BOOM! Studios, a division of
Boom Entertainment, inc. Once & Future
is ™ & © 2020 Kieron Gillen, Ltd. Originally
published in single magazine form as ONCE
& FUTURE No. 1-6. ™ & © 2019 Kieron Gillen, Ltd. All rights reserved.
BOOM! Studios™ and the BOOM! Studios logo are trademarks of Boom
Entertainment, inc., registered in various countries and categories.
All characters, events, and institutions depicted herein are fictional.
Any similarity between any of the names, characters, persons, events,
and/or institutions in this publication to actual names, characters,
and persons, whether living or dead, events, and/or institutions is
unintended and purely coincidental. BOOM! Studios does not read or
accept unsolicited submissions of ideas, stories, or artwork.

For information regarding the CPSIA on this printed material, call: (203)
595-3636 and provide reference #RICH – 879549.

BOOM! Studios, 5670 Wilshire Boulevard, Suite 450, Los Angeles, CA
90036-5679. Printed in USA. First Printing.

ISBN: 978-1-68415-491-3, eISBN: 978-1-64144-649-5

Forbidden Planet, Big Bang Comics, & Jetpack Comics Exclusive Edition
ISBN: 978-1-68415-643-6

WRITTEN BY
KIERON GILLEN

ILLUSTRATED BY
DAN MORA

COLORED BY
TAMRA BONVILLAIN

LETTERED BY
ED DUKESHIRE

COVER BY
DAN MORA

FORBIDDEN PLANET, BIG BANG COMICS,
& JETPACK COMICS EXCLUSIVE VARIANT COVER BY
DAVID LAFUENTE
WITH COLORS BY GERMÁN GARCÍA

ONCE & FUTURE ™

CREATED BY **KIERON GILLEN** AND **DAN MORA**

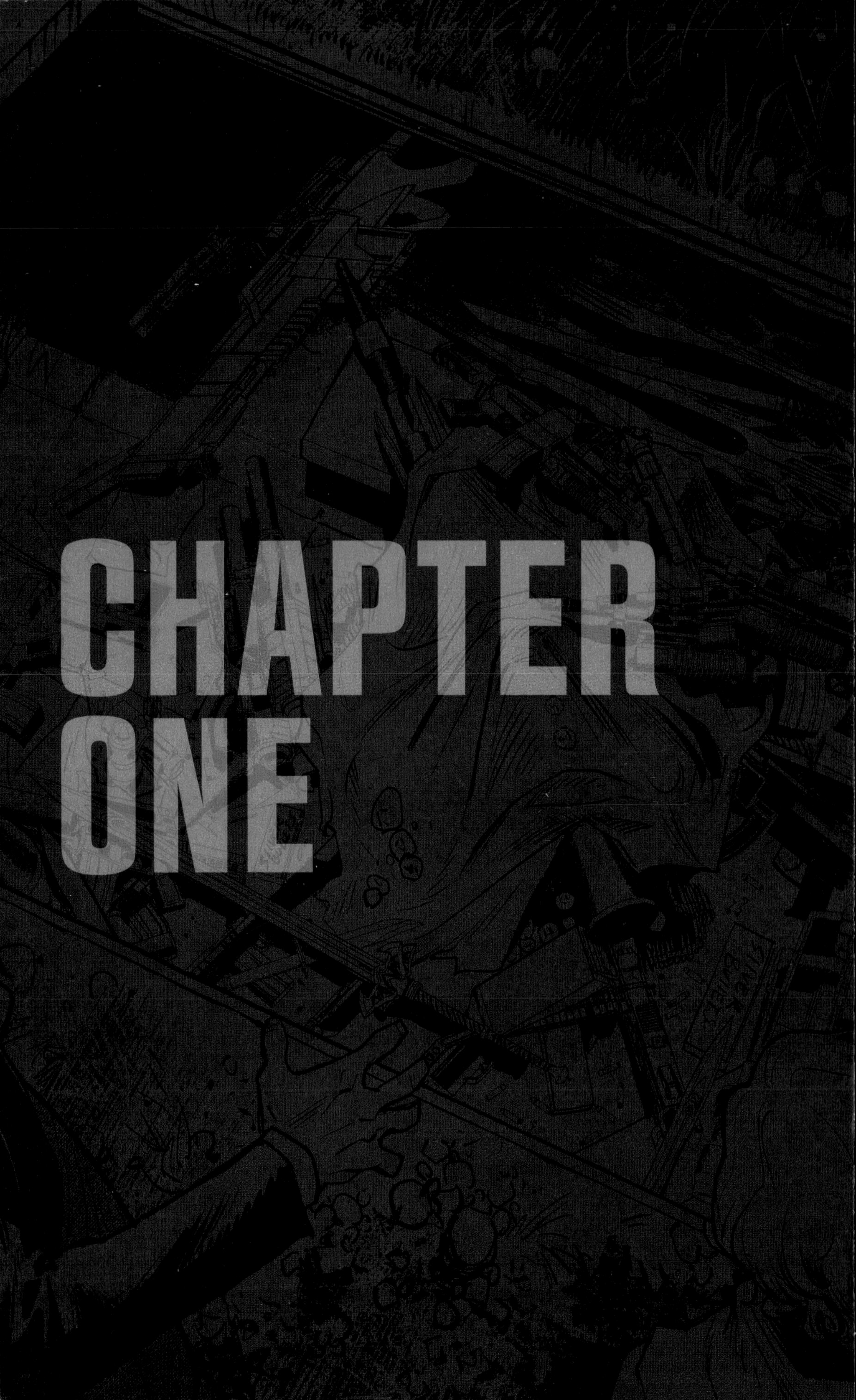

CHAPTER ONE

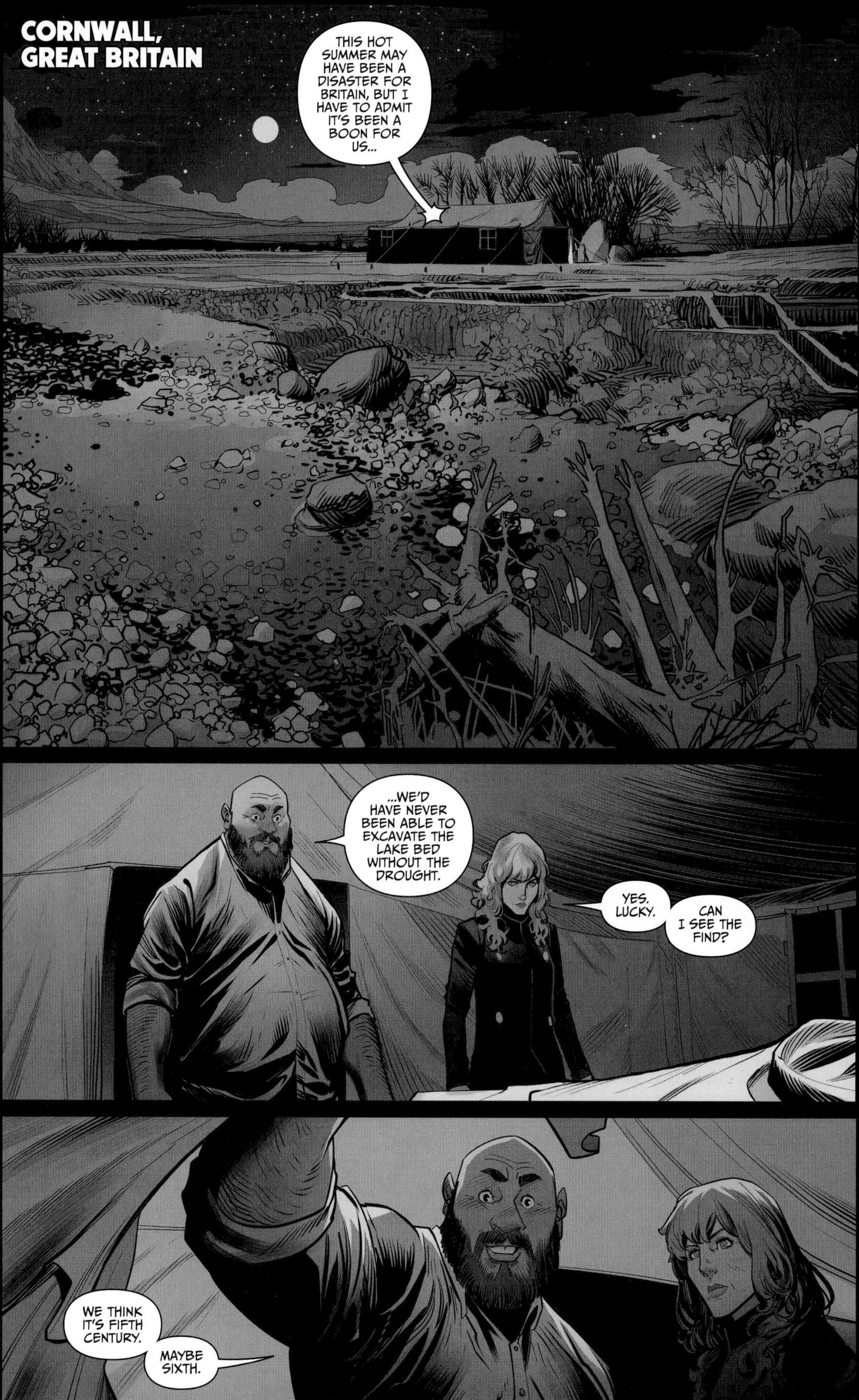
CORNWALL, GREAT BRITAIN
THIS HOT SUMMER MAY HAVE BEEN A DISASTER FOR BRITAIN, BUT I HAVE TO ADMIT IT'S BEEN A BOON FOR US...
...WE'D HAVE NEVER BEEN ABLE TO EXCAVATE THE LAKE BED WITHOUT THE DROUGHT.
YES. LUCKY.
CAN I SEE THE FIND?
WE THINK IT'S FIFTH CENTURY.
MAYBE SIXTH.

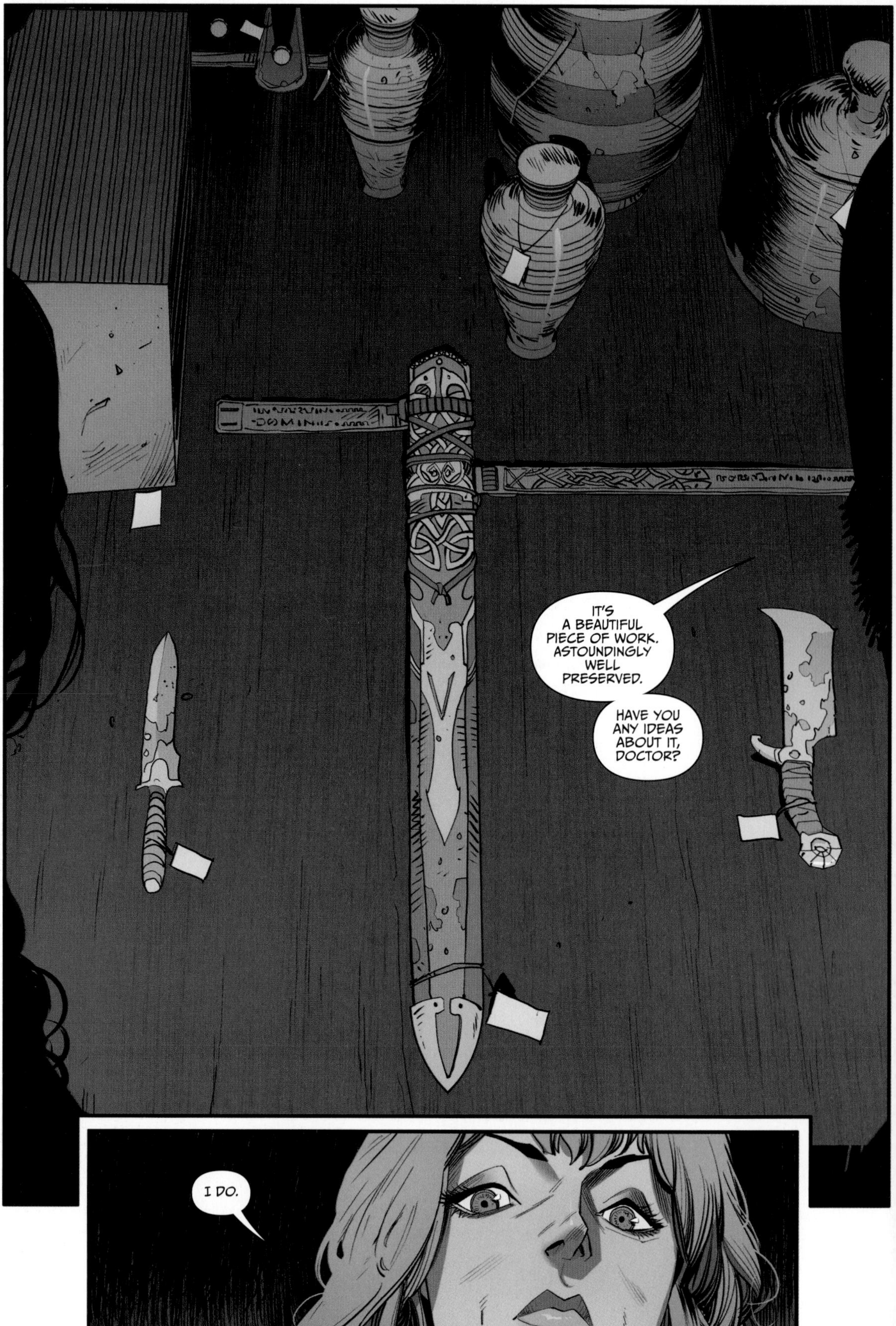
IT'S A BEAUTIFUL PIECE OF WORK. ASTOUNDINGLY WELL PRESERVED.
HAVE YOU ANY IDEAS ABOUT IT, DOCTOR?

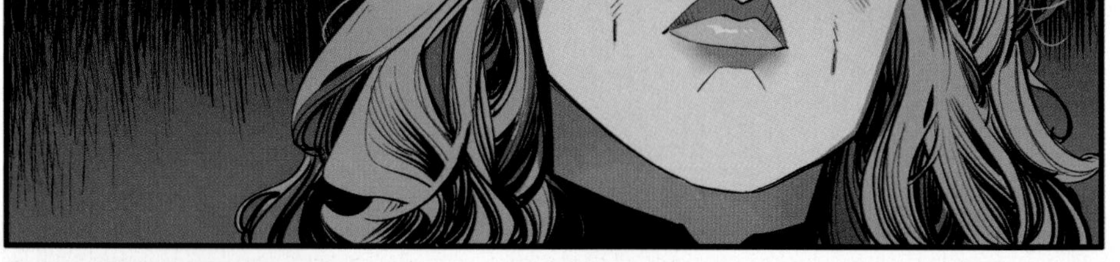
I DO.

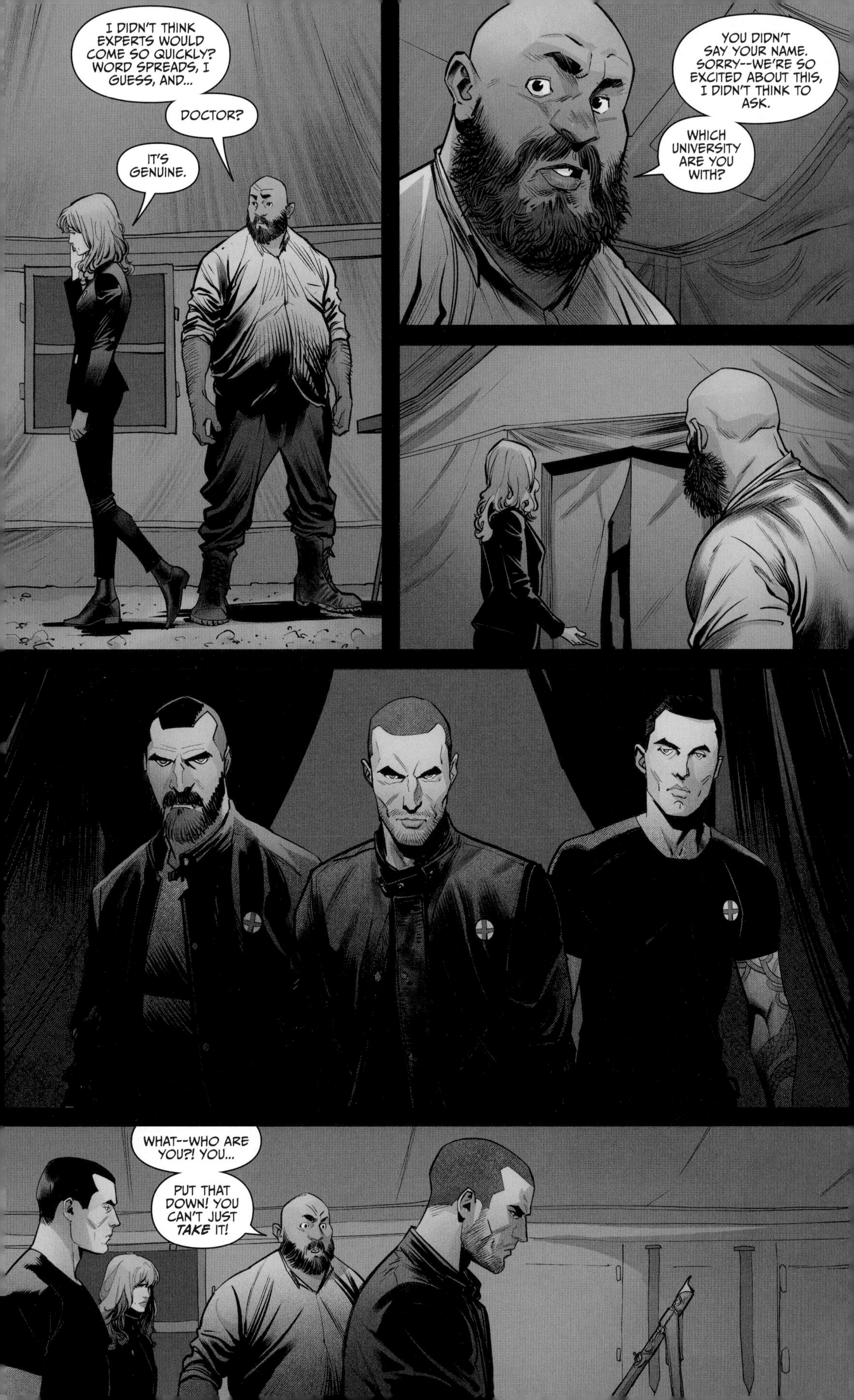
I DIDN'T THINK EXPERTS WOULD COME SO QUICKLY? WORD SPREADS, I GUESS, AND...
DOCTOR?
IT'S GENUINE.
YOU DIDN'T SAY YOUR NAME. SORRY--WE'RE SO EXCITED ABOUT THIS, I DIDN'T THINK TO ASK.
WHICH UNIVERSITY ARE YOU WITH?
WHAT--WHO ARE YOU?! YOU...
PUT THAT DOWN! YOU CAN'T JUST *TAKE* IT!

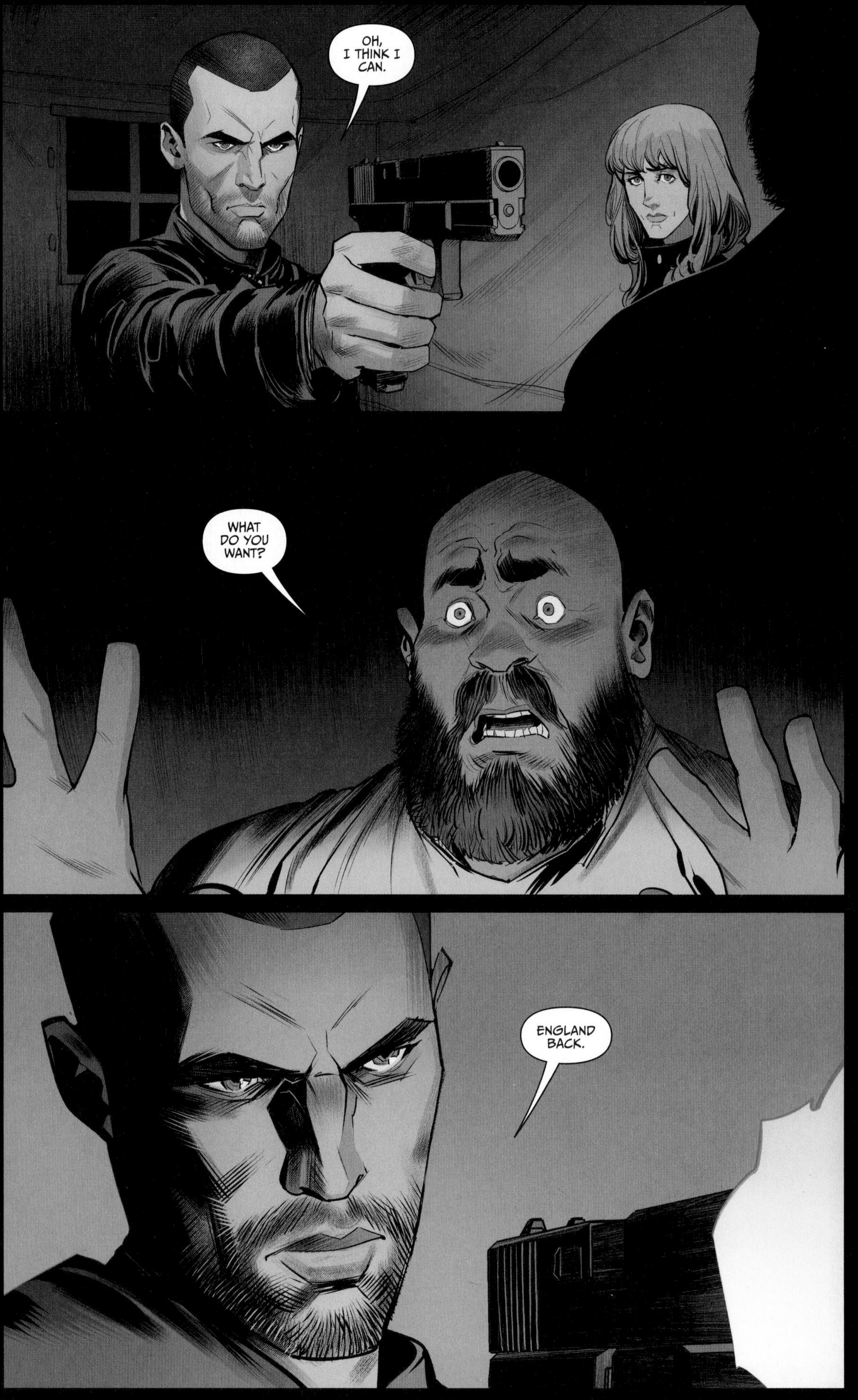
OH, I THINK I CAN.
WHAT DO YOU WANT?
ENGLAND BACK.

ONCE & FUTURE™

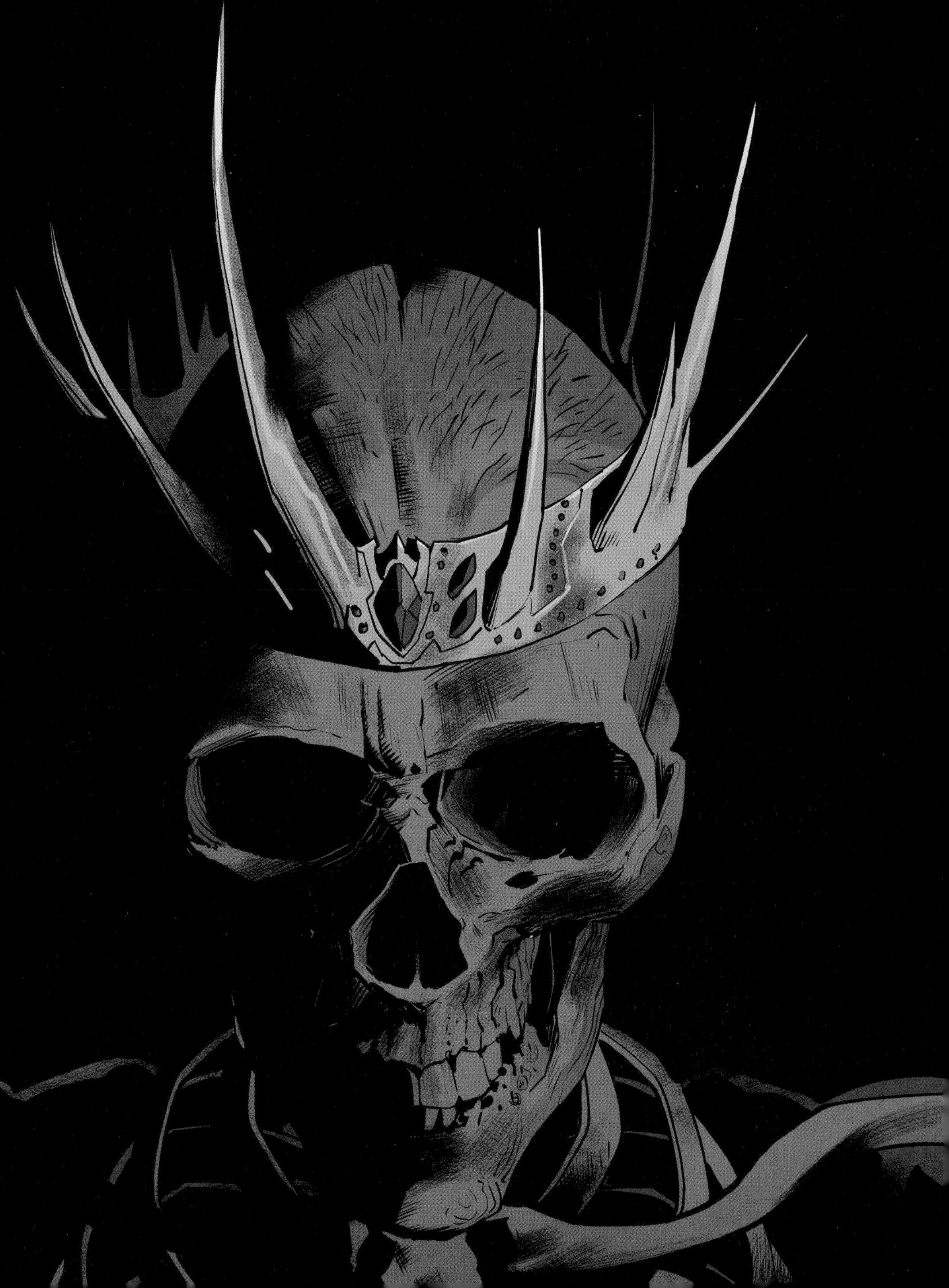

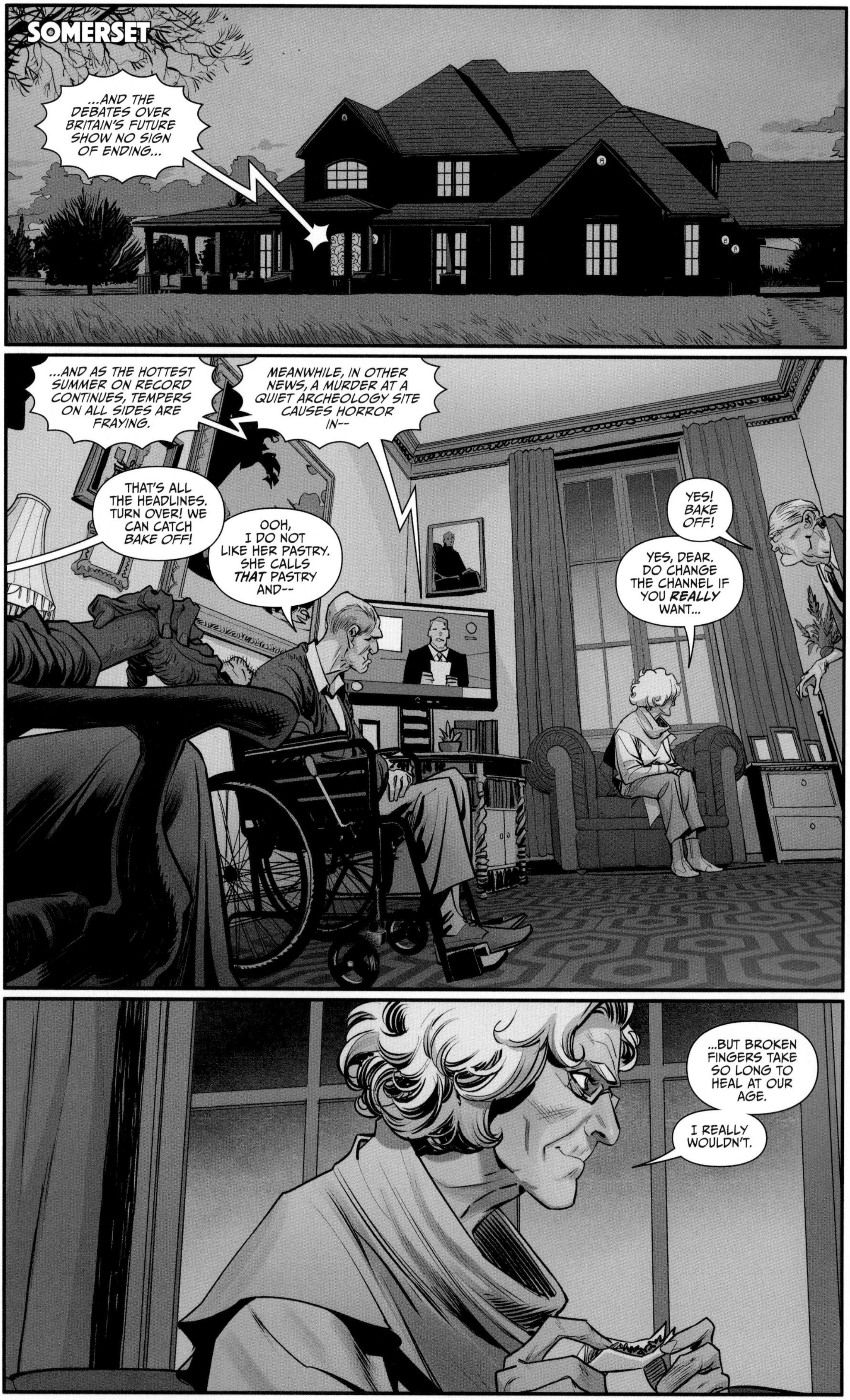

SOMERSET
...AND THE DEBATES OVER BRITAIN'S FUTURE SHOW NO SIGN OF ENDING...
...AND AS THE HOTTEST SUMMER ON RECORD CONTINUES, TEMPERS ON ALL SIDES ARE FRAYING.
MEANWHILE, IN OTHER NEWS, A MURDER AT A QUIET ARCHEOLOGY SITE CAUSES HORROR IN--
THAT'S ALL THE HEADLINES. TURN OVER! WE CAN CATCH BAKE OFF!
OOH, I DO NOT LIKE HER PASTRY. SHE CALLS THAT PASTRY AND--
YES! BAKE OFF!
YES, DEAR. DO CHANGE THE CHANNEL IF YOU REALLY WANT...
...BUT BROKEN FINGERS TAKE SO LONG TO HEAL AT OUR AGE.
I REALLY WOULDN'T.

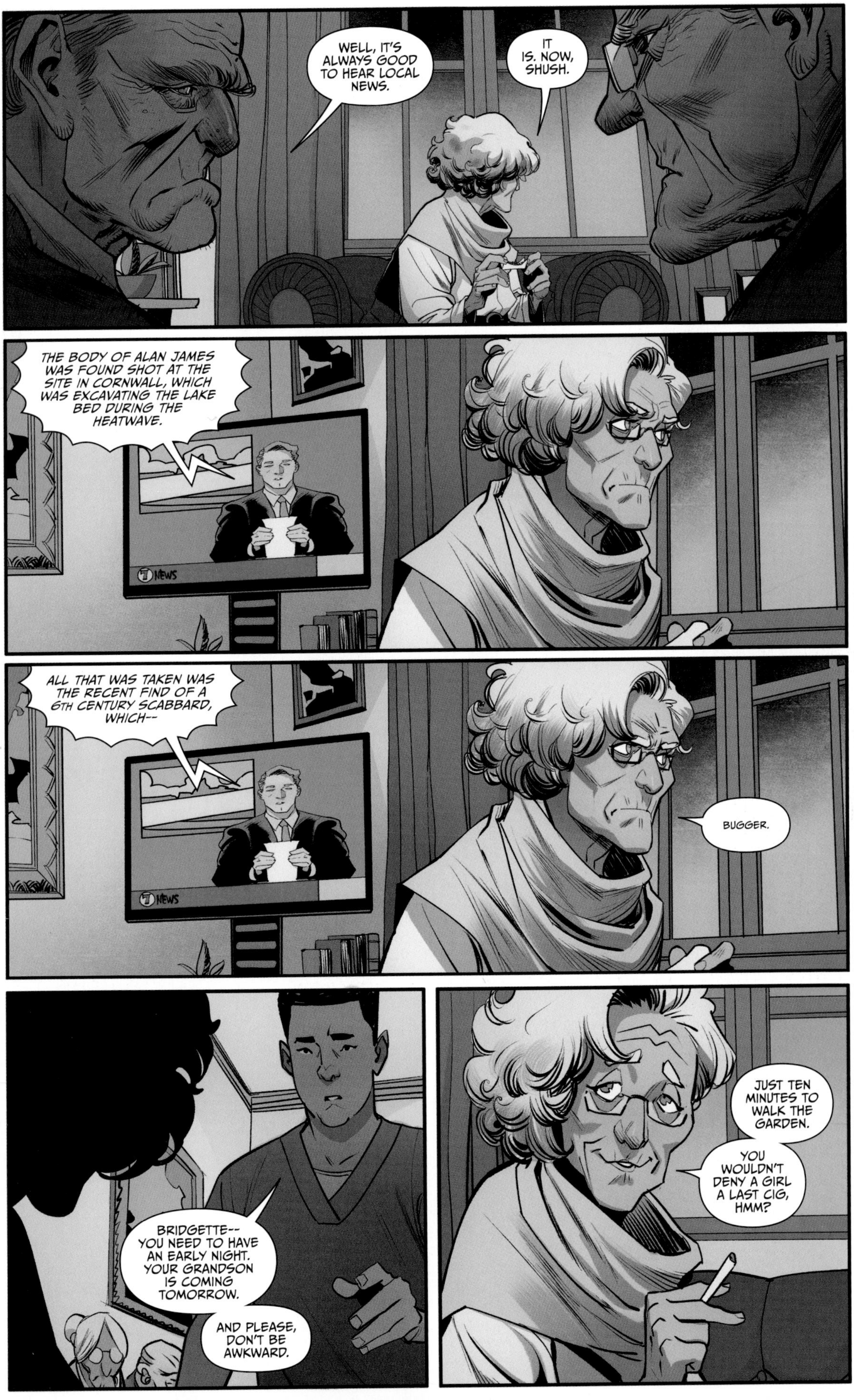
WELL, IT'S ALWAYS GOOD TO HEAR LOCAL NEWS.
IT IS. NOW, SHUSH.
THE BODY OF ALAN JAMES WAS FOUND SHOT AT THE SITE IN CORNWALL, WHICH WAS EXCAVATING THE LAKE BED DURING THE HEATWAVE.
NEWS
ALL THAT WAS TAKEN WAS THE RECENT FIND OF A 6TH CENTURY SCABBARD, WHICH--
NEWS
BUGGER.
BRIDGETTE-- YOU NEED TO HAVE AN EARLY NIGHT. YOUR GRANDSON IS COMING TOMORROW.
AND PLEASE, DON'T BE AWKWARD.
JUST TEN MINUTES TO WALK THE GARDEN.
YOU WOULDN'T DENY A GIRL A LAST CIG, HMM?

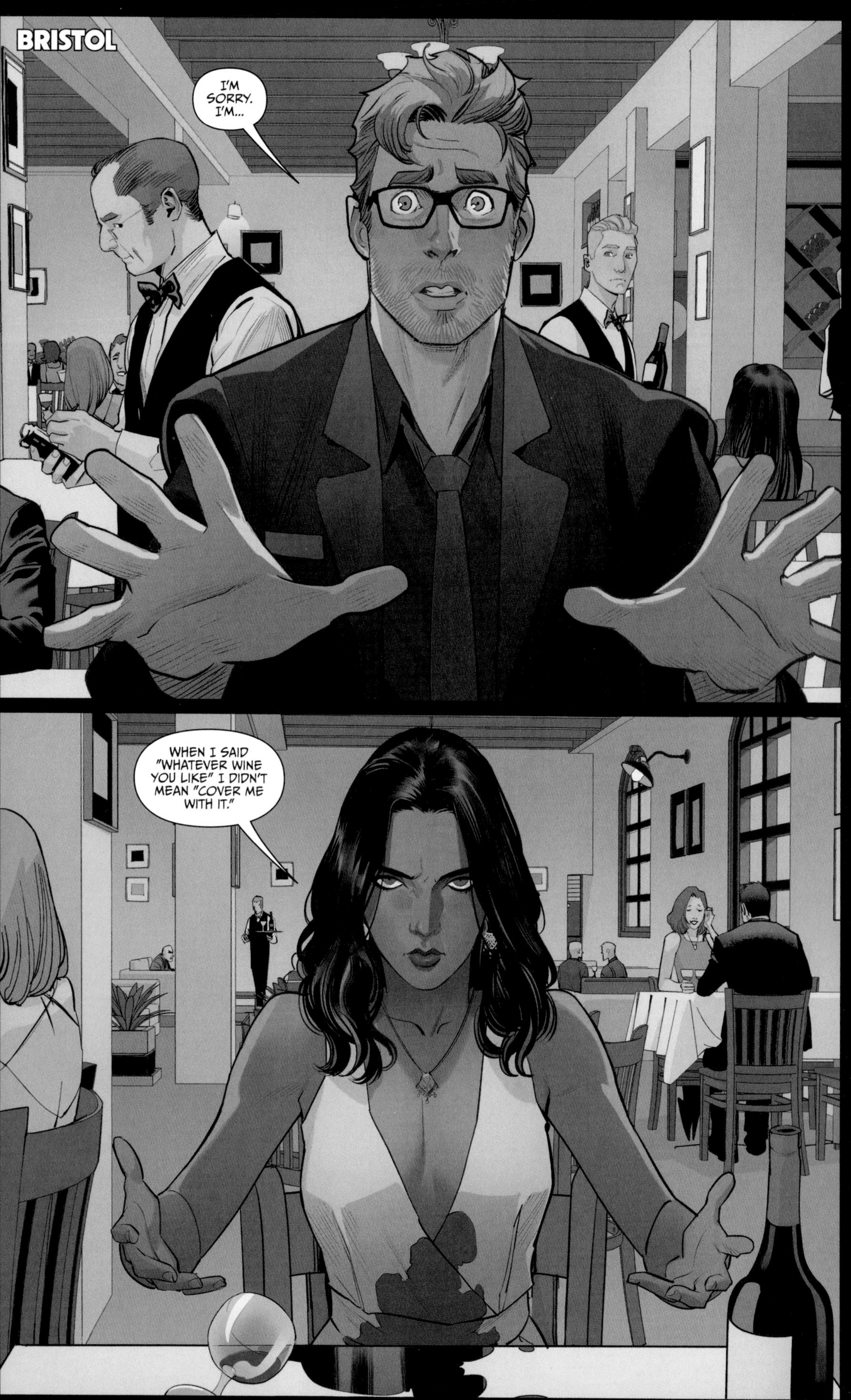
BRISTOL
I'M SORRY. I'M...
WHEN I SAID "WHATEVER WINE YOU LIKE" I DIDN'T MEAN "COVER ME WITH IT."

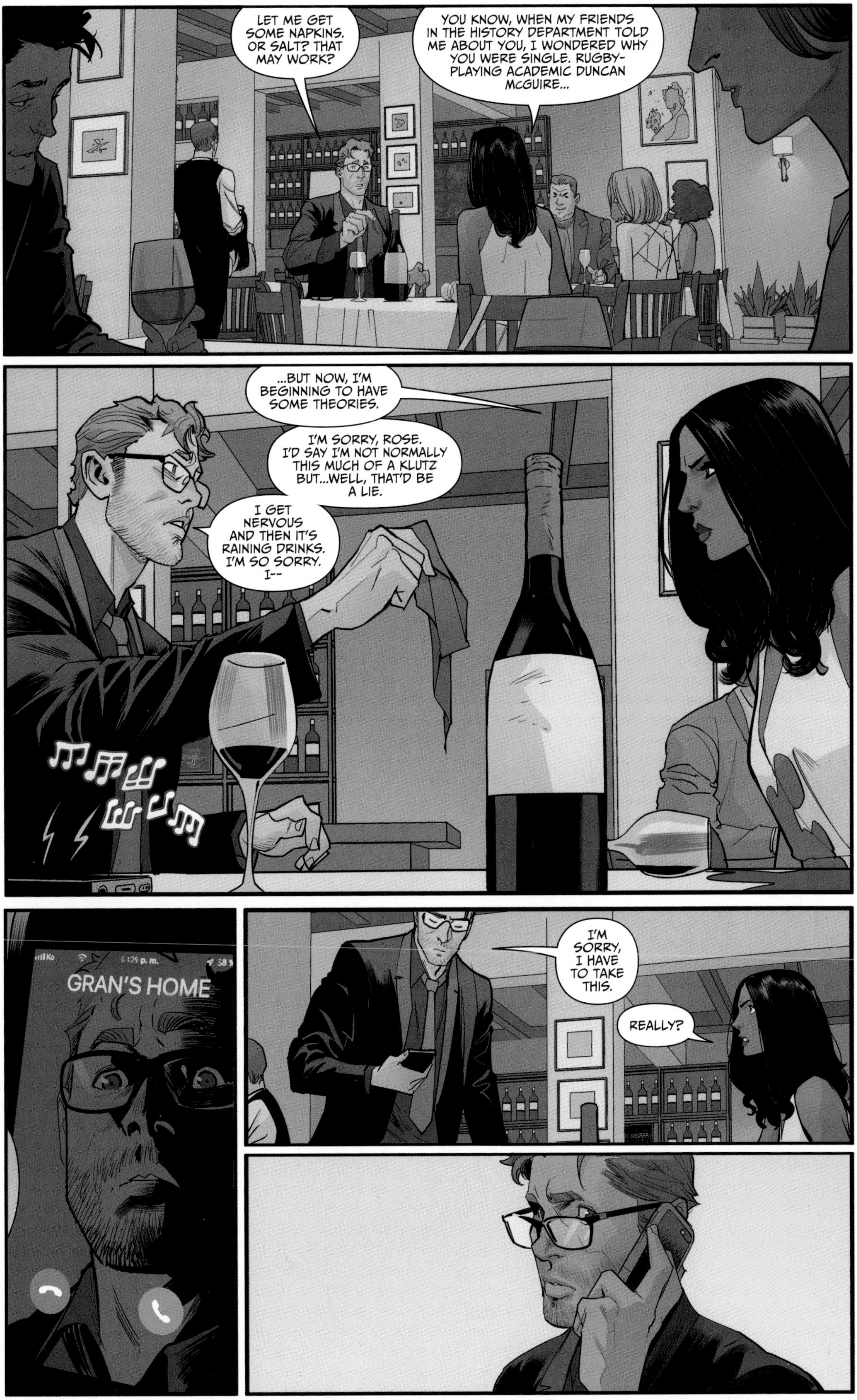
LET ME GET SOME NAPKINS. OR SALT? THAT MAY WORK?
YOU KNOW, WHEN MY FRIENDS IN THE HISTORY DEPARTMENT TOLD ME ABOUT YOU, I WONDERED WHY YOU WERE SINGLE. RUGBY-PLAYING ACADEMIC DUNCAN McGUIRE...
...BUT NOW, I'M BEGINNING TO HAVE SOME THEORIES.
I'M SORRY, ROSE. I'D SAY I'M NOT NORMALLY THIS MUCH OF A KLUTZ BUT...WELL, THAT'D BE A LIE.
I GET NERVOUS AND THEN IT'S RAINING DRINKS. I'M SO SORRY. I--
6:29 p. m.
GRAN'S HOME
I'M SORRY, I HAVE TO TAKE THIS.
REALLY?

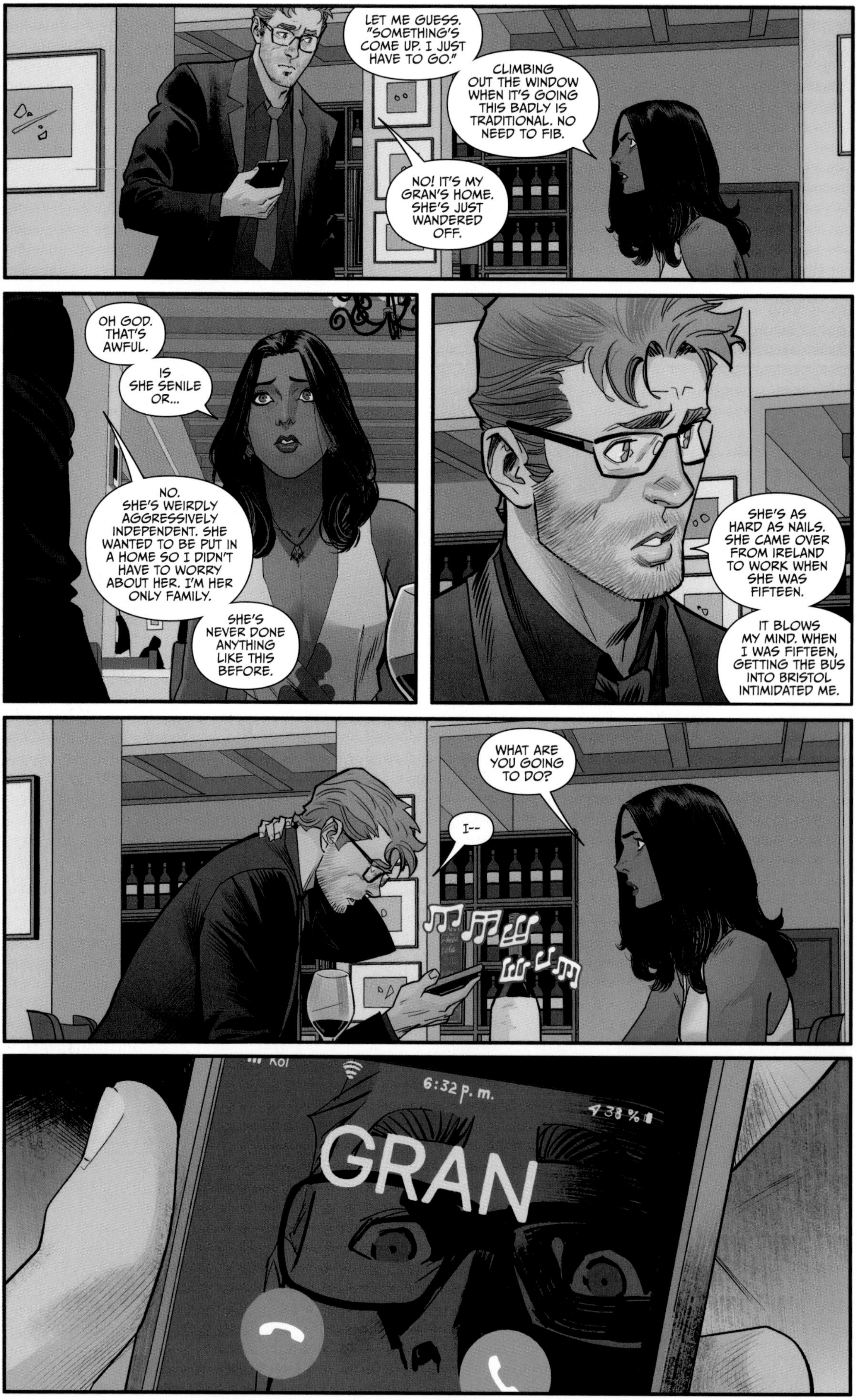
LET ME GUESS. "SOMETHING'S COME UP. I JUST HAVE TO GO."
CLIMBING OUT THE WINDOW WHEN IT'S GOING THIS BADLY IS TRADITIONAL. NO NEED TO FIB.
NO! IT'S MY GRAN'S HOME. SHE'S JUST WANDERED OFF.
OH GOD. THAT'S AWFUL.
IS SHE SENILE OR...
NO. SHE'S WEIRDLY AGGRESSIVELY INDEPENDENT. SHE WANTED TO BE PUT IN A HOME SO I DIDN'T HAVE TO WORRY ABOUT HER. I'M HER ONLY FAMILY.
SHE'S NEVER DONE ANYTHING LIKE THIS BEFORE.
SHE'S AS HARD AS NAILS. SHE CAME OVER FROM IRELAND TO WORK WHEN SHE WAS FIFTEEN.
IT BLOWS MY MIND. WHEN I WAS FIFTEEN, GETTING THE BUS INTO BRISTOL INTIMIDATED ME.
WHAT ARE YOU GOING TO DO?
I--
6:32 p. m.
38 %
GRAN

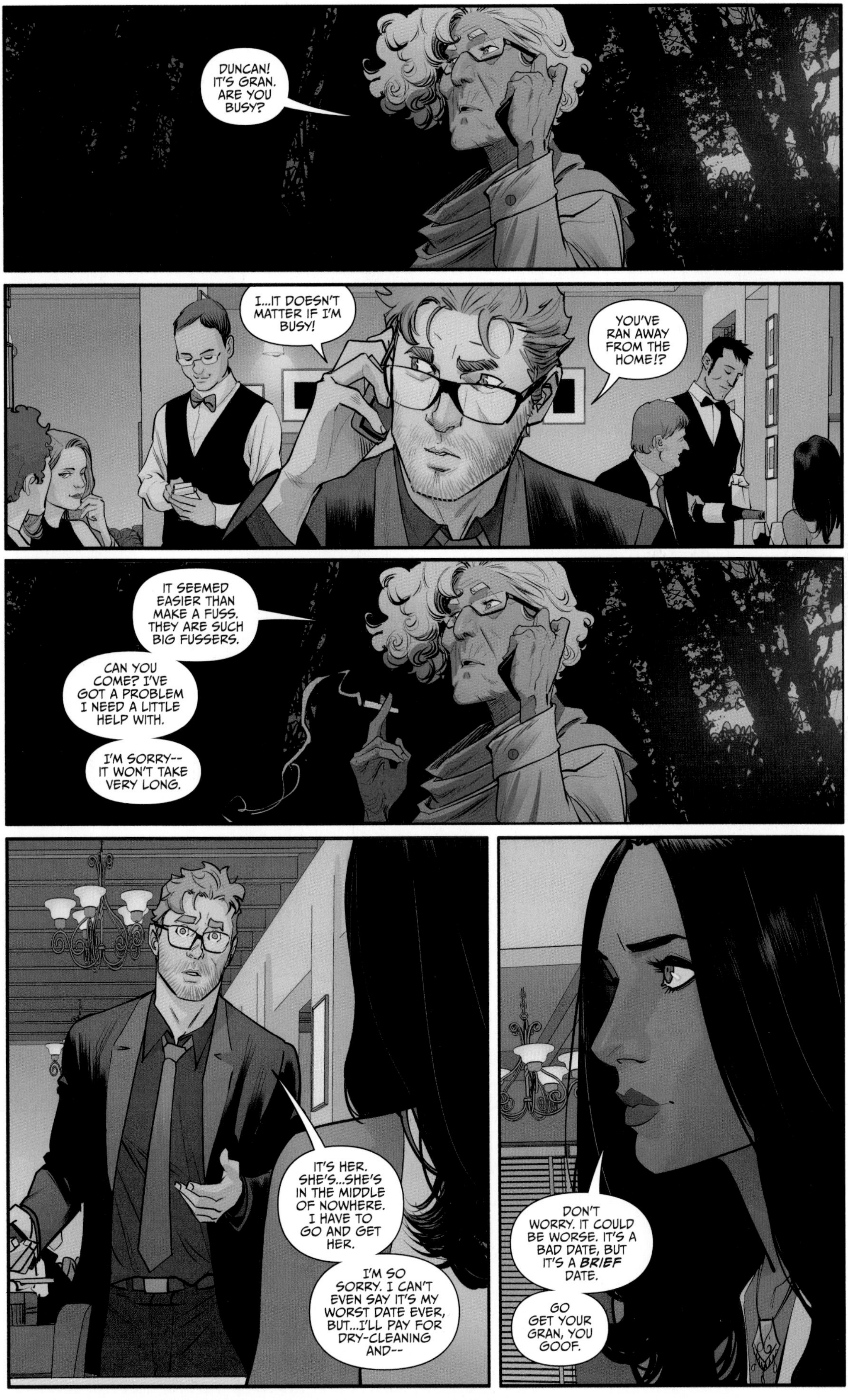
DUNCAN! IT'S GRAN. ARE YOU BUSY?
I...IT DOESN'T MATTER IF I'M BUSY!
YOU'VE RAN AWAY FROM THE HOME!?
IT SEEMED EASIER THAN MAKE A FUSS. THEY ARE SUCH BIG FUSSERS.
CAN YOU COME? I'VE GOT A PROBLEM I NEED A LITTLE HELP WITH.
I'M SORRY-- IT WON'T TAKE VERY LONG.
IT'S HER. SHE'S...SHE'S IN THE MIDDLE OF NOWHERE. I HAVE TO GO AND GET HER.
I'M SO SORRY. I CAN'T EVEN SAY IT'S MY WORST DATE EVER, BUT...I'LL PAY FOR DRY-CLEANING AND--
DON'T WORRY. IT COULD BE WORSE. IT'S A BAD DATE, BUT IT'S A *BRIEF* DATE.
GO GET YOUR GRAN, YOU GOOF.

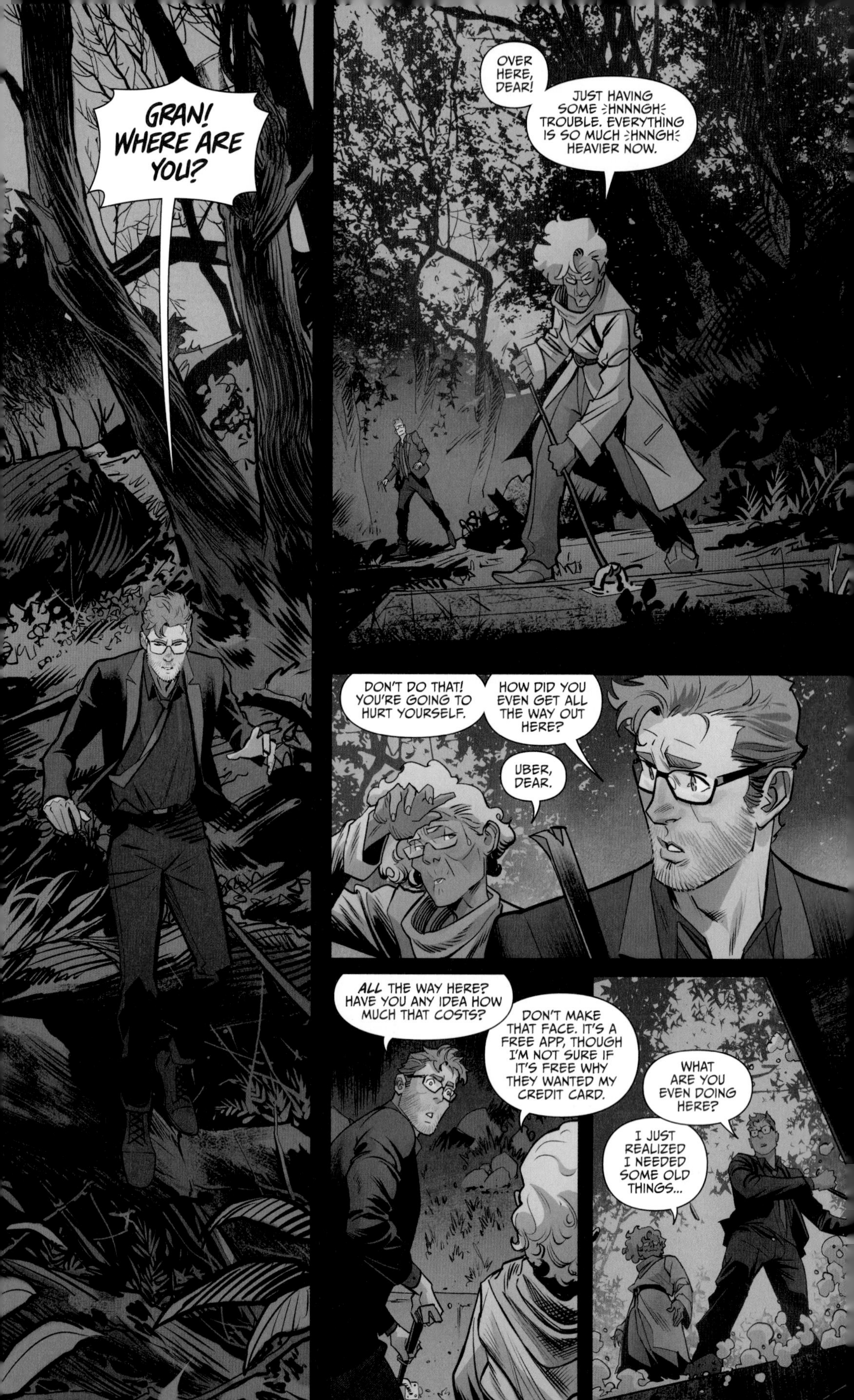
GRAN! WHERE ARE YOU?
OVER HERE, DEAR!
JUST HAVING SOME ≶HNNNGH≷ TROUBLE. EVERYTHING IS SO MUCH ≶HNNGH≷ HEAVIER NOW.
DON'T DO THAT! YOU'RE GOING TO HURT YOURSELF.
HOW DID YOU EVEN GET ALL THE WAY OUT HERE?
UBER, DEAR.
ALL THE WAY HERE? HAVE YOU ANY IDEA HOW MUCH THAT COSTS?
DON'T MAKE THAT FACE. IT'S A FREE APP, THOUGH I'M NOT SURE IF IT'S FREE WHY THEY WANTED MY CREDIT CARD.
WHAT ARE YOU EVEN DOING HERE?
I JUST REALIZED I NEEDED SOME OLD THINGS...

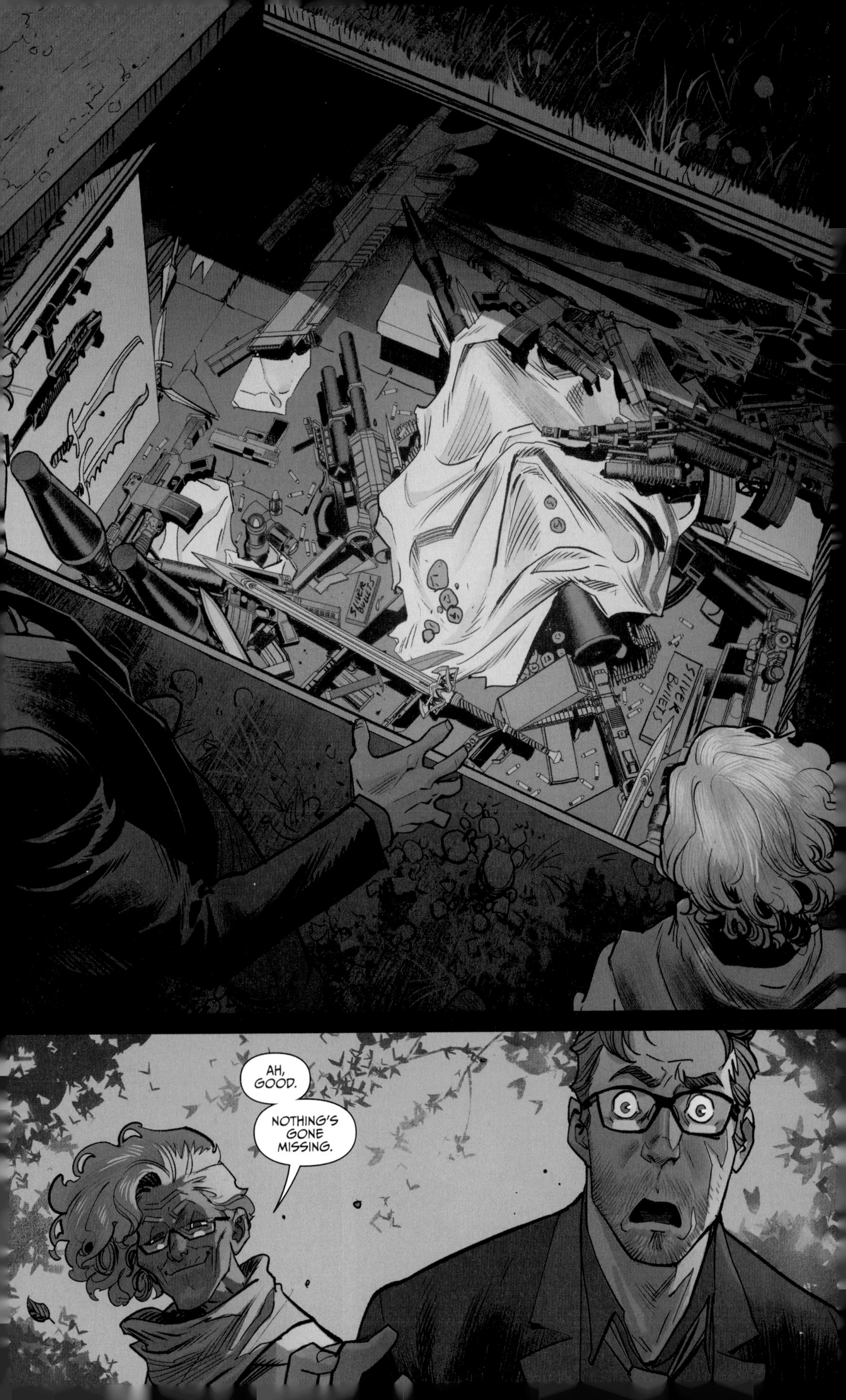
SILVER BULLETS
SILVER BULLETS
AH, GOOD.
NOTHING'S GONE MISSING.

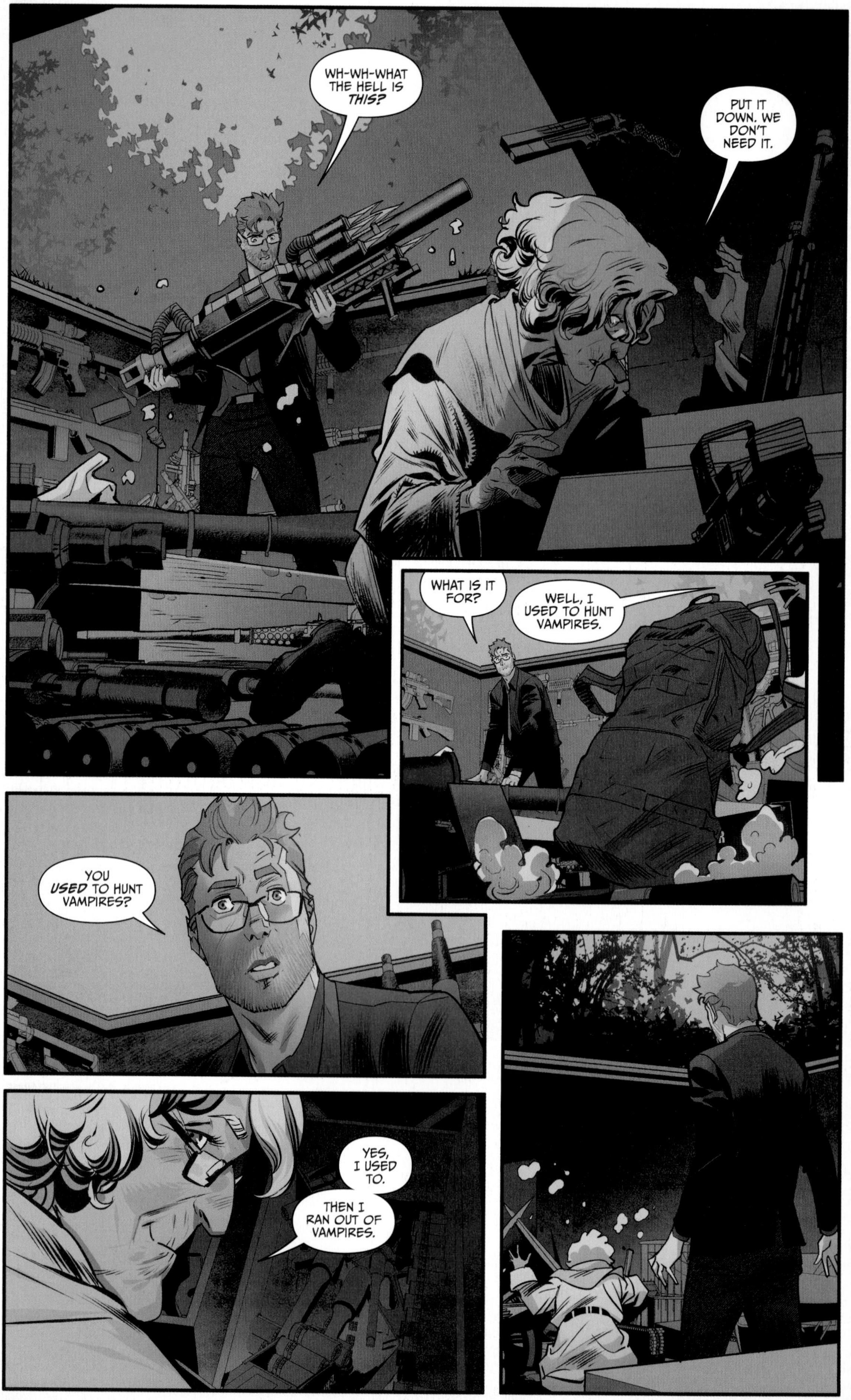
WH-WH-WHAT THE HELL IS *THIS?*
PUT IT DOWN. WE DON'T NEED IT.
WHAT IS IT FOR?
WELL, I USED TO HUNT VAMPIRES.
YOU *USED* TO HUNT VAMPIRES?
YES, I USED TO.
THEN I RAN OUT OF VAMPIRES.

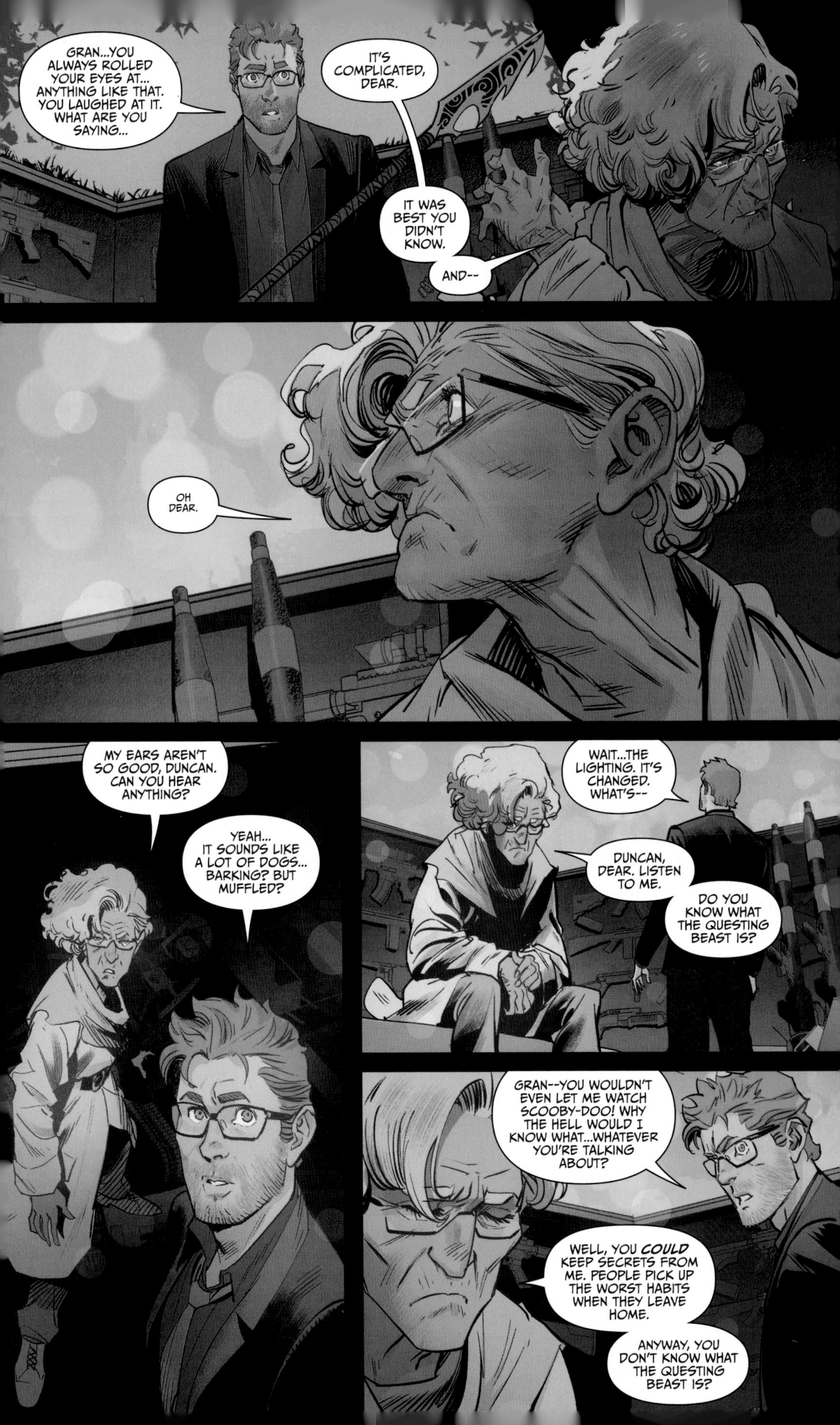
GRAN...YOU ALWAYS ROLLED YOUR EYES AT... ANYTHING LIKE THAT. YOU LAUGHED AT IT. WHAT ARE YOU SAYING...
IT'S COMPLICATED, DEAR.
IT WAS BEST YOU DIDN'T KNOW.
AND--
OH DEAR.
MY EARS AREN'T SO GOOD, DUNCAN. CAN YOU HEAR ANYTHING?
YEAH... IT SOUNDS LIKE A LOT OF DOGS... BARKING? BUT MUFFLED?
WAIT...THE LIGHTING. IT'S CHANGED. WHAT'S--
DUNCAN, DEAR. LISTEN TO ME.
DO YOU KNOW WHAT THE QUESTING BEAST IS?
GRAN--YOU WOULDN'T EVEN LET ME WATCH SCOOBY-DOO! WHY THE HELL WOULD I KNOW WHAT...WHATEVER YOU'RE TALKING ABOUT?
WELL, YOU *COULD* KEEP SECRETS FROM ME. PEOPLE PICK UP THE WORST HABITS WHEN THEY LEAVE HOME.
ANYWAY, YOU DON'T KNOW WHAT THE QUESTING BEAST IS?

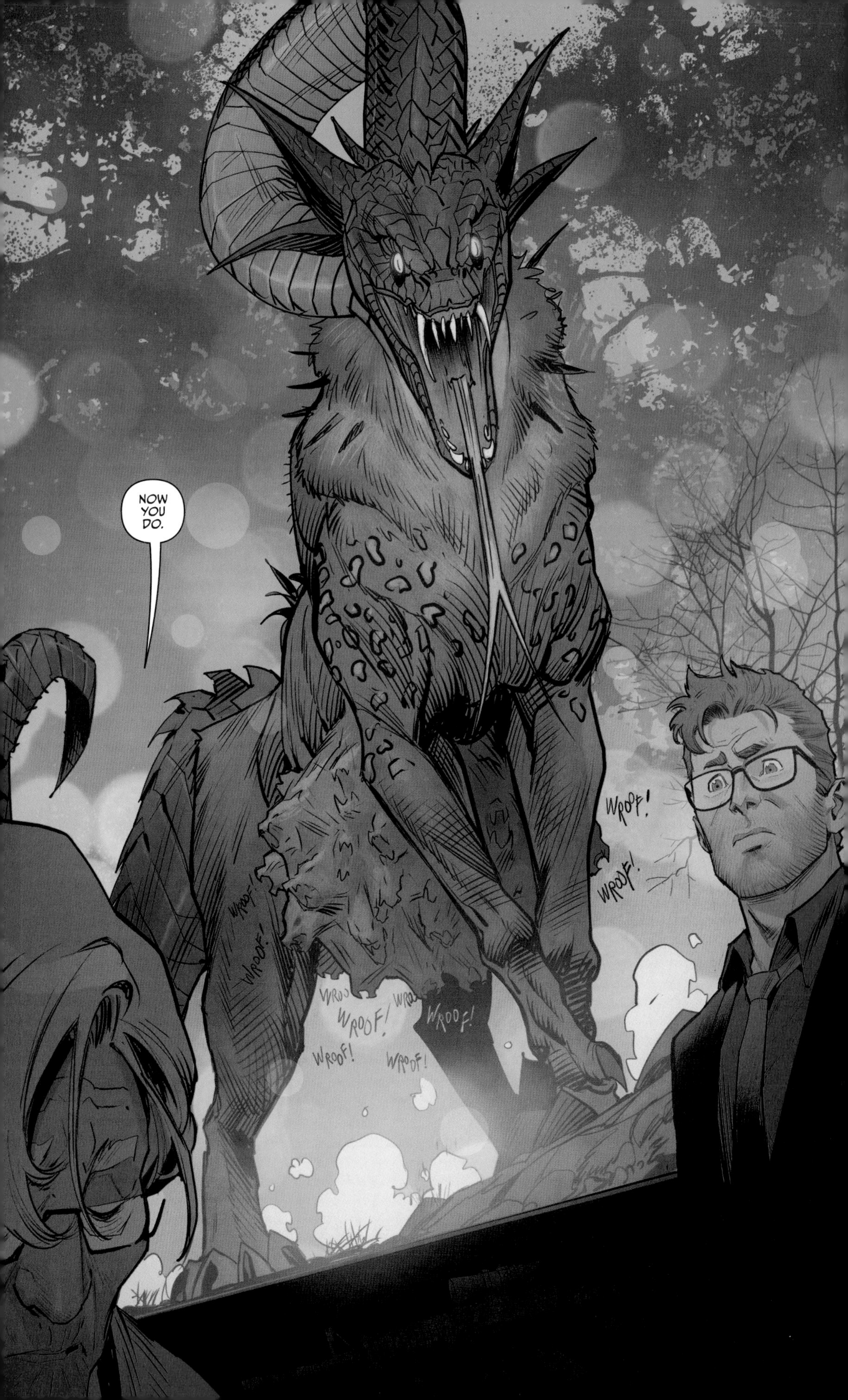
NOW YOU DO.
WROOF!
WROOF!
WROOF!
WROOF!
WROOF!
WROOF!
WROOF!
WROOF!

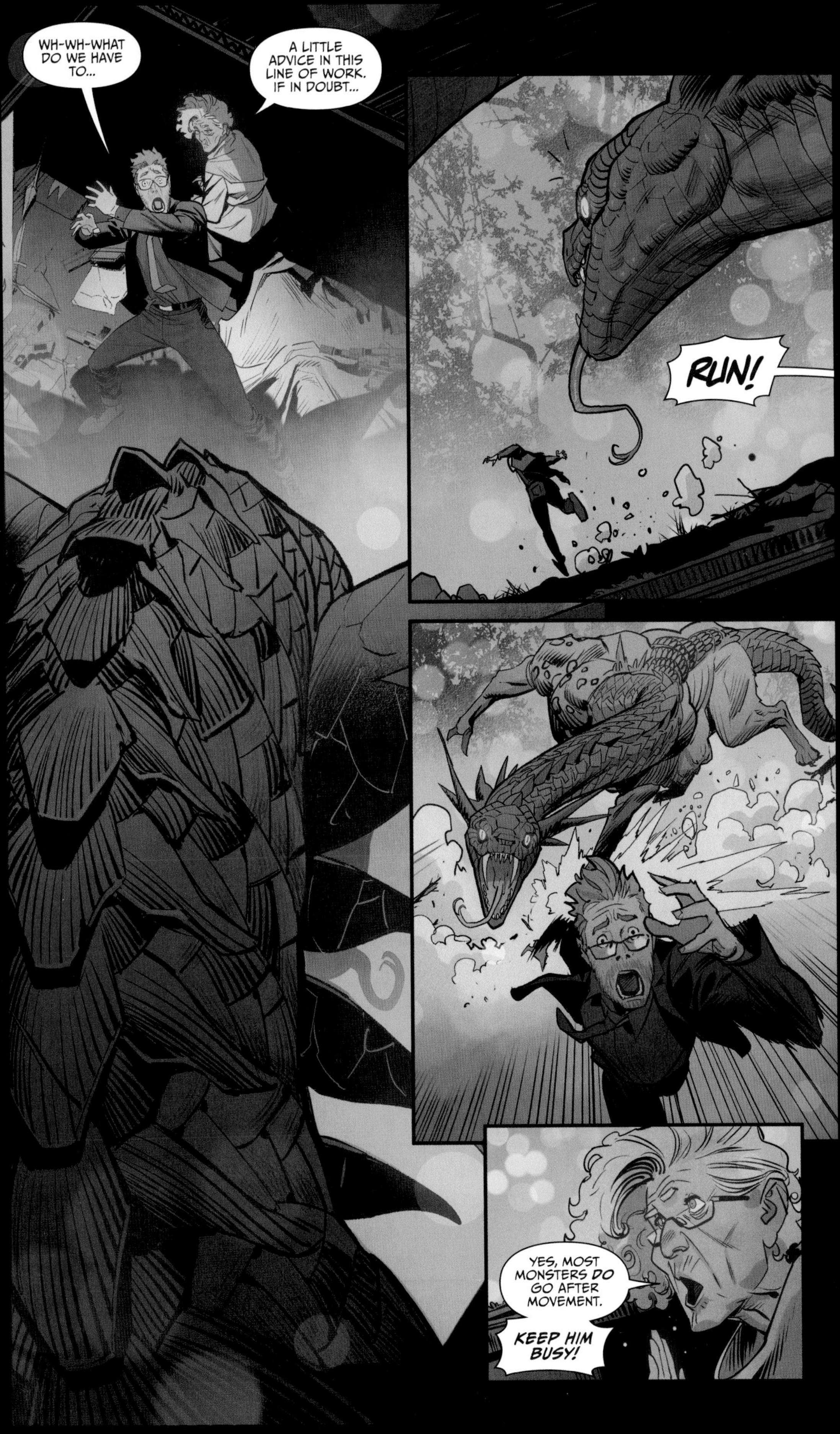
WH-WH-WHAT DO WE HAVE TO...
A LITTLE ADVICE IN THIS LINE OF WORK. IF IN DOUBT...
RUN!
YES, MOST MONSTERS DO GO AFTER MOVEMENT.
KEEP HIM BUSY!

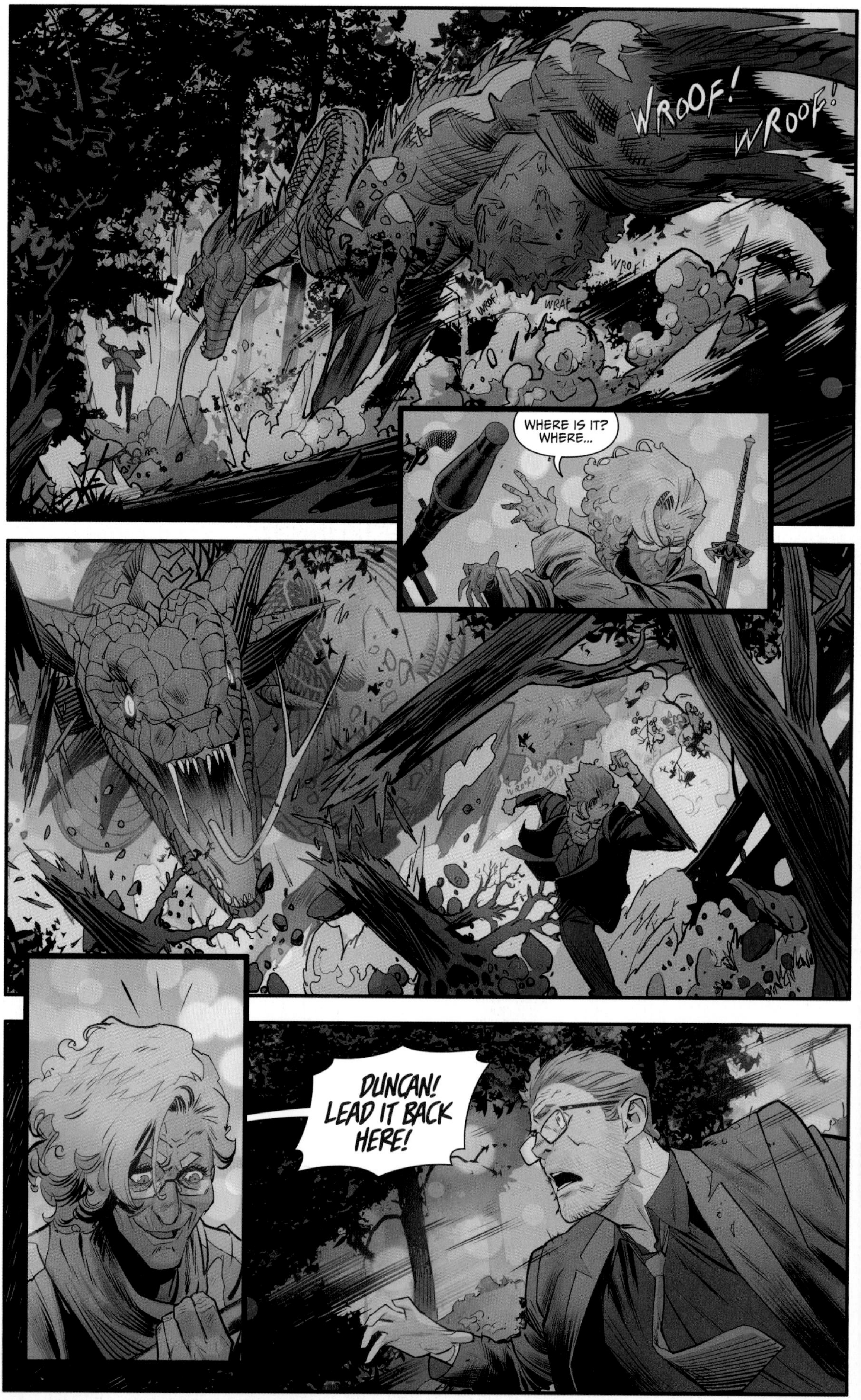
WROOF!
WROOF!
WROF!
WRAF
WROF!
WHERE IS IT? WHERE...
DUNCAN! LEAD IT BACK HERE!

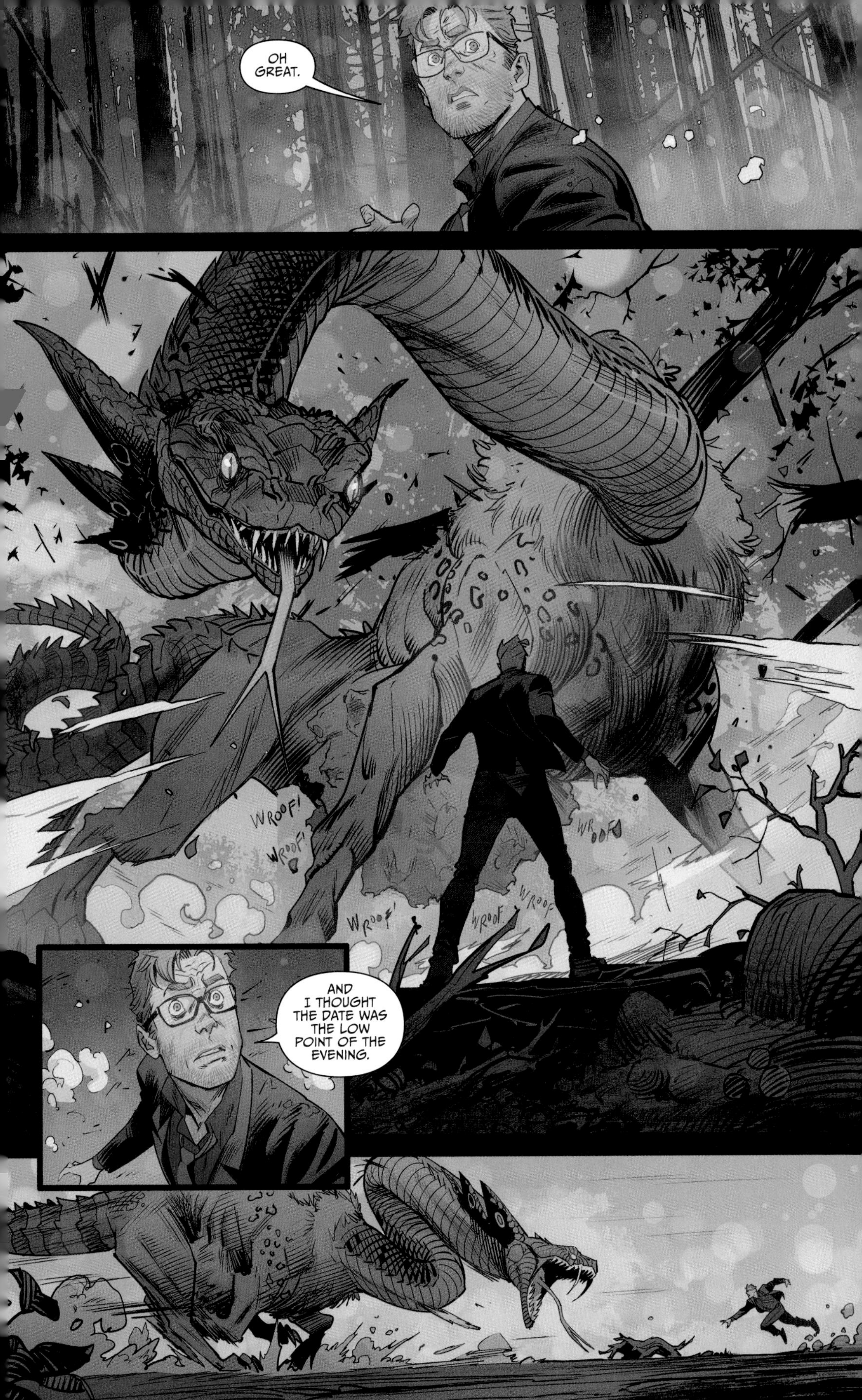
OH GREAT.
WROOF!
WROOF!
WROOF!
WROOF!
WROOF!
WROOF!
AND I THOUGHT THE DATE WAS THE LOW POINT OF THE EVENING.

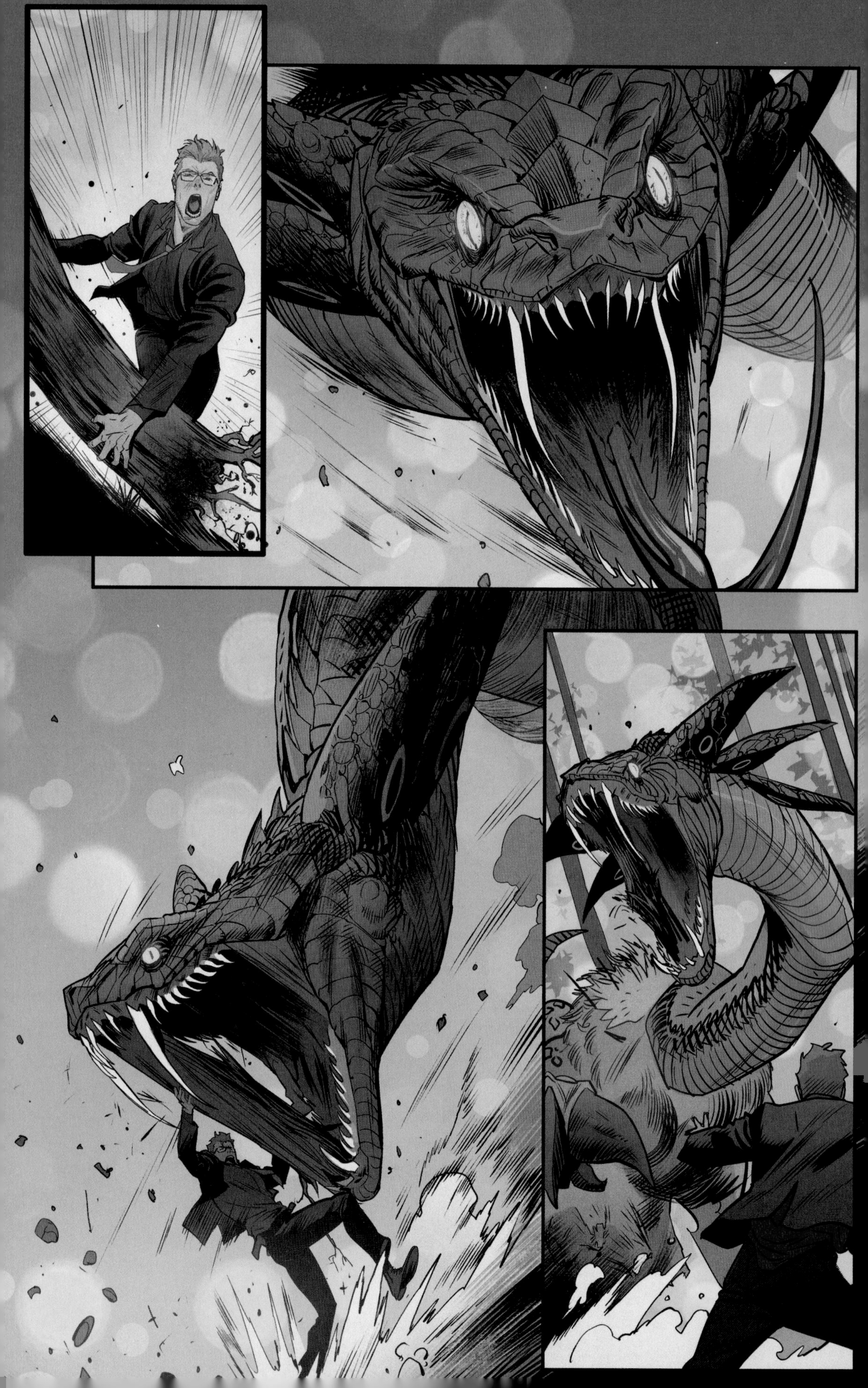

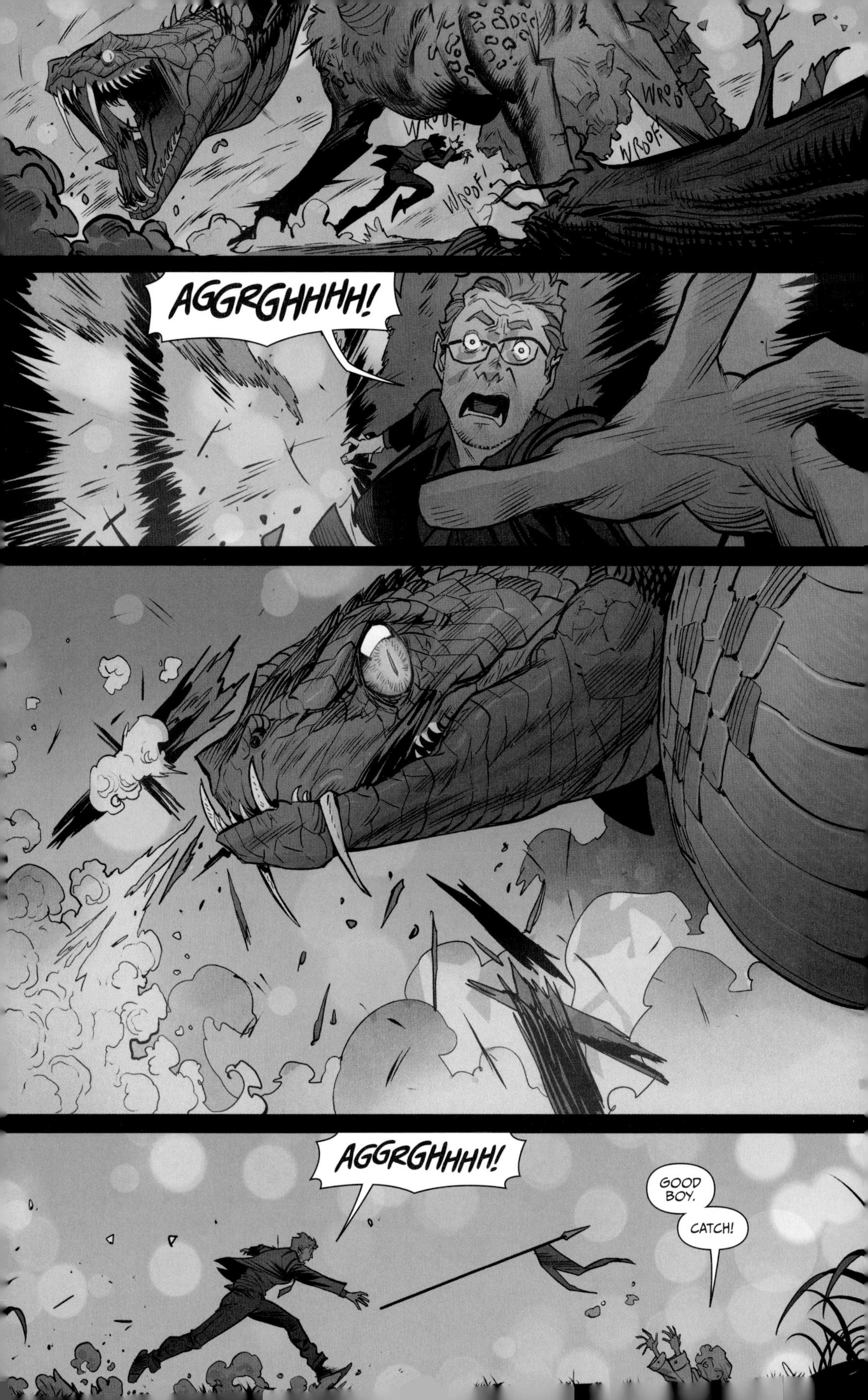
WROOF!
WROOF!
WROOF!
WROOF!
AGGRGHHHH!
AGGRGHHHH!
GOOD BOY.
CATCH!

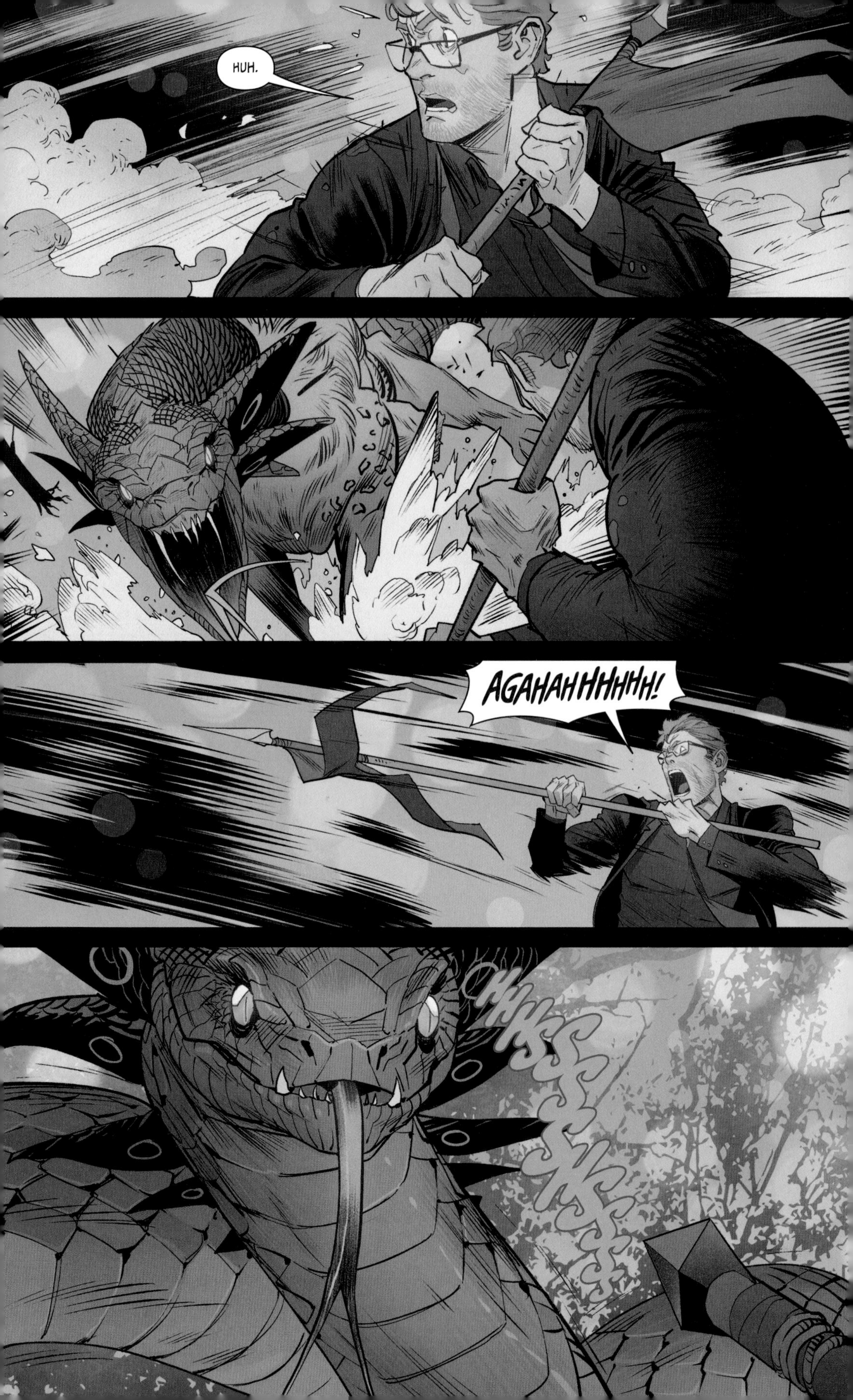
HUH.
AGAHAHHHHHH!
HHHSSSSSHCCCCSSSS

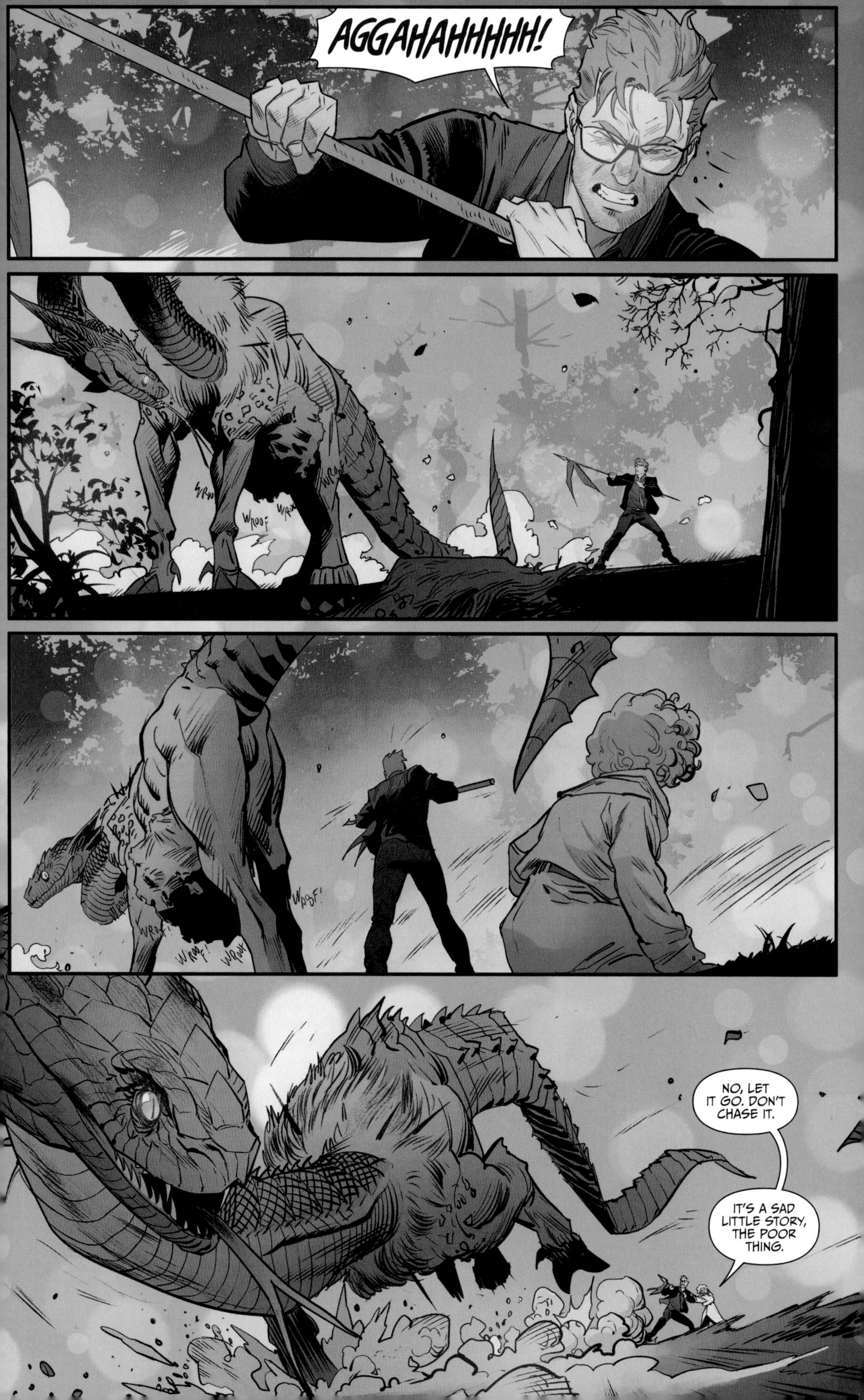
AGGAHAHHHH!
NO, LET IT GO. DON'T CHASE IT.
IT'S A SAD LITTLE STORY, THE POOR THING.

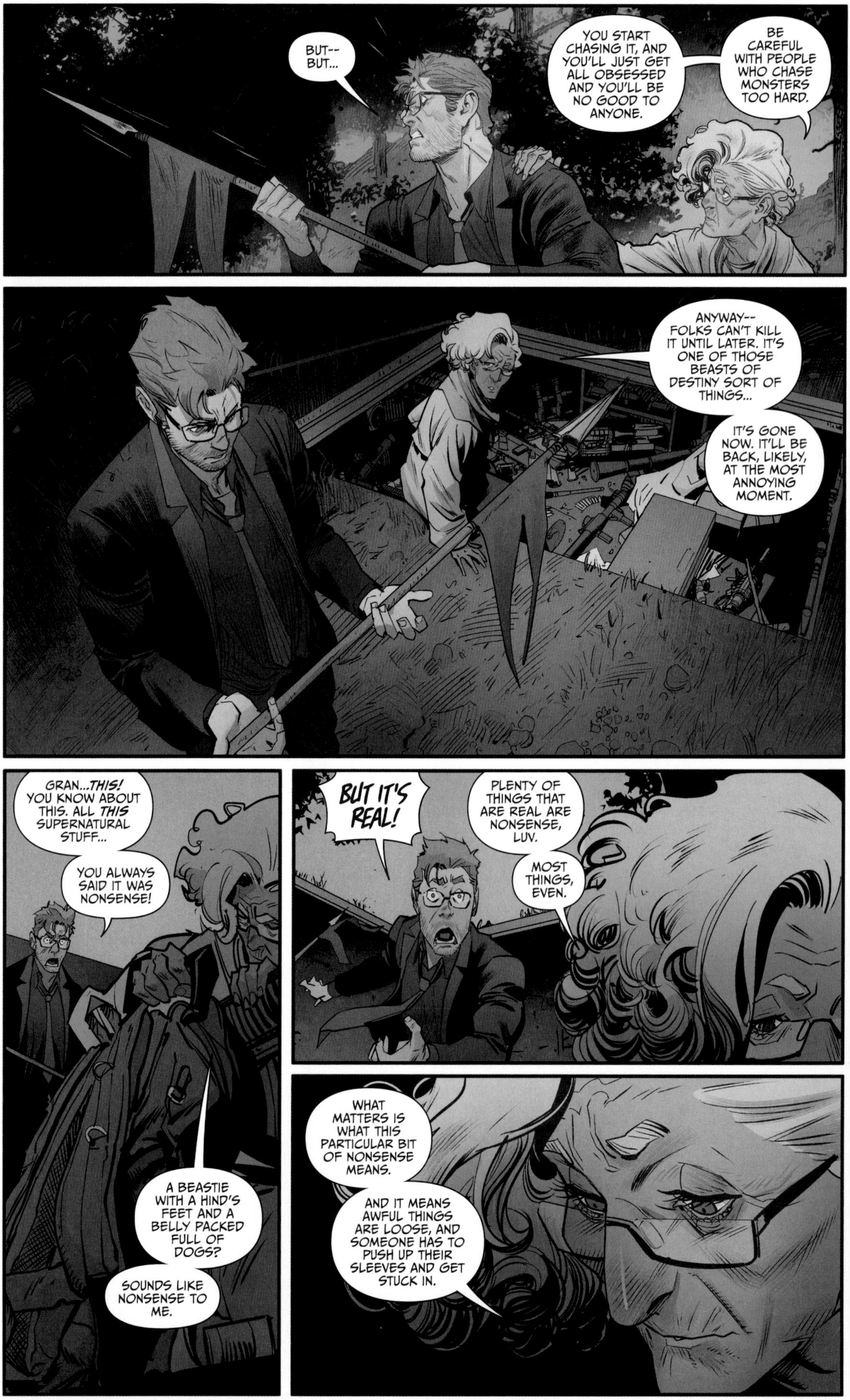

BUT-- BUT...
YOU START CHASING IT, AND YOU'LL JUST GET ALL OBSESSED AND YOU'LL BE NO GOOD TO ANYONE.
BE CAREFUL WITH PEOPLE WHO CHASE MONSTERS TOO HARD.
ANYWAY-- FOLKS CAN'T KILL IT UNTIL LATER. IT'S ONE OF THOSE BEASTS OF DESTINY SORT OF THINGS...
IT'S GONE NOW. IT'LL BE BACK, LIKELY, AT THE MOST ANNOYING MOMENT.
GRAN...THIS! YOU KNOW ABOUT THIS. ALL THIS SUPERNATURAL STUFF...
YOU ALWAYS SAID IT WAS NONSENSE!
A BEASTIE WITH A HIND'S FEET AND A BELLY PACKED FULL OF DOGS?
SOUNDS LIKE NONSENSE TO ME.
BUT IT'S REAL!
PLENTY OF THINGS THAT ARE REAL ARE NONSENSE, LUV.
MOST THINGS, EVEN.
WHAT MATTERS IS WHAT THIS PARTICULAR BIT OF NONSENSE MEANS.
AND IT MEANS AWFUL THINGS ARE LOOSE, AND SOMEONE HAS TO PUSH UP THEIR SLEEVES AND GET STUCK IN.

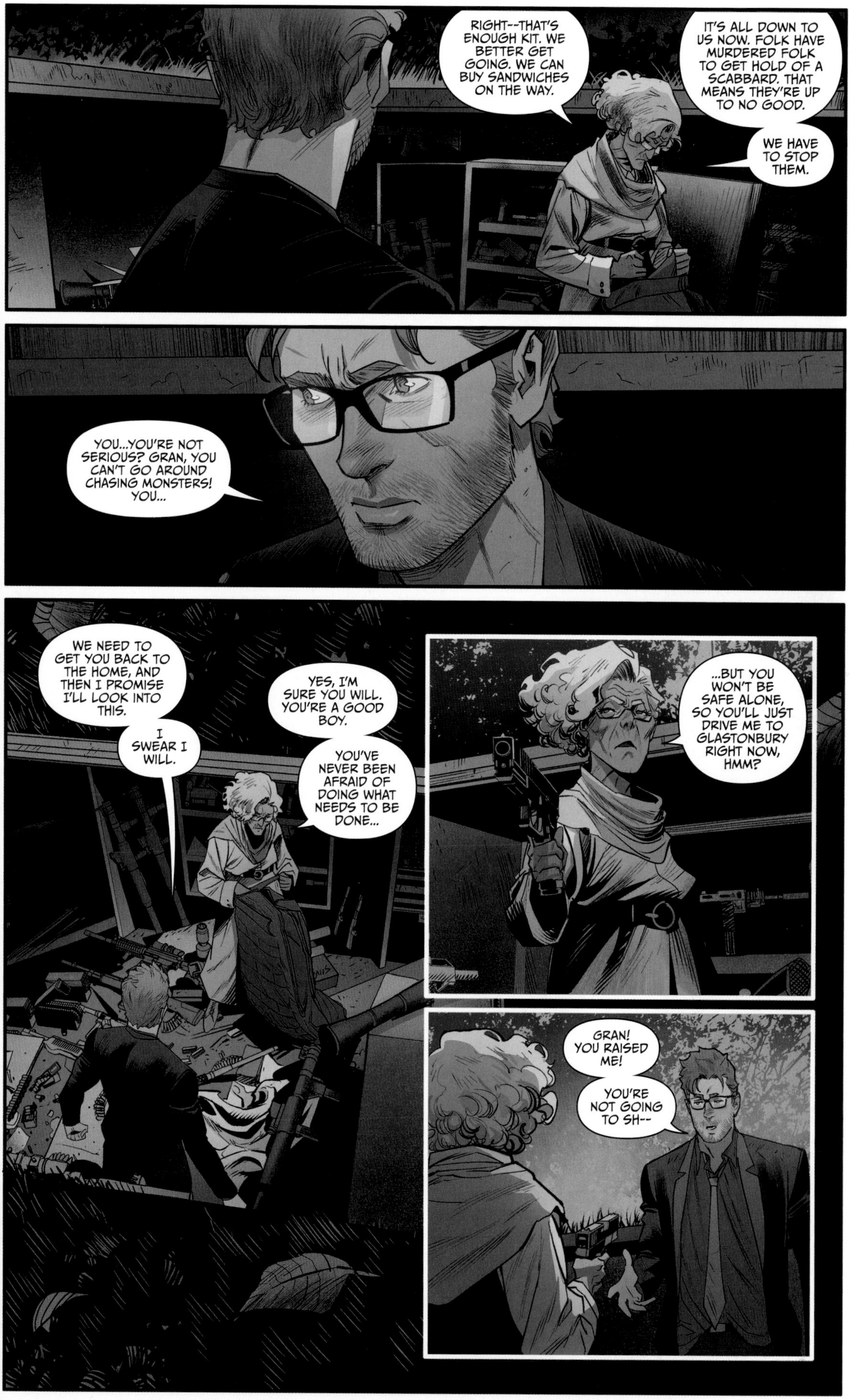
RIGHT--THAT'S ENOUGH KIT. WE BETTER GET GOING. WE CAN BUY SANDWICHES ON THE WAY.
IT'S ALL DOWN TO US NOW. FOLK HAVE MURDERED FOLK TO GET HOLD OF A SCABBARD. THAT MEANS THEY'RE UP TO NO GOOD.
WE HAVE TO STOP THEM.
YOU...YOU'RE NOT SERIOUS? GRAN, YOU CAN'T GO AROUND CHASING MONSTERS! YOU...
WE NEED TO GET YOU BACK TO THE HOME, AND THEN I PROMISE I'LL LOOK INTO THIS.
I SWEAR I WILL.
YES, I'M SURE YOU WILL. YOU'RE A GOOD BOY.
YOU'VE NEVER BEEN AFRAID OF DOING WHAT NEEDS TO BE DONE...
...BUT YOU WON'T BE SAFE ALONE, SO YOU'LL JUST DRIVE ME TO GLASTONBURY RIGHT NOW, HMM?
GRAN! YOU RAISED ME!
YOU'RE NOT GOING TO SH--

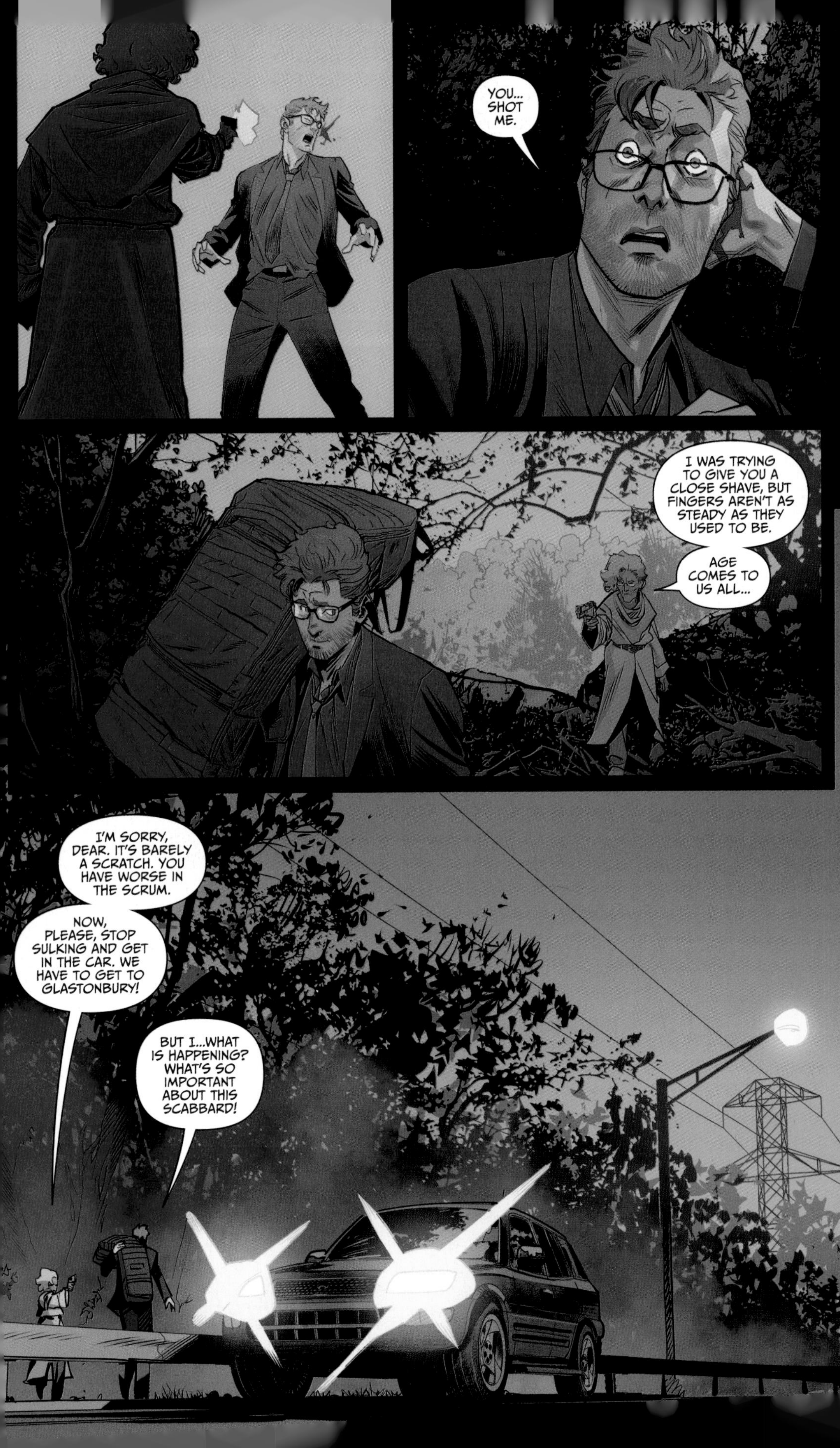
YOU... SHOT ME.
I WAS TRYING TO GIVE YOU A CLOSE SHAVE, BUT FINGERS AREN'T AS STEADY AS THEY USED TO BE.
AGE COMES TO US ALL...
I'M SORRY, DEAR. IT'S BARELY A SCRATCH. YOU HAVE WORSE IN THE SCRUM.
NOW, PLEASE, STOP SULKING AND GET IN THE CAR. WE HAVE TO GET TO GLASTONBURY!
BUT I...WHAT IS HAPPENING? WHAT'S SO IMPORTANT ABOUT THIS SCABBARD!

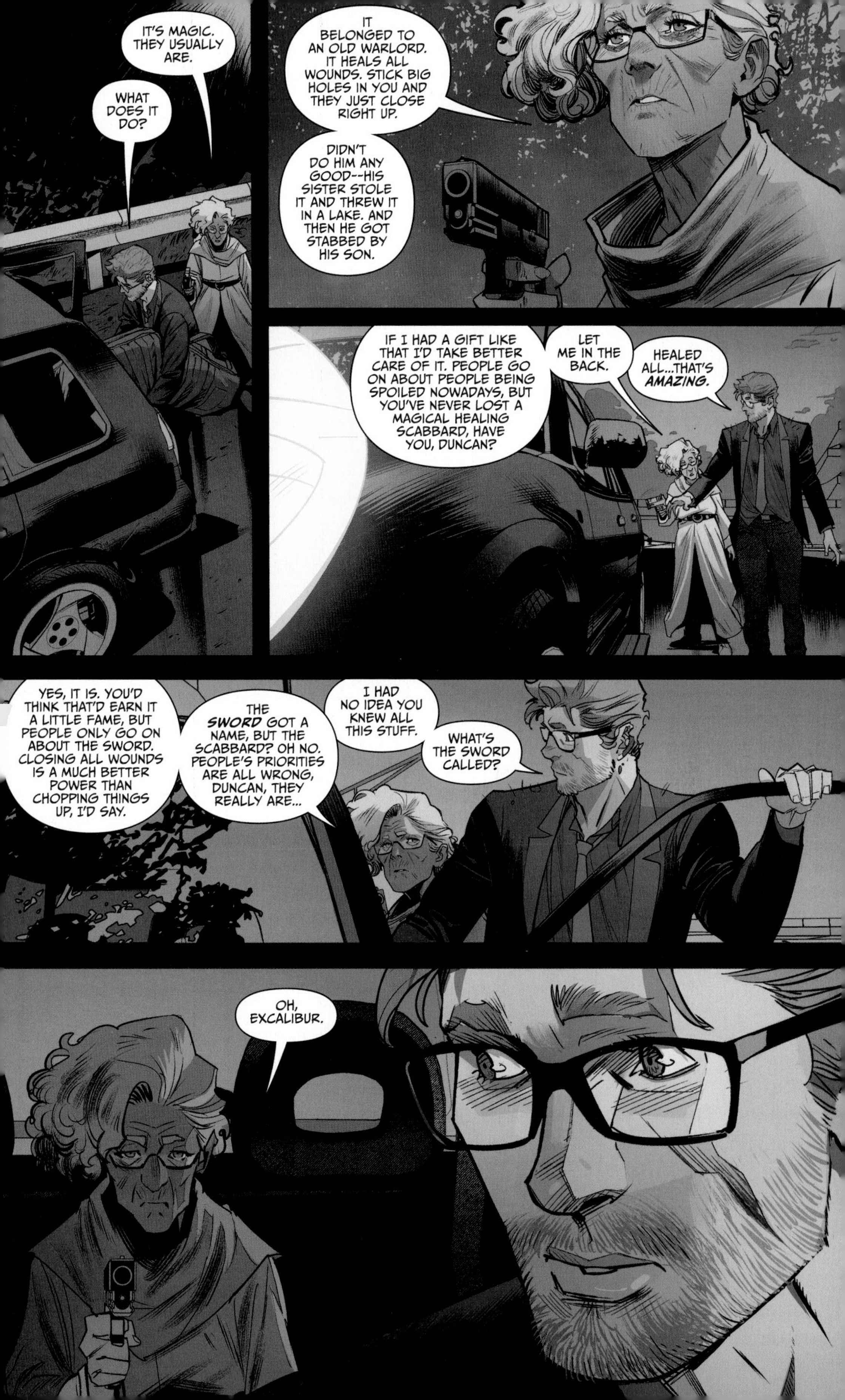
WHAT DOES IT DO?
IT'S MAGIC. THEY USUALLY ARE.
IT BELONGED TO AN OLD WARLORD. IT HEALS ALL WOUNDS. STICK BIG HOLES IN YOU AND THEY JUST CLOSE RIGHT UP.
DIDN'T DO HIM ANY GOOD--HIS SISTER STOLE IT AND THREW IT IN A LAKE. AND THEN HE GOT STABBED BY HIS SON.
HEALED ALL...THAT'S *AMAZING.*
LET ME IN THE BACK.
IF I HAD A GIFT LIKE THAT I'D TAKE BETTER CARE OF IT. PEOPLE GO ON ABOUT PEOPLE BEING SPOILED NOWADAYS, BUT YOU'VE NEVER LOST A MAGICAL HEALING SCABBARD, HAVE YOU, DUNCAN?
YES, IT IS. YOU'D THINK THAT'D EARN IT A LITTLE FAME, BUT PEOPLE ONLY GO ON ABOUT THE SWORD. CLOSING ALL WOUNDS IS A MUCH BETTER POWER THAN CHOPPING THINGS UP, I'D SAY.
THE *SWORD* GOT A NAME, BUT THE SCABBARD? OH NO. PEOPLE'S PRIORITIES ARE ALL WRONG, DUNCAN, THEY REALLY ARE...
I HAD NO IDEA YOU KNEW ALL THIS STUFF.
WHAT'S THE SWORD CALLED?
OH, EXCALIBUR.

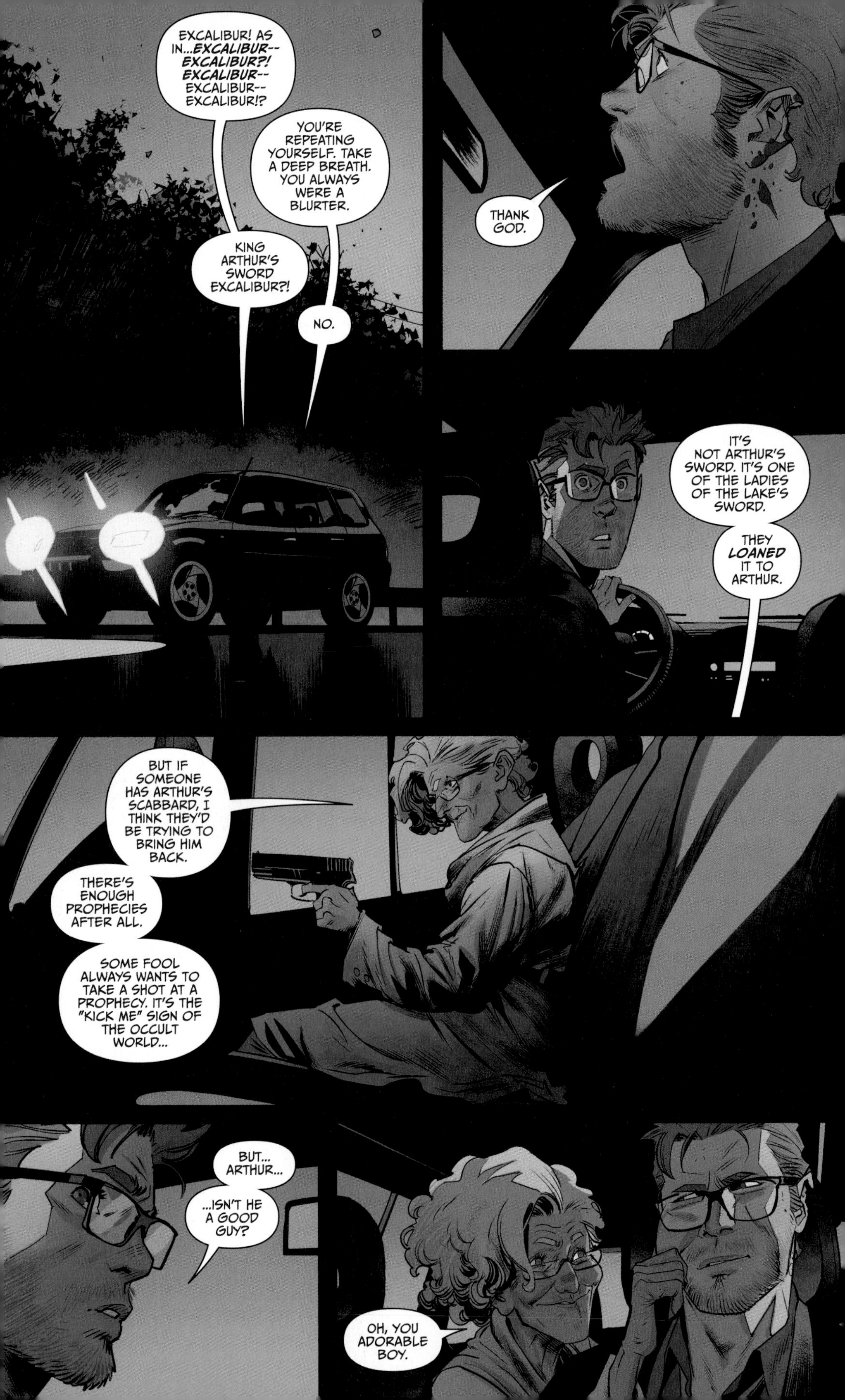
EXCALIBUR! AS IN...EXCALIBUR-- EXCALIBUR?! EXCALIBUR-- EXCALIBUR-- EXCALIBUR!?
YOU'RE REPEATING YOURSELF. TAKE A DEEP BREATH. YOU ALWAYS WERE A BLURTER.
KING ARTHUR'S SWORD EXCALIBUR?!
NO.
THANK GOD.
IT'S NOT ARTHUR'S SWORD. IT'S ONE OF THE LADIES OF THE LAKE'S SWORD.
THEY LOANED IT TO ARTHUR.
BUT IF SOMEONE HAS ARTHUR'S SCABBARD, I THINK THEY'D BE TRYING TO BRING HIM BACK.
THERE'S ENOUGH PROPHECIES AFTER ALL.
SOME FOOL ALWAYS WANTS TO TAKE A SHOT AT A PROPHECY. IT'S THE "KICK ME" SIGN OF THE OCCULT WORLD...
BUT... ARTHUR...
...ISN'T HE A GOOD GUY?
OH, YOU ADORABLE BOY.

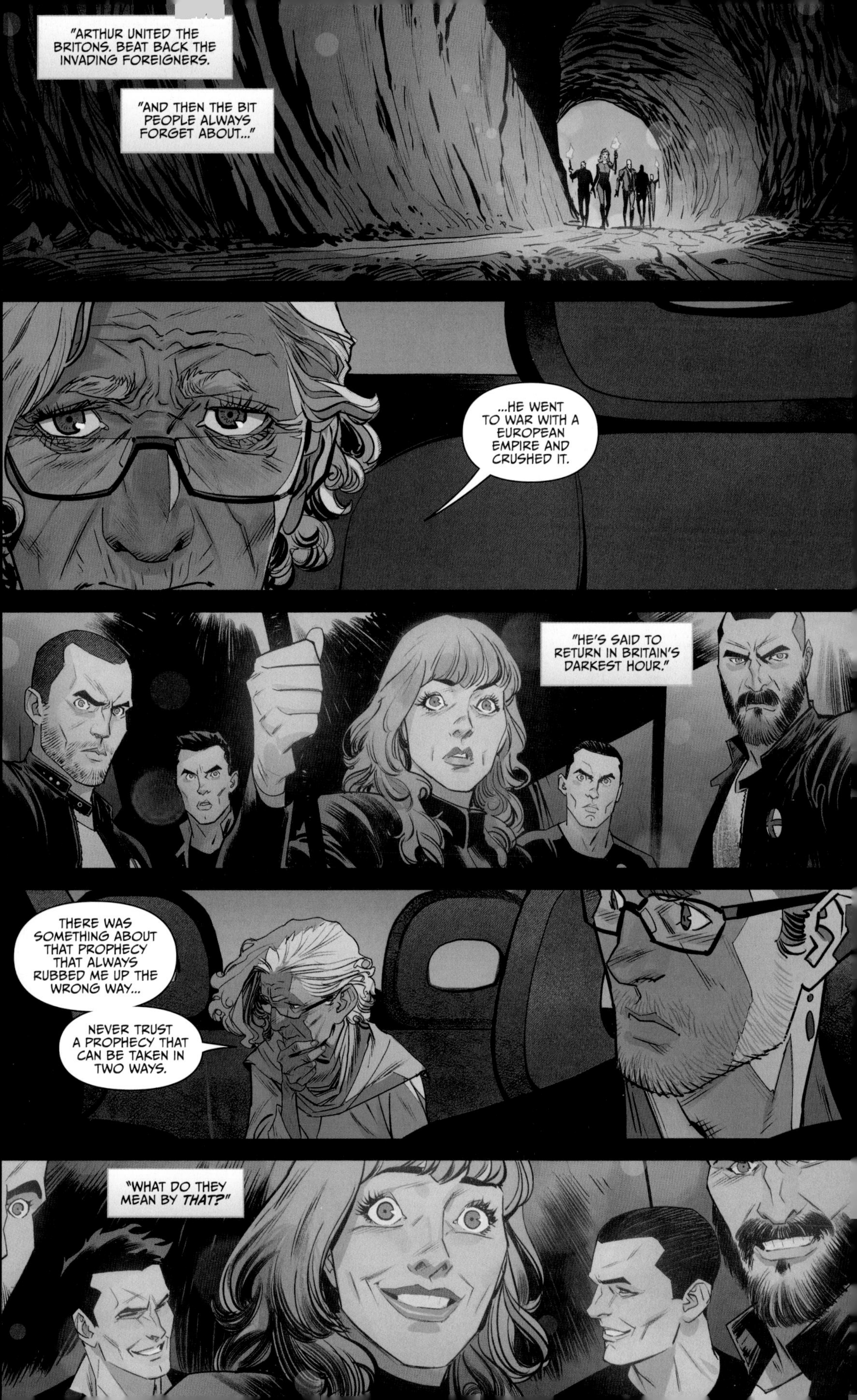
"ARTHUR UNITED THE BRITONS. BEAT BACK THE INVADING FOREIGNERS.
"AND THEN THE BIT PEOPLE ALWAYS FORGET ABOUT..."
...HE WENT TO WAR WITH A EUROPEAN EMPIRE AND CRUSHED IT.
"HE'S SAID TO RETURN IN BRITAIN'S DARKEST HOUR."
THERE WAS SOMETHING ABOUT THAT PROPHECY THAT ALWAYS RUBBED ME UP THE WRONG WAY...
NEVER TRUST A PROPHECY THAT CAN BE TAKEN IN TWO WAYS.
"WHAT DO THEY MEAN BY *THAT?*"

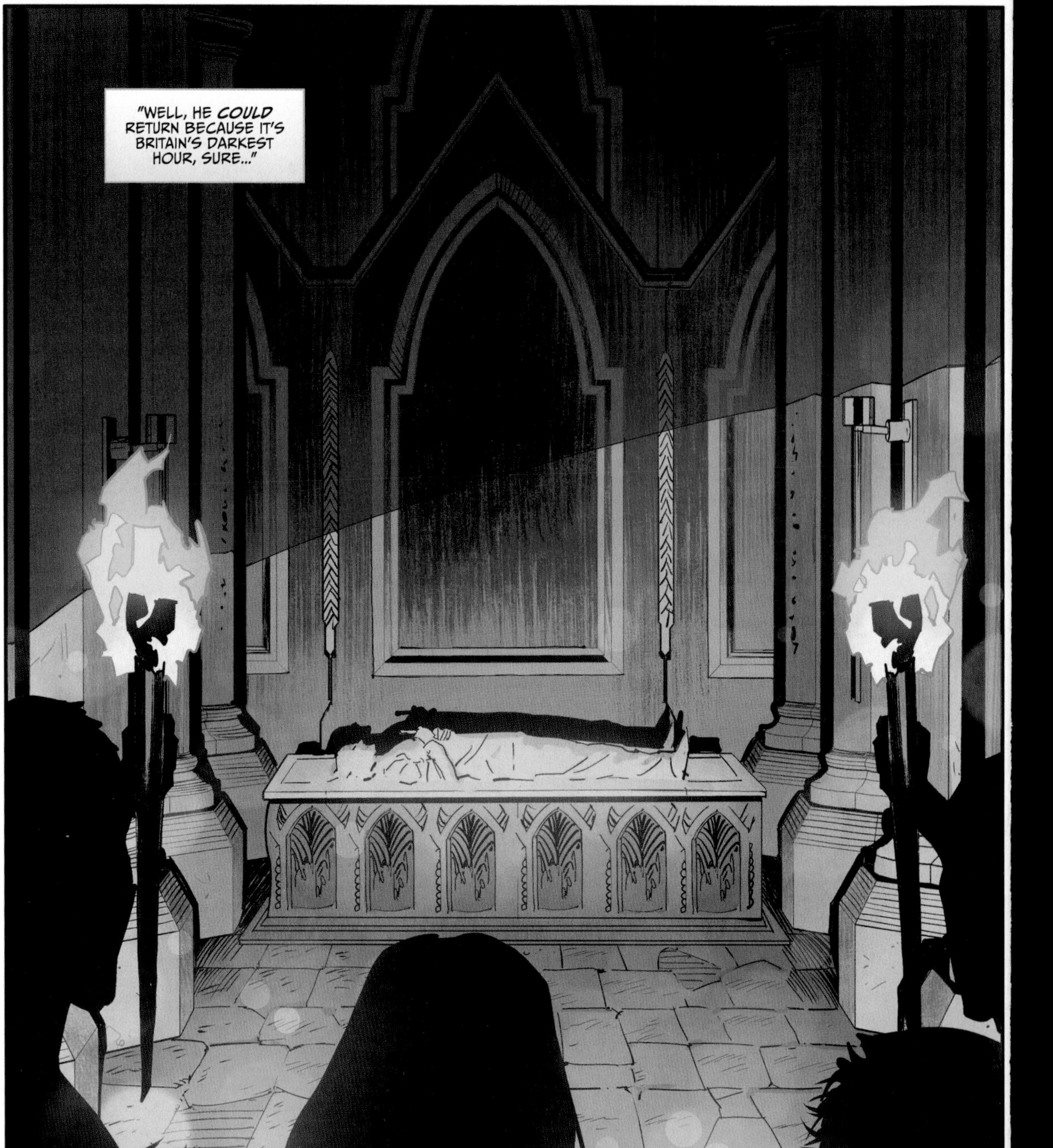
"WELL, HE COULD RETURN BECAUSE IT'S BRITAIN'S DARKEST HOUR, SURE..."

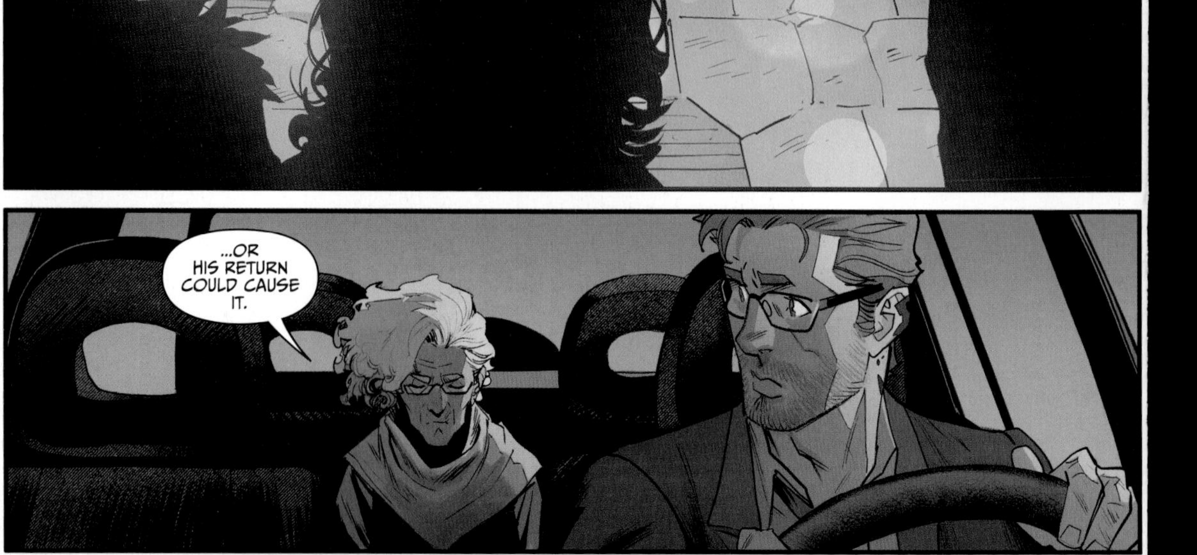
...OR HIS RETURN COULD CAUSE IT.

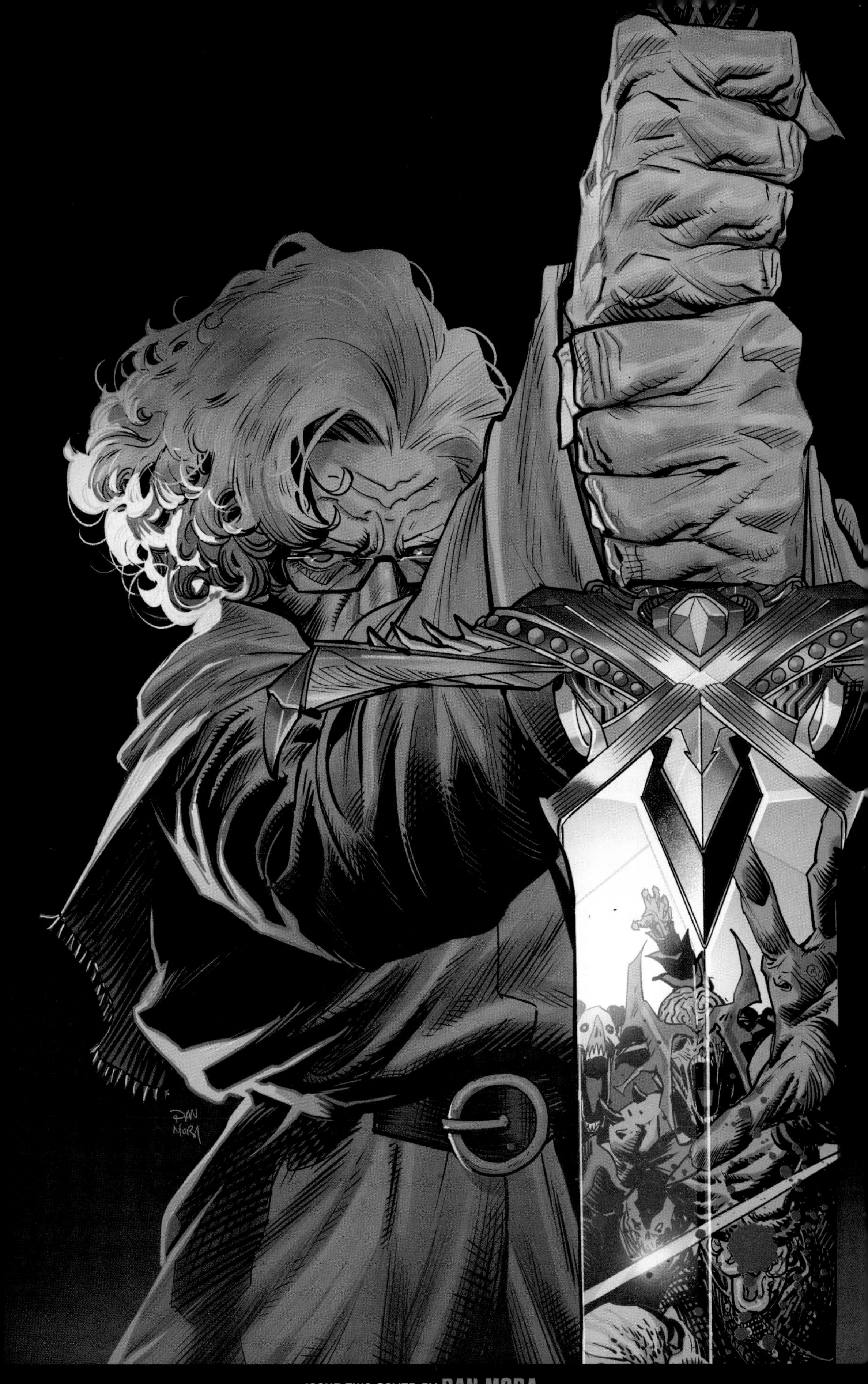
DAN
MORA

ISSUE TWO COVER BY **DAN MORA**

CHAPTER TWO

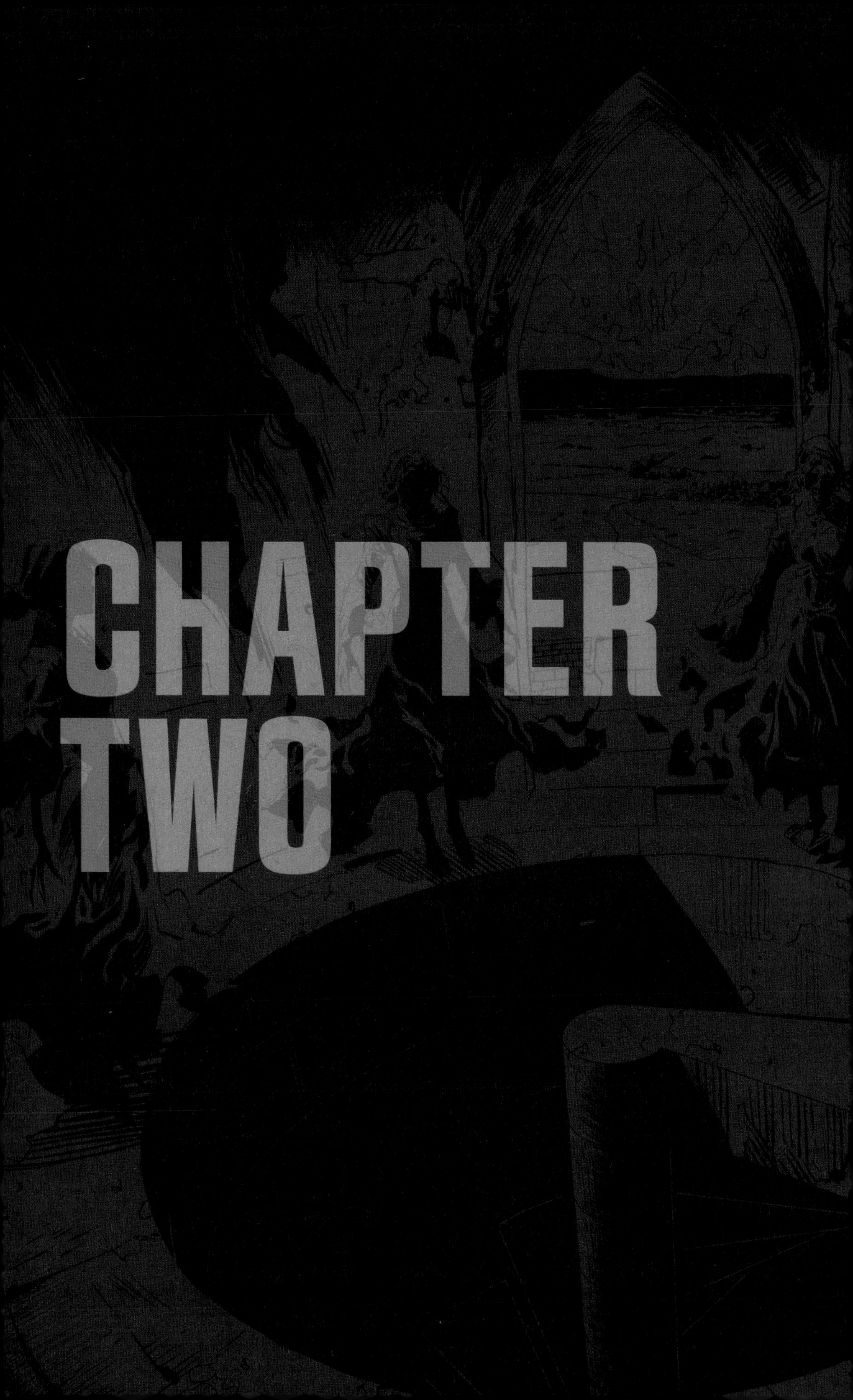

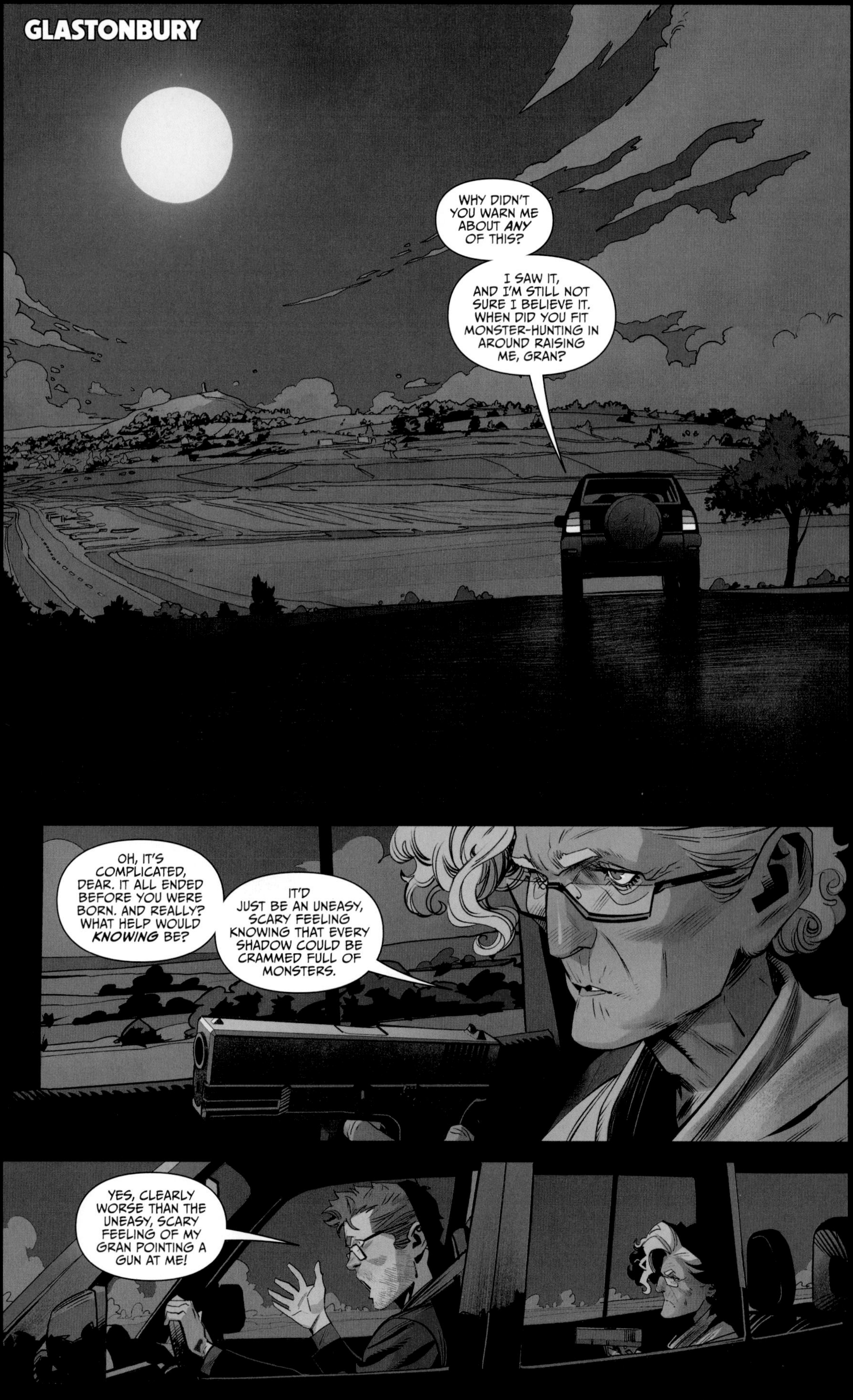
GLASTONBURY
WHY DIDN'T YOU WARN ME ABOUT *ANY* OF THIS?
I SAW IT, AND I'M STILL NOT SURE I BELIEVE IT. WHEN DID YOU FIT MONSTER-HUNTING IN AROUND RAISING ME, GRAN?
OH, IT'S COMPLICATED, DEAR. IT ALL ENDED BEFORE YOU WERE BORN. AND REALLY? WHAT HELP WOULD *KNOWING* BE?
IT'D JUST BE AN UNEASY, SCARY FEELING KNOWING THAT EVERY SHADOW COULD BE CRAMMED FULL OF MONSTERS.
YES, CLEARLY WORSE THAN THE UNEASY, SCARY FEELING OF MY GRAN POINTING A GUN AT ME!

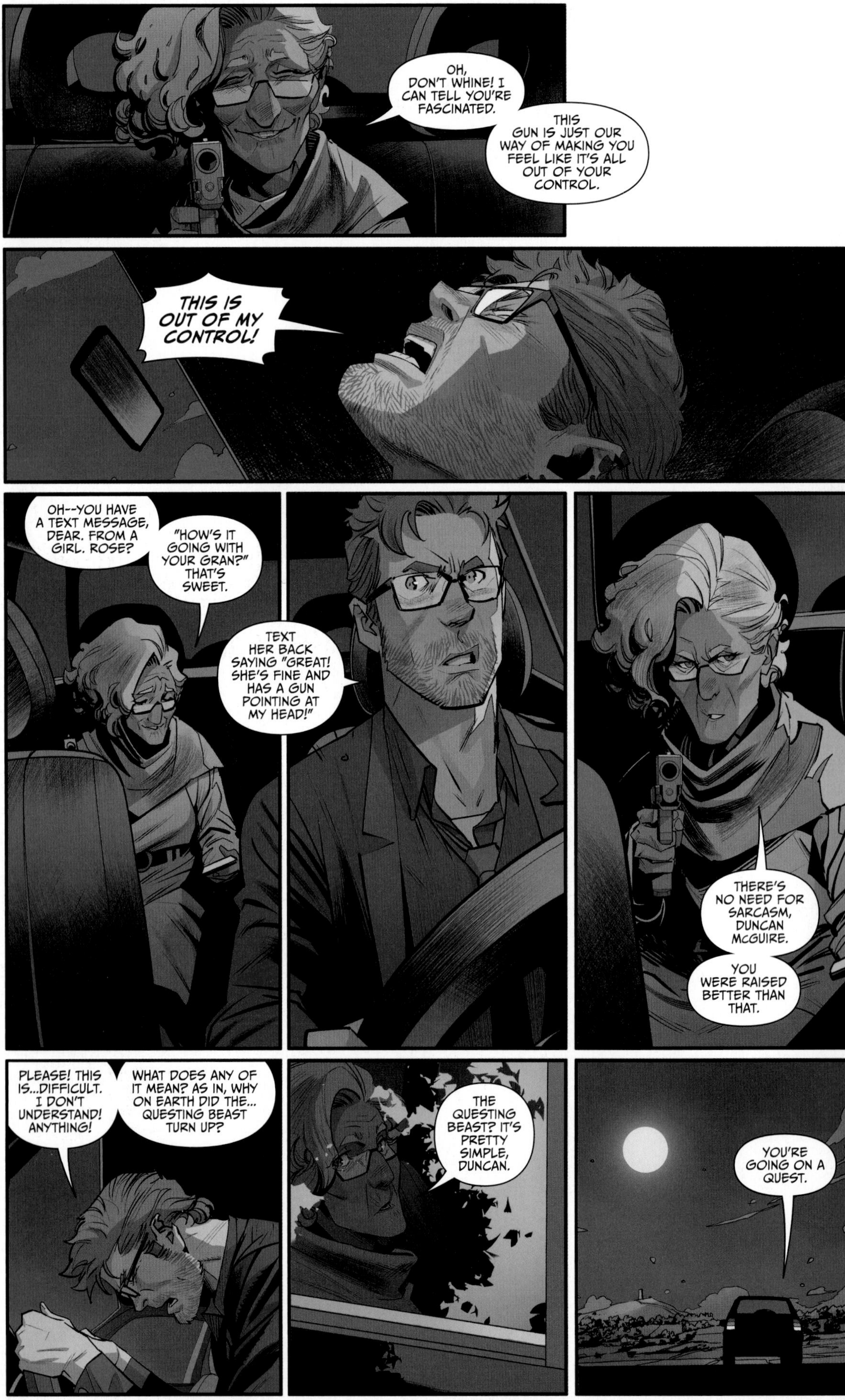
OH, DON'T WHINE! I CAN TELL YOU'RE FASCINATED.
THIS GUN IS JUST OUR WAY OF MAKING YOU FEEL LIKE IT'S ALL OUT OF YOUR CONTROL.
THIS IS OUT OF MY CONTROL!
OH--YOU HAVE A TEXT MESSAGE, DEAR. FROM A GIRL. ROSE?
"HOW'S IT GOING WITH YOUR GRAN?" THAT'S SWEET.
TEXT HER BACK SAYING "GREAT! SHE'S FINE AND HAS A GUN POINTING AT MY HEAD!"
THERE'S NO NEED FOR SARCASM, DUNCAN McGUIRE.
YOU WERE RAISED BETTER THAN THAT.
PLEASE! THIS IS...DIFFICULT. I DON'T UNDERSTAND! ANYTHING!
WHAT DOES ANY OF IT MEAN? AS IN, WHY ON EARTH DID THE... QUESTING BEAST TURN UP?
THE QUESTING BEAST? IT'S PRETTY SIMPLE, DUNCAN.
YOU'RE GOING ON A QUEST.

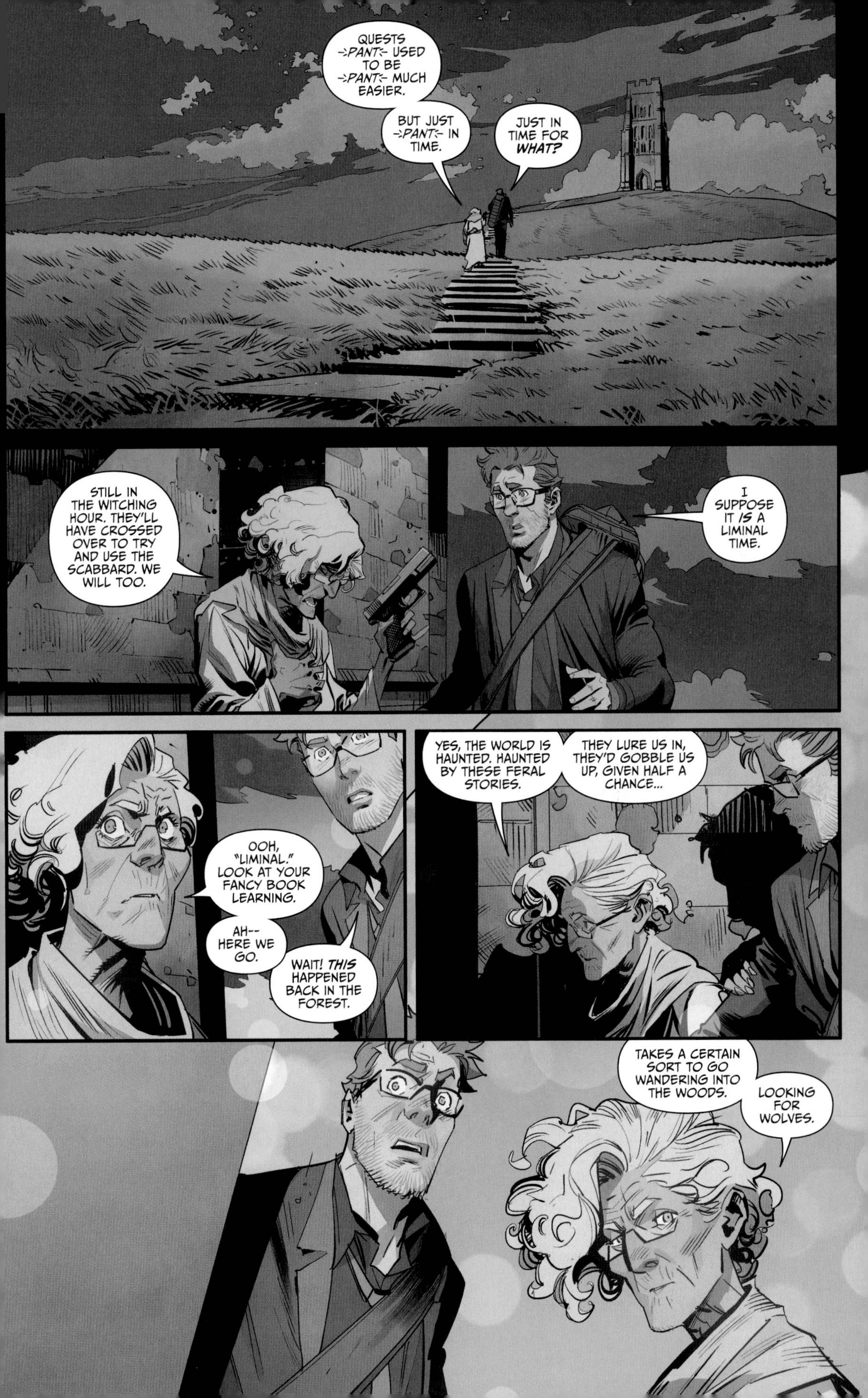
QUESTS -PANT- USED TO BE -PANT- MUCH EASIER.
BUT JUST -PANT- IN TIME.
JUST IN TIME FOR *WHAT?*
STILL IN THE WITCHING HOUR. THEY'LL HAVE CROSSED OVER TO TRY AND USE THE SCABBARD. WE WILL TOO.
I SUPPOSE IT *IS* A LIMINAL TIME.
OOH, "LIMINAL." LOOK AT YOUR FANCY BOOK LEARNING.
AH-- HERE WE GO.
WAIT! *THIS* HAPPENED BACK IN THE FOREST.
YES, THE WORLD IS HAUNTED. HAUNTED BY THESE FERAL STORIES.
THEY LURE US IN, THEY'D GOBBLE US UP, GIVEN HALF A CHANCE...
TAKES A CERTAIN SORT TO GO WANDERING INTO THE WOODS.
LOOKING FOR WOLVES.

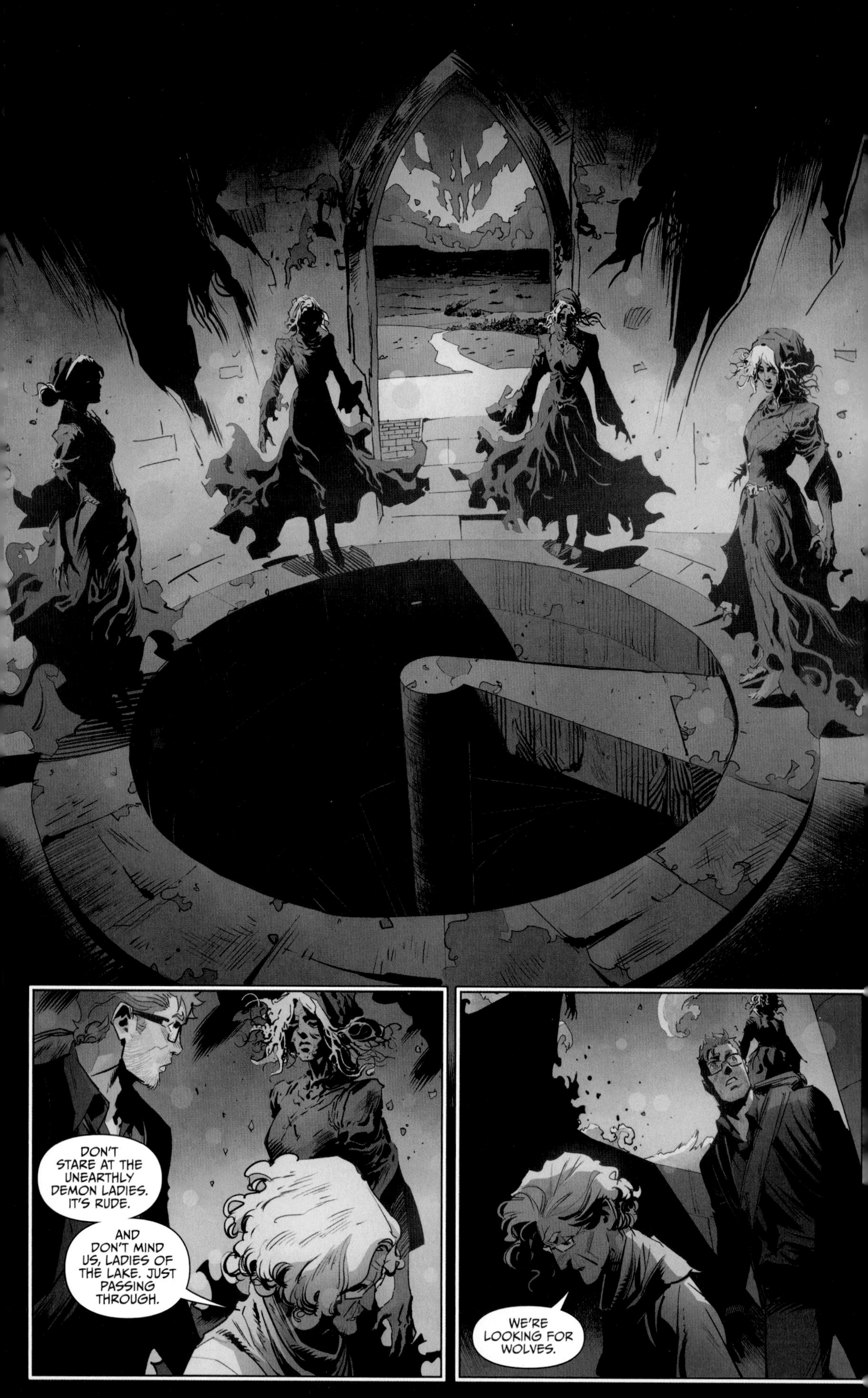
DON'T STARE AT THE UNEARTHLY DEMON LADIES. IT'S RUDE.
AND DON'T MIND US, LADIES OF THE LAKE. JUST PASSING THROUGH.
WE'RE LOOKING FOR WOLVES.

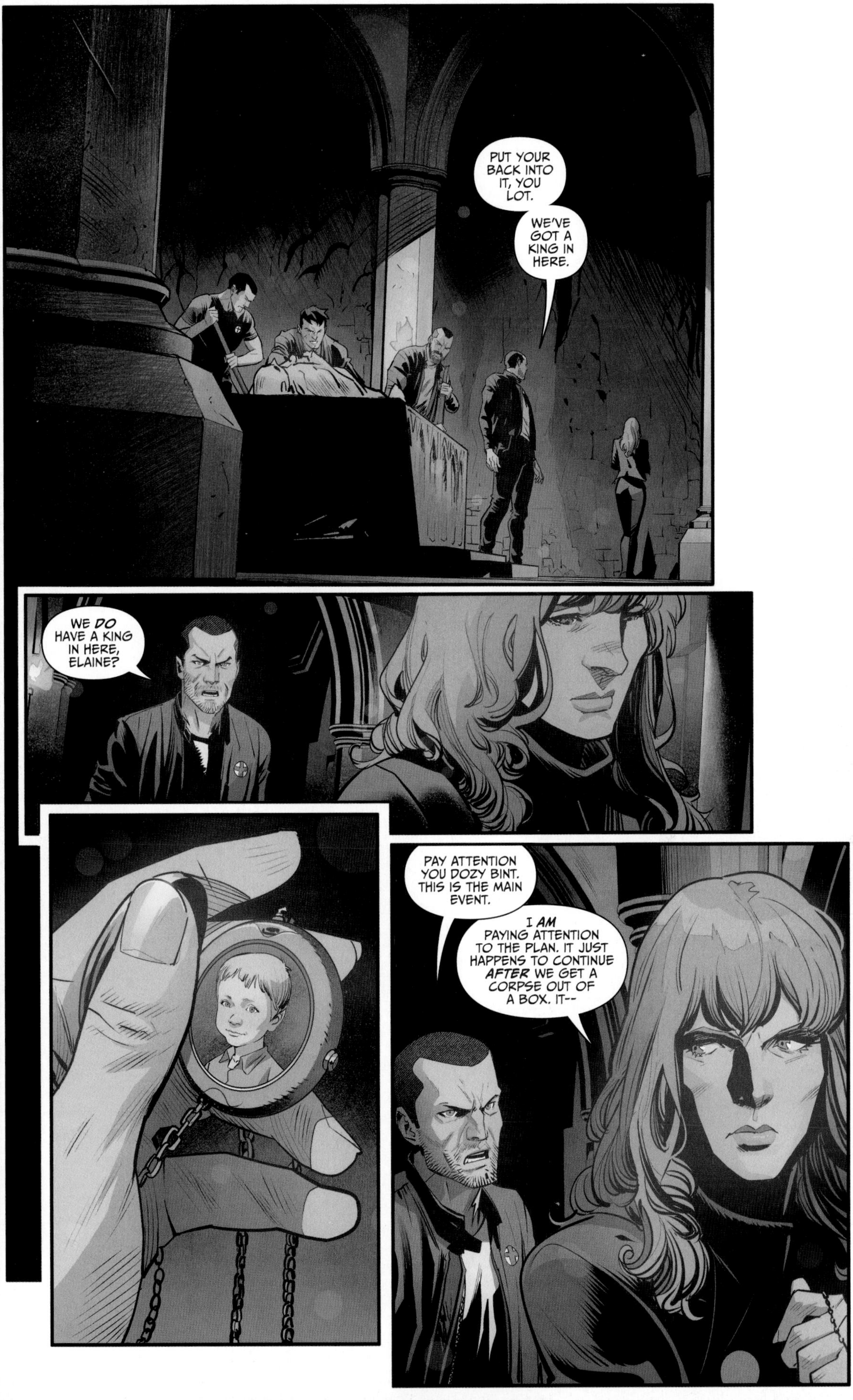
PUT YOUR BACK INTO IT, YOU LOT.
WE'VE GOT A KING IN HERE.
WE *DO* HAVE A KING IN HERE, ELAINE?
PAY ATTENTION YOU DOZY BINT. THIS IS THE MAIN EVENT.
I ***AM*** PAYING ATTENTION TO THE PLAN. IT JUST HAPPENS TO CONTINUE ***AFTER*** WE GET A CORPSE OUT OF A BOX. IT--

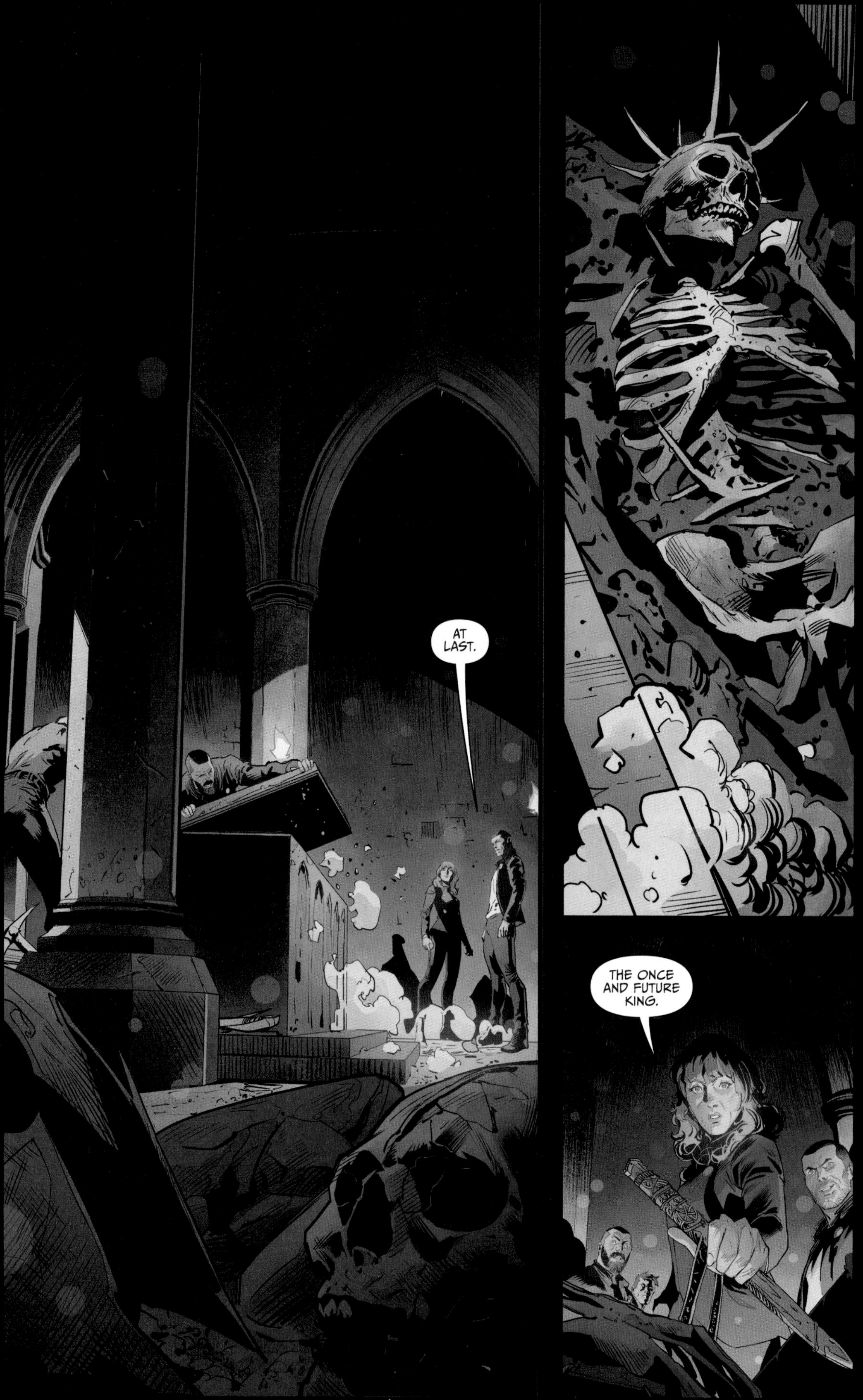
AT LAST.
THE ONCE AND FUTURE KING.

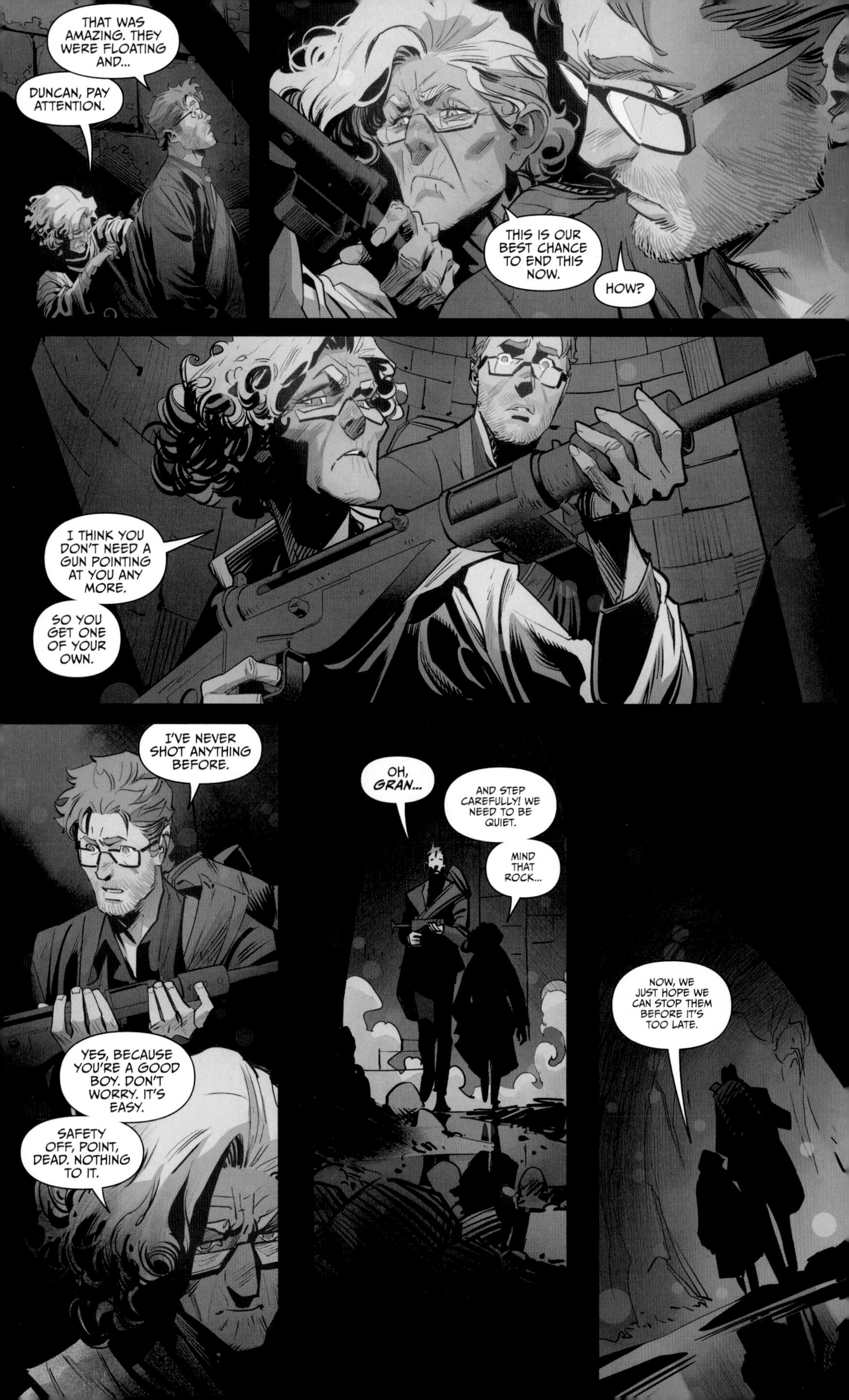
THAT WAS AMAZING. THEY WERE FLOATING AND...
DUNCAN, PAY ATTENTION.
THIS IS OUR BEST CHANCE TO END THIS NOW.
HOW?
I THINK YOU DON'T NEED A GUN POINTING AT YOU ANY MORE.
SO YOU GET ONE OF YOUR OWN.
I'VE NEVER SHOT ANYTHING BEFORE.
YES, BECAUSE YOU'RE A GOOD BOY. DON'T WORRY. IT'S EASY.
SAFETY OFF, POINT, DEAD. NOTHING TO IT.
OH, GRAN...
AND STEP CAREFULLY! WE NEED TO BE QUIET.
MIND THAT ROCK...
NOW, WE JUST HOPE WE CAN STOP THEM BEFORE IT'S TOO LATE.

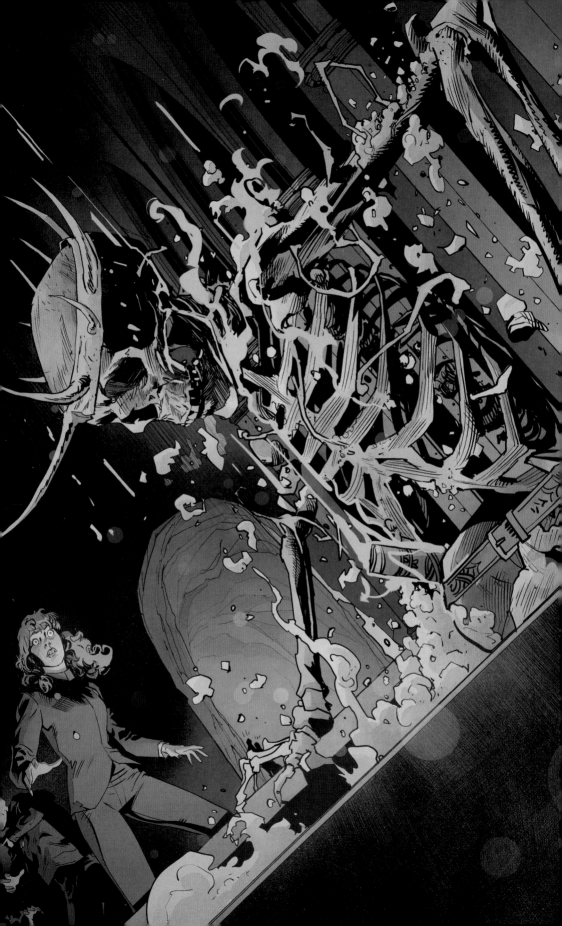

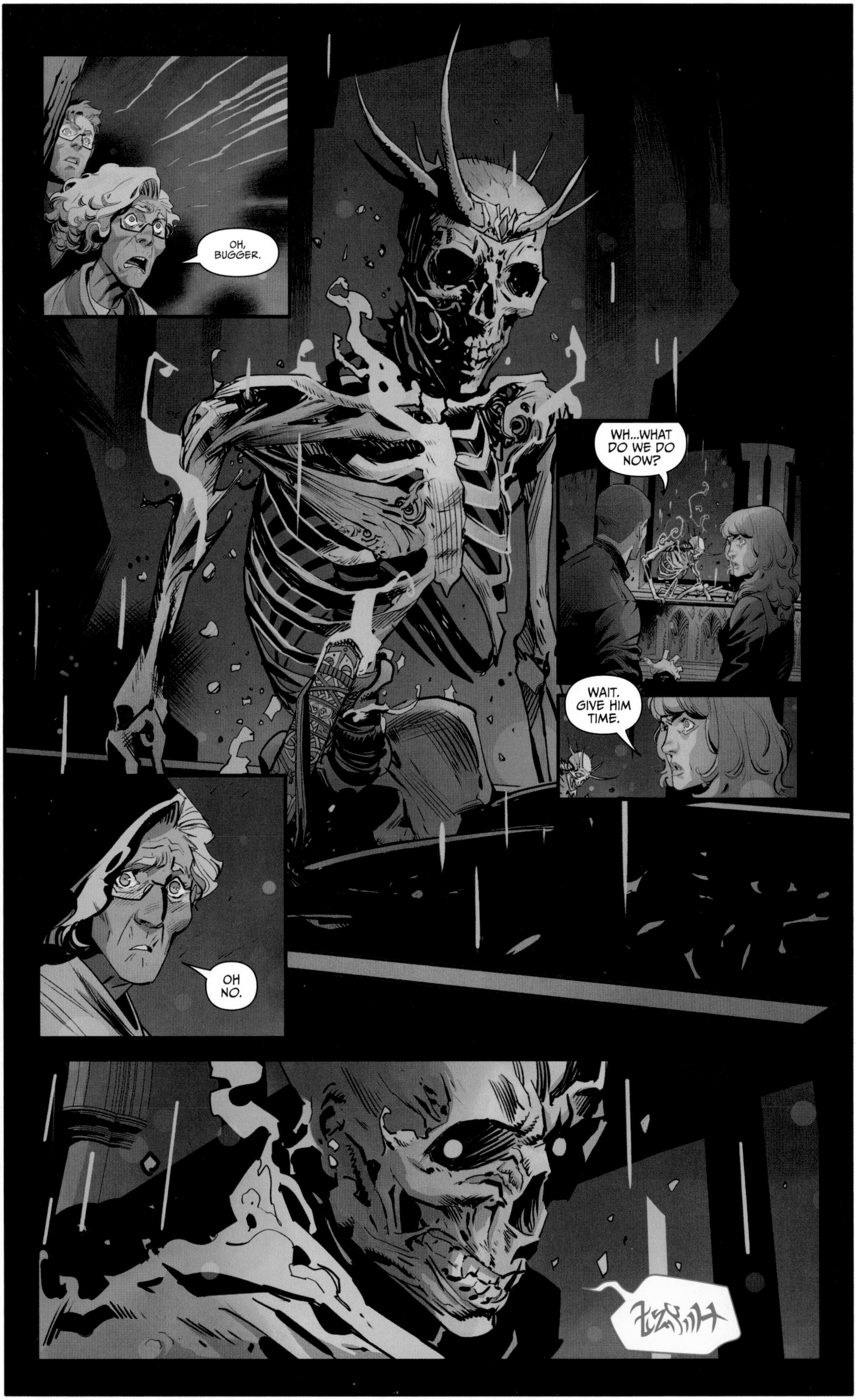
OH, BUGGER.
WH...WHAT DO WE DO NOW?
WAIT. GIVE HIM TIME.
OH NO.

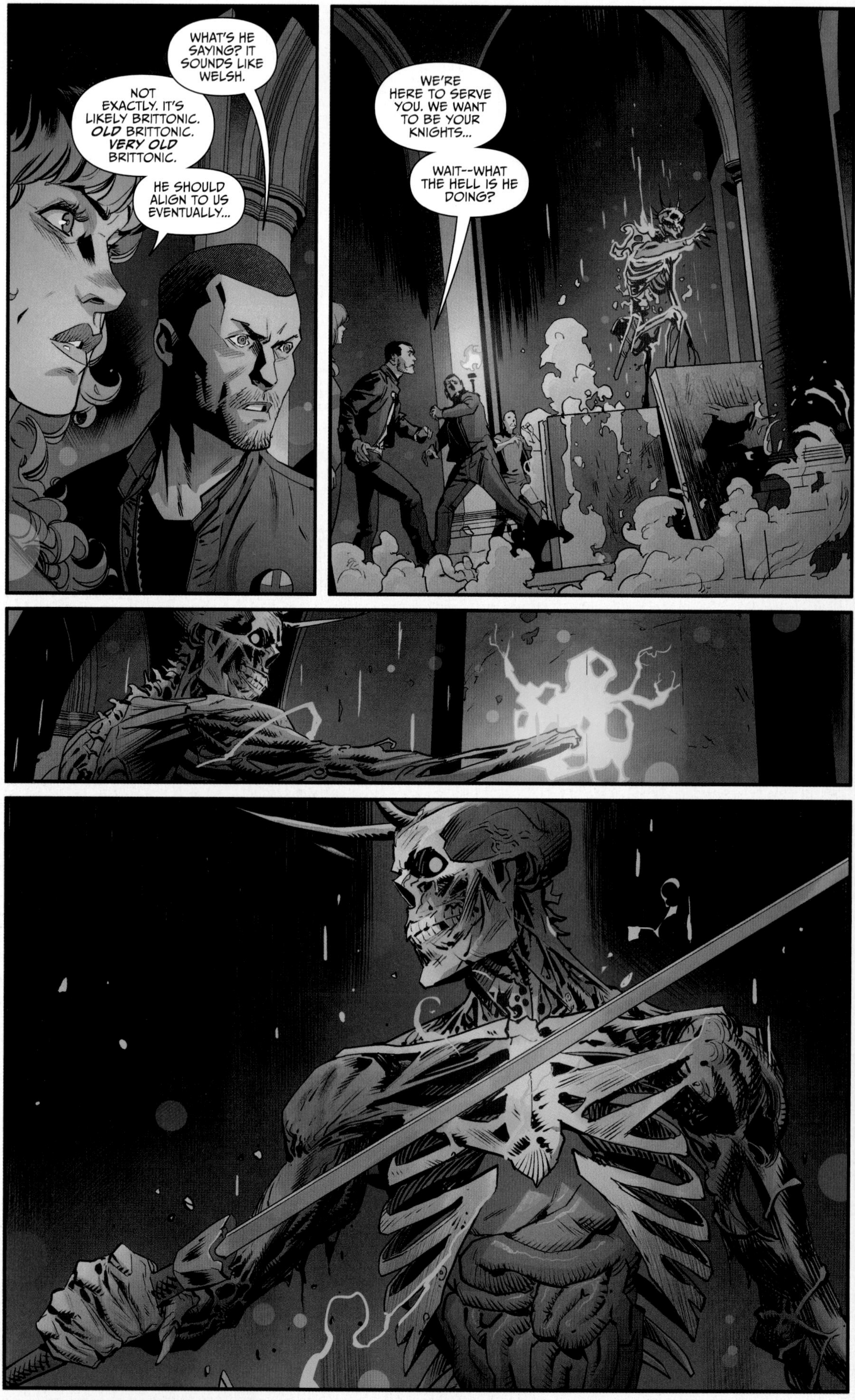
WHAT'S HE SAYING? IT SOUNDS LIKE WELSH.
NOT EXACTLY. IT'S LIKELY BRITTONIC. OLD BRITTONIC. VERY OLD BRITTONIC.
HE SHOULD ALIGN TO US EVENTUALLY...
WE'RE HERE TO SERVE YOU. WE WANT TO BE YOUR KNIGHTS...
WAIT--WHAT THE HELL IS HE DOING?

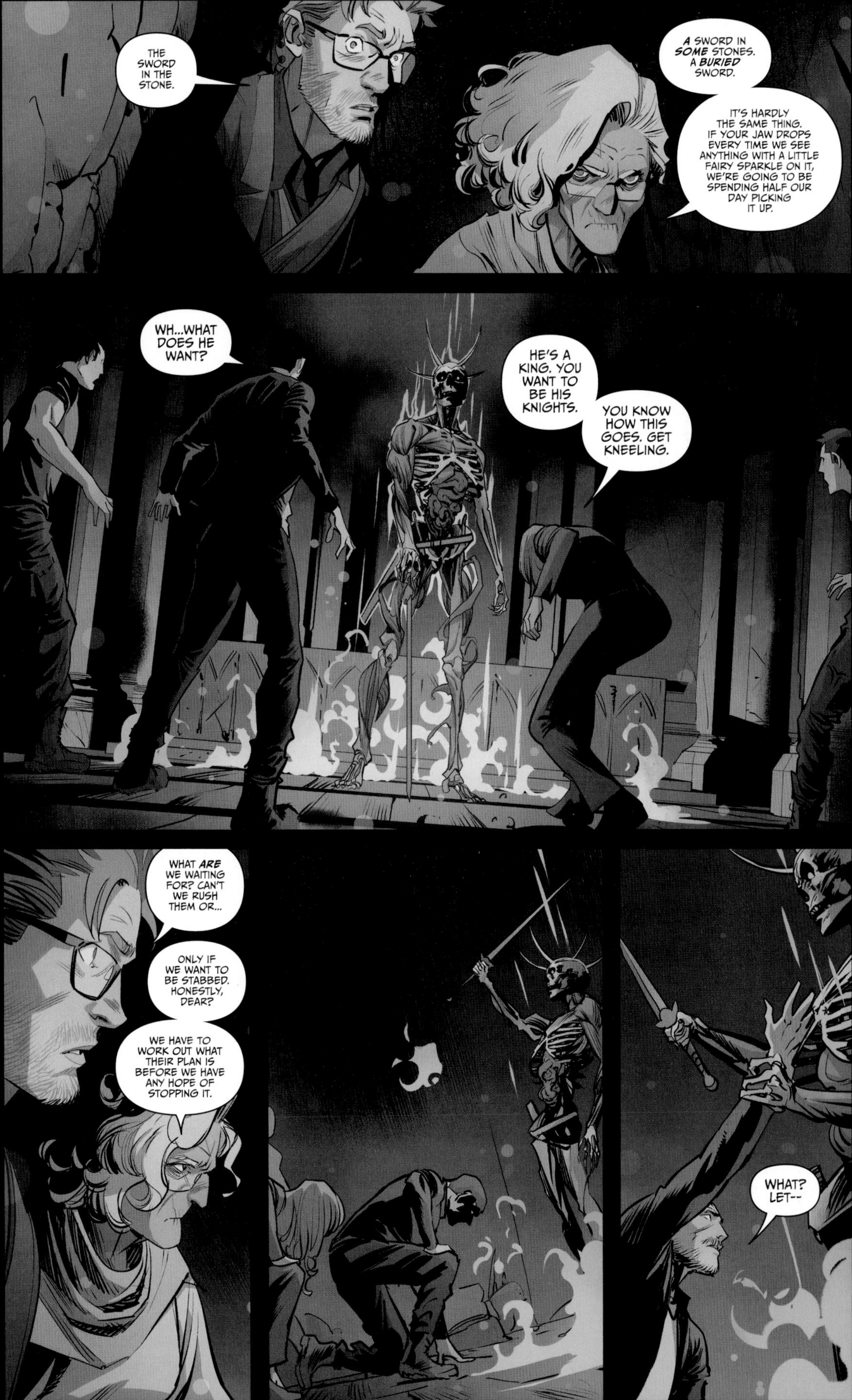
THE SWORD IN THE STONE.
A SWORD IN SOME STONES. A BURIED SWORD.
IT'S HARDLY THE SAME THING. IF YOUR JAW DROPS EVERY TIME WE SEE ANYTHING WITH A LITTLE FAIRY SPARKLE ON IT, WE'RE GOING TO BE SPENDING HALF OUR DAY PICKING IT UP.
WH...WHAT DOES HE WANT?
HE'S A KING. YOU WANT TO BE HIS KNIGHTS.
YOU KNOW HOW THIS GOES. GET KNEELING.
WHAT ARE WE WAITING FOR? CAN'T WE RUSH THEM OR...
ONLY IF WE WANT TO BE STABBED. HONESTLY, DEAR?
WE HAVE TO WORK OUT WHAT THEIR PLAN IS BEFORE WE HAVE ANY HOPE OF STOPPING IT.
WHAT? LET--

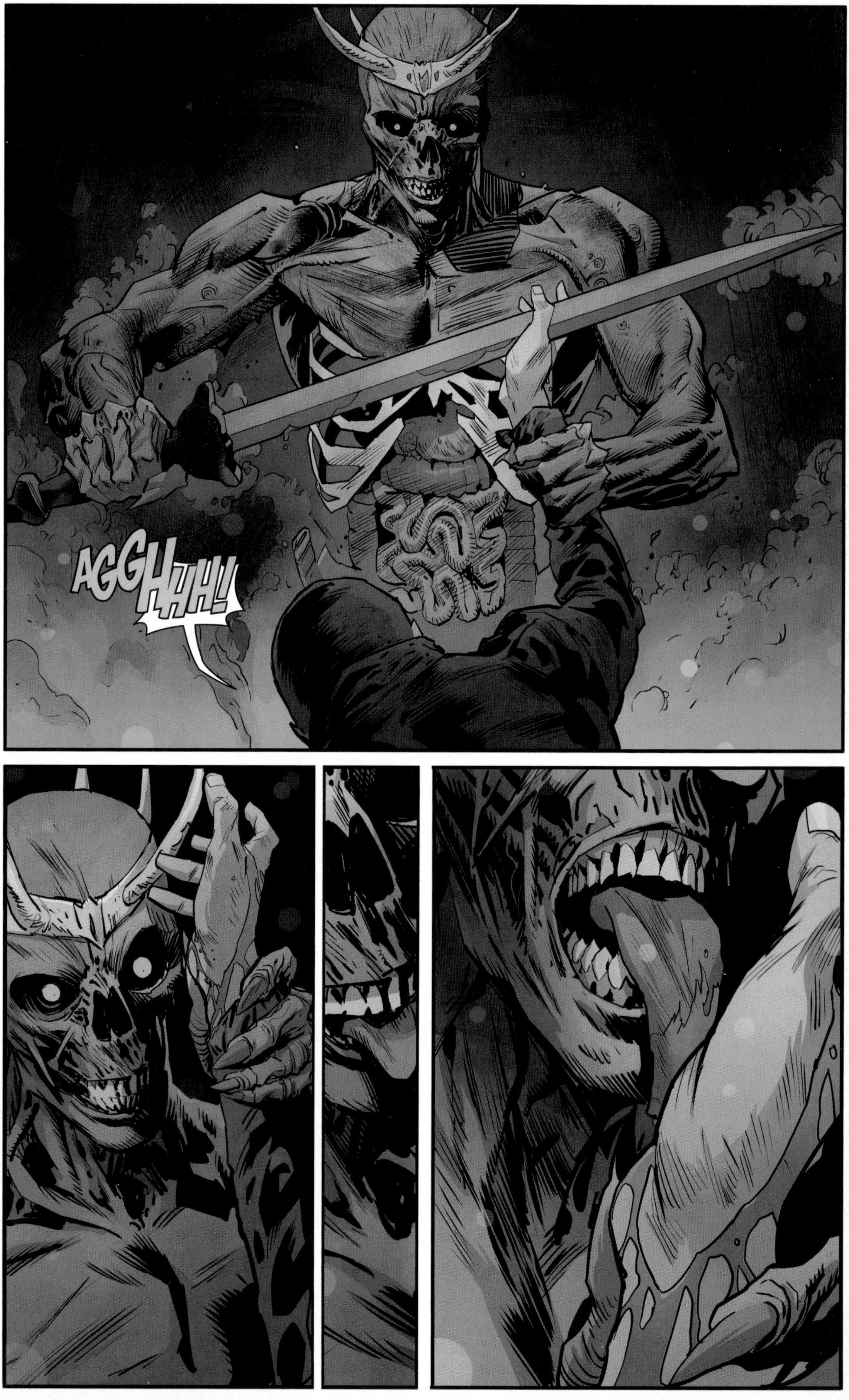
AGGHHH!

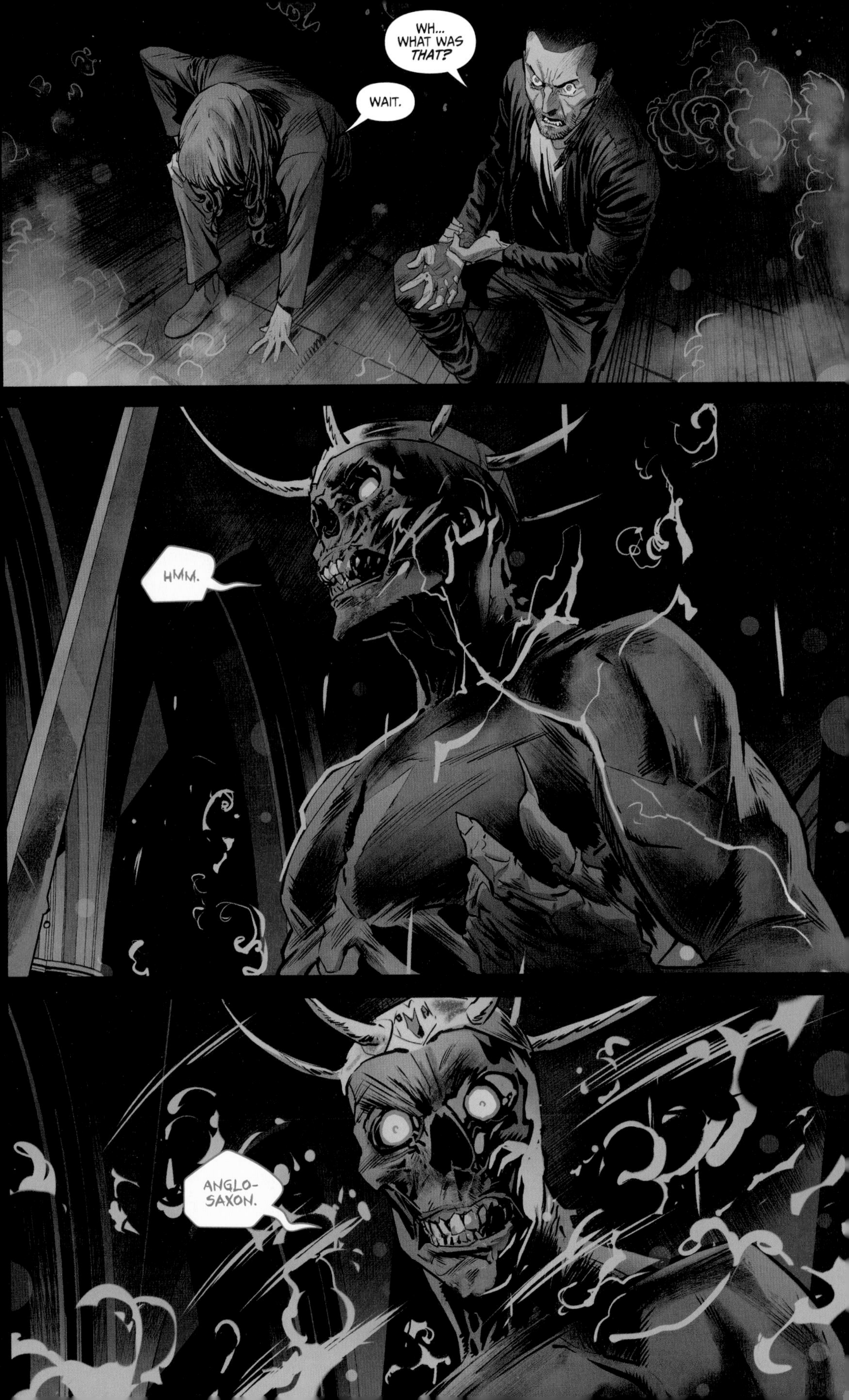
WH... WHAT WAS *THAT?*
WAIT.
HMM.
ANGLO-SAXON.

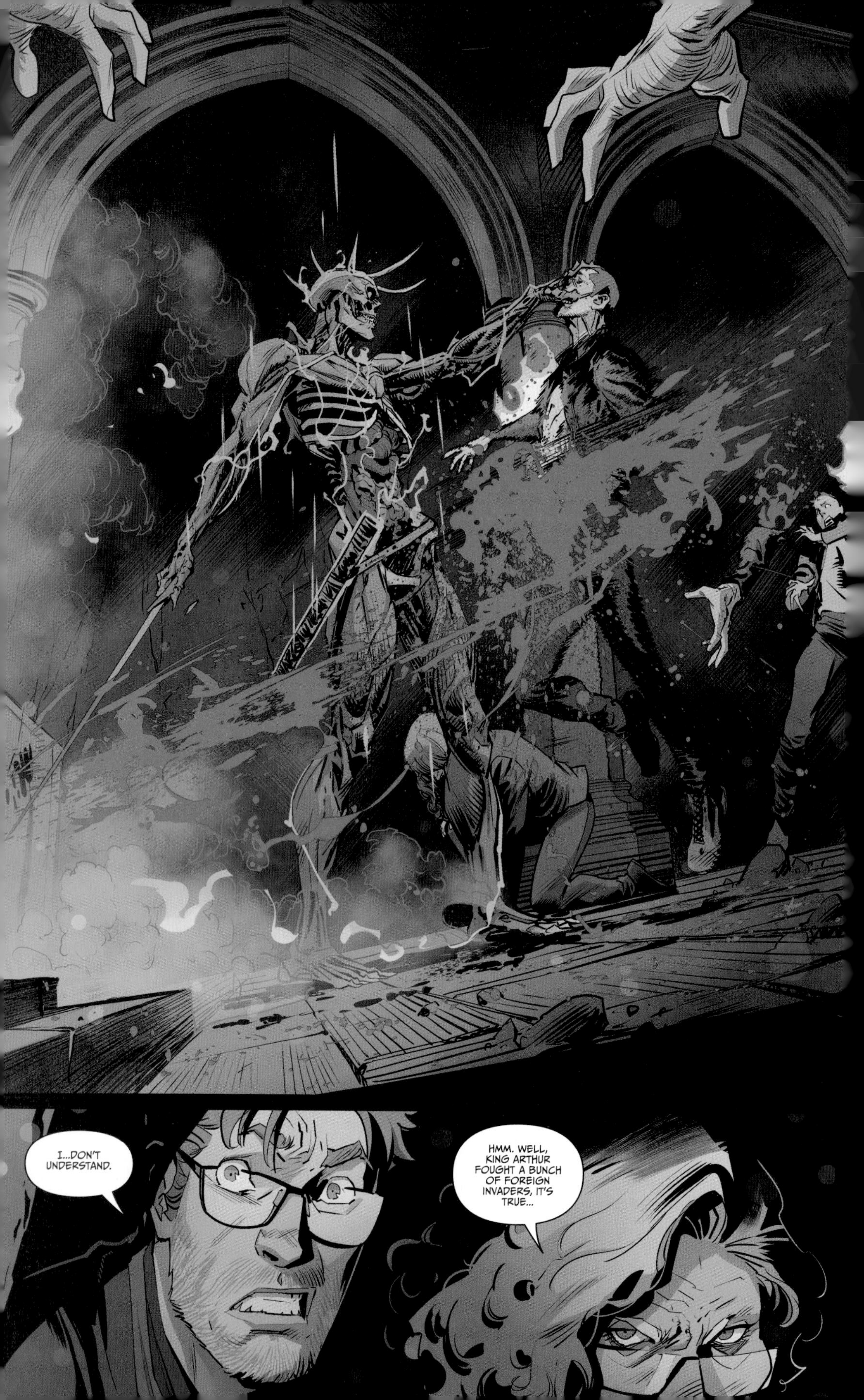
I...DON'T UNDERSTAND.
HMM. WELL, KING ARTHUR FOUGHT A BUNCH OF FOREIGN INVADERS, IT'S TRUE...

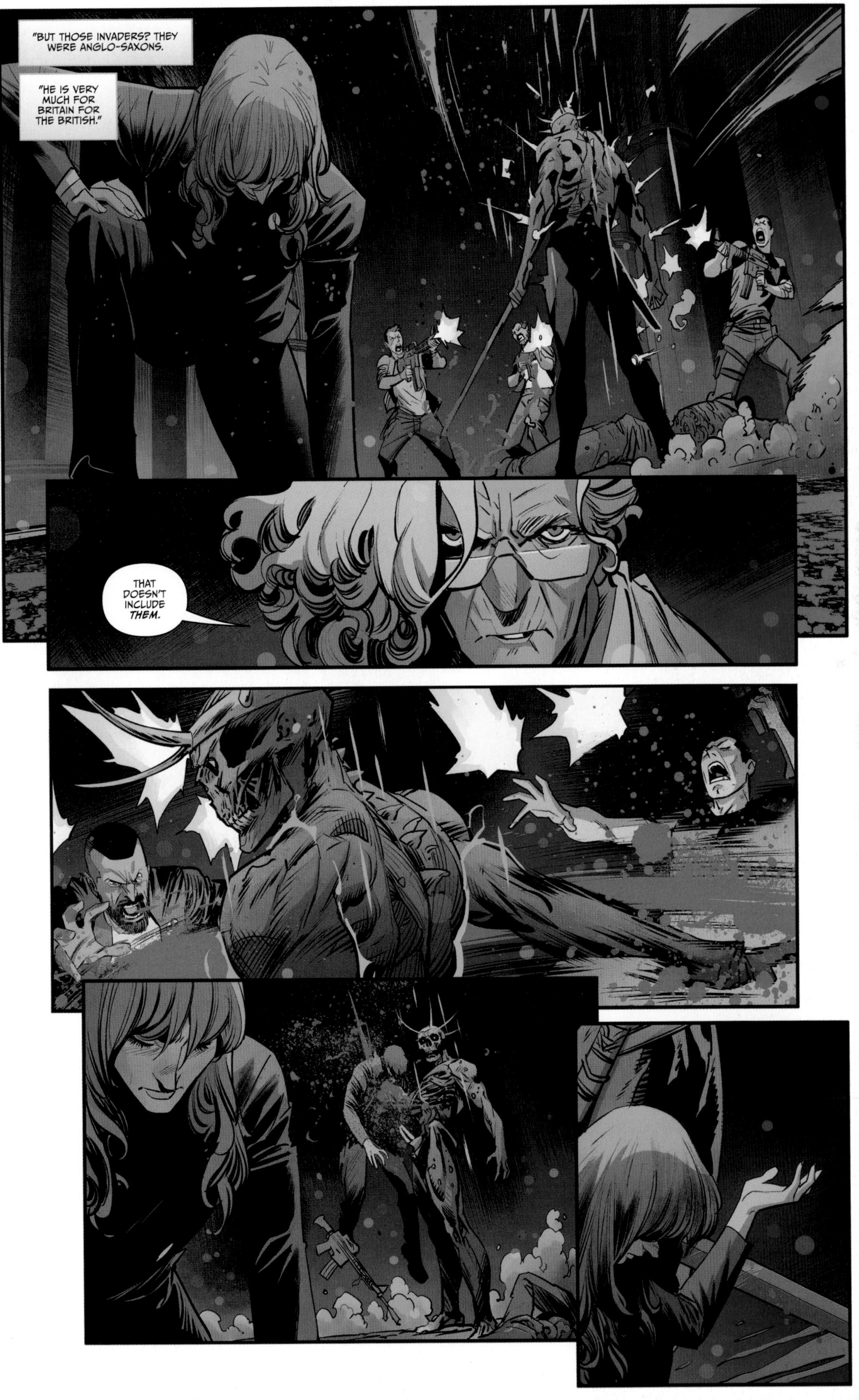
"BUT THOSE INVADERS? THEY WERE ANGLO-SAXONS.
"HE IS VERY MUCH FOR BRITAIN FOR THE BRITISH."
THAT DOESN'T INCLUDE *THEM.*

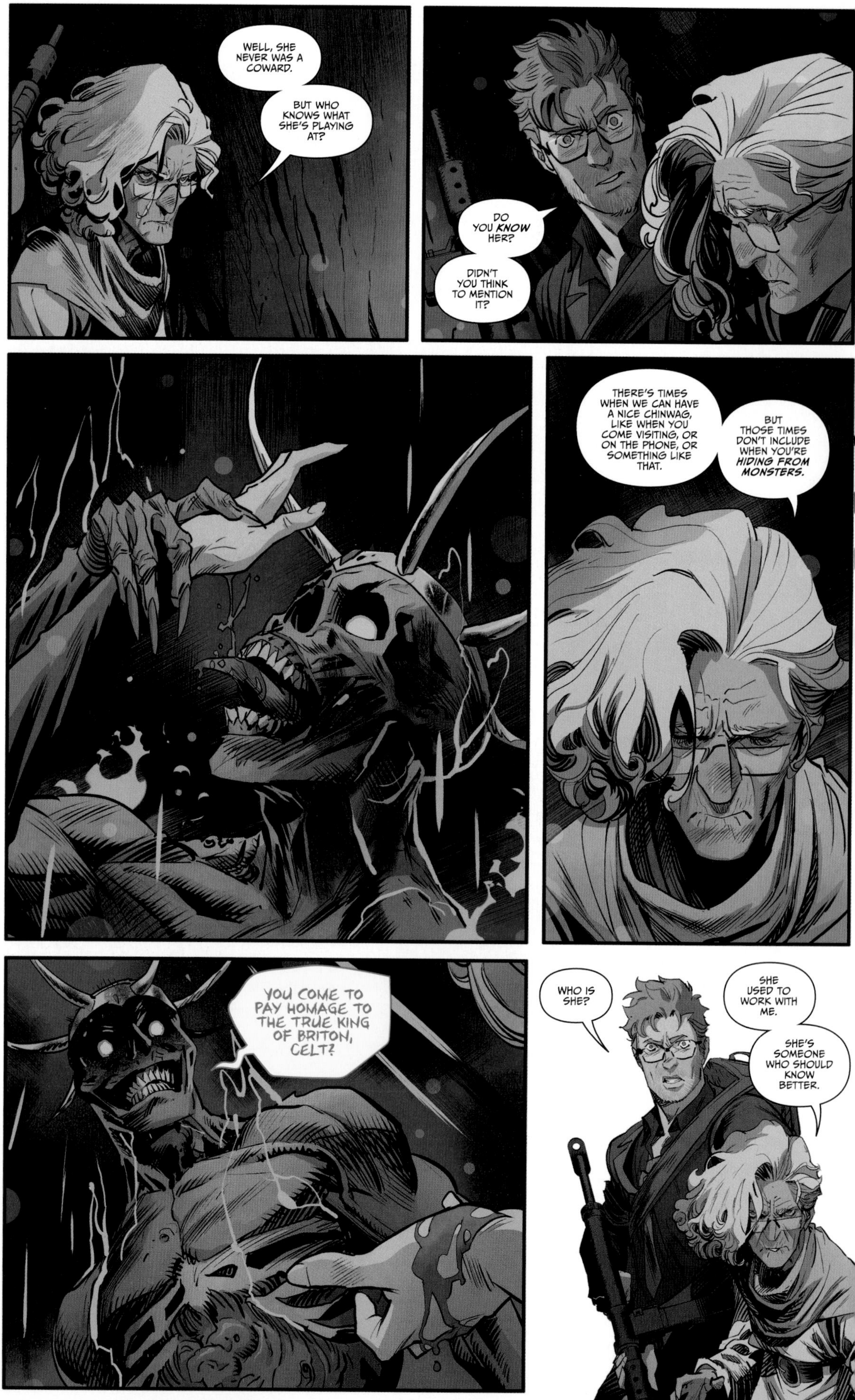

WELL, SHE NEVER WAS A COWARD.
BUT WHO KNOWS WHAT SHE'S PLAYING AT?
DO YOU *KNOW* HER?
DIDN'T YOU THINK TO MENTION IT?
THERE'S TIMES WHEN WE CAN HAVE A NICE CHINWAG, LIKE WHEN YOU COME VISITING, OR ON THE PHONE, OR SOMETHING LIKE THAT.
BUT THOSE TIMES DON'T INCLUDE WHEN YOU'RE *HIDING FROM MONSTERS.*
YOU COME TO PAY HOMAGE TO THE TRUE KING OF BRITON, CELT?
WHO IS SHE?
SHE USED TO WORK WITH ME.
SHE'S SOMEONE WHO SHOULD KNOW BETTER.

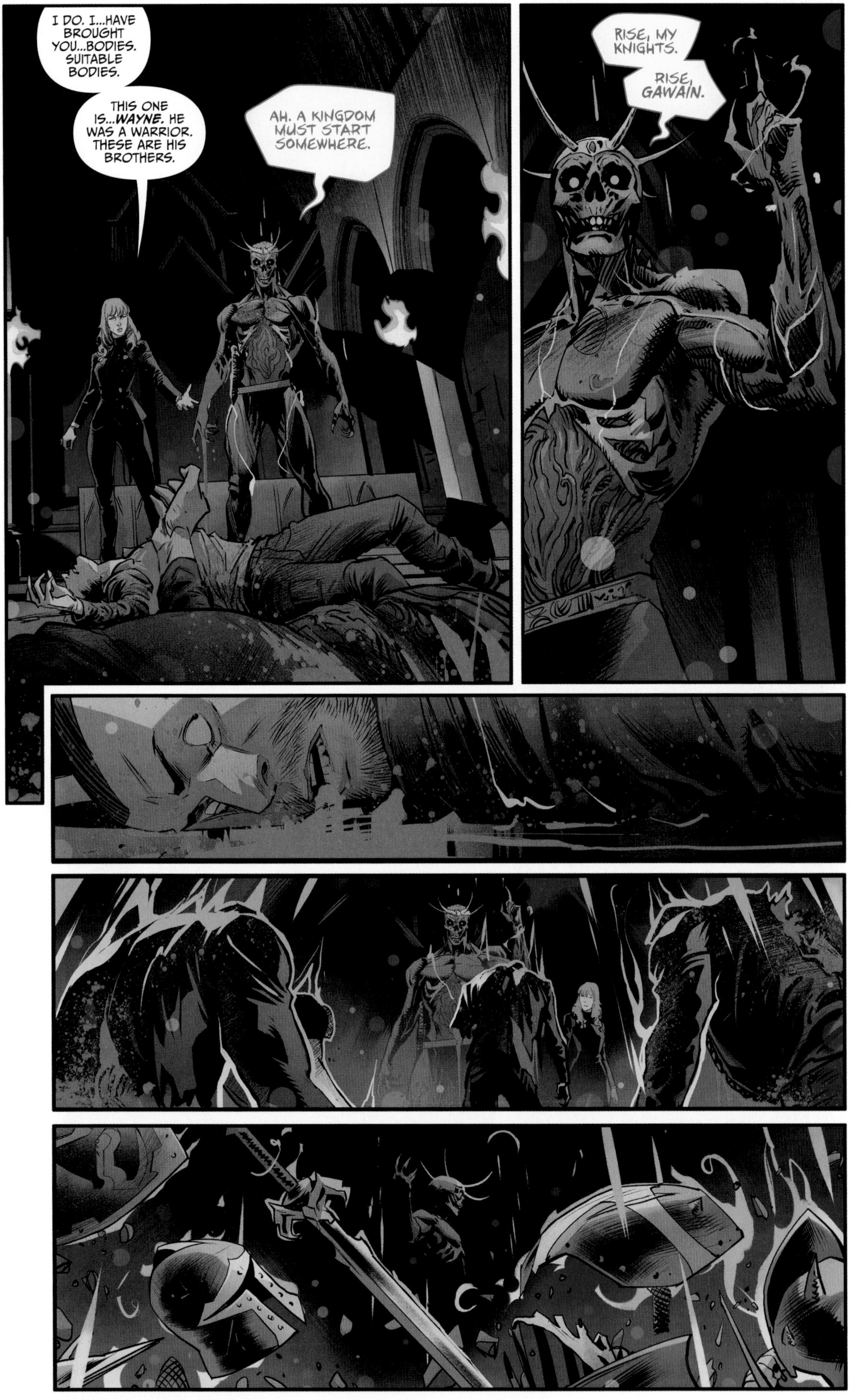
I DO. I...HAVE BROUGHT YOU...BODIES. SUITABLE BODIES.
THIS ONE IS...WAYNE. HE WAS A WARRIOR. THESE ARE HIS BROTHERS.
AH. A KINGDOM MUST START SOMEWHERE.
RISE, MY KNIGHTS.
RISE, GAWAIN.

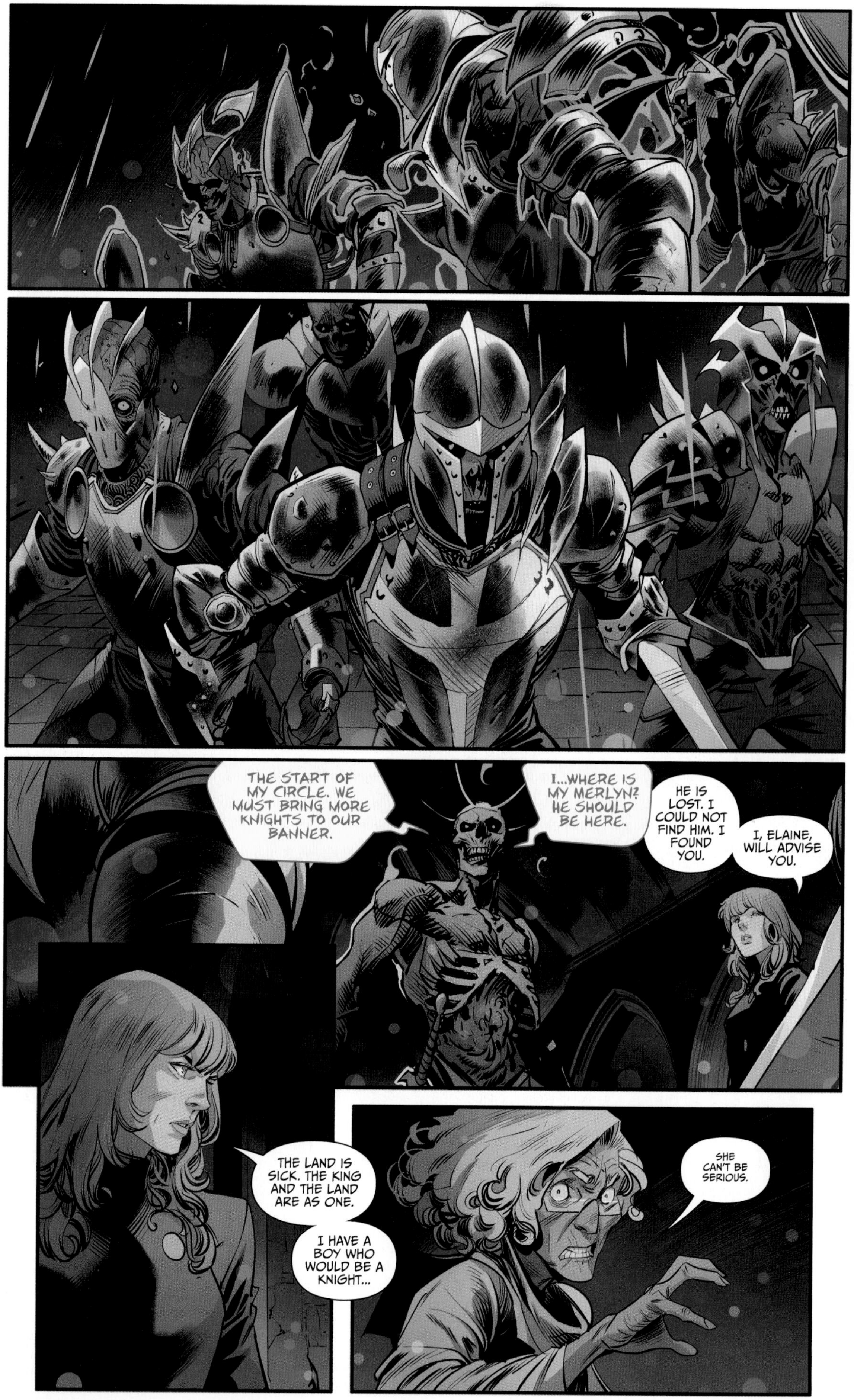
THE START OF MY CIRCLE. WE MUST BRING MORE KNIGHTS TO OUR BANNER.
I...WHERE IS MY MERLYN? HE SHOULD BE HERE.
HE IS LOST. I COULD NOT FIND HIM. I FOUND YOU.
I, ELAINE, WILL ADVISE YOU.
THE LAND IS SICK. THE KING AND THE LAND ARE AS ONE.
I HAVE A BOY WHO WOULD BE A KNIGHT...
SHE CAN'T BE SERIOUS.

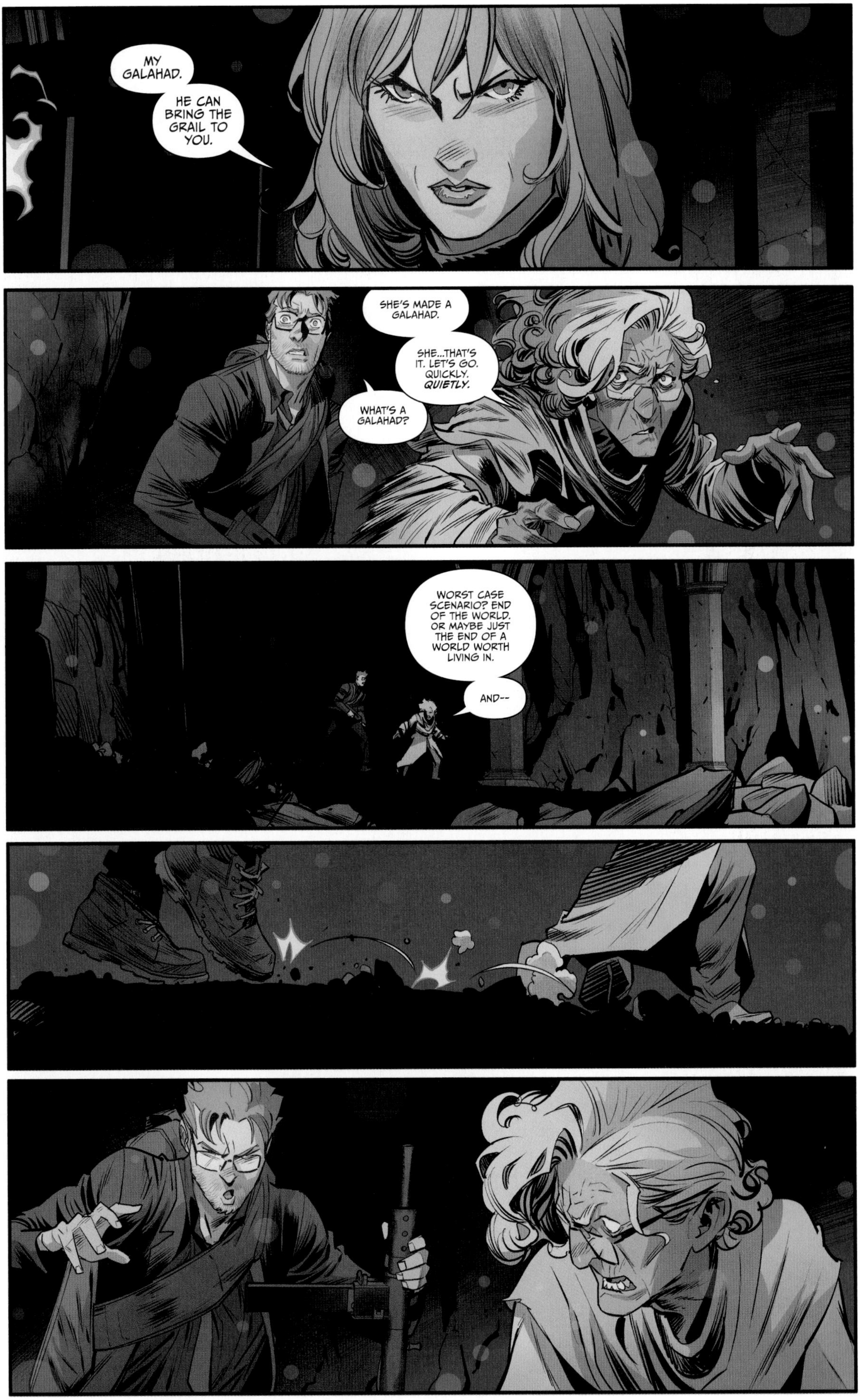
MY GALAHAD.
HE CAN BRING THE GRAIL TO YOU.
SHE'S MADE A GALAHAD.
SHE...THAT'S IT. LET'S GO. QUICKLY. *QUIETLY.*
WHAT'S A GALAHAD?
WORST CASE SCENARIO? END OF THE WORLD. OR MAYBE JUST THE END OF A WORLD WORTH LIVING IN.
AND--

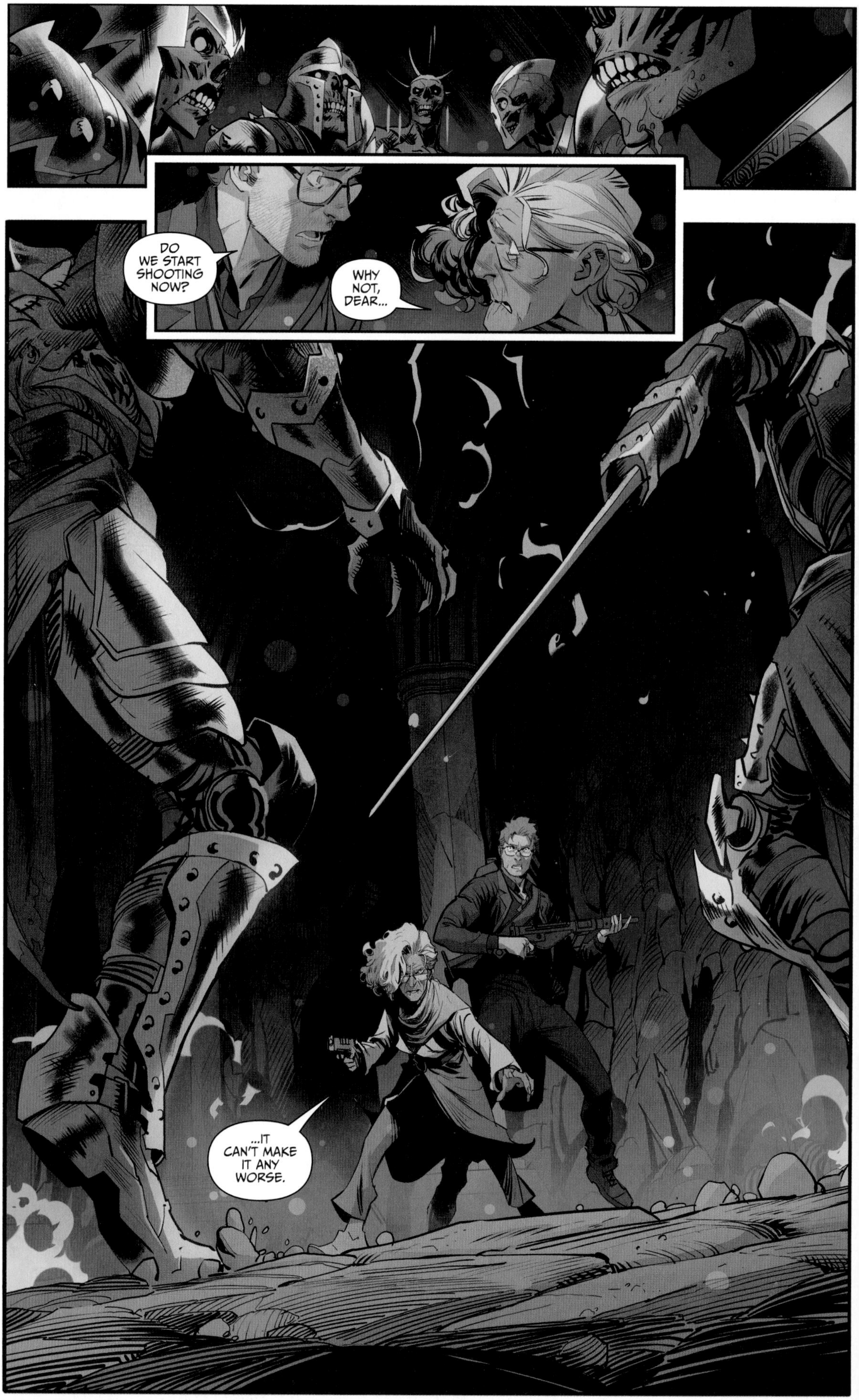
DO WE START SHOOTING NOW?
WHY NOT, DEAR...
...IT CAN'T MAKE IT ANY WORSE.

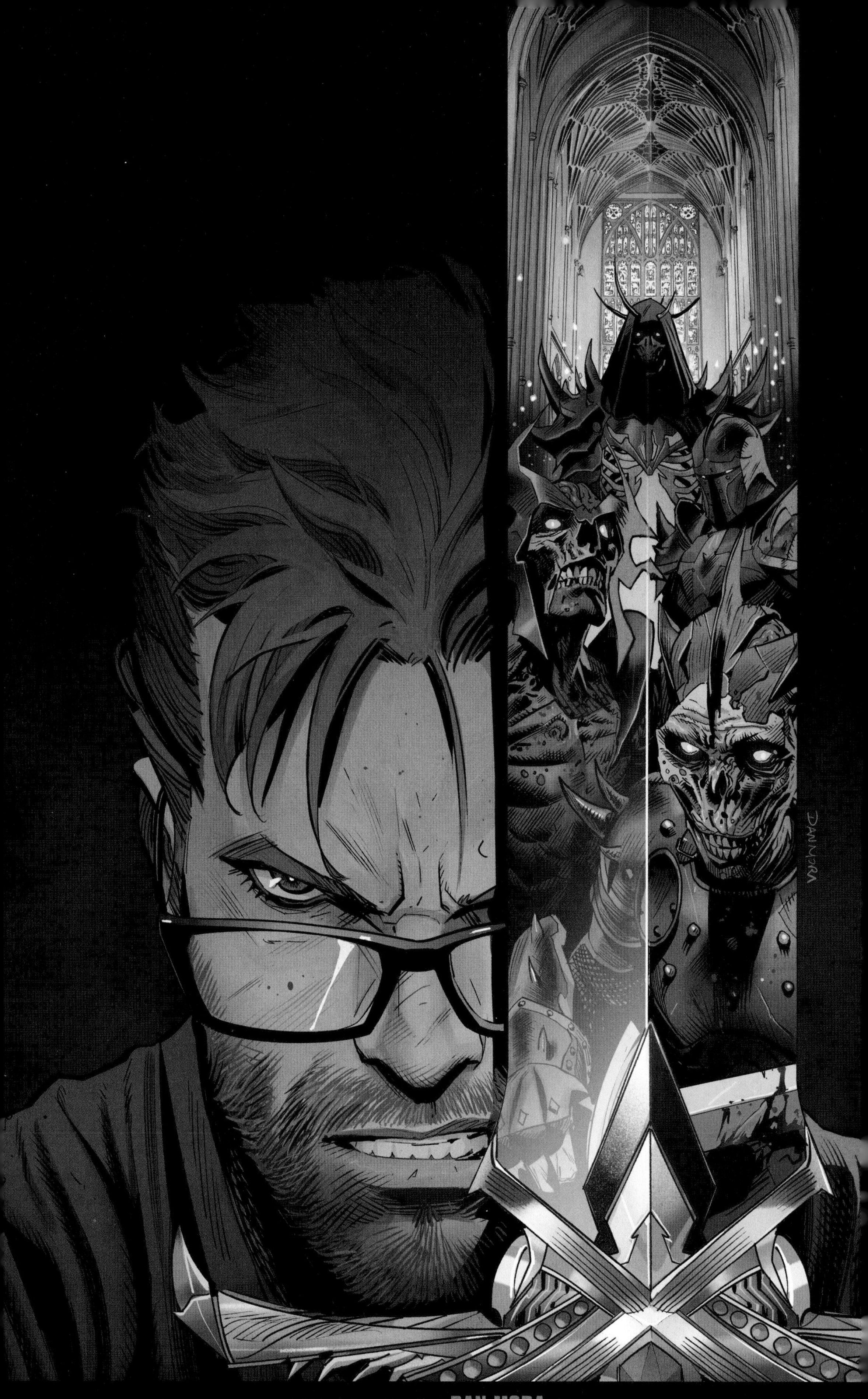
DANMORA

ISSUE THREE COVER BY **DAN MORA**

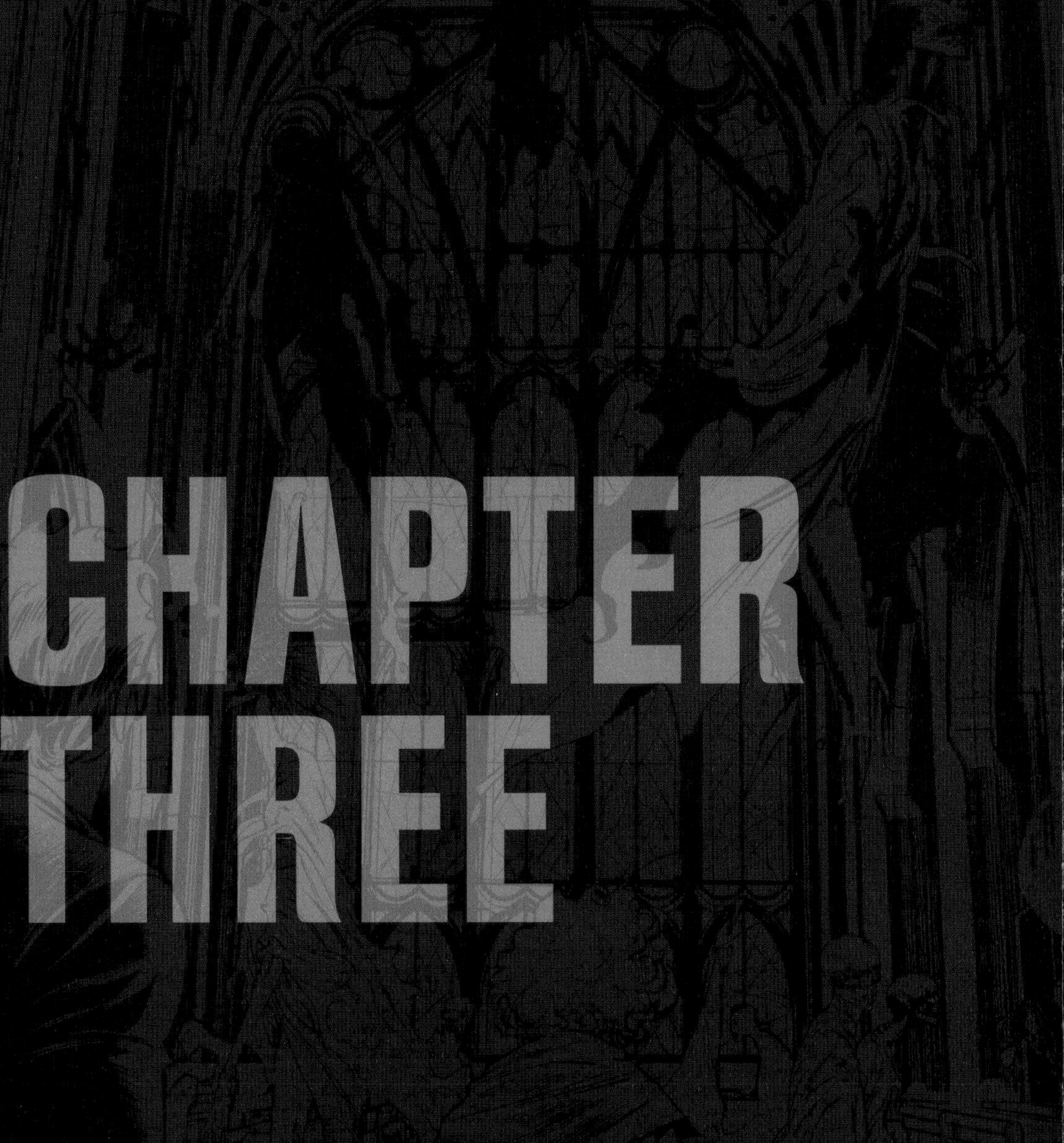

CHAPTER THREE

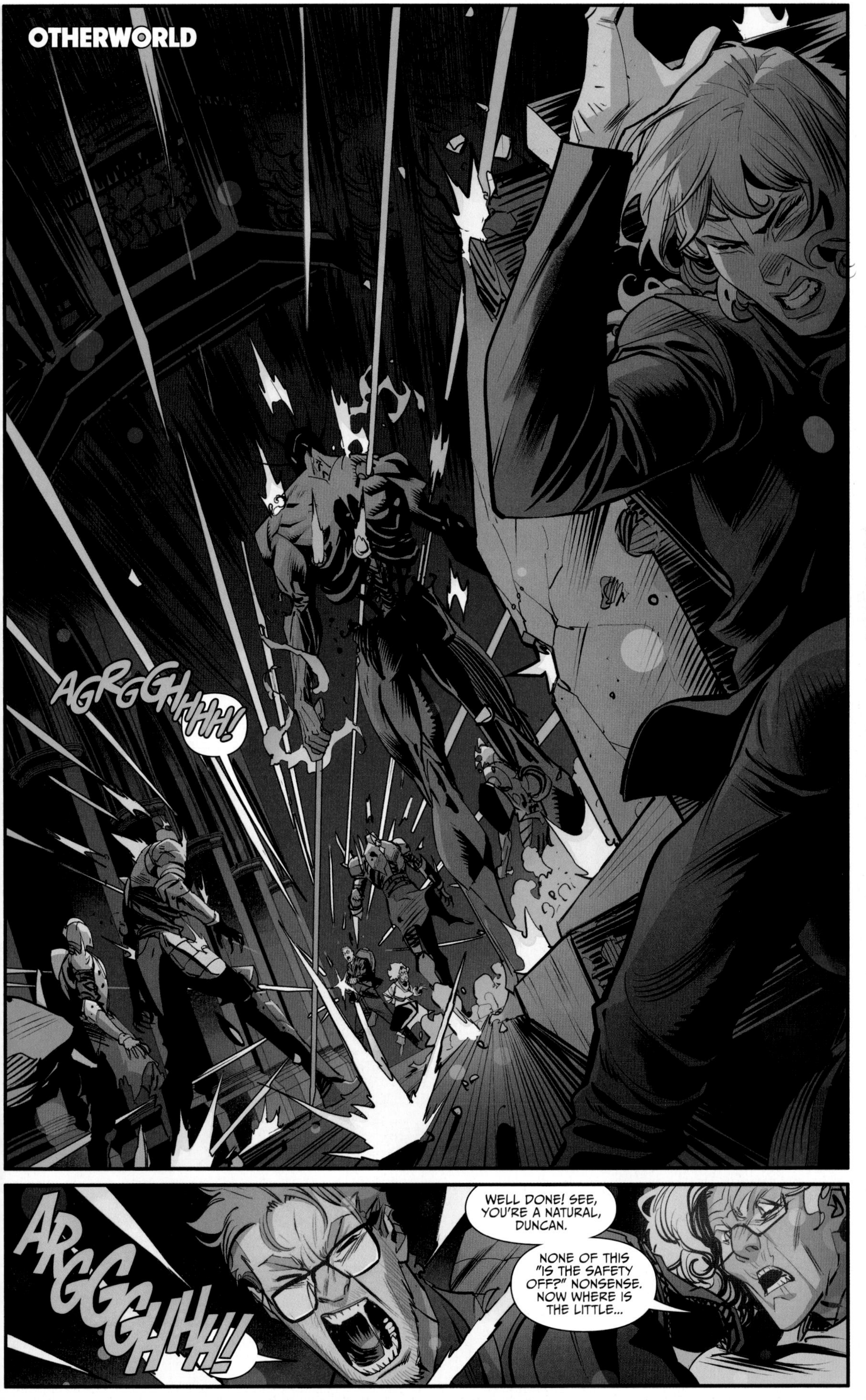
OTHERWORLD
AGRGGHHHH!
ARGGGHHH!!
WELL DONE! SEE, YOU'RE A NATURAL, DUNCAN.
NONE OF THIS "IS THE SAFETY OFF?" NONSENSE. NOW WHERE IS THE LITTLE...

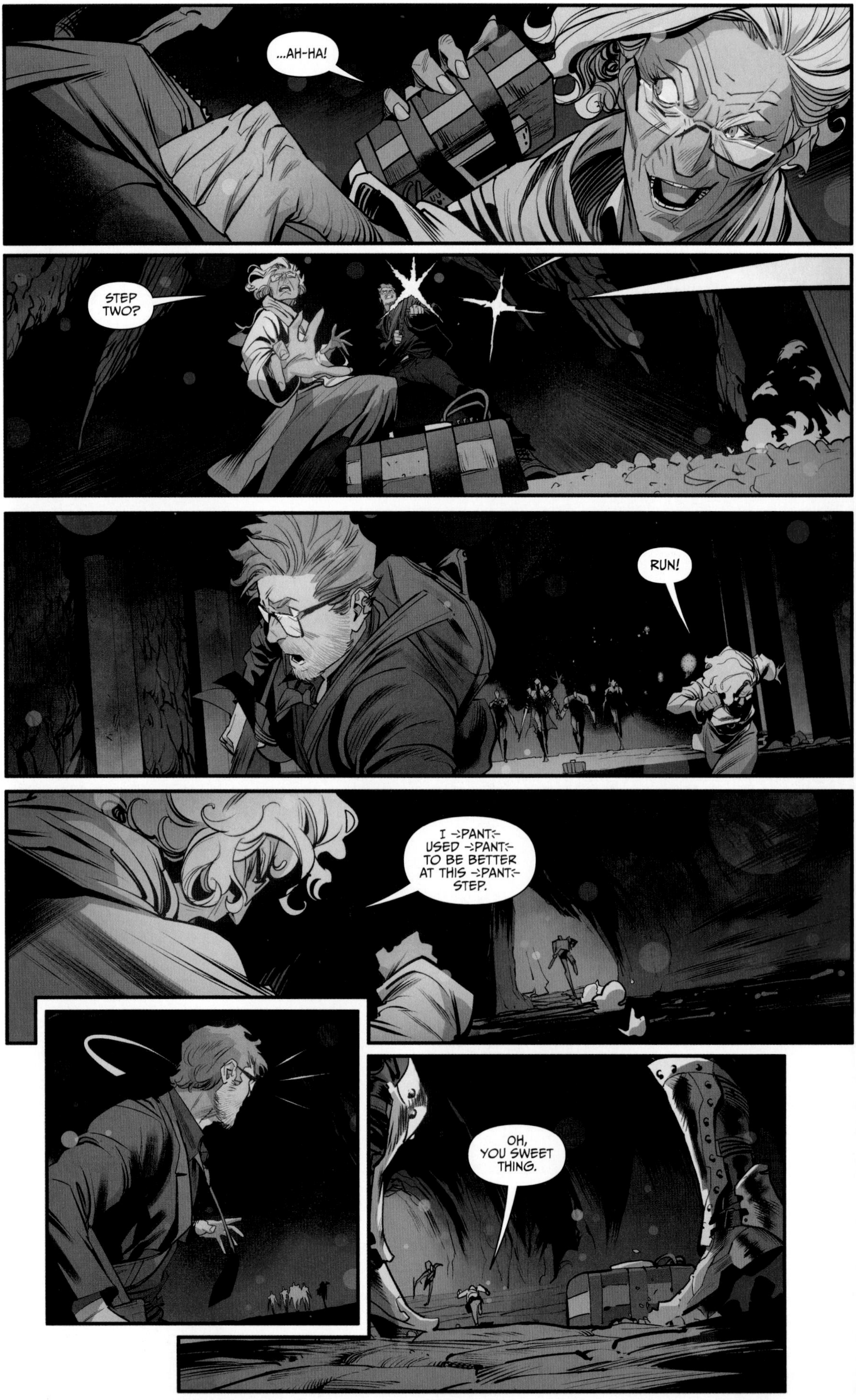
...AH-HA!
STEP TWO?
RUN!
I -›PANT‹- USED -›PANT‹- TO BE BETTER AT THIS -›PANT‹- STEP.
OH, YOU SWEET THING.

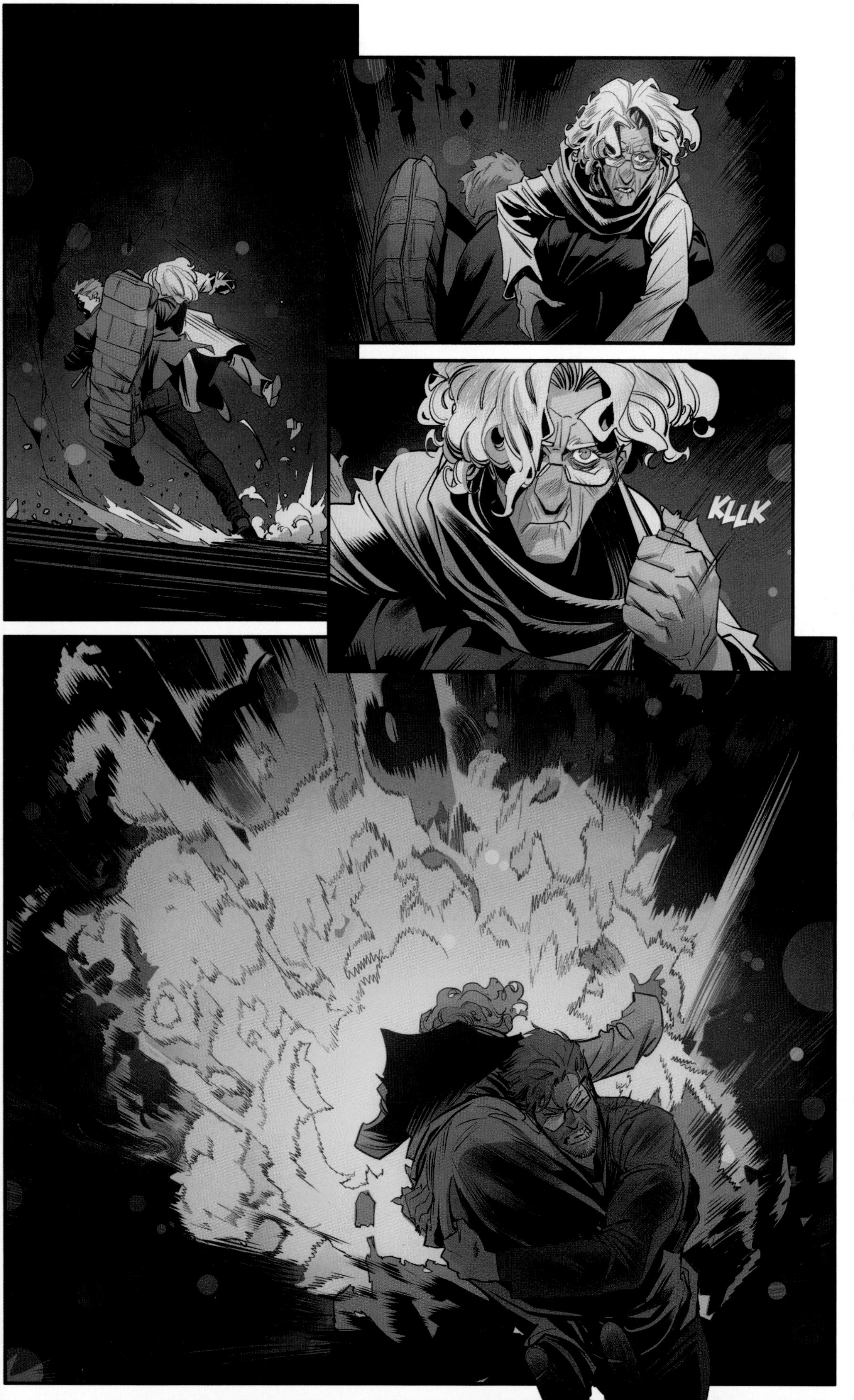
KLLK

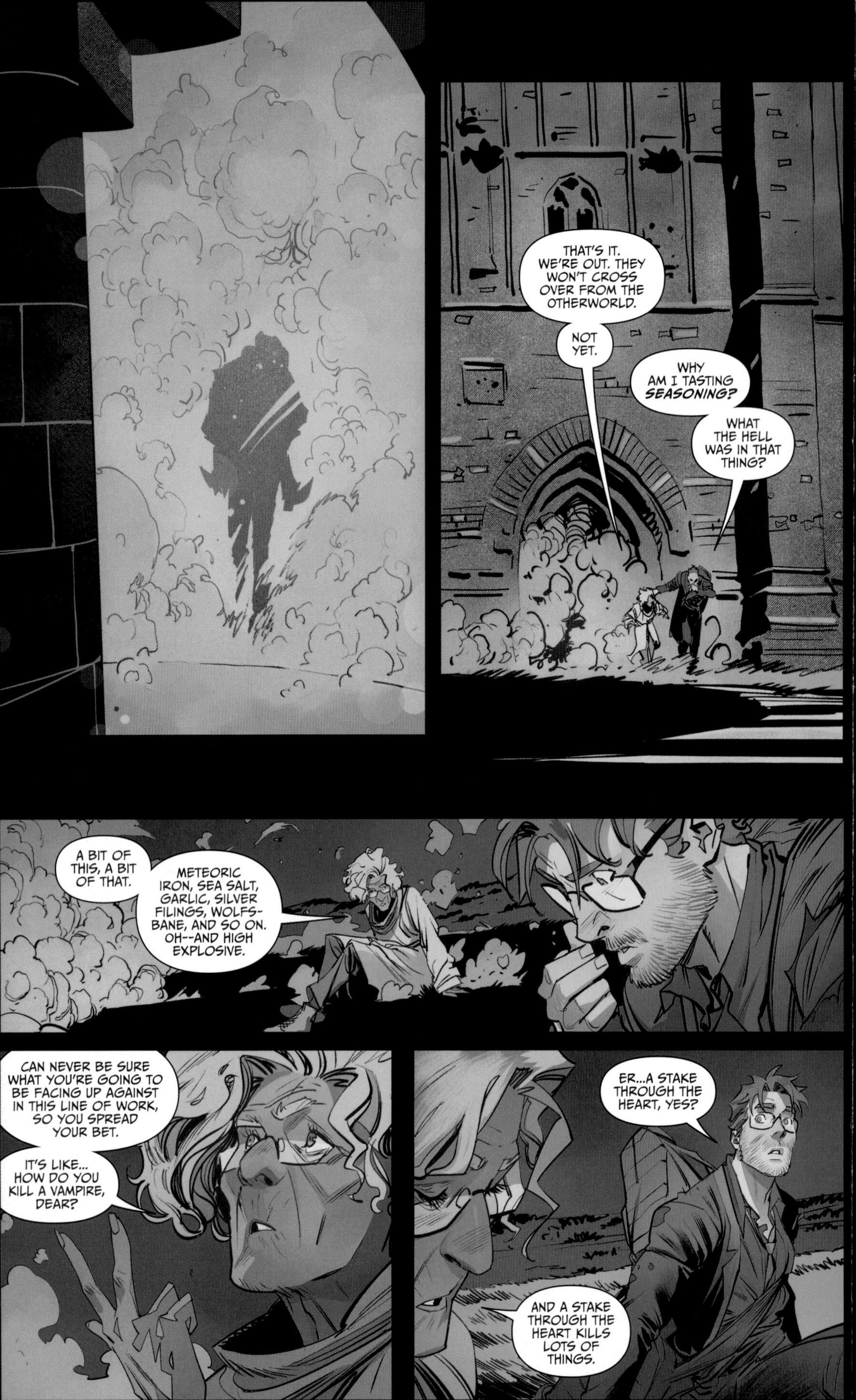
THAT'S IT. WE'RE OUT. THEY WON'T CROSS OVER FROM THE OTHERWORLD.
NOT YET.
WHY AM I TASTING SEASONING?
WHAT THE HELL WAS IN THAT THING?
A BIT OF THIS, A BIT OF THAT.
METEORIC IRON, SEA SALT, GARLIC, SILVER FILINGS, WOLFS-BANE, AND SO ON. OH--AND HIGH EXPLOSIVE.
CAN NEVER BE SURE WHAT YOU'RE GOING TO BE FACING UP AGAINST IN THIS LINE OF WORK, SO YOU SPREAD YOUR BET.
IT'S LIKE... HOW DO YOU KILL A VAMPIRE, DEAR?
ER...A STAKE THROUGH THE HEART, YES?
AND A STAKE THROUGH THE HEART KILLS LOTS OF THINGS.

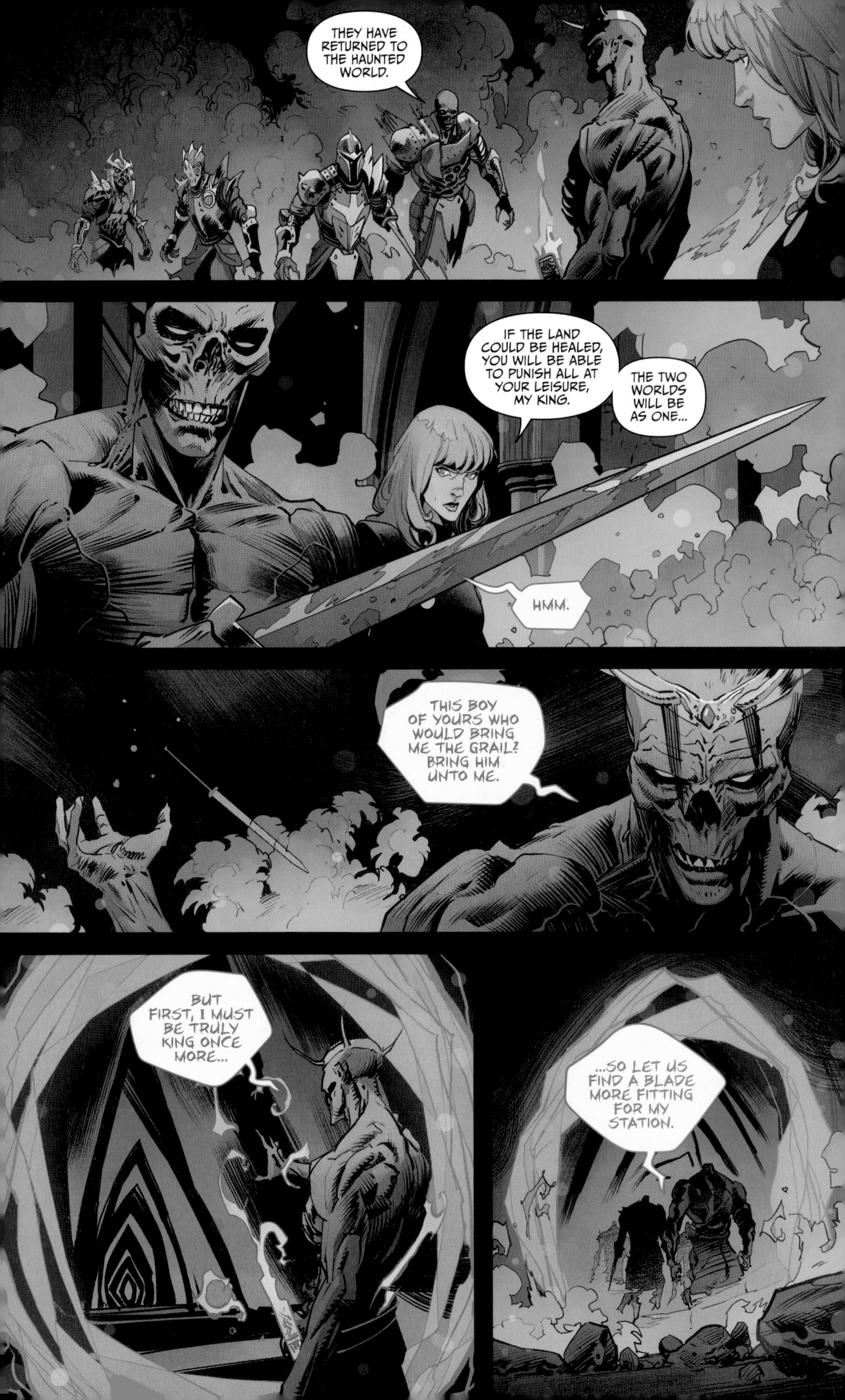
THEY HAVE RETURNED TO THE HAUNTED WORLD.
IF THE LAND COULD BE HEALED, YOU WILL BE ABLE TO PUNISH ALL AT YOUR LEISURE, MY KING.
THE TWO WORLDS WILL BE AS ONE...
HMM.
THIS BOY OF YOURS WHO WOULD BRING ME THE GRAIL? BRING HIM UNTO ME.
BUT FIRST, I MUST BE TRULY KING ONCE MORE...
...SO LET US FIND A BLADE MORE FITTING FOR MY STATION.

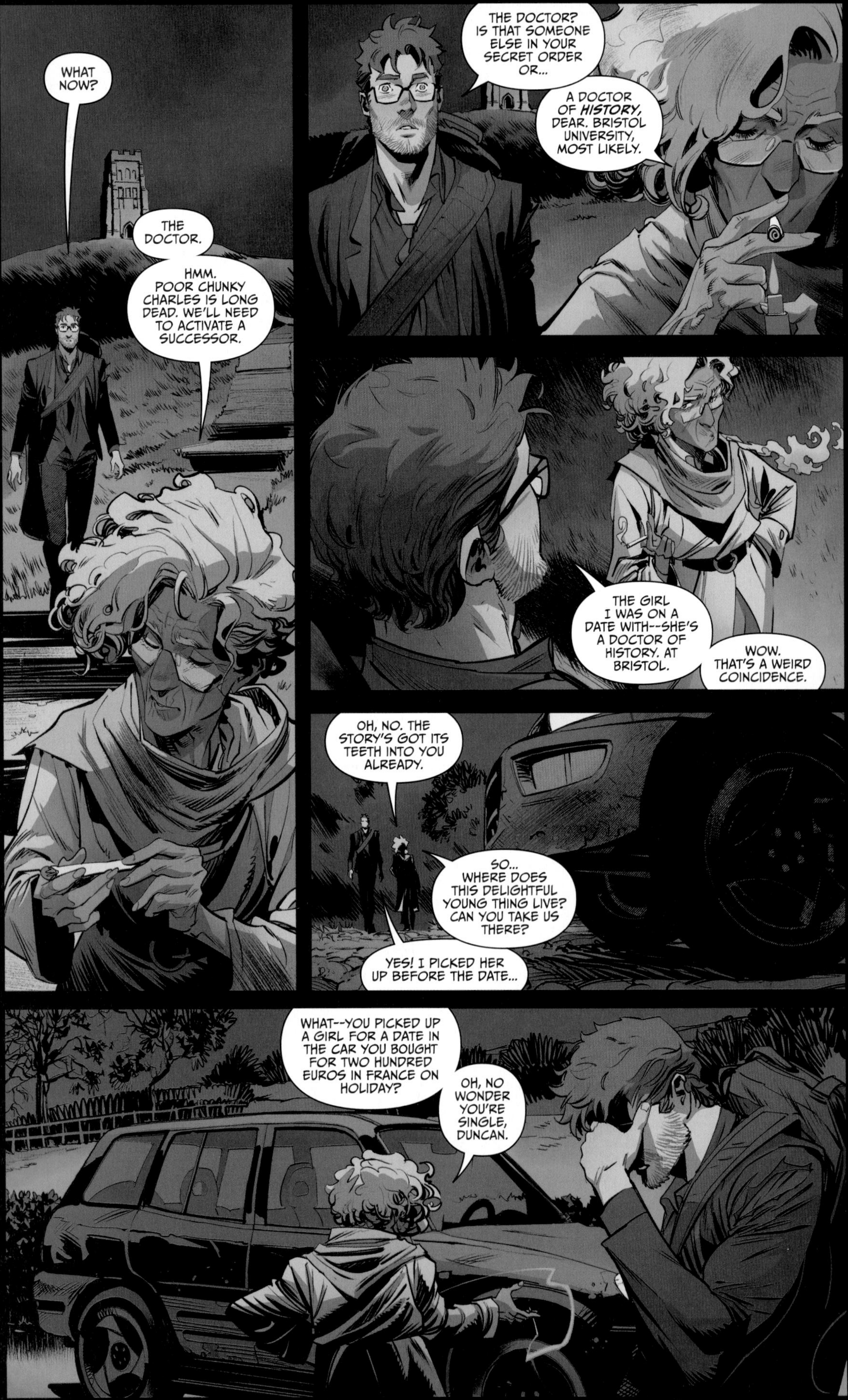
WHAT NOW?
THE DOCTOR.
HMM. POOR CHUNKY CHARLES IS LONG DEAD. WE'LL NEED TO ACTIVATE A SUCCESSOR.
THE DOCTOR? IS THAT SOMEONE ELSE IN YOUR SECRET ORDER OR...
A DOCTOR OF *HISTORY*, DEAR. BRISTOL UNIVERSITY, MOST LIKELY.
THE GIRL I WAS ON A DATE WITH--SHE'S A DOCTOR OF HISTORY. AT BRISTOL.
WOW. THAT'S A WEIRD COINCIDENCE.
OH, NO. THE STORY'S GOT ITS TEETH INTO YOU ALREADY.
SO... WHERE DOES THIS DELIGHTFUL YOUNG THING LIVE? CAN YOU TAKE US THERE?
YES! I PICKED HER UP BEFORE THE DATE...
WHAT--YOU PICKED UP A GIRL FOR A DATE IN THE CAR YOU BOUGHT FOR TWO HUNDRED EUROS IN FRANCE ON HOLIDAY?
OH, NO WONDER YOU'RE SINGLE, DUNCAN.

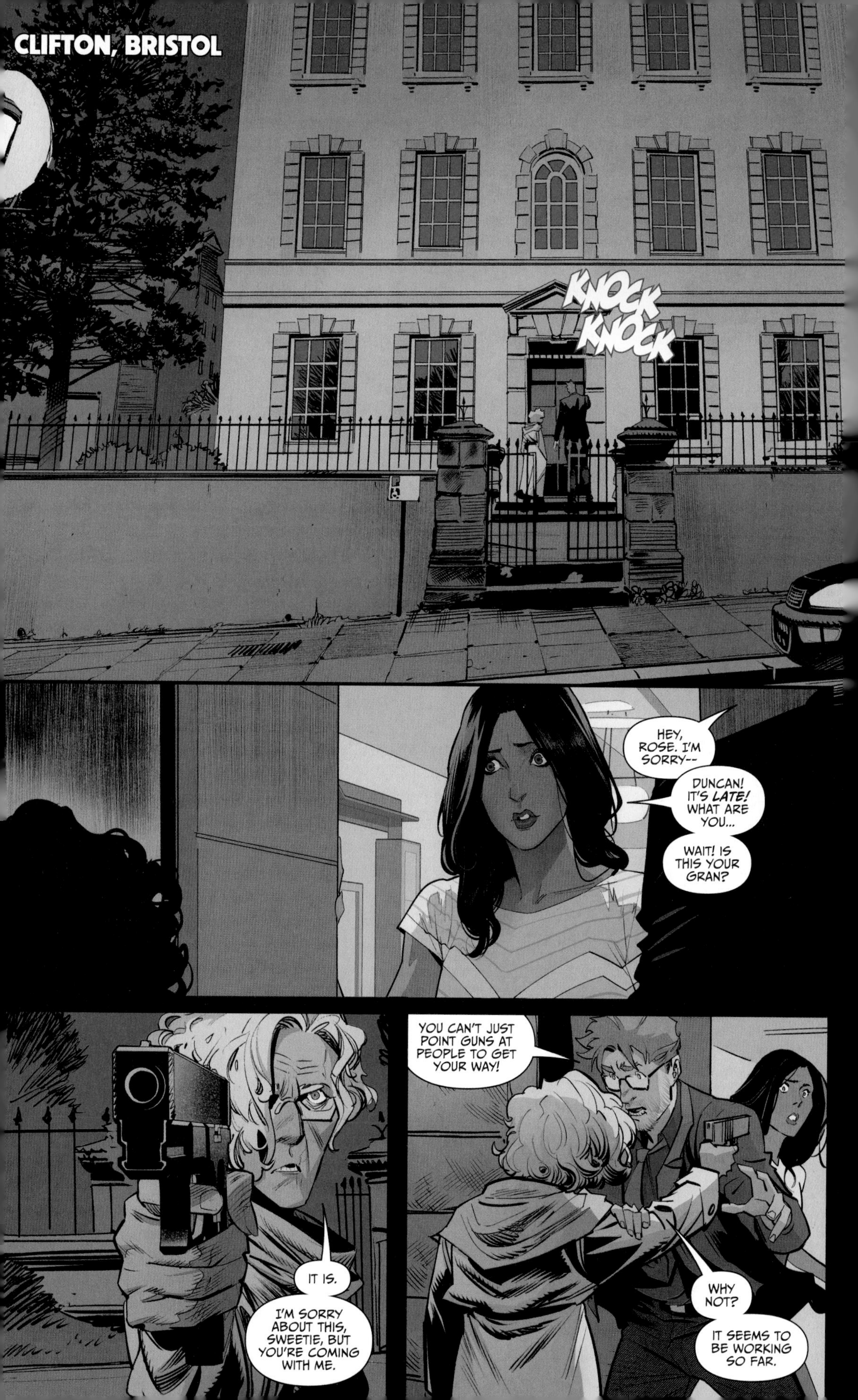
CLIFTON, BRISTOL
KNOCK KNOCK
HEY, ROSE. I'M SORRY--
DUNCAN! IT'S *LATE!* WHAT ARE YOU...
WAIT! IS THIS YOUR GRAN?
IT IS.
I'M SORRY ABOUT THIS, SWEETIE, BUT YOU'RE COMING WITH ME.
YOU CAN'T JUST POINT GUNS AT PEOPLE TO GET YOUR WAY!
WHY NOT?
IT SEEMS TO BE WORKING SO FAR.

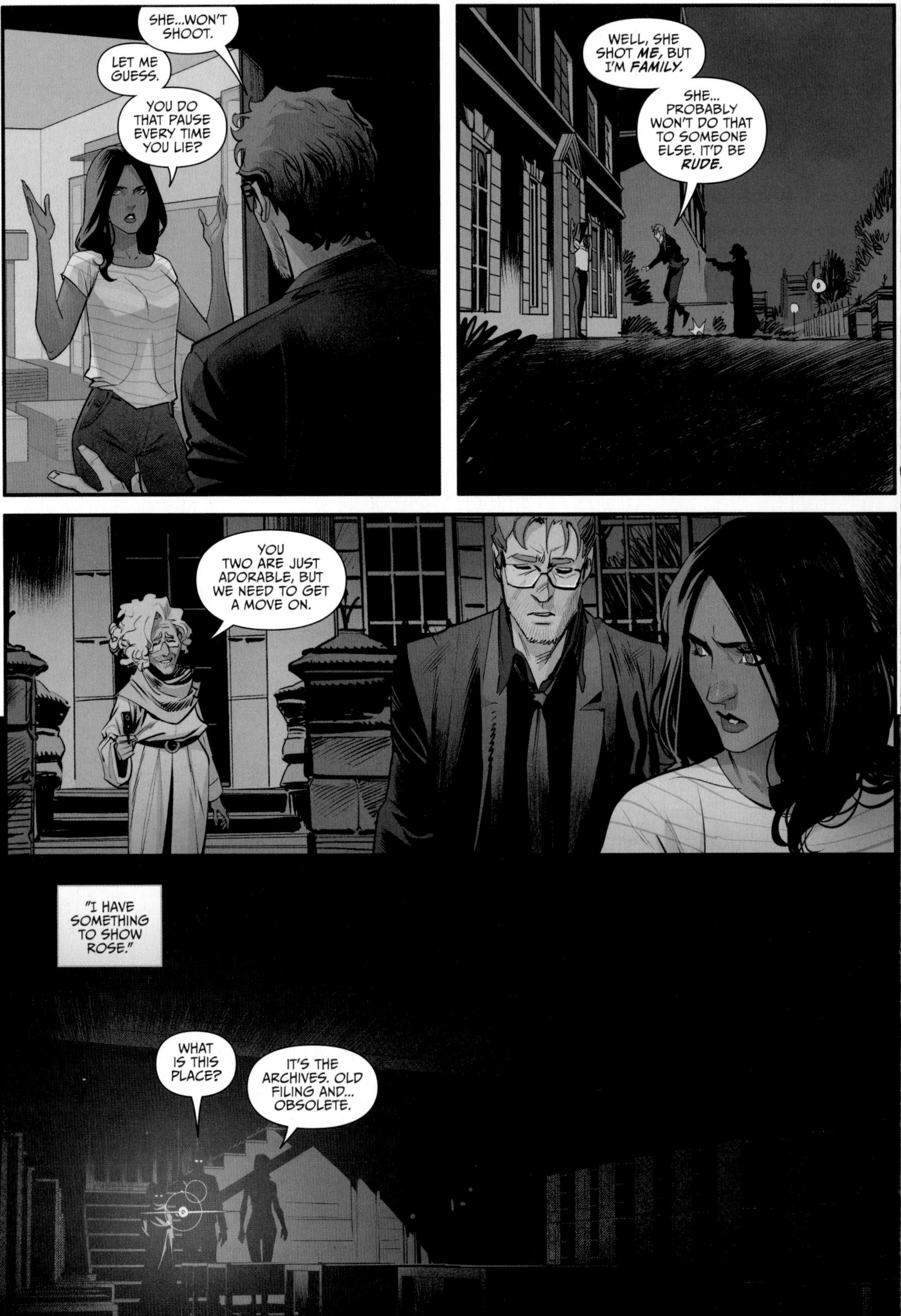
SHE...WON'T SHOOT.
LET ME GUESS.
YOU DO THAT PAUSE EVERY TIME YOU LIE?
WELL, SHE SHOT *ME*, BUT I'M *FAMILY.*
SHE... PROBABLY WON'T DO THAT TO SOMEONE ELSE. IT'D BE *RUDE.*
YOU TWO ARE JUST ADORABLE, BUT WE NEED TO GET A MOVE ON.
"I HAVE SOMETHING TO SHOW ROSE."
WHAT IS THIS PLACE?
IT'S THE ARCHIVES. OLD FILING AND... OBSOLETE.

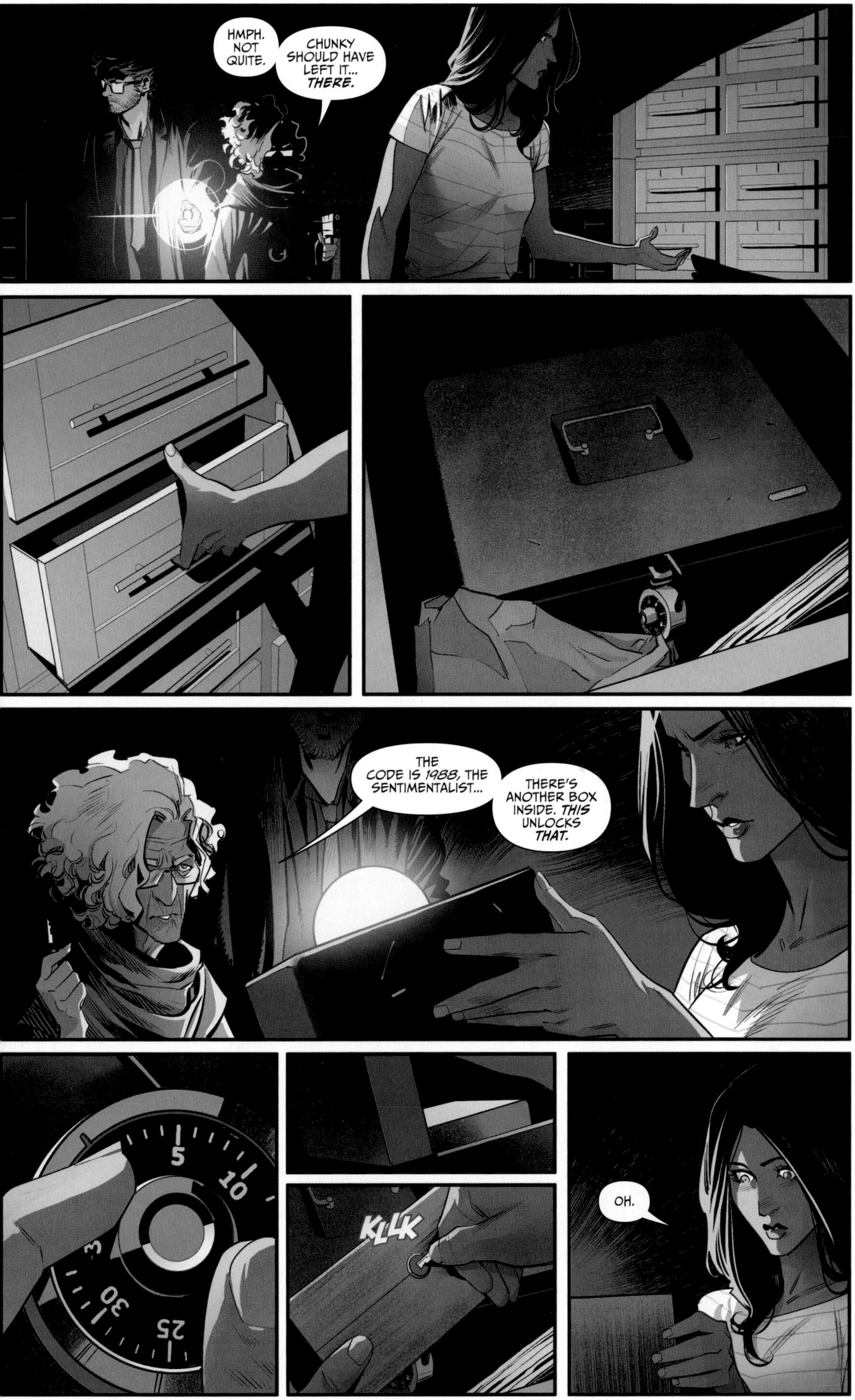
HMPH. NOT QUITE.
CHUNKY SHOULD HAVE LEFT IT... THERE.
THE CODE IS 1988, THE SENTIMENTALIST...
THERE'S ANOTHER BOX INSIDE. THIS UNLOCKS THAT.
KLIK
OH.

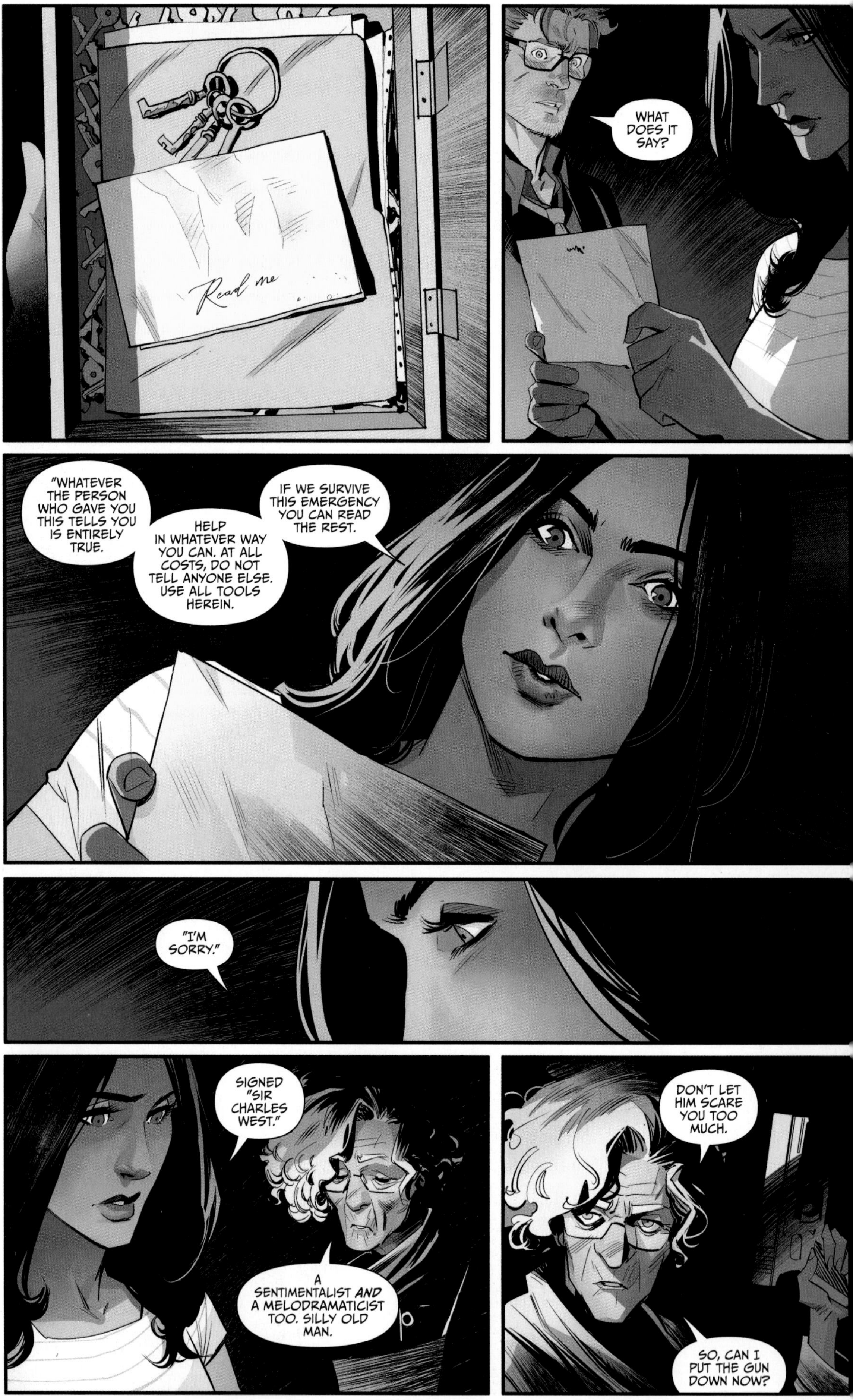
Read me
WHAT DOES IT SAY?
"WHATEVER THE PERSON WHO GAVE YOU THIS TELLS YOU IS ENTIRELY TRUE.
HELP IN WHATEVER WAY YOU CAN. AT ALL COSTS, DO NOT TELL ANYONE ELSE. USE ALL TOOLS HEREIN.
IF WE SURVIVE THIS EMERGENCY YOU CAN READ THE REST.
"I'M SORRY."
SIGNED "SIR CHARLES WEST."
A SENTIMENTALIST *AND* A MELODRAMATICIST TOO. SILLY OLD MAN.
DON'T LET HIM SCARE YOU TOO MUCH.
SO, CAN I PUT THE GUN DOWN NOW?

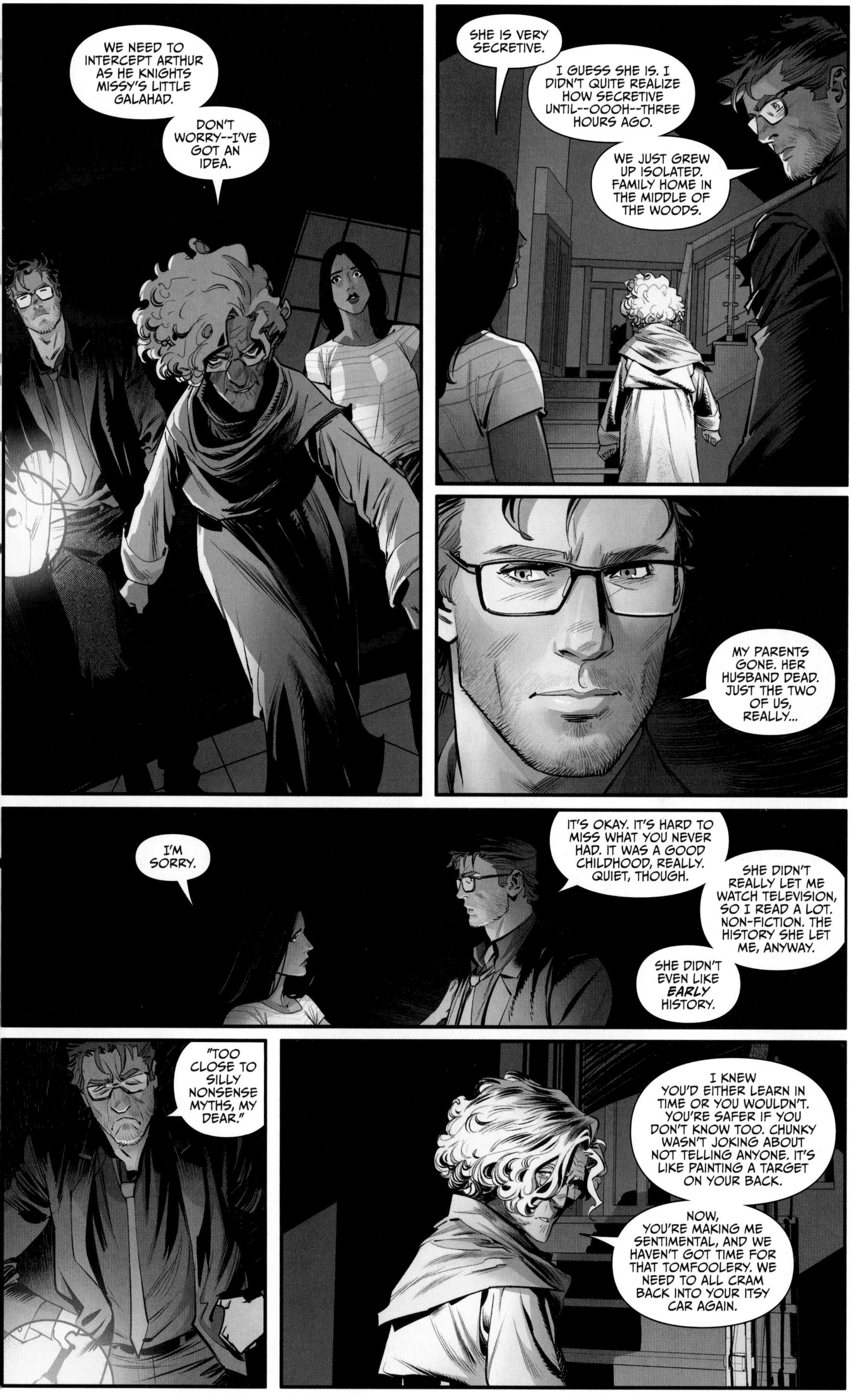

WE NEED TO INTERCEPT ARTHUR AS HE KNIGHTS MISSY'S LITTLE GALAHAD.
DON'T WORRY--I'VE GOT AN IDEA.
SHE IS VERY SECRETIVE.
I GUESS SHE IS. I DIDN'T QUITE REALIZE HOW SECRETIVE UNTIL--OOOH--THREE HOURS AGO.
WE JUST GREW UP ISOLATED. FAMILY HOME IN THE MIDDLE OF THE WOODS.
MY PARENTS GONE. HER HUSBAND DEAD. JUST THE TWO OF US, REALLY...
I'M SORRY.
IT'S OKAY. IT'S HARD TO MISS WHAT YOU NEVER HAD. IT WAS A GOOD CHILDHOOD, REALLY. QUIET, THOUGH.
SHE DIDN'T REALLY LET ME WATCH TELEVISION, SO I READ A LOT. NON-FICTION. THE HISTORY SHE LET ME, ANYWAY.
SHE DIDN'T EVEN LIKE *EARLY* HISTORY.
"TOO CLOSE TO SILLY NONSENSE MYTHS, MY DEAR."
I KNEW YOU'D EITHER LEARN IN TIME OR YOU WOULDN'T. YOU'RE SAFER IF YOU DON'T KNOW TOO. CHUNKY WASN'T JOKING ABOUT NOT TELLING ANYONE. IT'S LIKE PAINTING A TARGET ON YOUR BACK.
NOW, YOU'RE MAKING ME SENTIMENTAL, AND WE HAVEN'T GOT TIME FOR THAT TOMFOOLERY. WE NEED TO ALL CRAM BACK INTO YOUR ITSY CAR AGAIN.

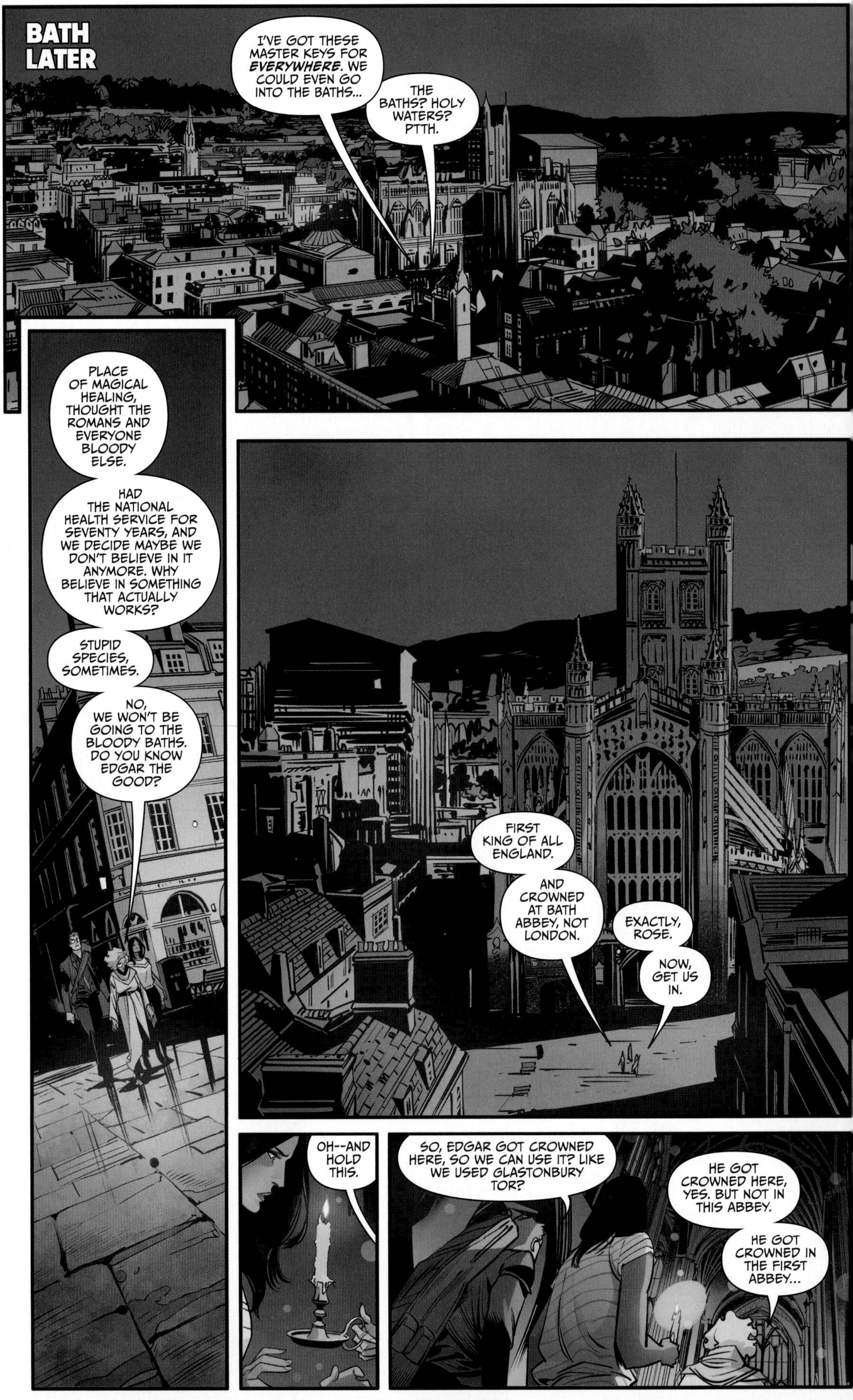
BATH
LATER
I'VE GOT THESE MASTER KEYS FOR EVERYWHERE. WE COULD EVEN GO INTO THE BATHS...
THE BATHS? HOLY WATERS? PTTH.
PLACE OF MAGICAL HEALING, THOUGHT THE ROMANS AND EVERYONE BLOODY ELSE.
HAD THE NATIONAL HEALTH SERVICE FOR SEVENTY YEARS, AND WE DECIDE MAYBE WE DON'T BELIEVE IN IT ANYMORE. WHY BELIEVE IN SOMETHING THAT ACTUALLY WORKS?
STUPID SPECIES, SOMETIMES.
NO, WE WON'T BE GOING TO THE BLOODY BATHS. DO YOU KNOW EDGAR THE GOOD?
FIRST KING OF ALL ENGLAND.
AND CROWNED AT BATH ABBEY, NOT LONDON.
EXACTLY, ROSE.
NOW, GET US IN.
OH--AND HOLD THIS.
SO, EDGAR GOT CROWNED HERE, SO WE CAN USE IT? LIKE WE USED GLASTONBURY TOR?
HE GOT CROWNED HERE, YES. BUT NOT IN THIS ABBEY.
HE GOT CROWNED IN THE FIRST ABBEY...

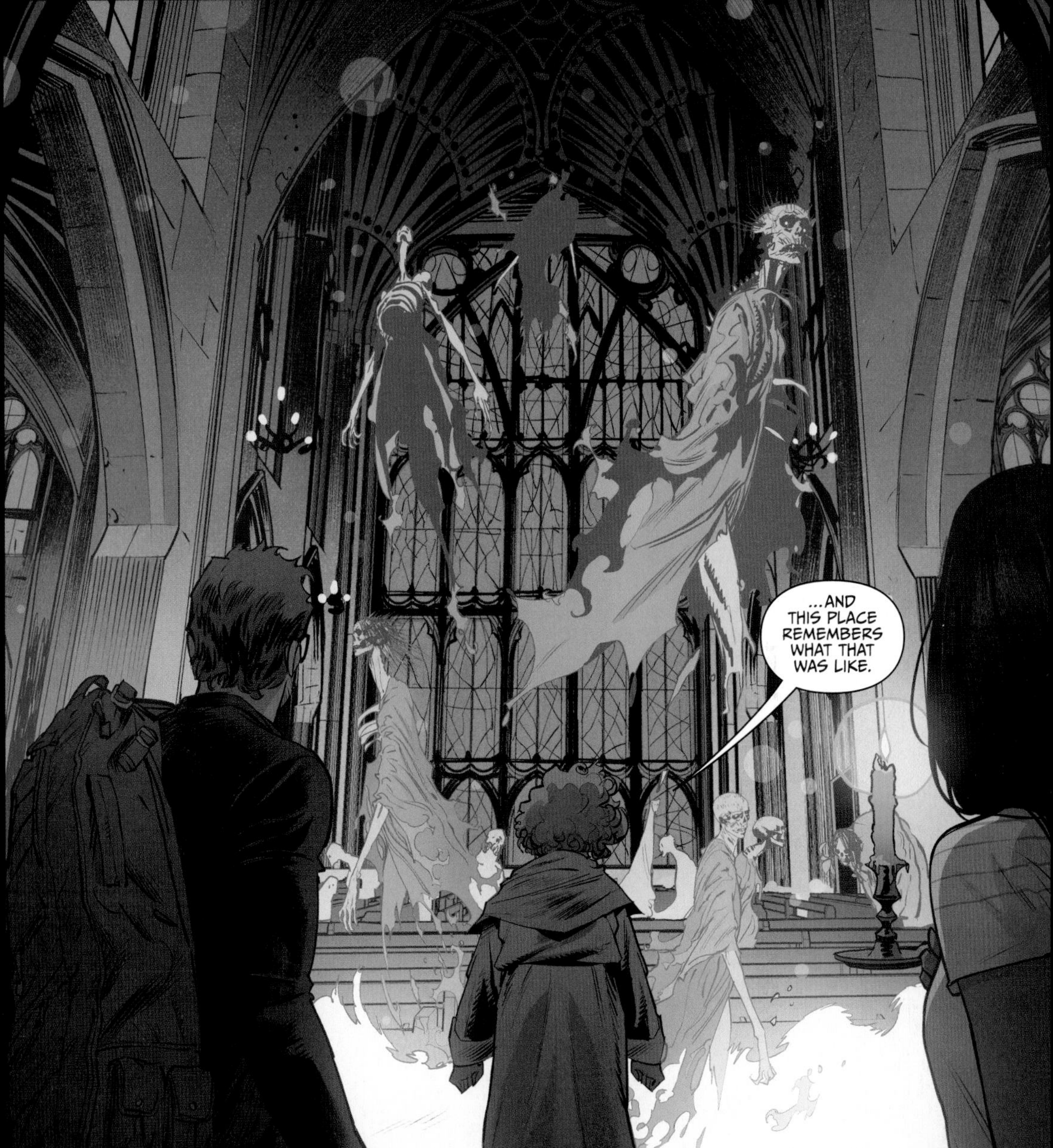
...AND THIS PLACE REMEMBERS WHAT THAT WAS LIKE.

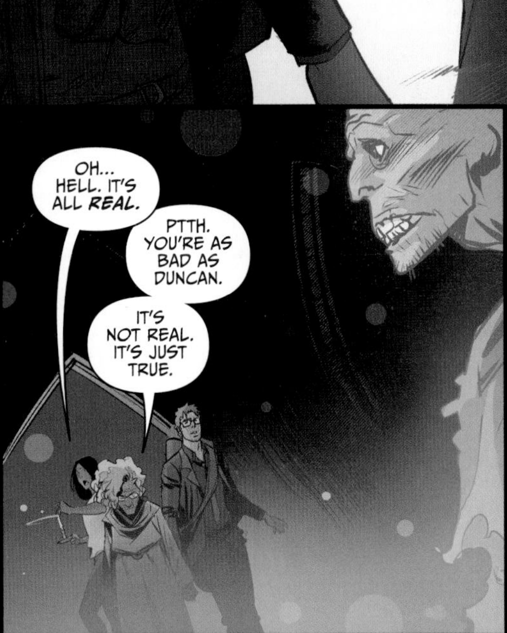
OH... HELL. IT'S ALL *REAL*.
PTTH. YOU'RE AS BAD AS DUNCAN.
IT'S NOT REAL. IT'S JUST TRUE.

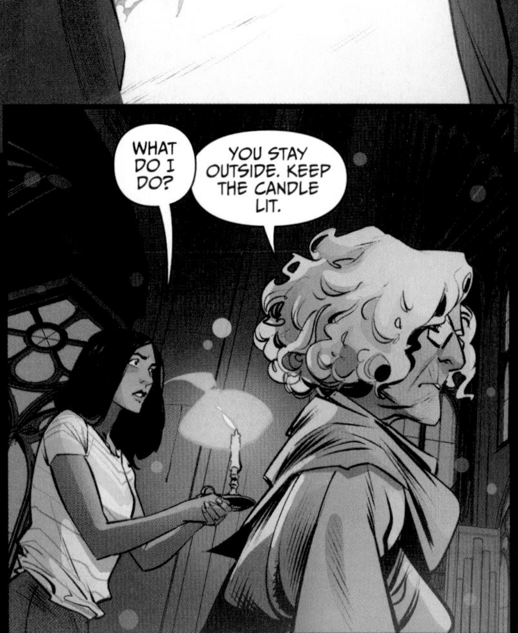
WHAT DO I DO?
YOU STAY OUTSIDE. KEEP THE CANDLE LIT.

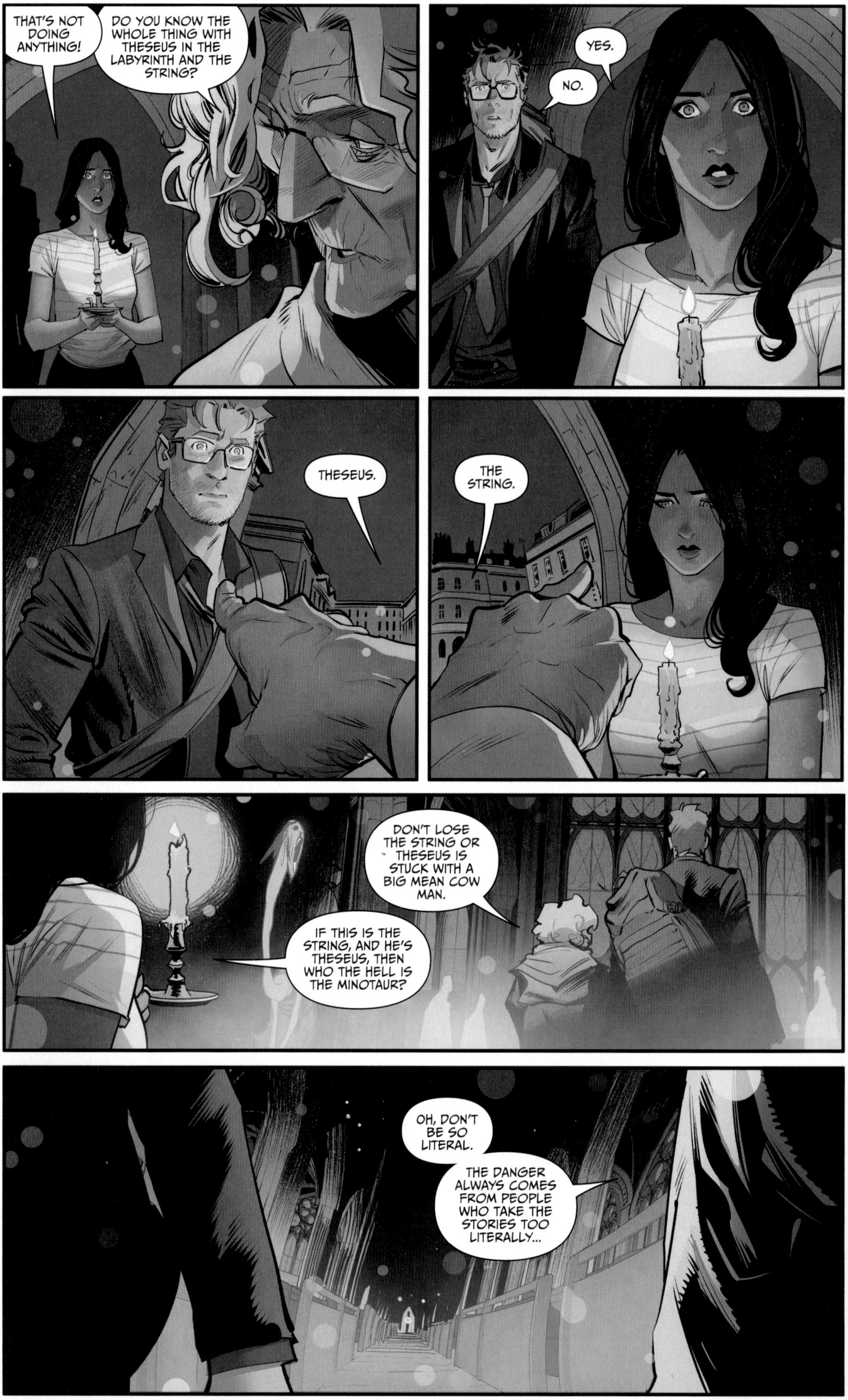
THAT'S NOT DOING ANYTHING!
DO YOU KNOW THE WHOLE THING WITH THESEUS IN THE LABYRINTH AND THE STRING?
YES.
NO.
THESEUS.
THE STRING.
DON'T LOSE THE STRING OR THESEUS IS STUCK WITH A BIG MEAN COW MAN.
IF THIS IS THE STRING, AND HE'S THESEUS, THEN WHO THE HELL IS THE MINOTAUR?
OH, DON'T BE SO LITERAL.
THE DANGER ALWAYS COMES FROM PEOPLE WHO TAKE THE STORIES TOO LITERALLY...

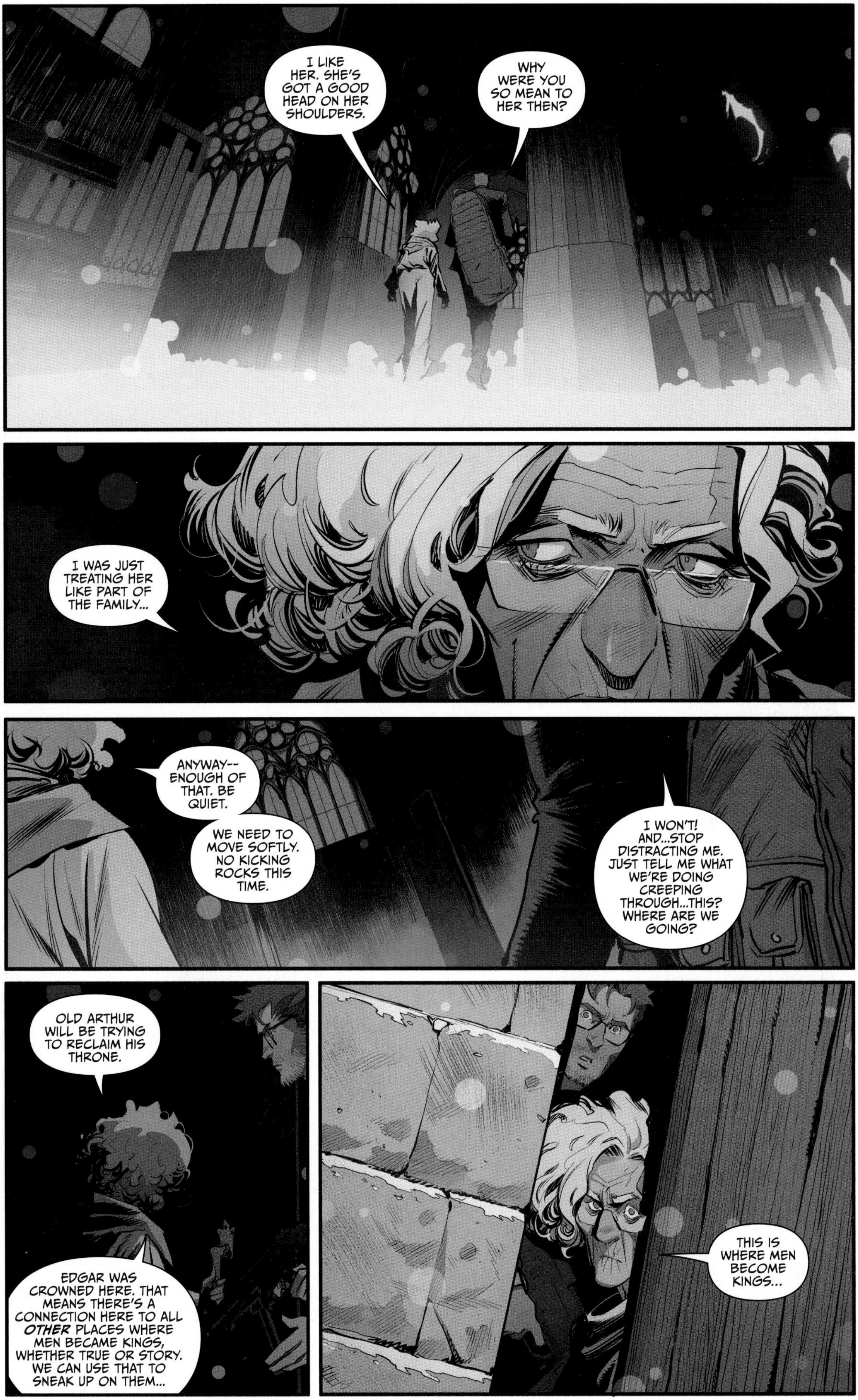
I LIKE HER. SHE'S GOT A GOOD HEAD ON HER SHOULDERS.
WHY WERE YOU SO MEAN TO HER THEN?
I WAS JUST TREATING HER LIKE PART OF THE FAMILY...
ANYWAY-- ENOUGH OF THAT. BE QUIET.
WE NEED TO MOVE SOFTLY. NO KICKING ROCKS THIS TIME.
I WON'T! AND...STOP DISTRACTING ME. JUST TELL ME WHAT WE'RE DOING CREEPING THROUGH...THIS? WHERE ARE WE GOING?
OLD ARTHUR WILL BE TRYING TO RECLAIM HIS THRONE.
EDGAR WAS CROWNED HERE. THAT MEANS THERE'S A CONNECTION HERE TO ALL *OTHER* PLACES WHERE MEN BECAME KINGS, WHETHER TRUE OR STORY. WE CAN USE THAT TO SNEAK UP ON THEM...
THIS IS WHERE MEN BECOME KINGS...

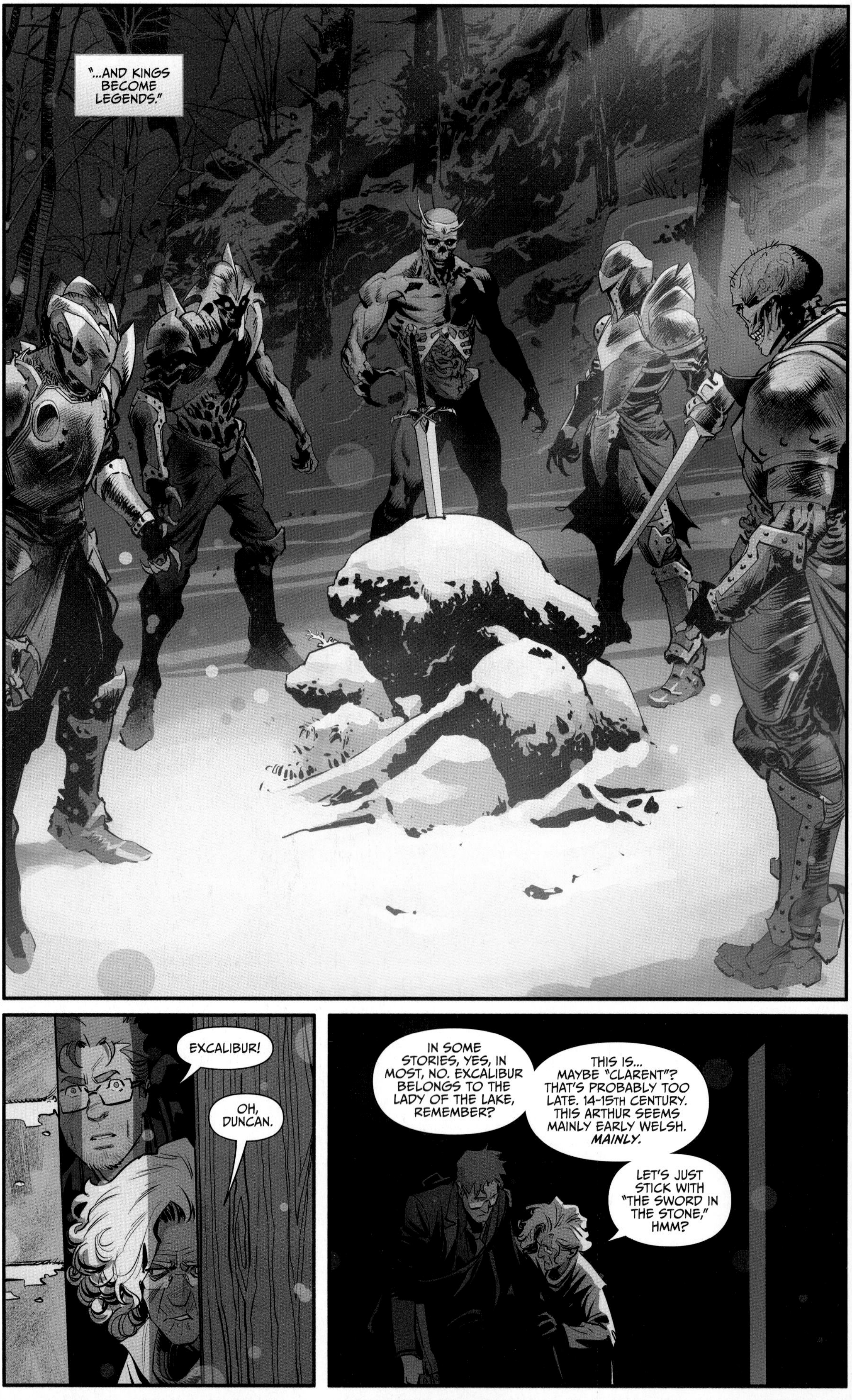
"...AND KINGS BECOME LEGENDS."
EXCALIBUR!
OH, DUNCAN.
IN SOME STORIES, YES, IN MOST, NO. EXCALIBUR BELONGS TO THE LADY OF THE LAKE, REMEMBER?
THIS IS... MAYBE "CLARENT"? THAT'S PROBABLY TOO LATE. 14-15TH CENTURY. THIS ARTHUR SEEMS MAINLY EARLY WELSH. *MAINLY.*
LET'S JUST STICK WITH "THE SWORD IN THE STONE," HMM?

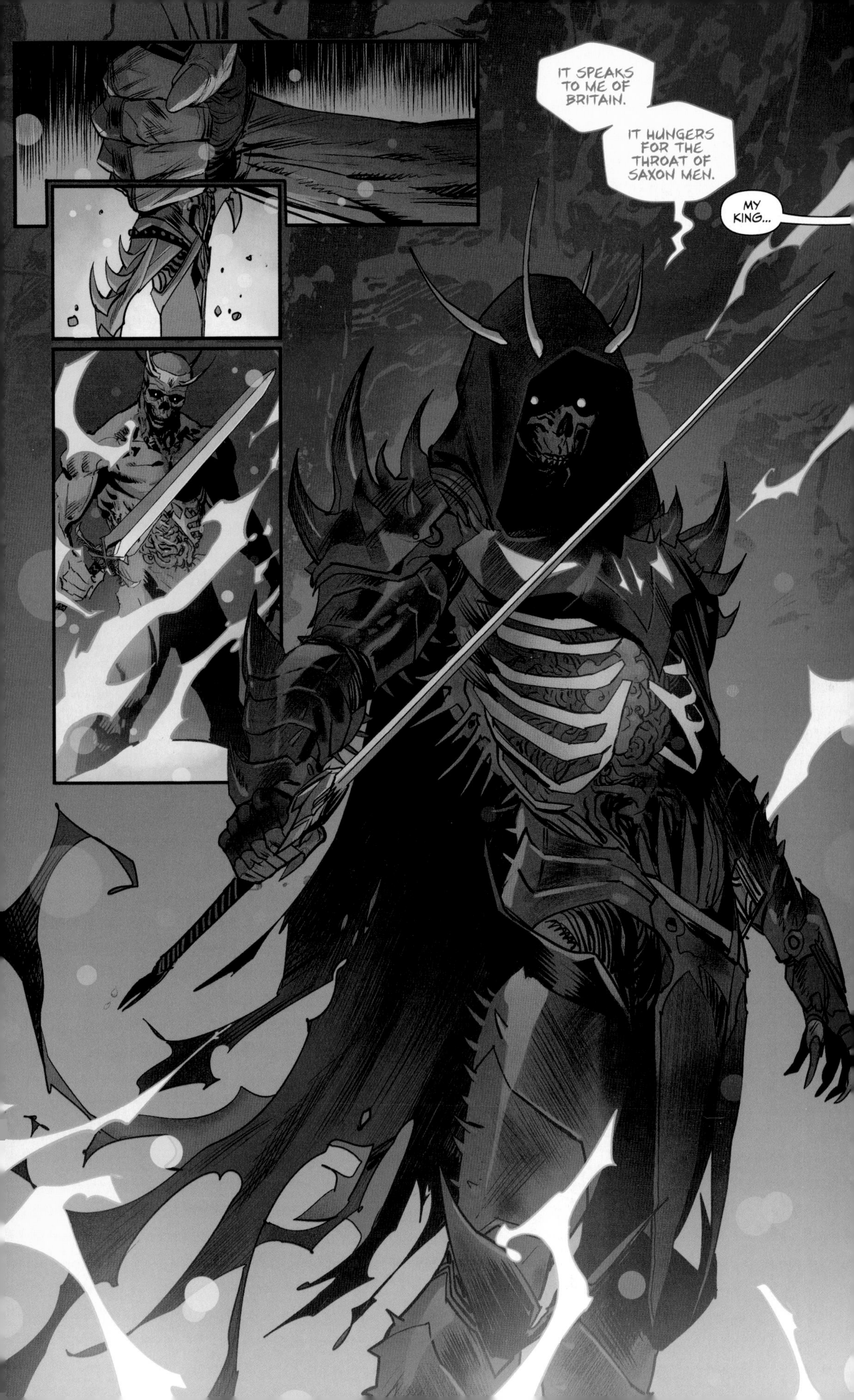
IT SPEAKS TO ME OF BRITAIN.
IT HUNGERS FOR THE THROAT OF SAXON MEN.
MY KING...

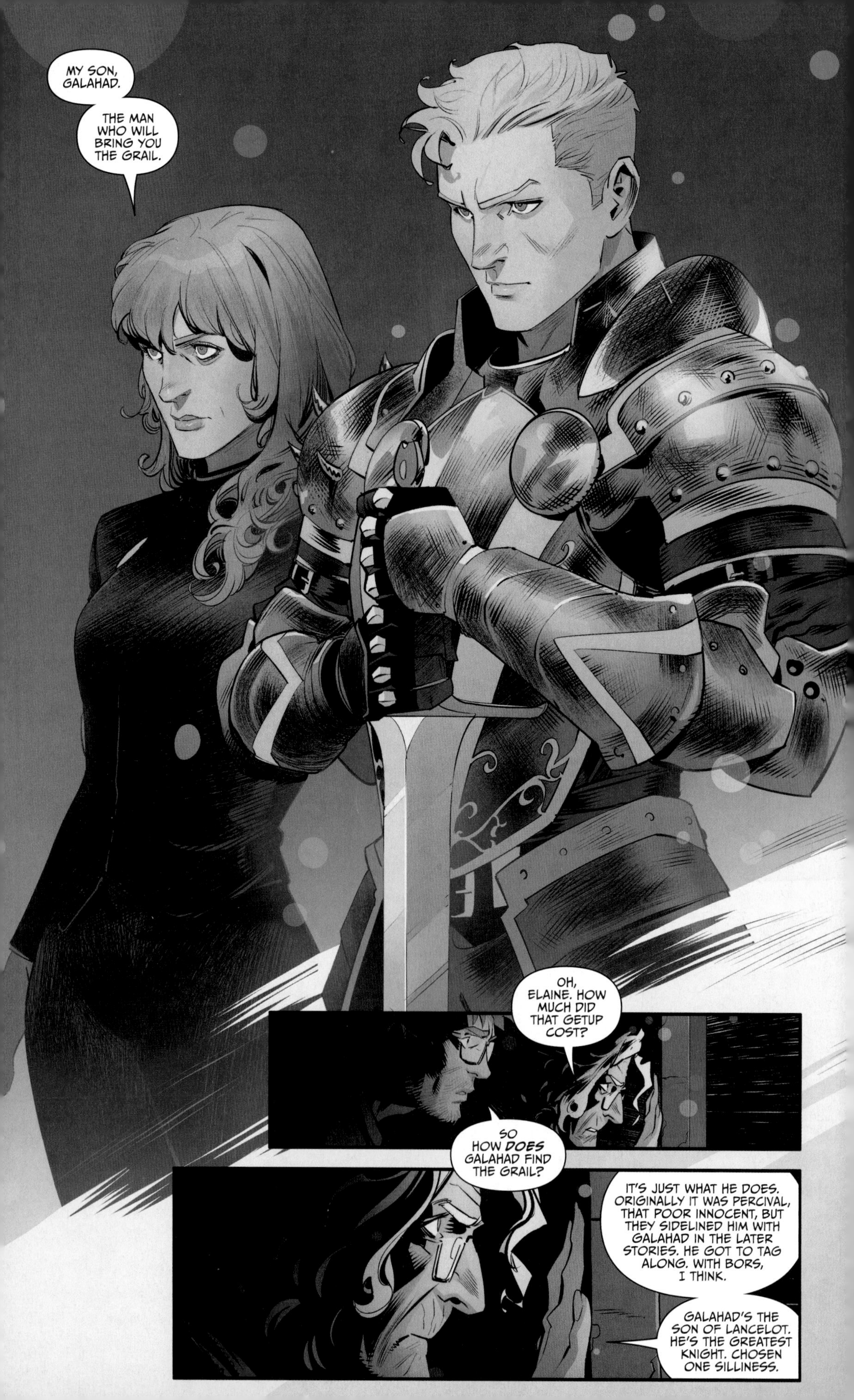
MY SON, GALAHAD.
THE MAN WHO WILL BRING YOU THE GRAIL.
OH, ELAINE. HOW MUCH DID THAT GETUP COST?
SO HOW *DOES* GALAHAD FIND THE GRAIL?
IT'S JUST WHAT HE DOES. ORIGINALLY IT WAS PERCIVAL, THAT POOR INNOCENT, BUT THEY SIDELINED HIM WITH GALAHAD IN THE LATER STORIES. HE GOT TO TAG ALONG. WITH BORS, I THINK.
GALAHAD'S THE SON OF LANCELOT. HE'S THE GREATEST KNIGHT. CHOSEN ONE SILLINESS.

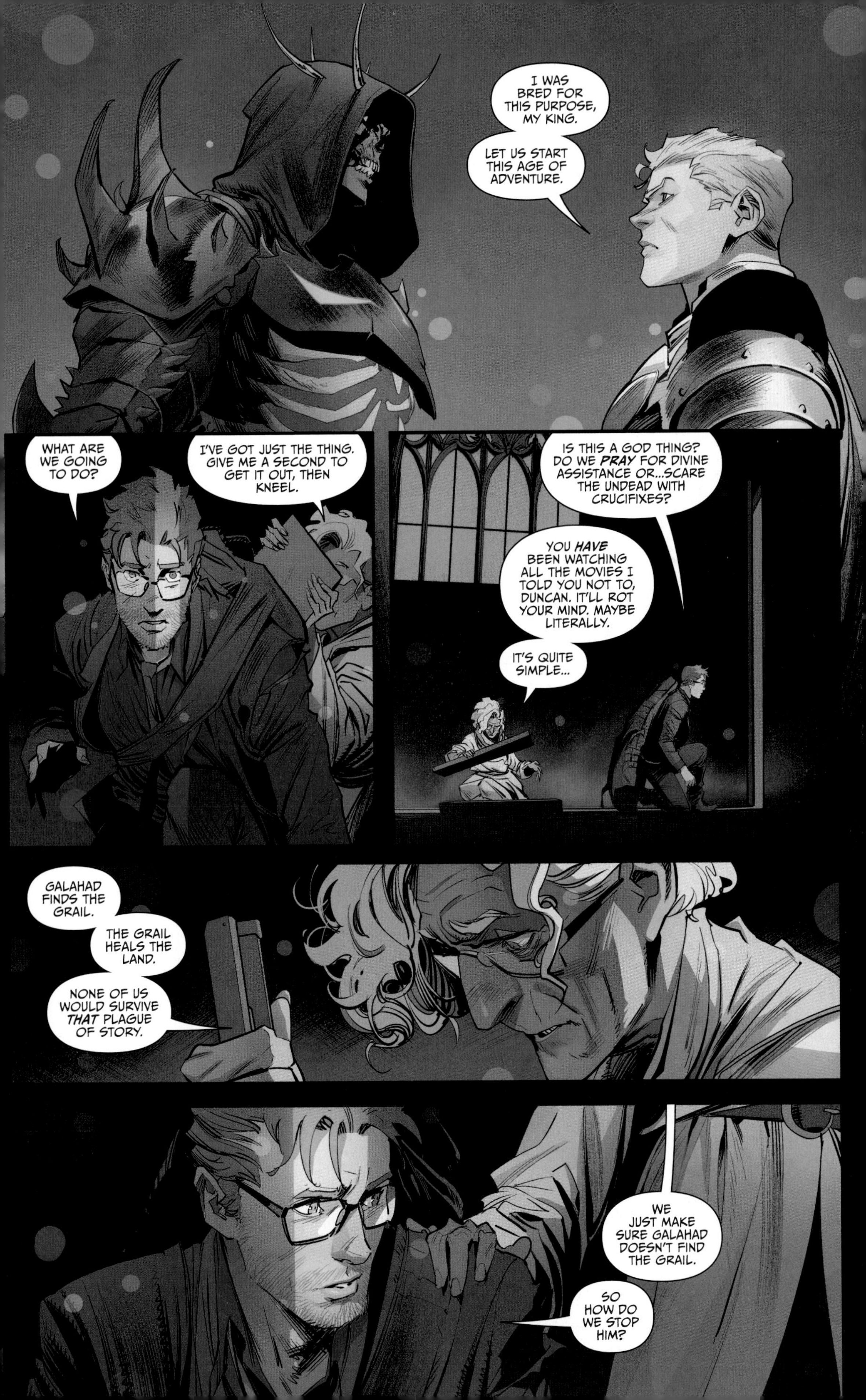
I WAS BRED FOR THIS PURPOSE, MY KING.
LET US START THIS AGE OF ADVENTURE.
WHAT ARE WE GOING TO DO?
I'VE GOT JUST THE THING. GIVE ME A SECOND TO GET IT OUT, THEN KNEEL.
IS THIS A GOD THING? DO WE PRAY FOR DIVINE ASSISTANCE OR...SCARE THE UNDEAD WITH CRUCIFIXES?
YOU HAVE BEEN WATCHING ALL THE MOVIES I TOLD YOU NOT TO, DUNCAN. IT'LL ROT YOUR MIND. MAYBE LITERALLY.
IT'S QUITE SIMPLE...
GALAHAD FINDS THE GRAIL.
THE GRAIL HEALS THE LAND.
NONE OF US WOULD SURVIVE THAT PLAGUE OF STORY.
WE JUST MAKE SURE GALAHAD DOESN'T FIND THE GRAIL.
SO HOW DO WE STOP HIM?

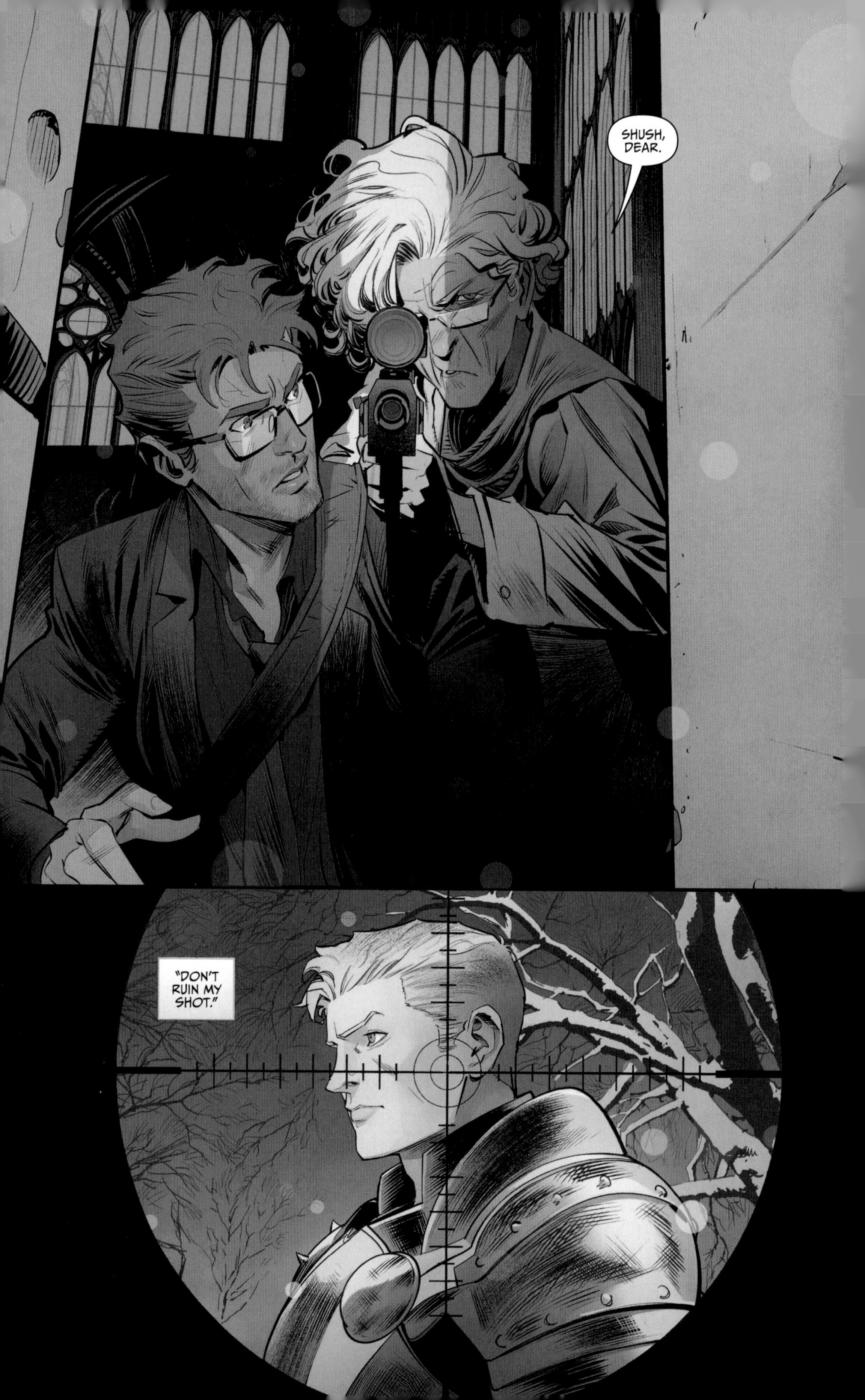
SHUSH, DEAR.
"DON'T RUIN MY SHOT."

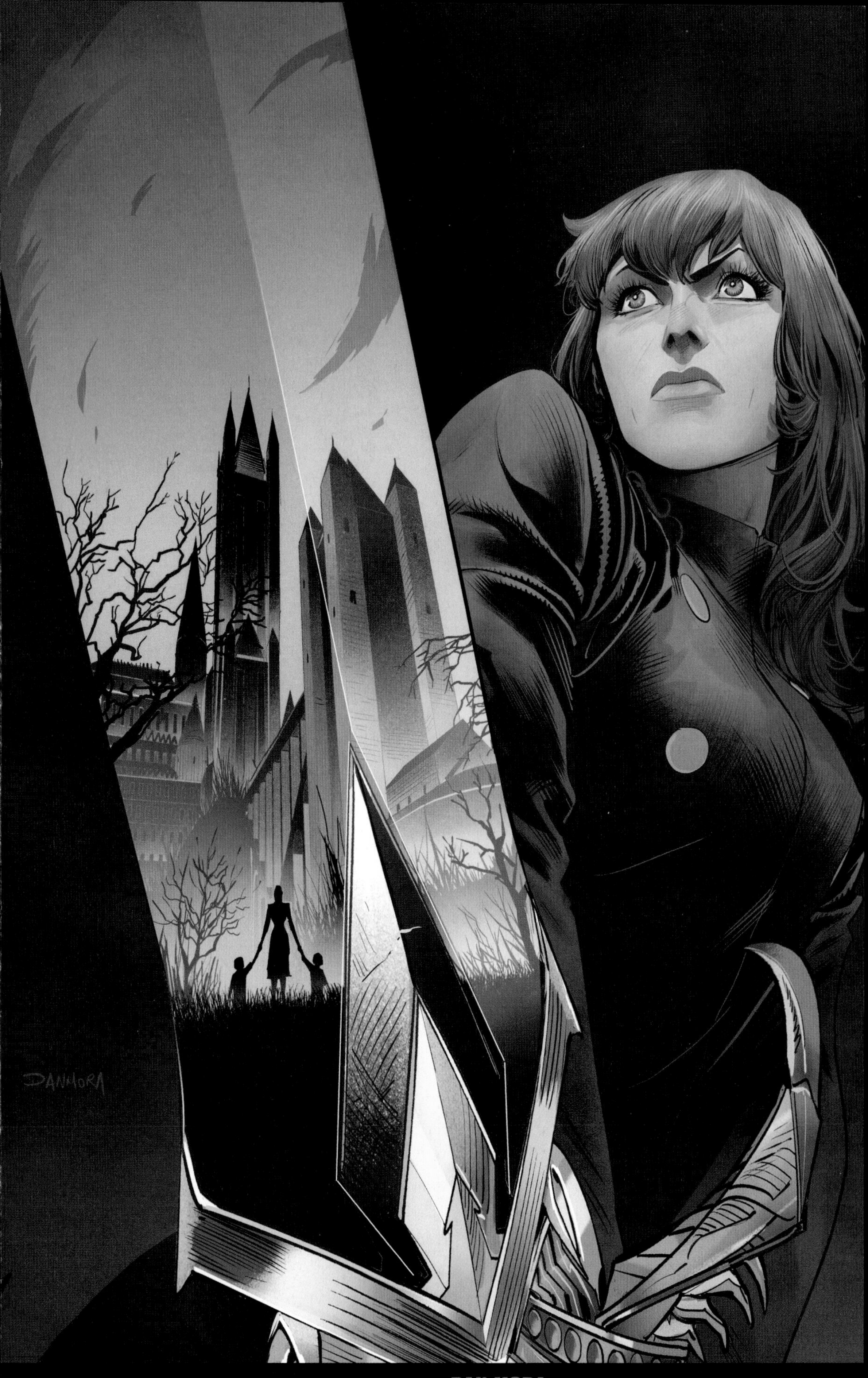
DANMORA

ISSUE FOUR COVER BY **DAN MORA**

CHAPTER FOUR

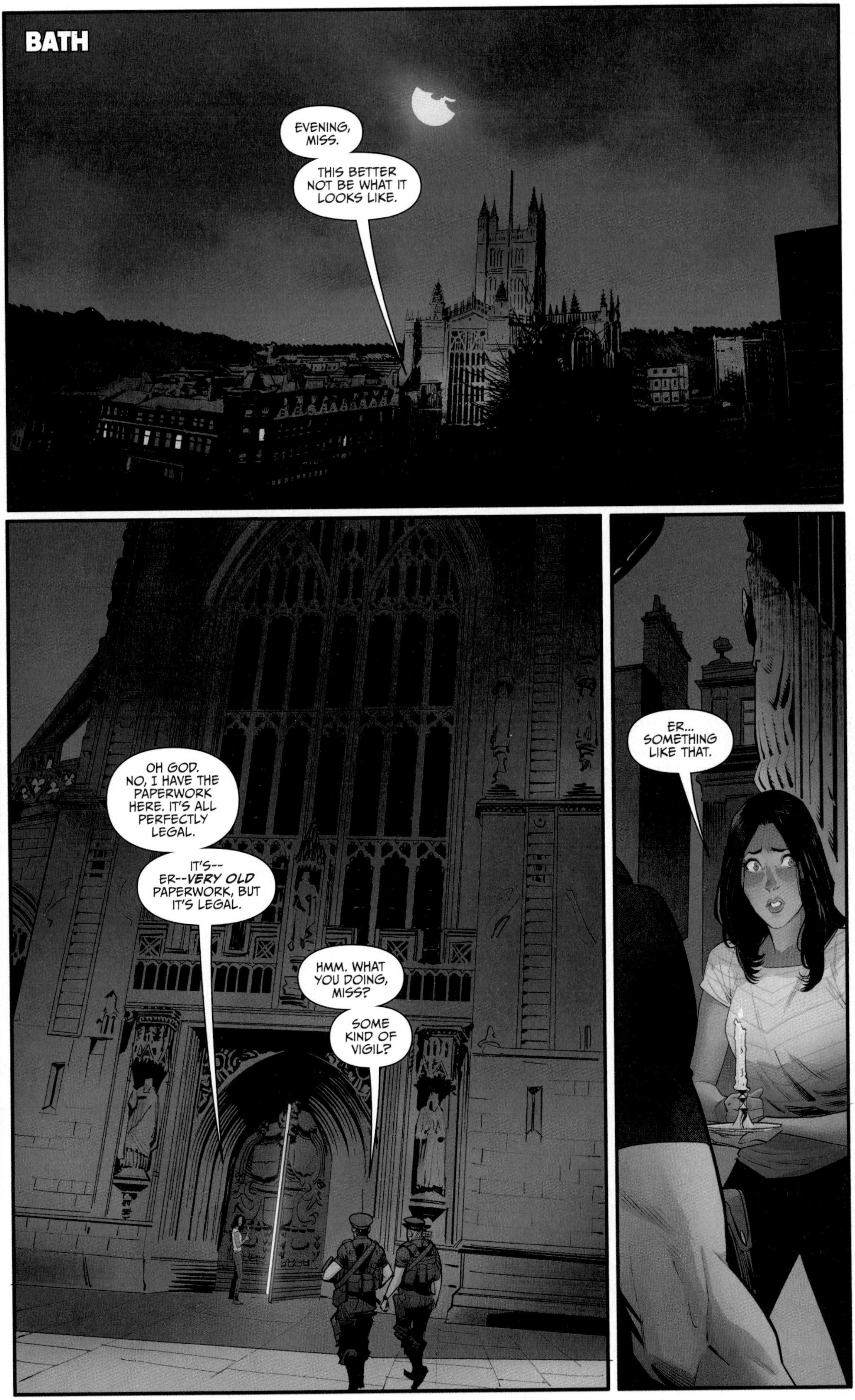
BATH
EVENING, MISS.
THIS BETTER NOT BE WHAT IT LOOKS LIKE.
OH GOD. NO, I HAVE THE PAPERWORK HERE. IT'S ALL PERFECTLY LEGAL.
IT'S-- ER--*VERY OLD* PAPERWORK, BUT IT'S LEGAL.
HMM. WHAT YOU DOING, MISS?
SOME KIND OF VIGIL?
ER... SOMETHING LIKE THAT.

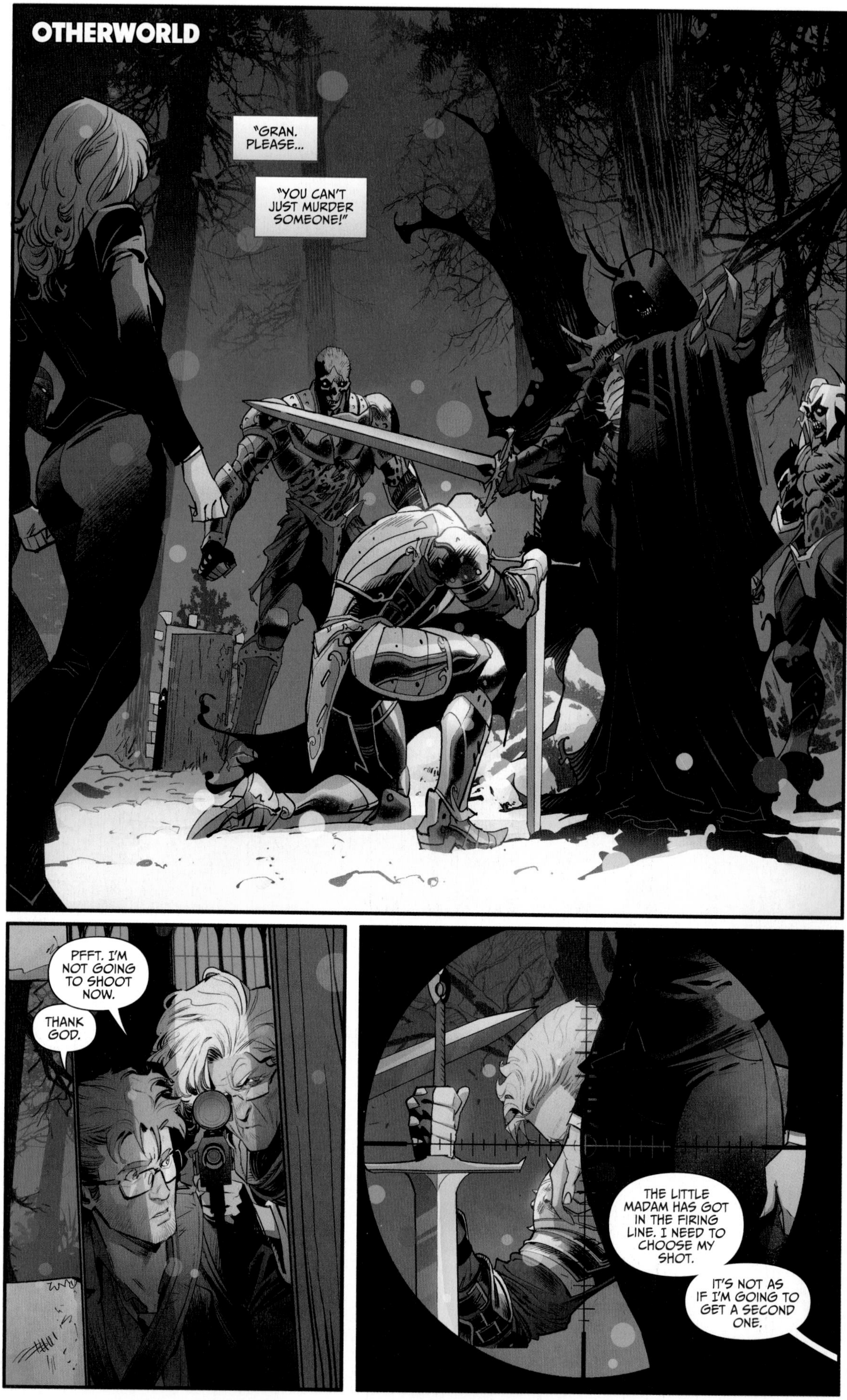
OTHERWORLD
"GRAN. PLEASE...
"YOU CAN'T JUST MURDER SOMEONE!"
PFFT. I'M NOT GOING TO SHOOT NOW.
THANK GOD.
THE LITTLE MADAM HAS GOT IN THE FIRING LINE. I NEED TO CHOOSE MY SHOT.
IT'S NOT AS IF I'M GOING TO GET A SECOND ONE.

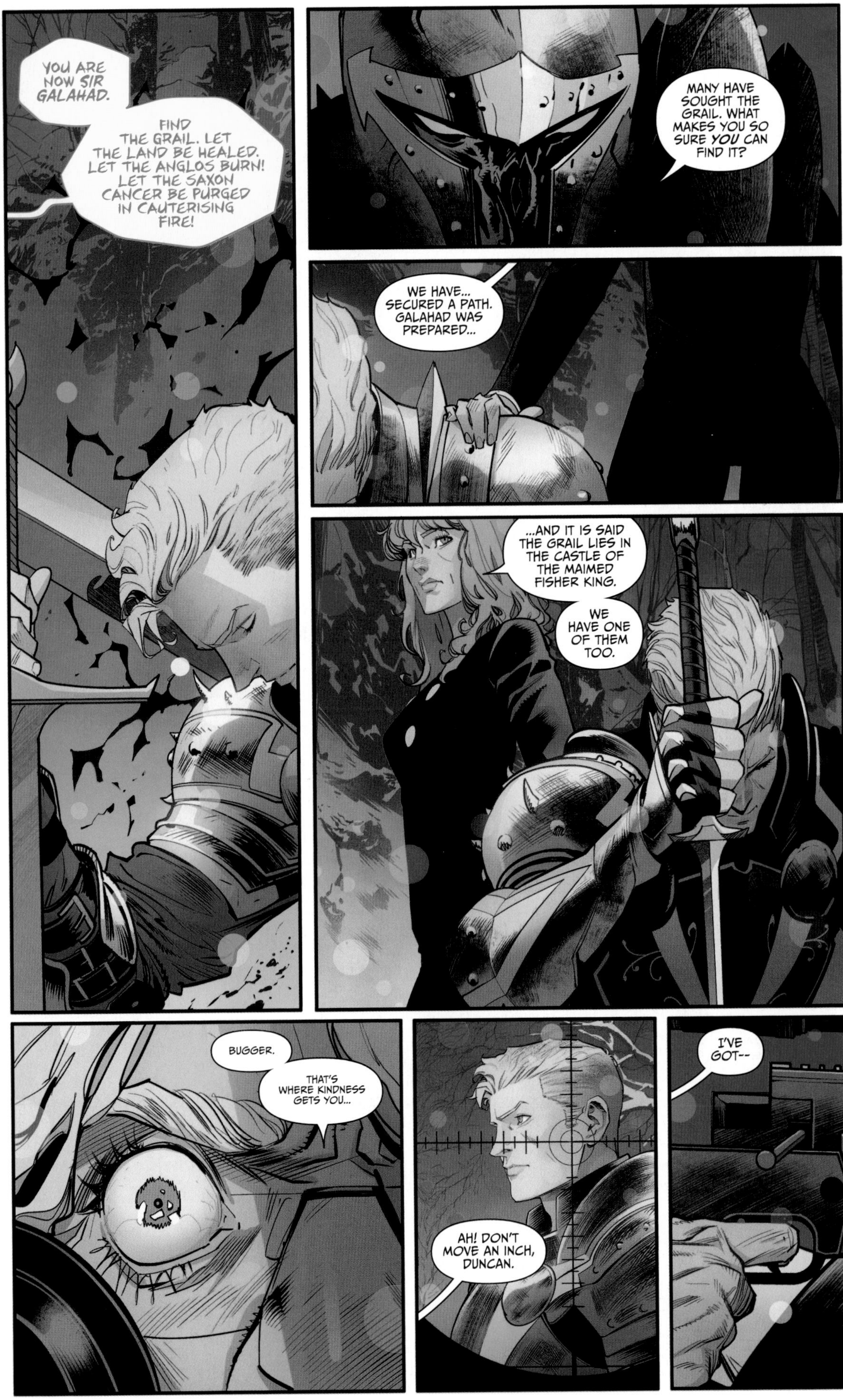
YOU ARE NOW SIR GALAHAD.
FIND THE GRAIL. LET THE LAND BE HEALED. LET THE ANGLOS BURN! LET THE SAXON CANCER BE PURGED IN CAUTERISING FIRE!
MANY HAVE SOUGHT THE GRAIL. WHAT MAKES YOU SO SURE YOU CAN FIND IT?
WE HAVE... SECURED A PATH. GALAHAD WAS PREPARED...
...AND IT IS SAID THE GRAIL LIES IN THE CASTLE OF THE MAIMED FISHER KING.
WE HAVE ONE OF THEM TOO.
BUGGER.
THAT'S WHERE KINDNESS GETS YOU...
AH! DON'T MOVE AN INCH, DUNCAN.
I'VE GOT--

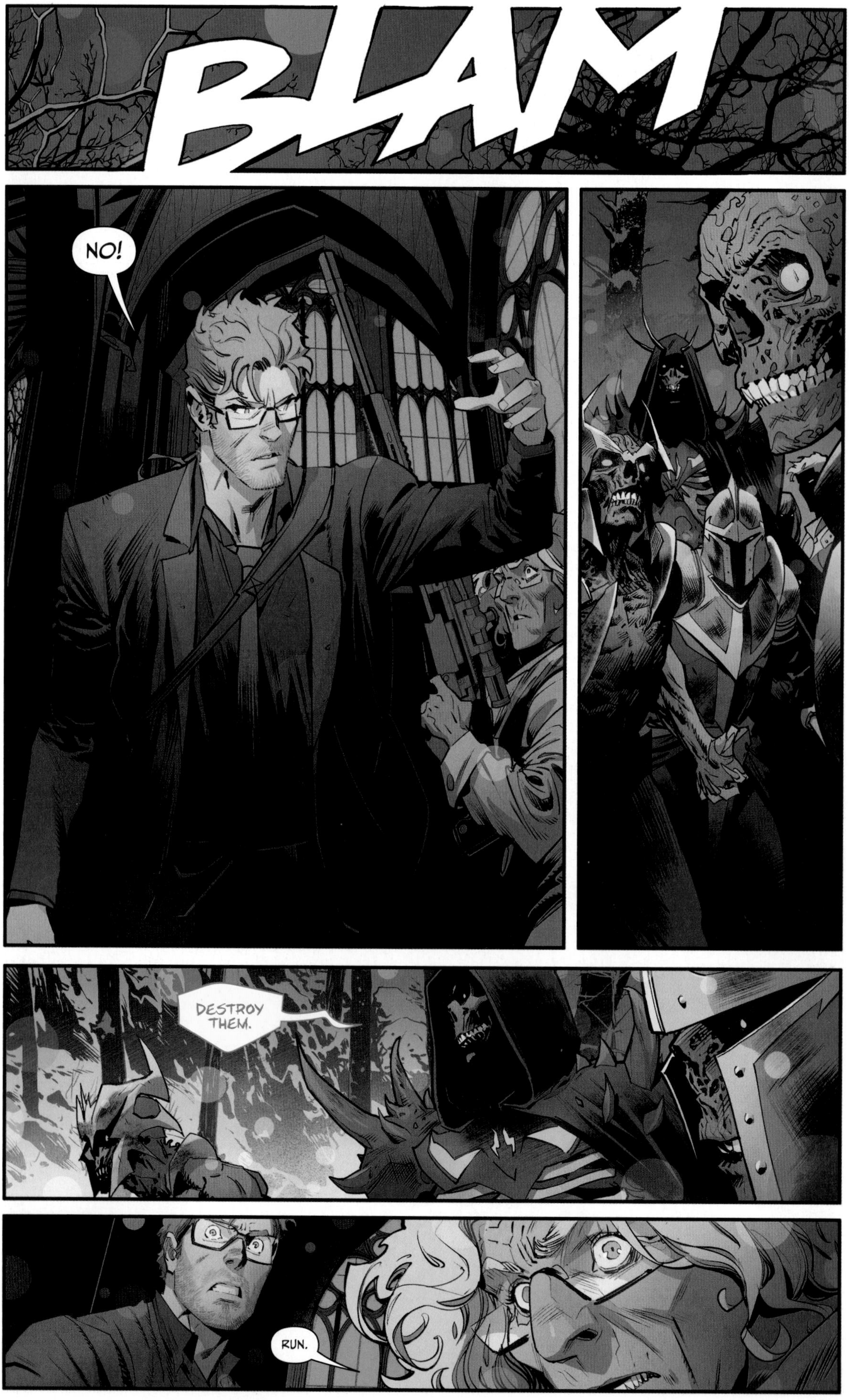
BLAM
NO!
DESTROY THEM.
RUN.

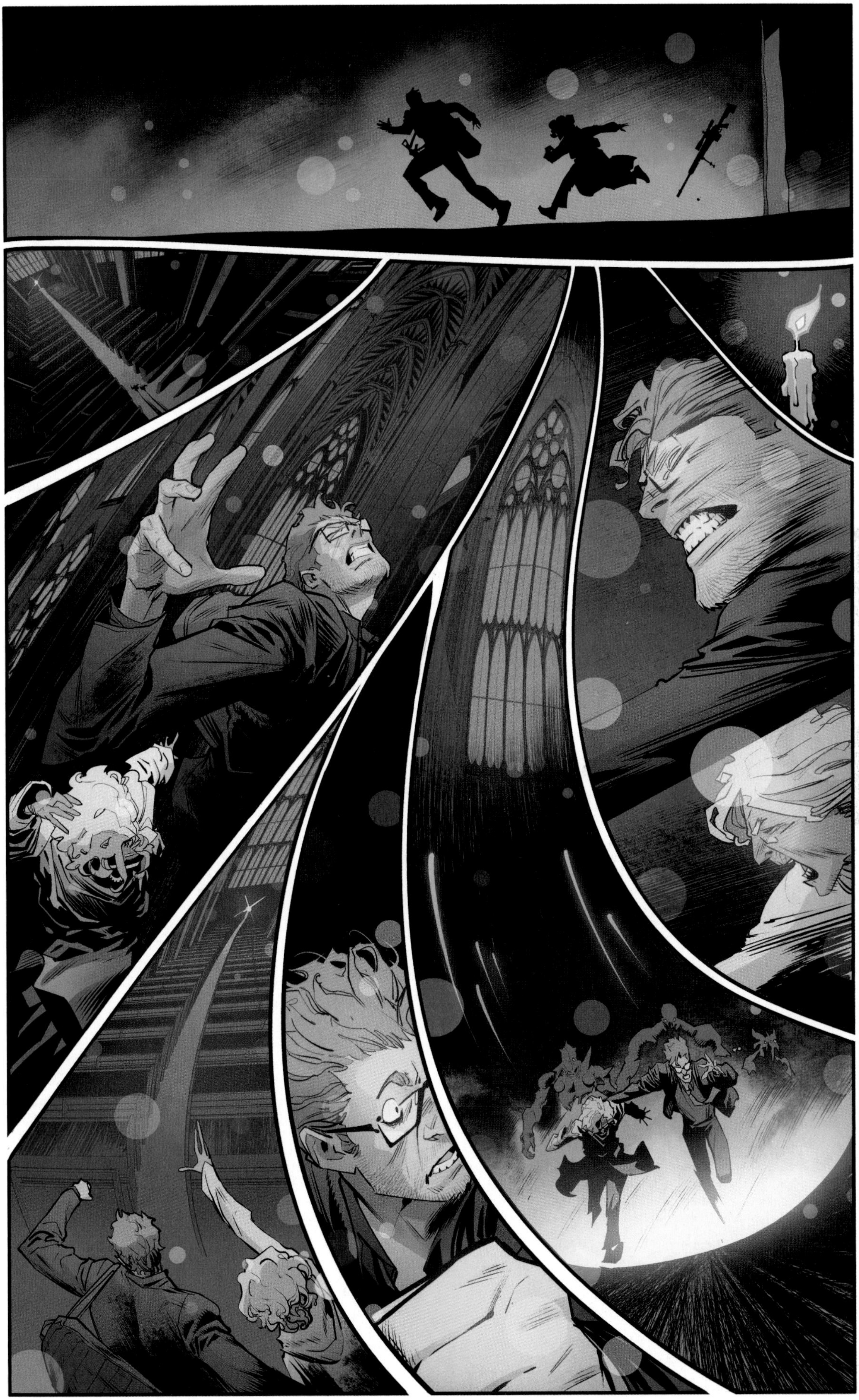

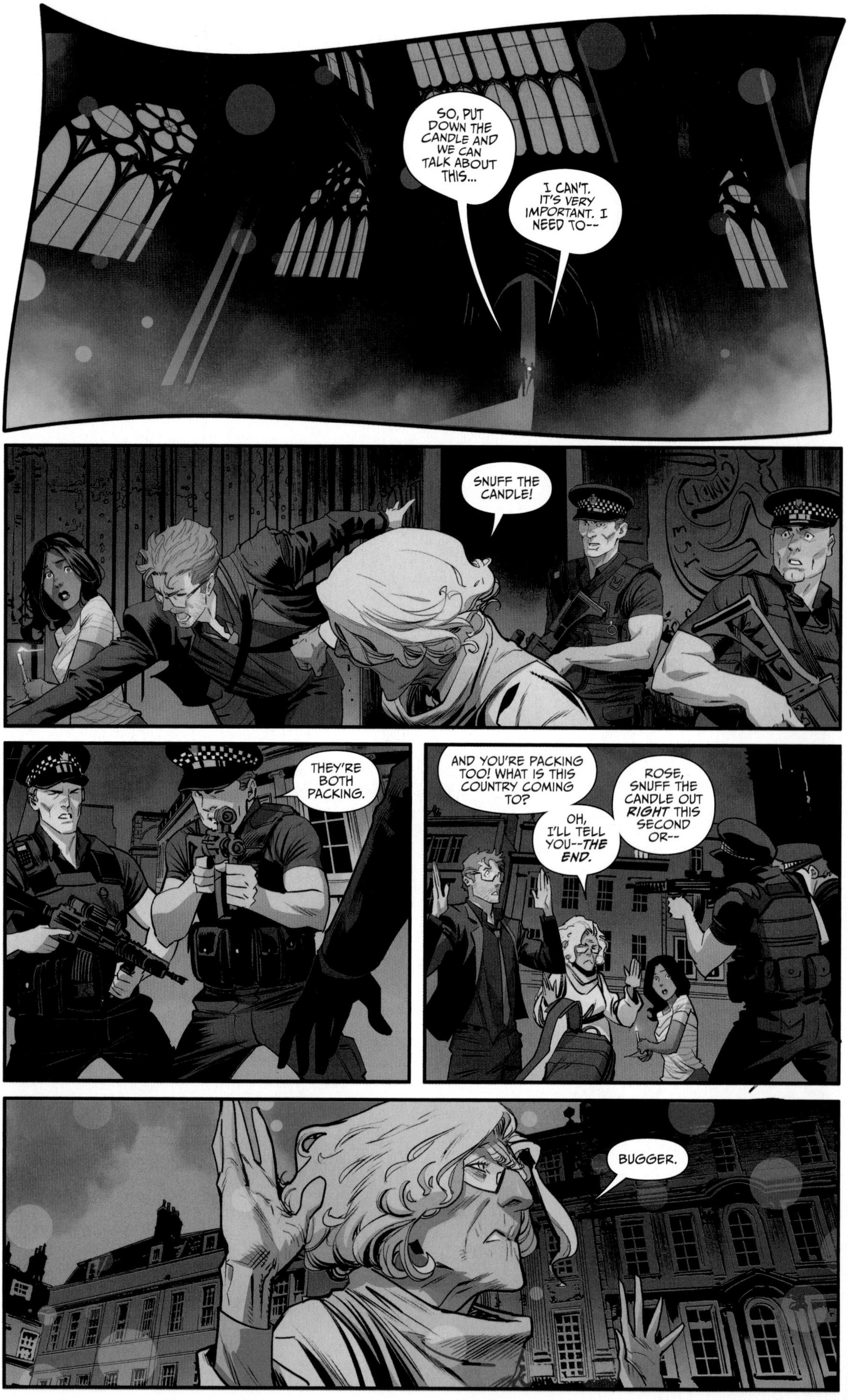
SO, PUT DOWN THE CANDLE AND WE CAN TALK ABOUT THIS...
I CAN'T. IT'S VERY IMPORTANT. I NEED TO--
SNUFF THE CANDLE!
THEY'RE BOTH PACKING.
AND YOU'RE PACKING TOO! WHAT IS THIS COUNTRY COMING TO?
OH, I'LL TELL YOU--*THE END.*
ROSE, SNUFF THE CANDLE OUT *RIGHT* THIS SECOND OR--
BUGGER.

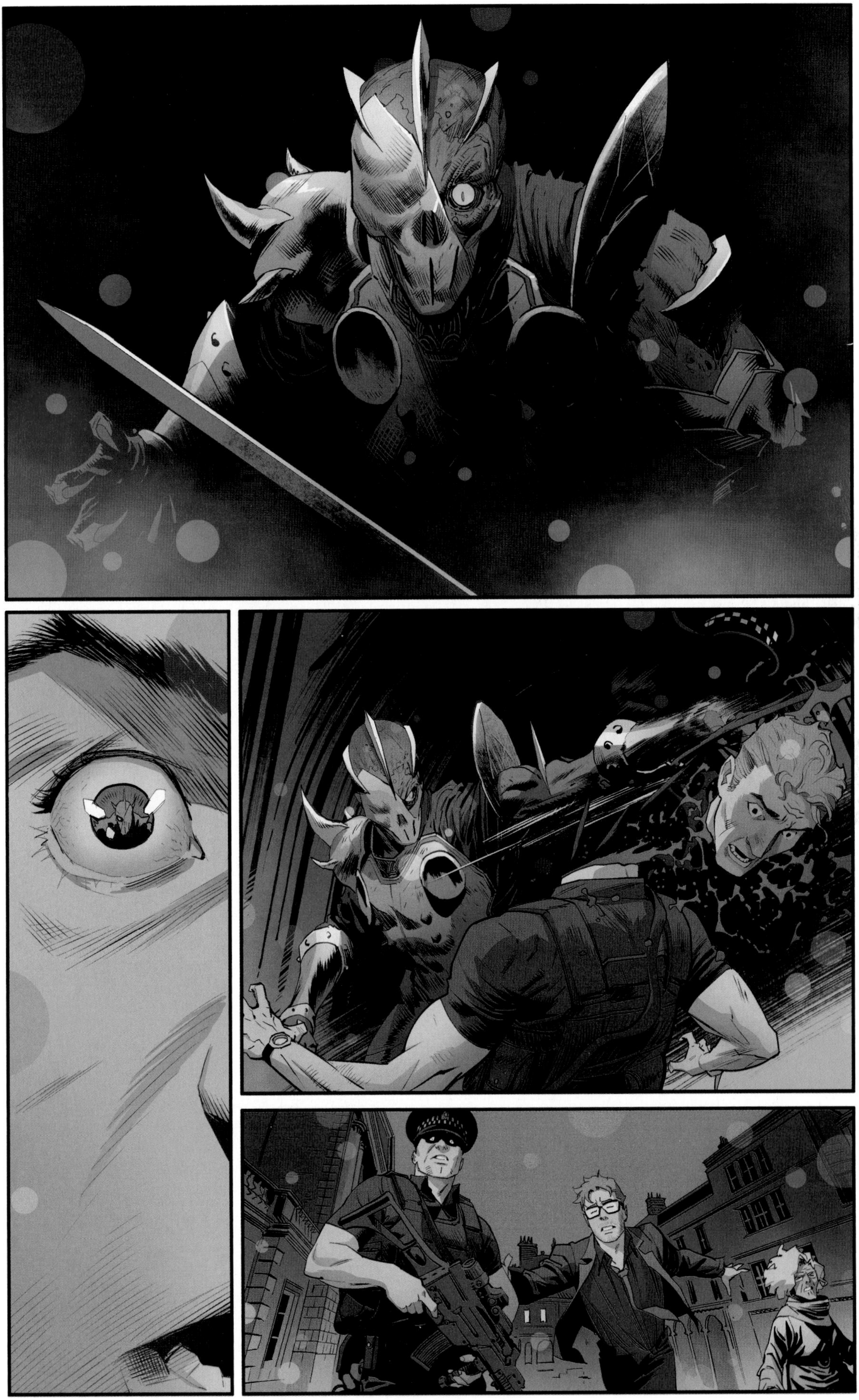

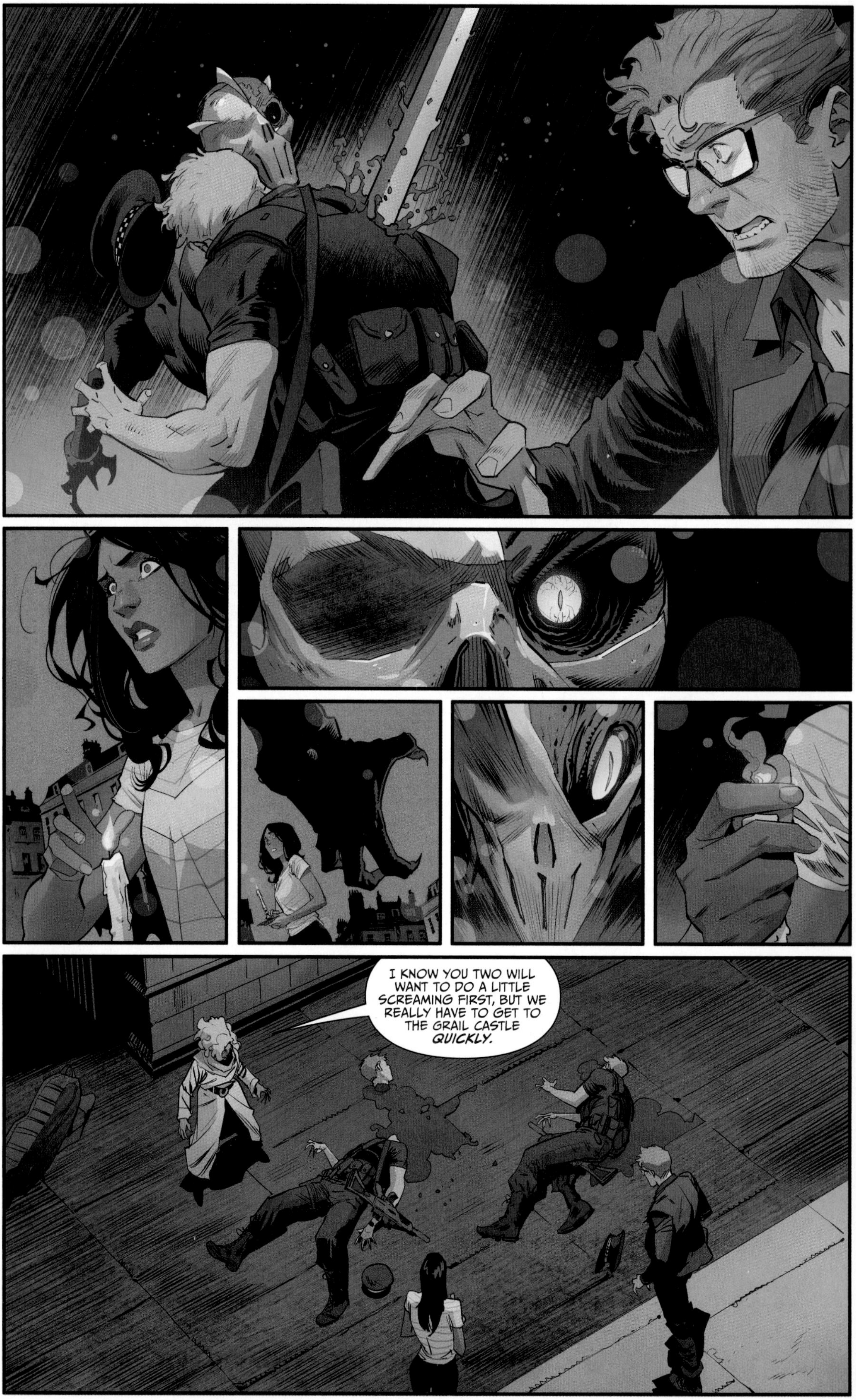
I KNOW YOU TWO WILL WANT TO DO A LITTLE SCREAMING FIRST, BUT WE REALLY HAVE TO GET TO THE GRAIL CASTLE *QUICKLY.*

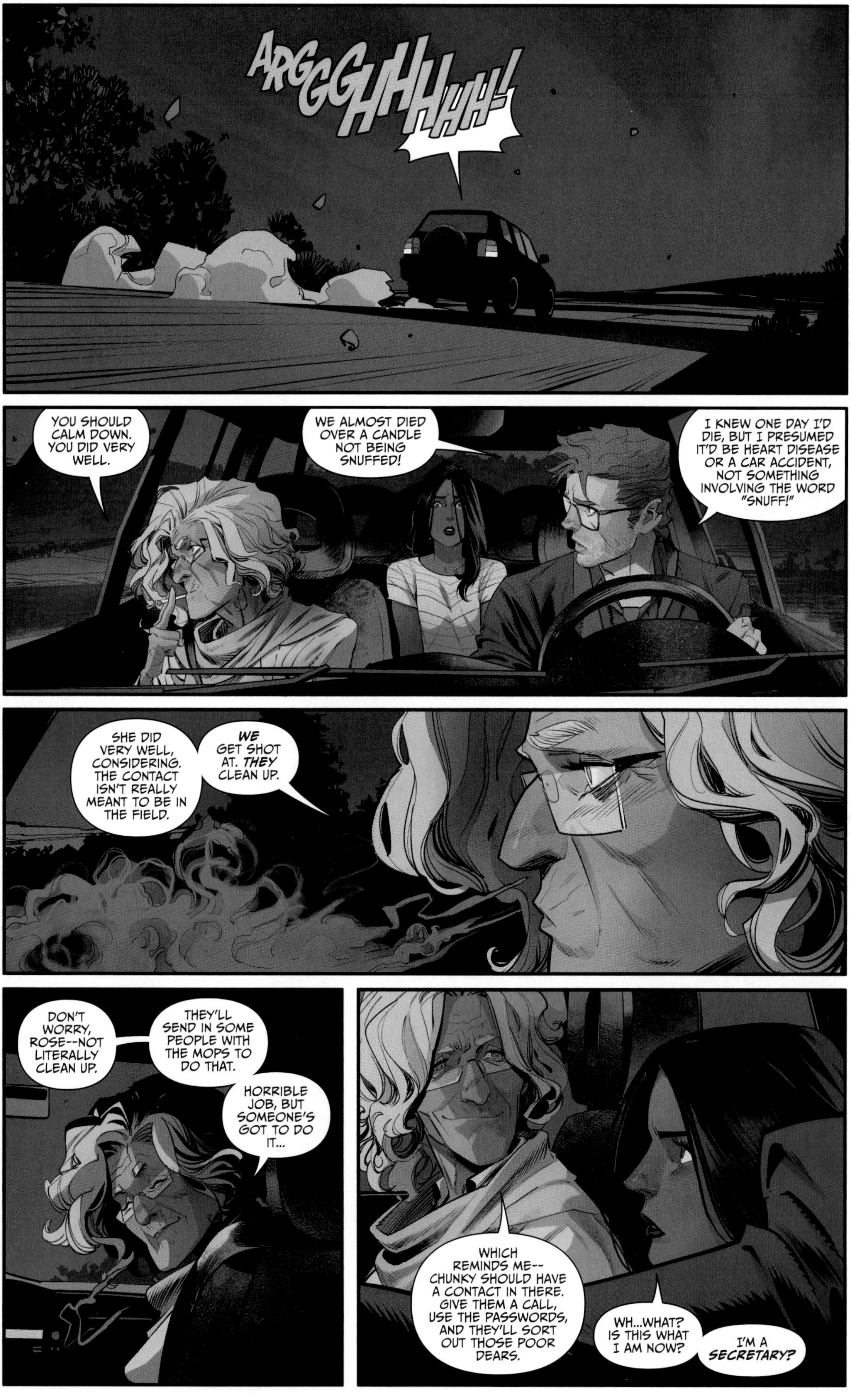
ARGGHHHHH-!
YOU SHOULD CALM DOWN. YOU DID VERY WELL.
WE ALMOST DIED OVER A CANDLE NOT BEING SNUFFED!
I KNEW ONE DAY I'D DIE, BUT I PRESUMED IT'D BE HEART DISEASE OR A CAR ACCIDENT, NOT SOMETHING INVOLVING THE WORD "SNUFF!"
SHE DID VERY WELL, CONSIDERING. THE CONTACT ISN'T REALLY MEANT TO BE IN THE FIELD.
WE GET SHOT AT. THEY CLEAN UP.
DON'T WORRY, ROSE--NOT LITERALLY CLEAN UP.
THEY'LL SEND IN SOME PEOPLE WITH THE MOPS TO DO THAT.
HORRIBLE JOB, BUT SOMEONE'S GOT TO DO IT...
WHICH REMINDS ME--CHUNKY SHOULD HAVE A CONTACT IN THERE. GIVE THEM A CALL, USE THE PASSWORDS, AND THEY'LL SORT OUT THOSE POOR DEARS.
WH...WHAT? IS THIS WHAT I AM NOW?
I'M A SECRETARY?

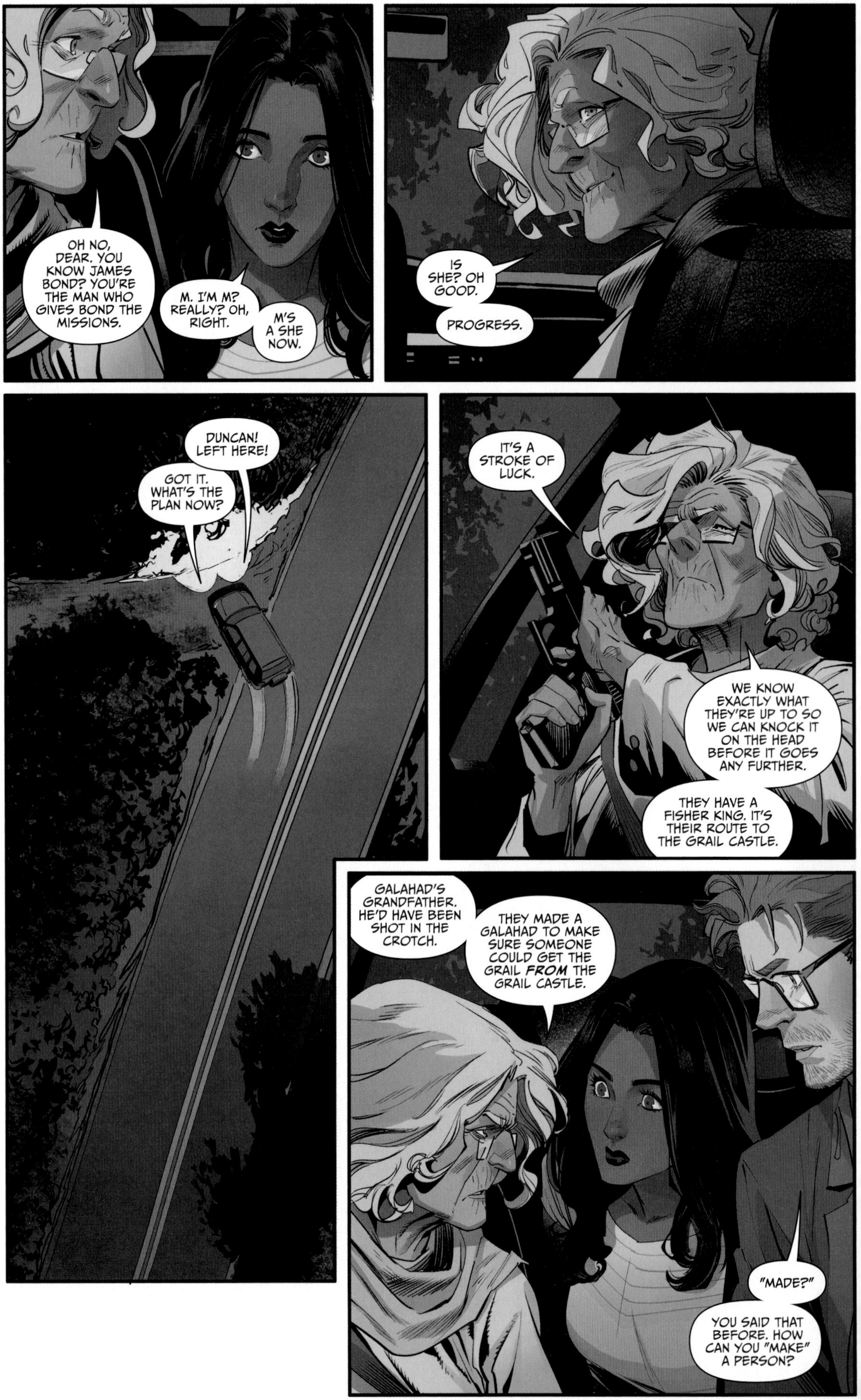
OH NO, DEAR. YOU KNOW JAMES BOND? YOU'RE THE MAN WHO GIVES BOND THE MISSIONS.
M. I'M M? REALLY? OH, RIGHT.
M'S A SHE NOW.
IS SHE? OH GOOD.
PROGRESS.
DUNCAN! LEFT HERE!
GOT IT. WHAT'S THE PLAN NOW?
IT'S A STROKE OF LUCK.
WE KNOW EXACTLY WHAT THEY'RE UP TO SO WE CAN KNOCK IT ON THE HEAD BEFORE IT GOES ANY FURTHER.
THEY HAVE A FISHER KING. IT'S THEIR ROUTE TO THE GRAIL CASTLE.
GALAHAD'S GRANDFATHER. HE'D HAVE BEEN SHOT IN THE CROTCH.
THEY MADE A GALAHAD TO MAKE SURE SOMEONE COULD GET THE GRAIL *FROM* THE GRAIL CASTLE.
"MADE?"
YOU SAID THAT BEFORE. HOW CAN YOU "MAKE" A PERSON?

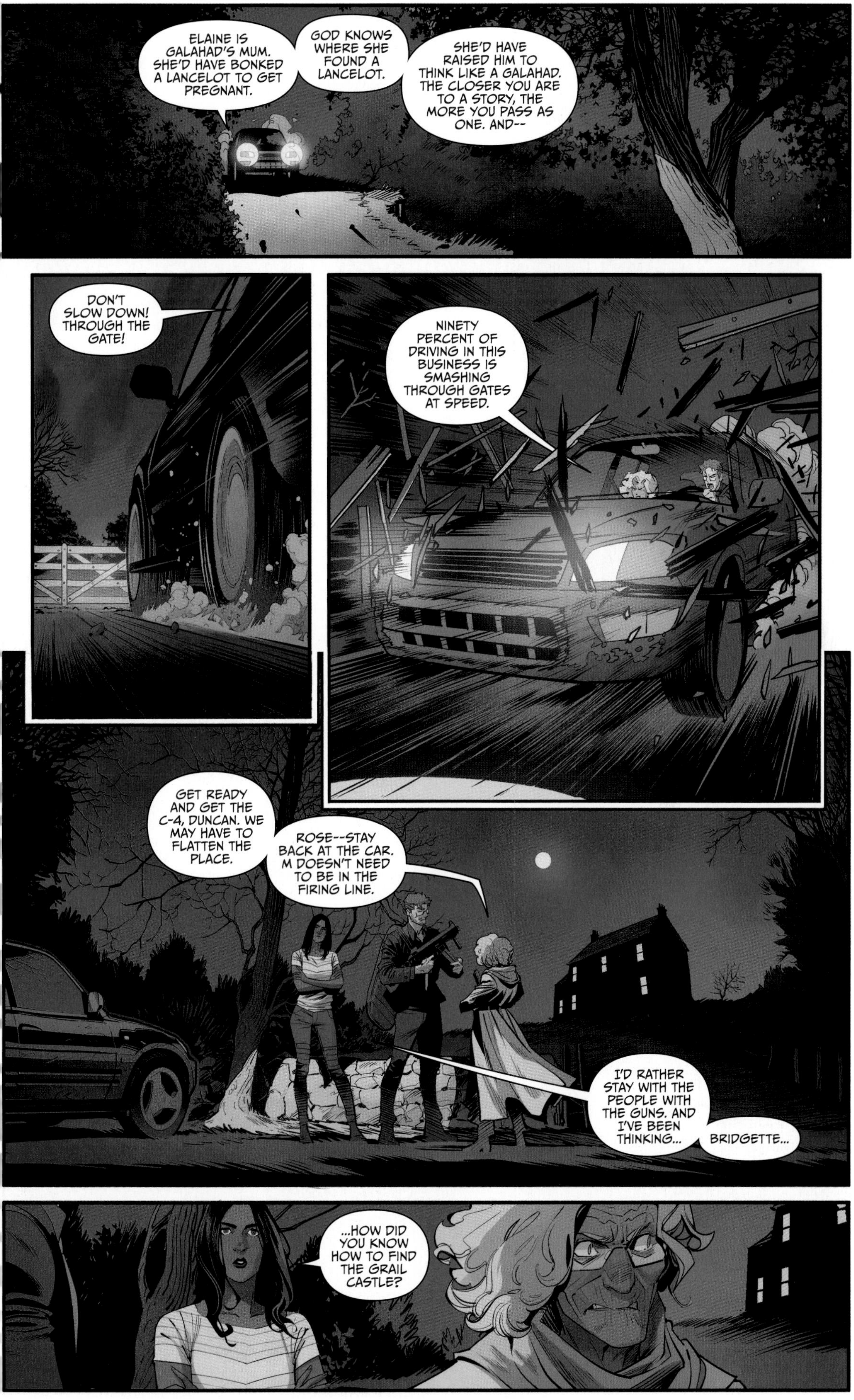
ELAINE IS GALAHAD'S MUM. SHE'D HAVE BONKED A LANCELOT TO GET PREGNANT.
GOD KNOWS WHERE SHE FOUND A LANCELOT.
SHE'D HAVE RAISED HIM TO THINK LIKE A GALAHAD. THE CLOSER YOU ARE TO A STORY, THE MORE YOU PASS AS ONE. AND--
DON'T SLOW DOWN! THROUGH THE GATE!
NINETY PERCENT OF DRIVING IN THIS BUSINESS IS SMASHING THROUGH GATES AT SPEED.
GET READY AND GET THE C-4, DUNCAN. WE MAY HAVE TO FLATTEN THE PLACE.
ROSE--STAY BACK AT THE CAR. M DOESN'T NEED TO BE IN THE FIRING LINE.
I'D RATHER STAY WITH THE PEOPLE WITH THE GUNS. AND I'VE BEEN THINKING...
BRIDGETTE...
...HOW DID YOU KNOW HOW TO FIND THE GRAIL CASTLE?

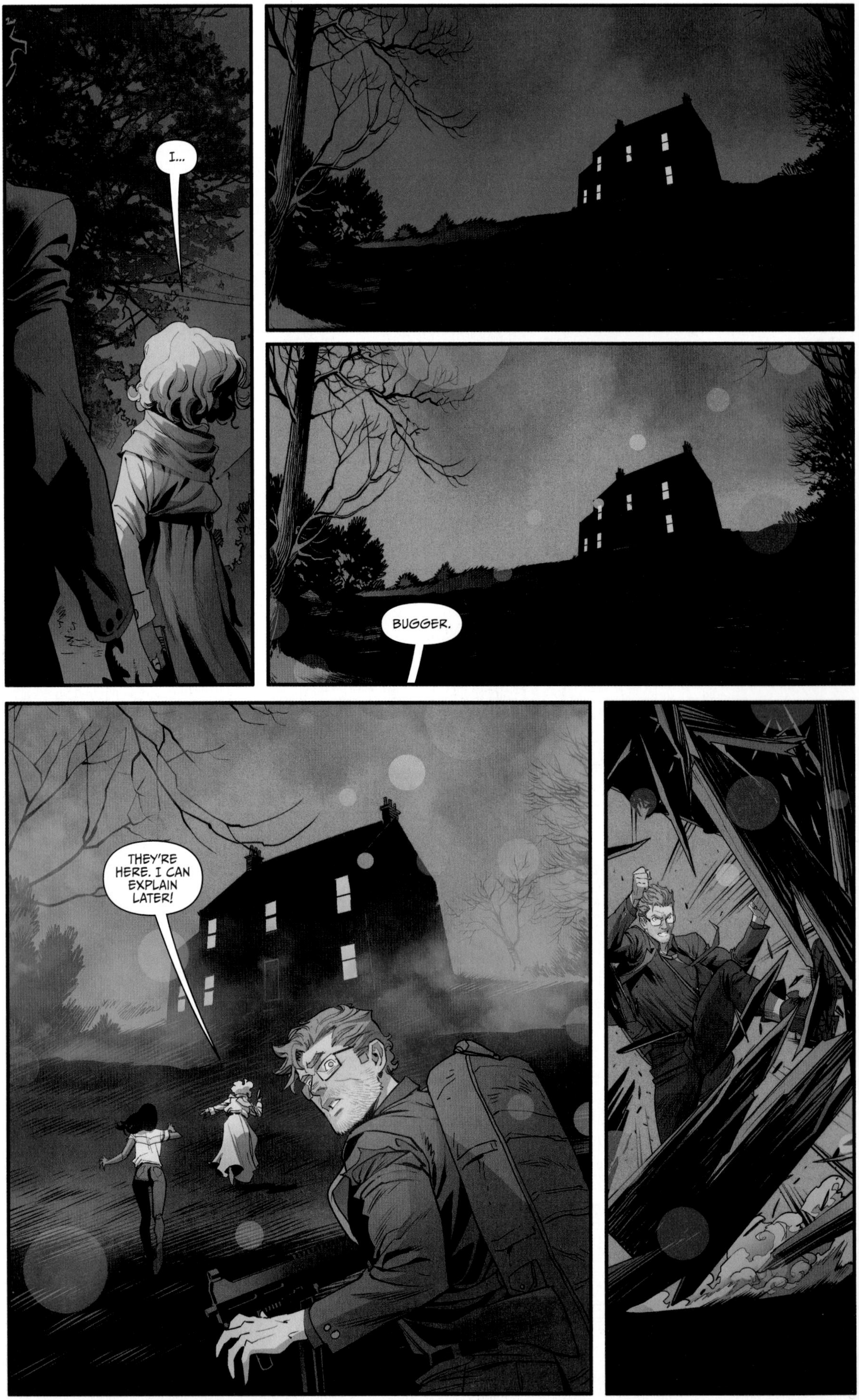
I...
BUGGER.
THEY'RE HERE. I CAN EXPLAIN LATER!

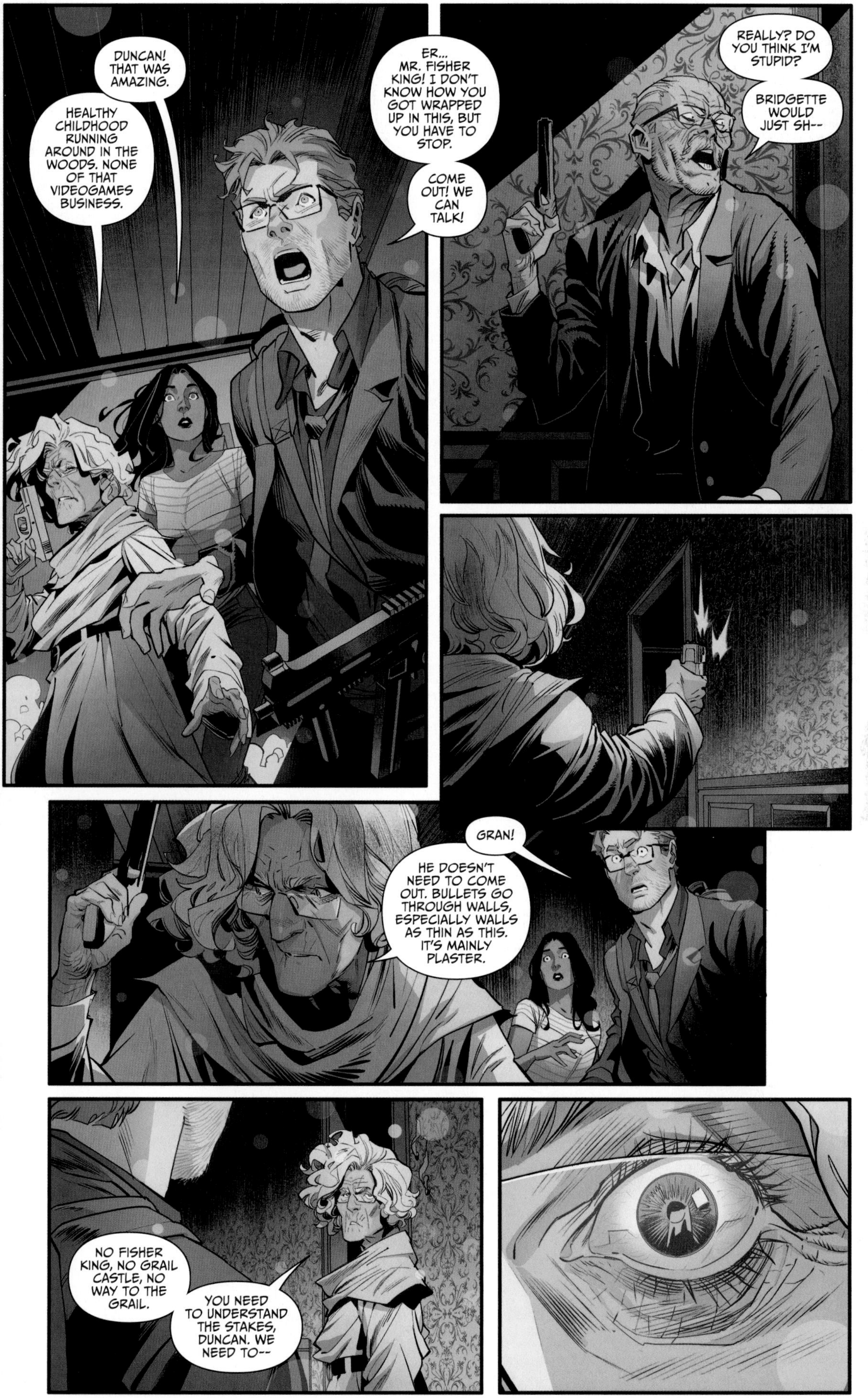
DUNCAN! THAT WAS AMAZING.
HEALTHY CHILDHOOD RUNNING AROUND IN THE WOODS. NONE OF THAT VIDEOGAMES BUSINESS.
ER... MR. FISHER KING! I DON'T KNOW HOW YOU GOT WRAPPED UP IN THIS, BUT YOU HAVE TO STOP.
COME OUT! WE CAN TALK!
REALLY? DO YOU THINK I'M STUPID?
BRIDGETTE WOULD JUST SH--
GRAN!
HE DOESN'T NEED TO COME OUT. BULLETS GO THROUGH WALLS, ESPECIALLY WALLS AS THIN AS THIS. IT'S MAINLY PLASTER.
NO FISHER KING, NO GRAIL CASTLE, NO WAY TO THE GRAIL.
YOU NEED TO UNDERSTAND THE STAKES, DUNCAN. WE NEED TO--

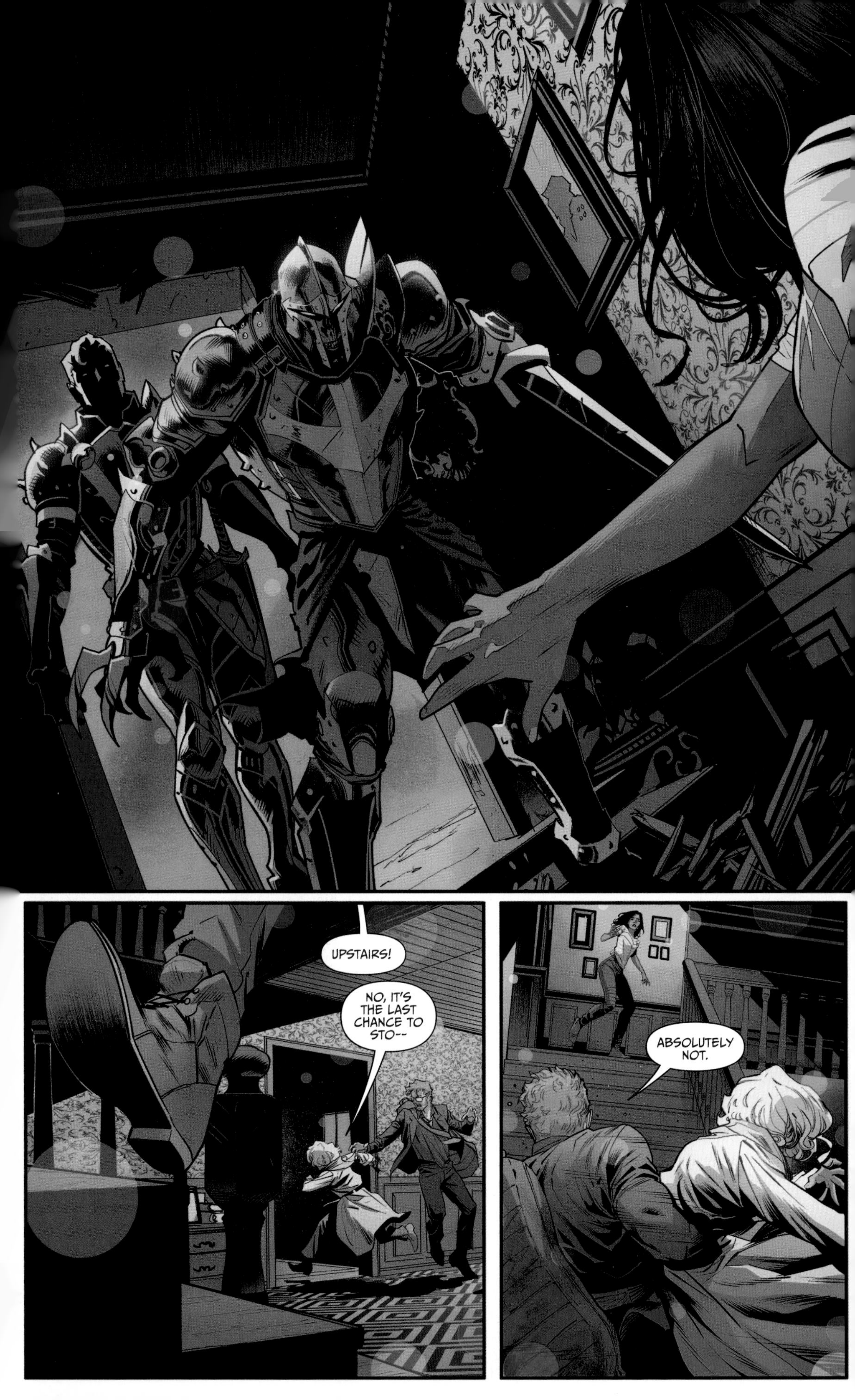
UPSTAIRS!
NO, IT'S THE LAST CHANCE TO STO--
ABSOLUTELY NOT.

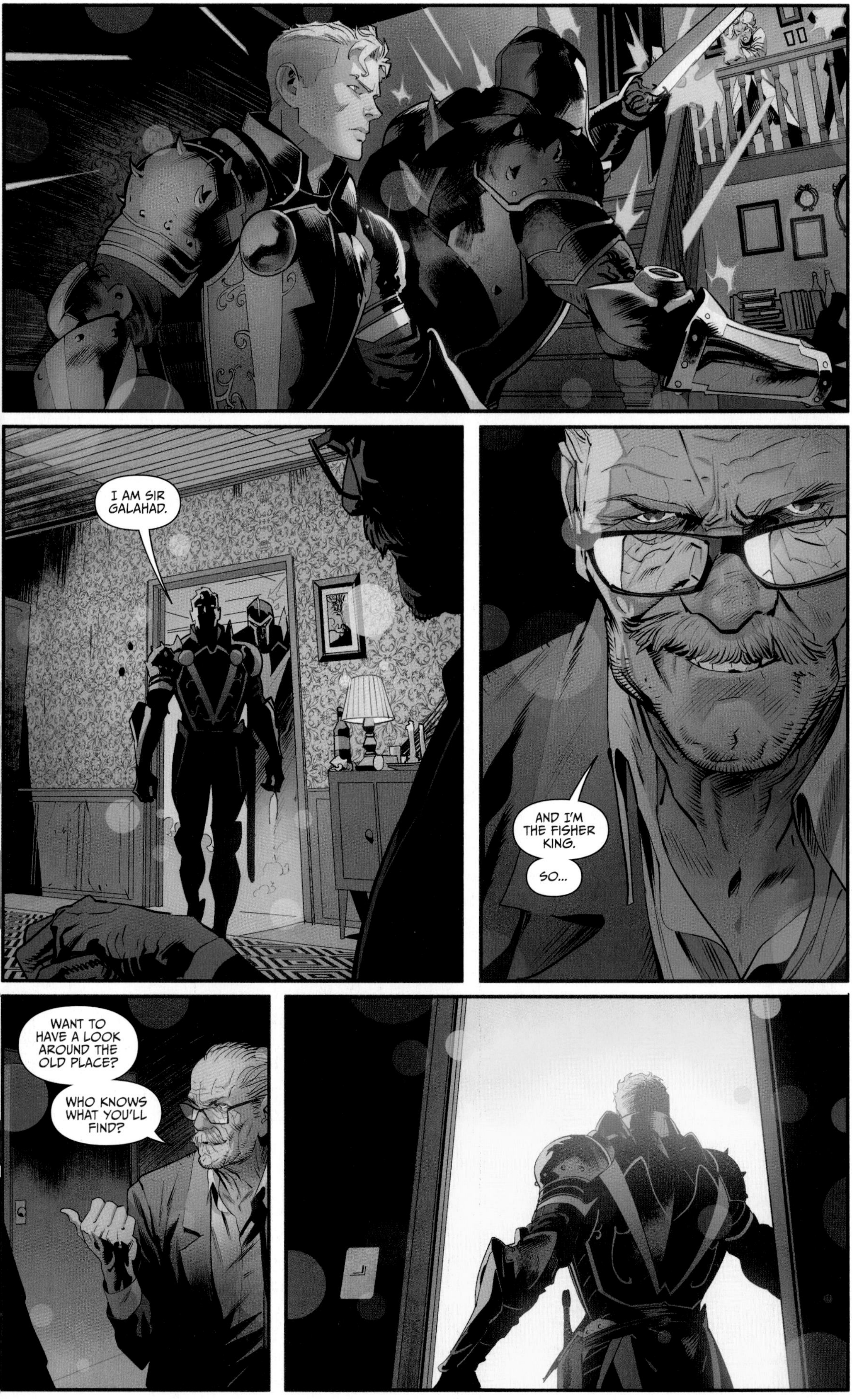
I AM SIR GALAHAD.
AND I'M THE FISHER KING.
SO...
WANT TO HAVE A LOOK AROUND THE OLD PLACE?
WHO KNOWS WHAT YOU'LL FIND?

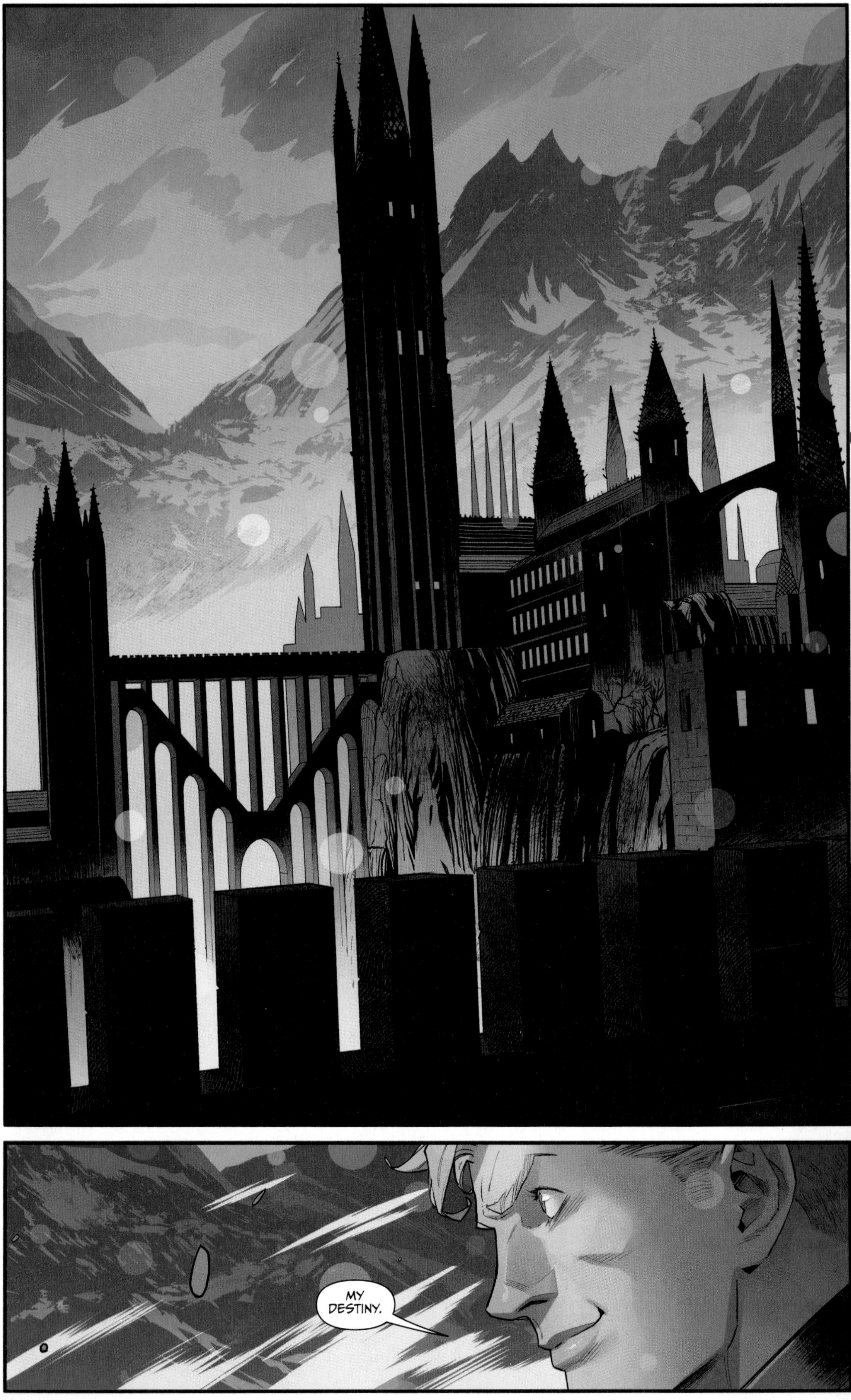
MY DESTINY.

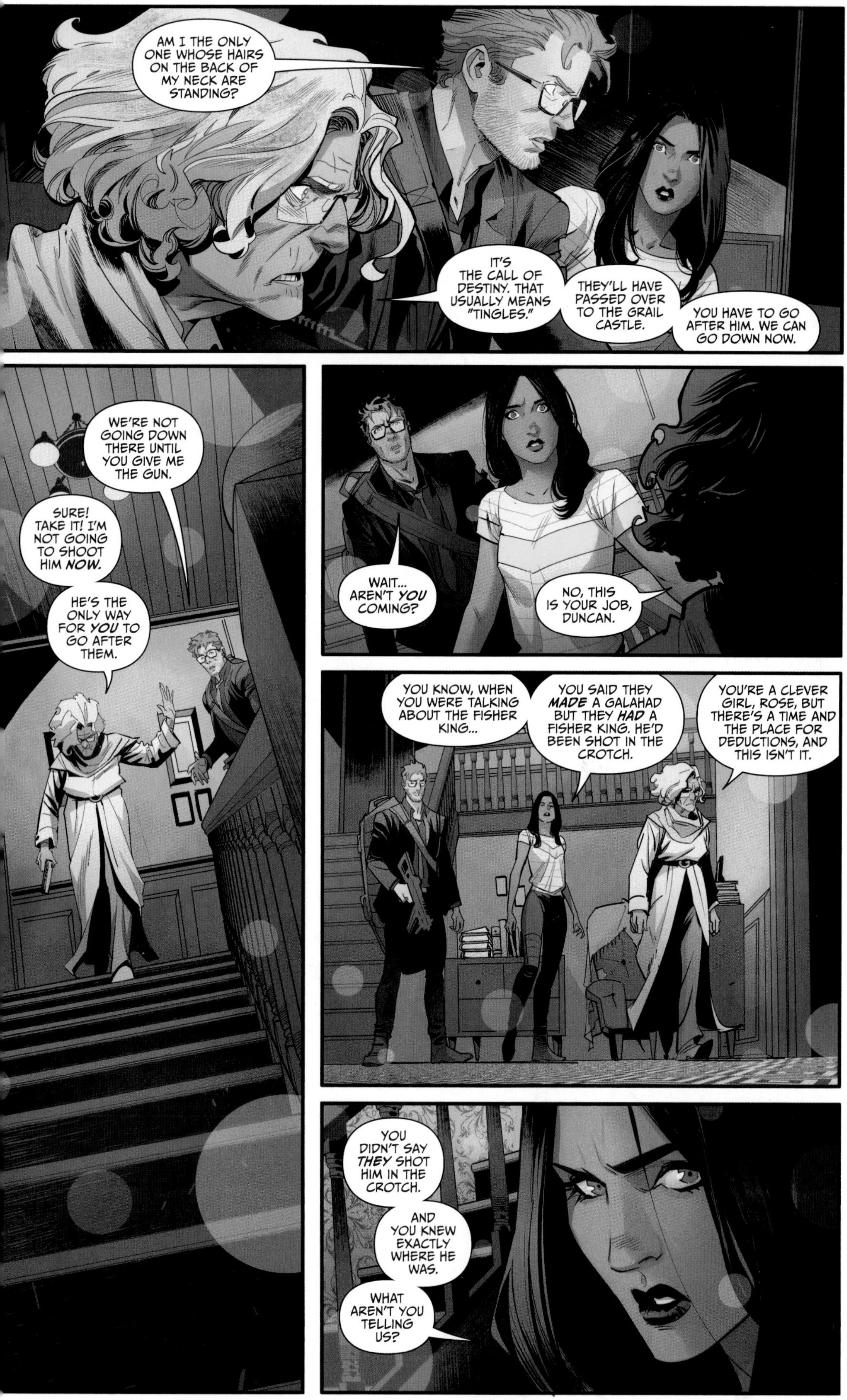
AM I THE ONLY ONE WHOSE HAIRS ON THE BACK OF MY NECK ARE STANDING?
IT'S THE CALL OF DESTINY. THAT USUALLY MEANS "TINGLES."
THEY'LL HAVE PASSED OVER TO THE GRAIL CASTLE.
YOU HAVE TO GO AFTER HIM. WE CAN GO DOWN NOW.
WE'RE NOT GOING DOWN THERE UNTIL YOU GIVE ME THE GUN.
SURE! TAKE IT! I'M NOT GOING TO SHOOT HIM *NOW.*
HE'S THE ONLY WAY FOR *YOU* TO GO AFTER THEM.
WAIT... AREN'T *YOU* COMING?
NO, THIS IS YOUR JOB, DUNCAN.
YOU KNOW, WHEN YOU WERE TALKING ABOUT THE FISHER KING...
YOU SAID THEY *MADE* A GALAHAD BUT THEY *HAD* A FISHER KING. HE'D BEEN SHOT IN THE CROTCH.
YOU'RE A CLEVER GIRL, ROSE, BUT THERE'S A TIME AND THE PLACE FOR DEDUCTIONS, AND THIS ISN'T IT.
YOU DIDN'T SAY *THEY* SHOT HIM IN THE CROTCH.
AND YOU KNEW EXACTLY WHERE HE WAS.
WHAT AREN'T YOU TELLING US?

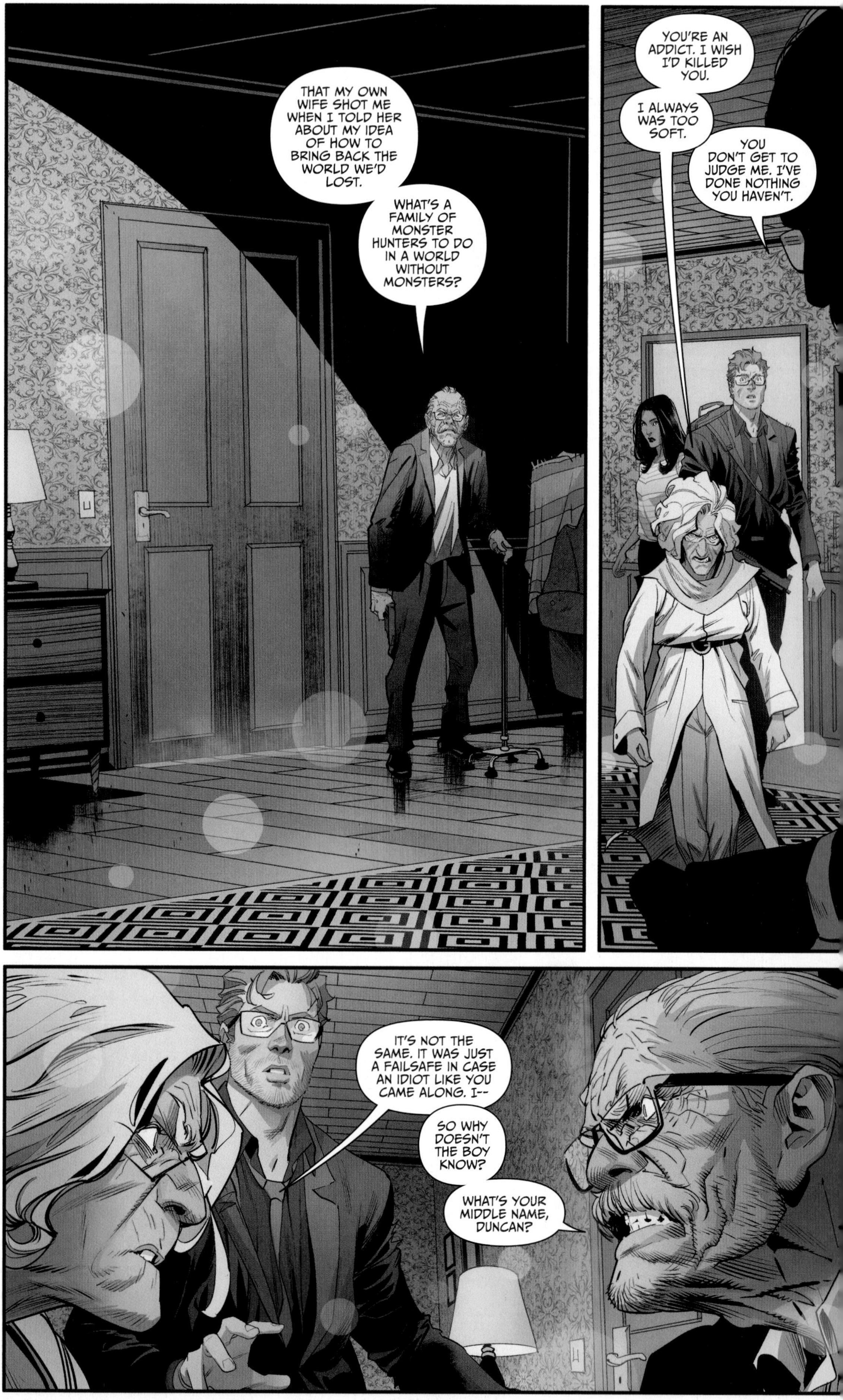
THAT MY OWN WIFE SHOT ME WHEN I TOLD HER ABOUT MY IDEA OF HOW TO BRING BACK THE WORLD WE'D LOST.
WHAT'S A FAMILY OF MONSTER HUNTERS TO DO IN A WORLD WITHOUT MONSTERS?
YOU'RE AN ADDICT. I WISH I'D KILLED YOU.
I ALWAYS WAS TOO SOFT.
YOU DON'T GET TO JUDGE ME. I'VE DONE NOTHING YOU HAVEN'T.
IT'S NOT THE SAME. IT WAS JUST A FAILSAFE IN CASE AN IDIOT LIKE YOU CAME ALONG. I--
SO WHY DOESN'T THE BOY KNOW?
WHAT'S YOUR MIDDLE NAME, DUNCAN?

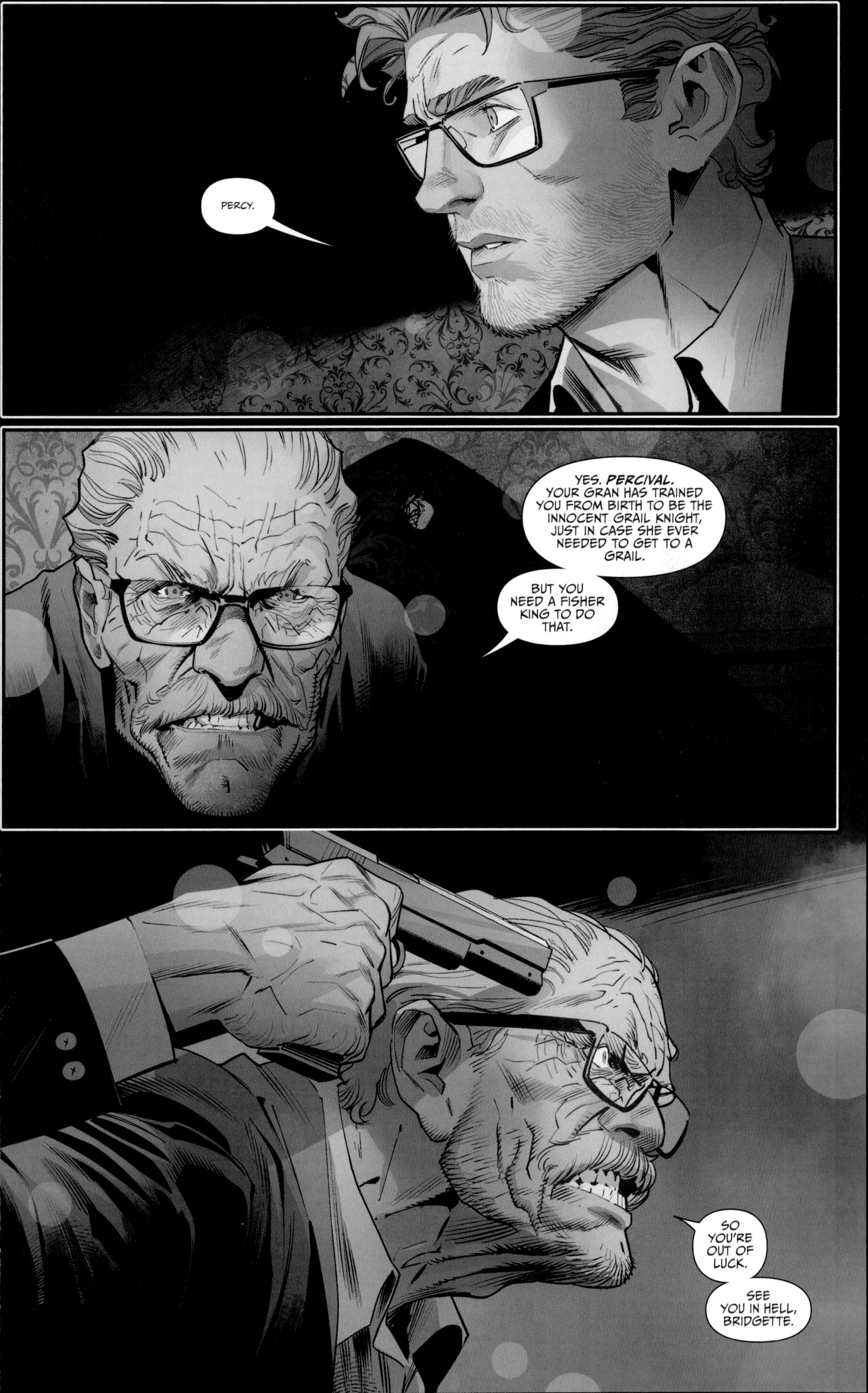
PERCY.
YES. PERCIVAL. YOUR GRAN HAS TRAINED YOU FROM BIRTH TO BE THE INNOCENT GRAIL KNIGHT, JUST IN CASE SHE EVER NEEDED TO GET TO A GRAIL.
BUT YOU NEED A FISHER KING TO DO THAT.
SO YOU'RE OUT OF LUCK.
SEE YOU IN HELL, BRIDGETTE.

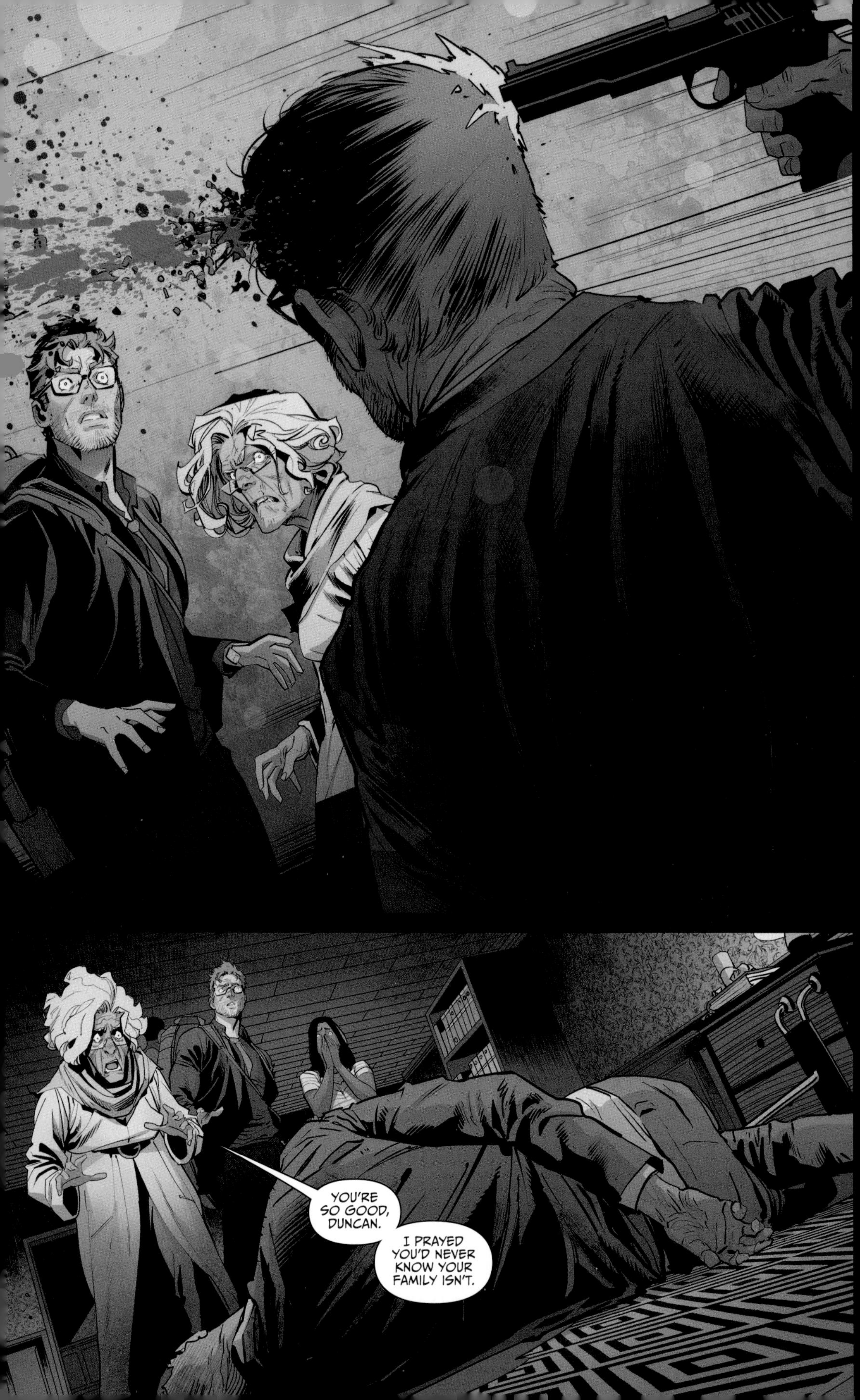
YOU'RE SO GOOD, DUNCAN.
I PRAYED YOU'D NEVER KNOW YOUR FAMILY ISN'T.

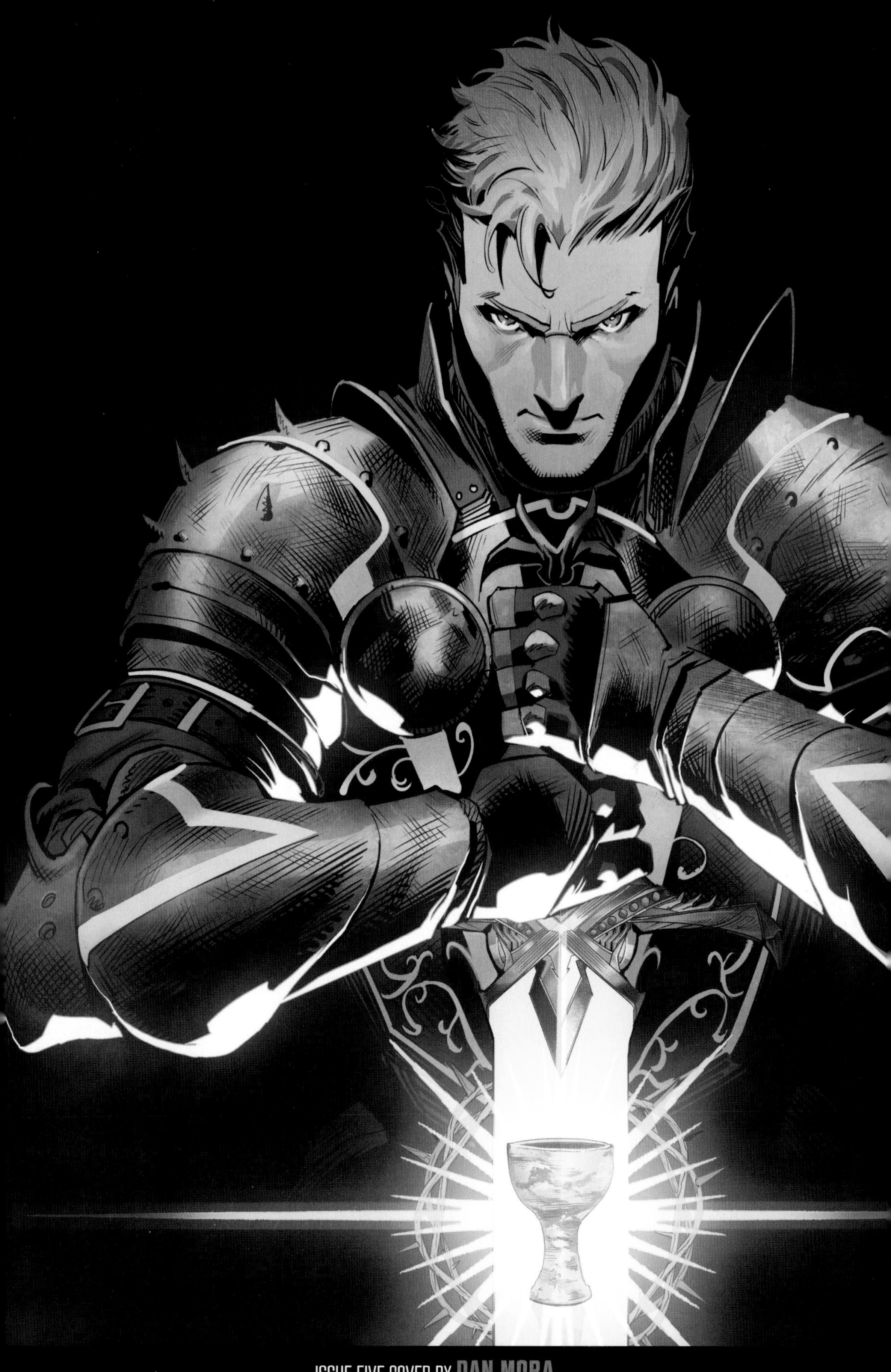

ISSUE FIVE COVER BY **DAN MORA**

CHAPTER FIVE

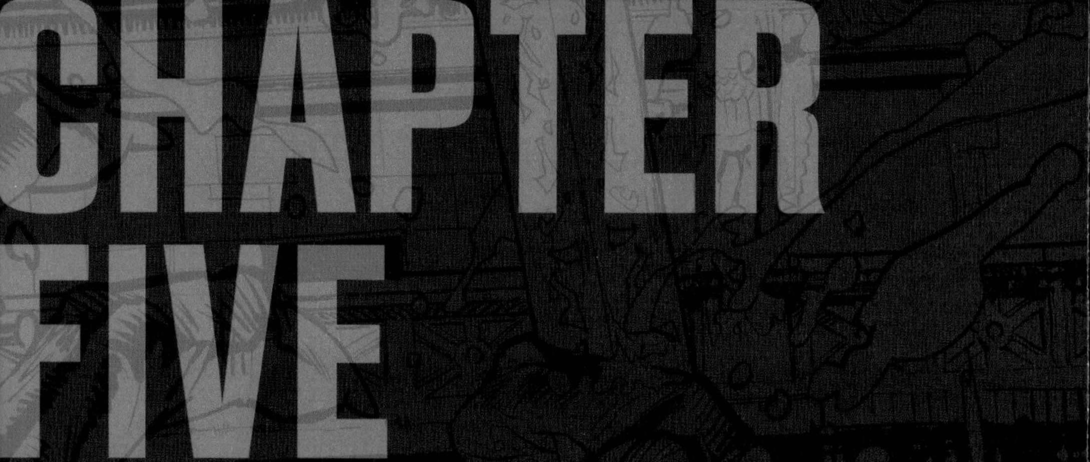

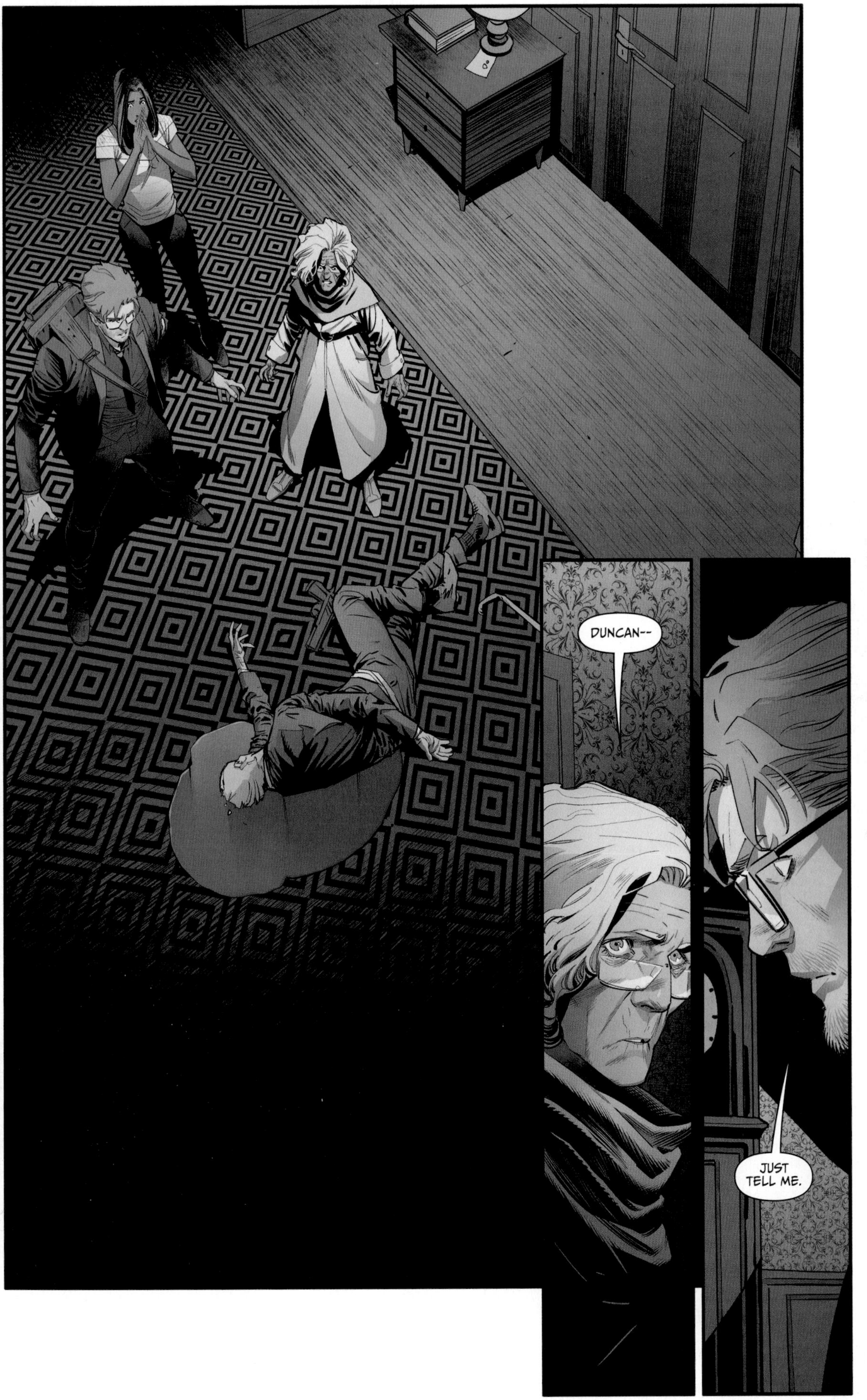
DUNCAN--
JUST TELL ME.

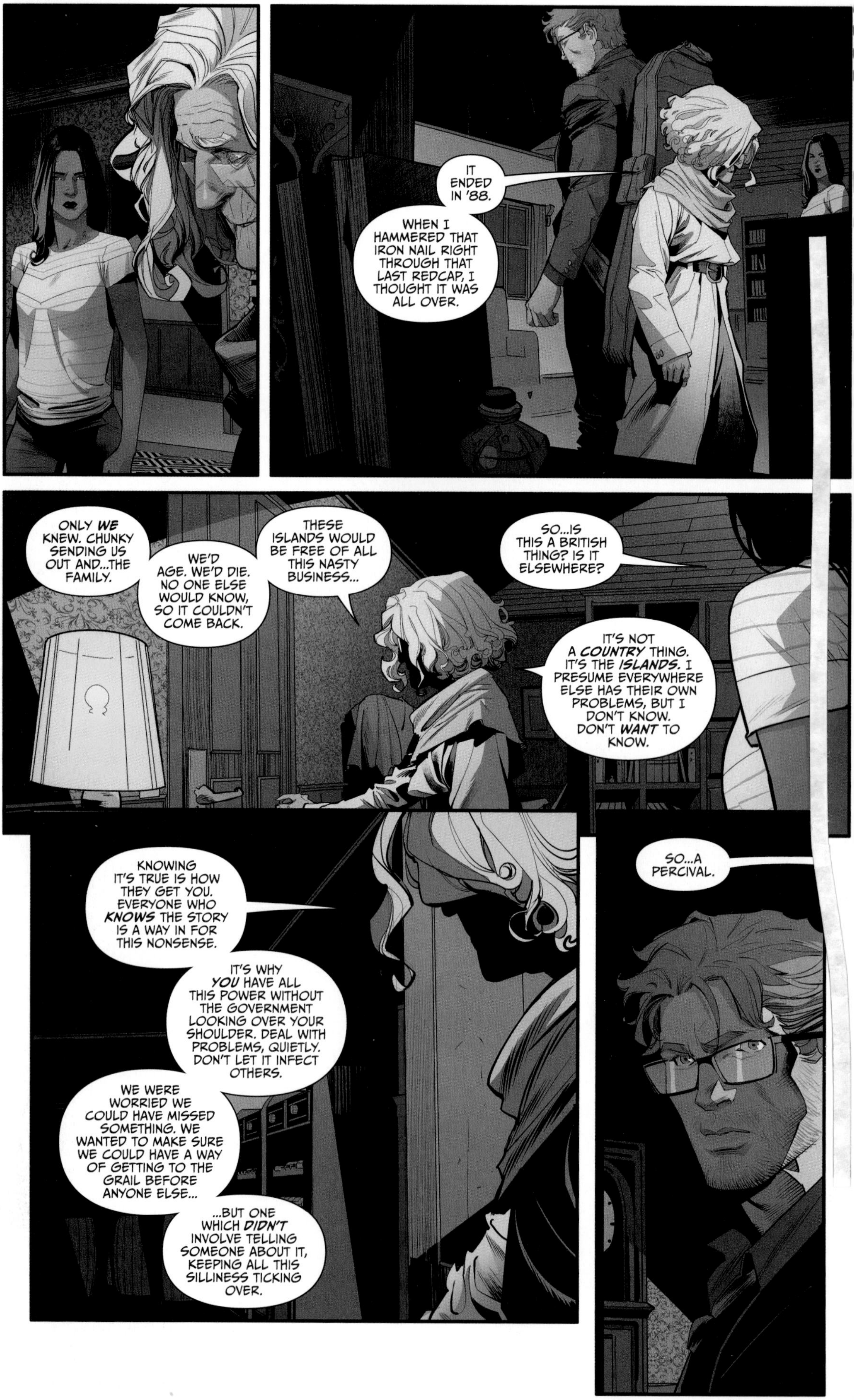
IT ENDED IN '88.
WHEN I HAMMERED THAT IRON NAIL RIGHT THROUGH THAT LAST REDCAP, I THOUGHT IT WAS ALL OVER.
ONLY **WE** KNEW. CHUNKY SENDING US OUT AND...THE FAMILY.
WE'D AGE. WE'D DIE. NO ONE ELSE WOULD KNOW, SO IT COULDN'T COME BACK.
THESE ISLANDS WOULD BE FREE OF ALL THIS NASTY BUSINESS...
SO...IS THIS A BRITISH THING? IS IT ELSEWHERE?
IT'S NOT A **COUNTRY** THING. IT'S THE **ISLANDS.** I PRESUME EVERYWHERE ELSE HAS THEIR OWN PROBLEMS, BUT I DON'T KNOW. DON'T **WANT** TO KNOW.
KNOWING IT'S TRUE IS HOW THEY GET YOU. EVERYONE WHO **KNOWS** THE STORY IS A WAY IN FOR THIS NONSENSE.
IT'S WHY **YOU** HAVE ALL THIS POWER WITHOUT THE GOVERNMENT LOOKING OVER YOUR SHOULDER. DEAL WITH PROBLEMS, QUIETLY. DON'T LET IT INFECT OTHERS.
WE WERE WORRIED WE COULD HAVE MISSED SOMETHING. WE WANTED TO MAKE SURE WE COULD HAVE A WAY OF GETTING TO THE GRAIL BEFORE ANYONE ELSE...
...BUT ONE WHICH **DIDN'T** INVOLVE TELLING SOMEONE ABOUT IT, KEEPING ALL THIS SILLINESS TICKING OVER.
SO...A PERCIVAL.

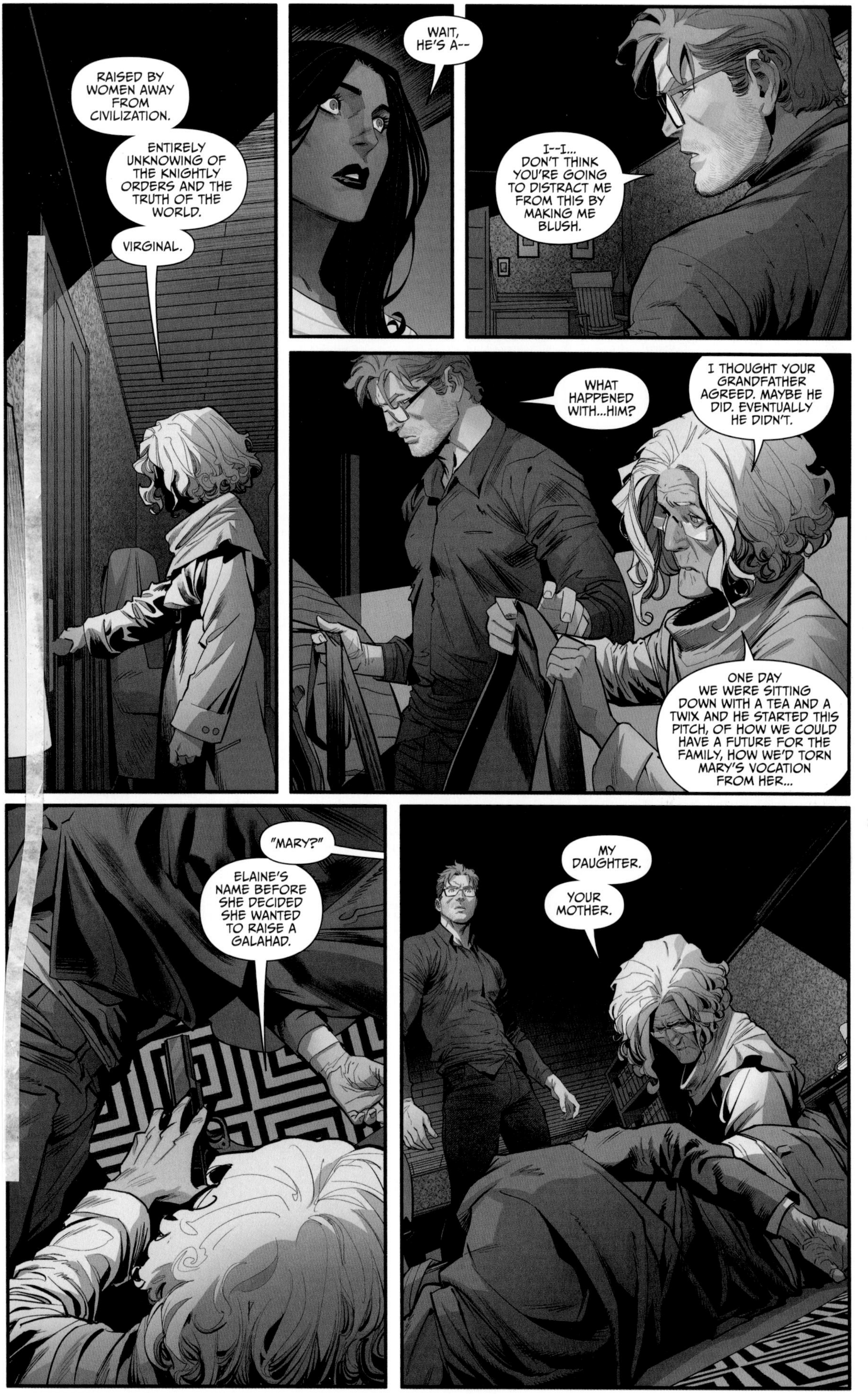
RAISED BY WOMEN AWAY FROM CIVILIZATION.
ENTIRELY UNKNOWING OF THE KNIGHTLY ORDERS AND THE TRUTH OF THE WORLD.
VIRGINAL.
WAIT, HE'S A--
I--I... DON'T THINK YOU'RE GOING TO DISTRACT ME FROM THIS BY MAKING ME BLUSH.
WHAT HAPPENED WITH...HIM?
I THOUGHT YOUR GRANDFATHER AGREED. MAYBE HE DID. EVENTUALLY HE DIDN'T.
ONE DAY WE WERE SITTING DOWN WITH A TEA AND A TWIX AND HE STARTED THIS PITCH, OF HOW WE COULD HAVE A FUTURE FOR THE FAMILY, HOW WE'D TORN MARY'S VOCATION FROM HER...
"MARY?"
ELAINE'S NAME BEFORE SHE DECIDED SHE WANTED TO RAISE A GALAHAD.
MY DAUGHTER.
YOUR MOTHER.

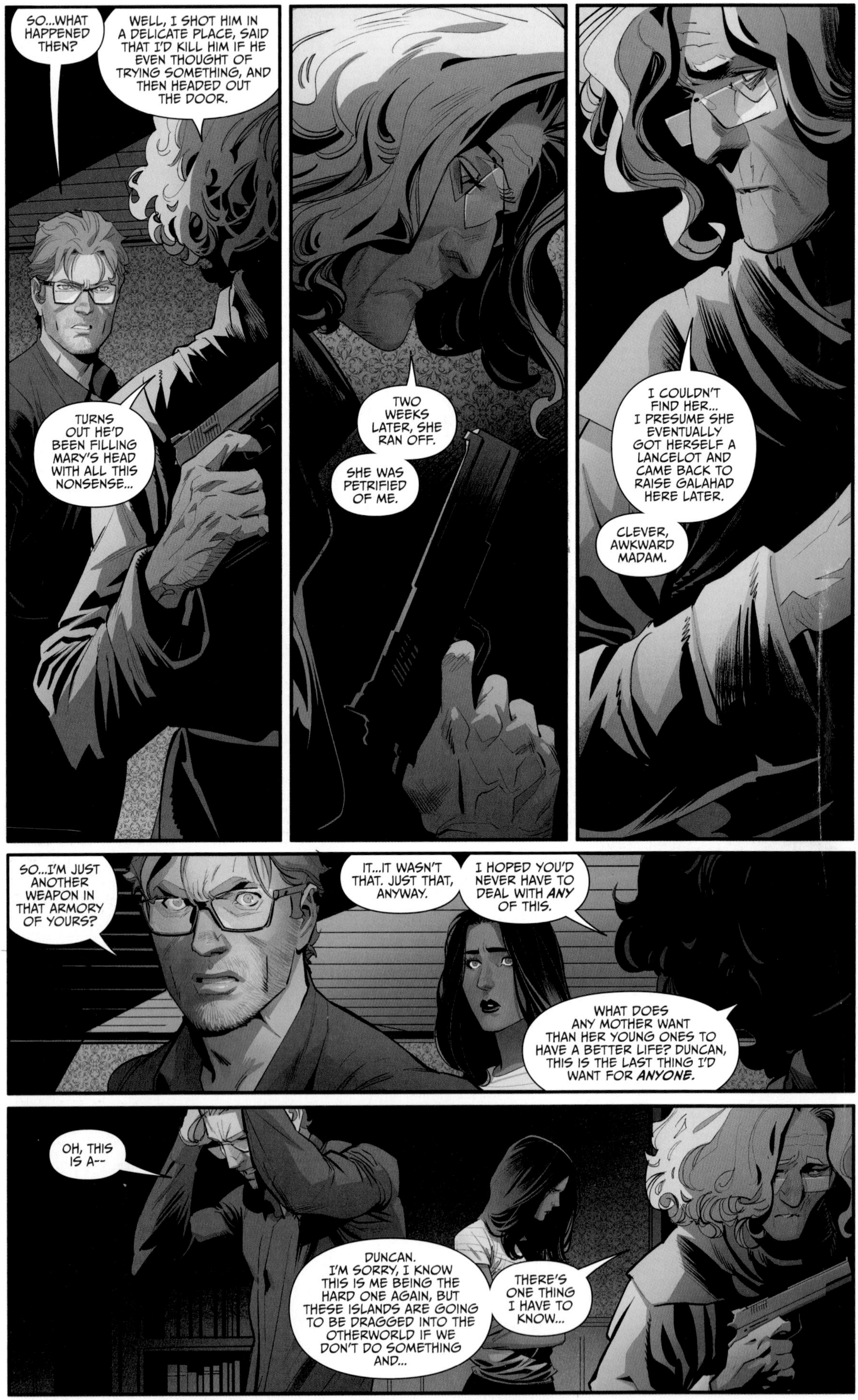

SO...WHAT HAPPENED THEN?
WELL, I SHOT HIM IN A DELICATE PLACE, SAID THAT I'D KILL HIM IF HE EVEN THOUGHT OF TRYING SOMETHING, AND THEN HEADED OUT THE DOOR.
TURNS OUT HE'D BEEN FILLING MARY'S HEAD WITH ALL THIS NONSENSE...
TWO WEEKS LATER, SHE RAN OFF.
SHE WAS PETRIFIED OF ME.
I COULDN'T FIND HER... I PRESUME SHE EVENTUALLY GOT HERSELF A LANCELOT AND CAME BACK TO RAISE GALAHAD HERE LATER.
CLEVER, AWKWARD MADAM.
SO...I'M JUST ANOTHER WEAPON IN THAT ARMORY OF YOURS?
IT...IT WASN'T THAT. JUST THAT, ANYWAY.
I HOPED YOU'D NEVER HAVE TO DEAL WITH ANY OF THIS.
WHAT DOES ANY MOTHER WANT THAN HER YOUNG ONES TO HAVE A BETTER LIFE? DUNCAN, THIS IS THE LAST THING I'D WANT FOR ANYONE.
OH, THIS IS A--
DUNCAN. I'M SORRY, I KNOW THIS IS ME BEING THE HARD ONE AGAIN, BUT THESE ISLANDS ARE GOING TO BE DRAGGED INTO THE OTHERWORLD IF WE DON'T DO SOMETHING AND...
THERE'S ONE THING I HAVE TO KNOW...

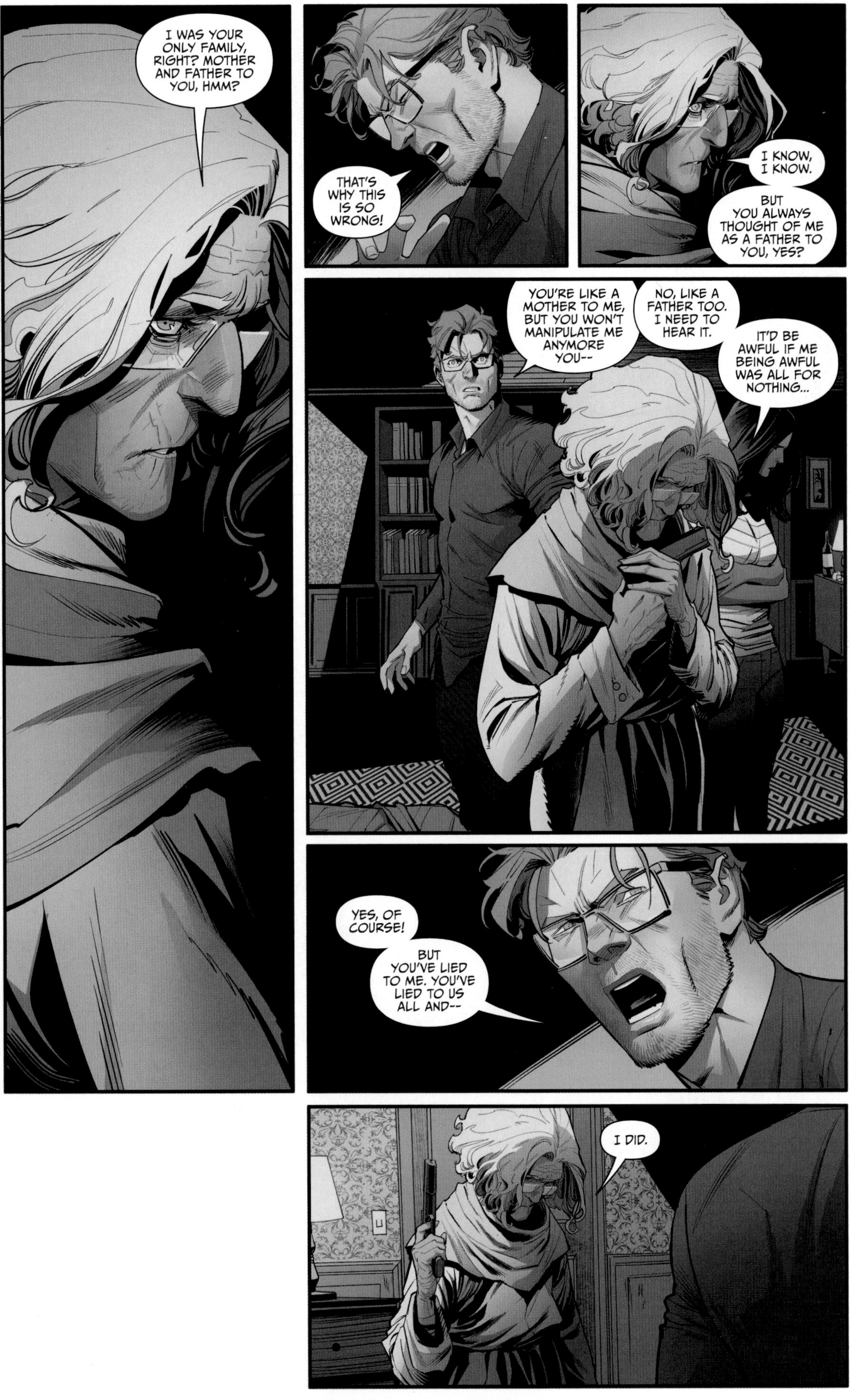
I WAS YOUR ONLY FAMILY, RIGHT? MOTHER AND FATHER TO YOU, HMM?
THAT'S WHY THIS IS SO WRONG!
I KNOW, I KNOW.
BUT YOU ALWAYS THOUGHT OF ME AS A FATHER TO YOU, YES?
YOU'RE LIKE A MOTHER TO ME, BUT YOU WON'T MANIPULATE ME ANYMORE YOU--
NO, LIKE A FATHER TOO. I NEED TO HEAR IT.
IT'D BE AWFUL IF ME BEING AWFUL WAS ALL FOR NOTHING...
YES, OF COURSE!
BUT YOU'VE LIED TO ME. YOU'VE LIED TO US ALL AND--
I DID.

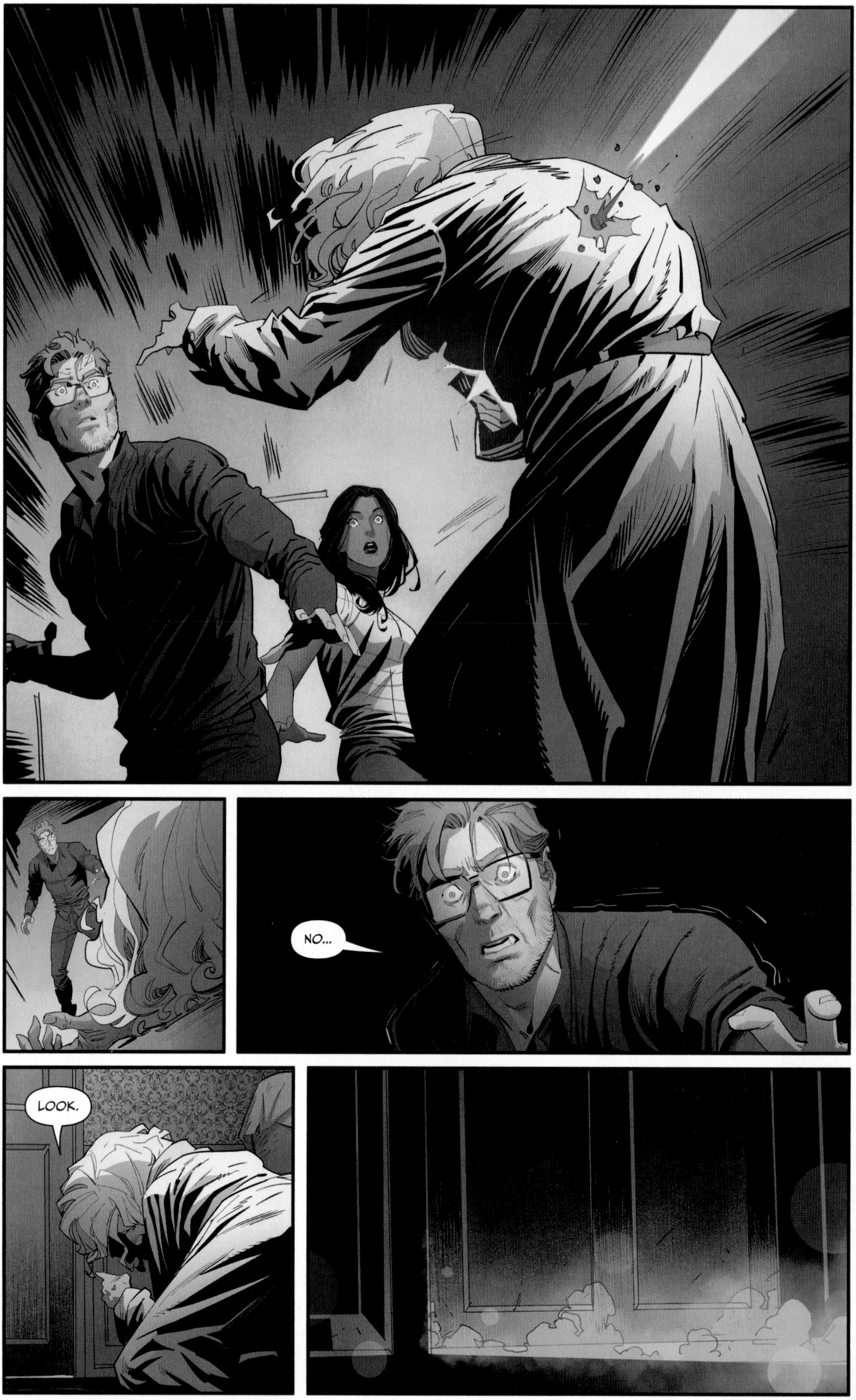
NO...
LOOK.

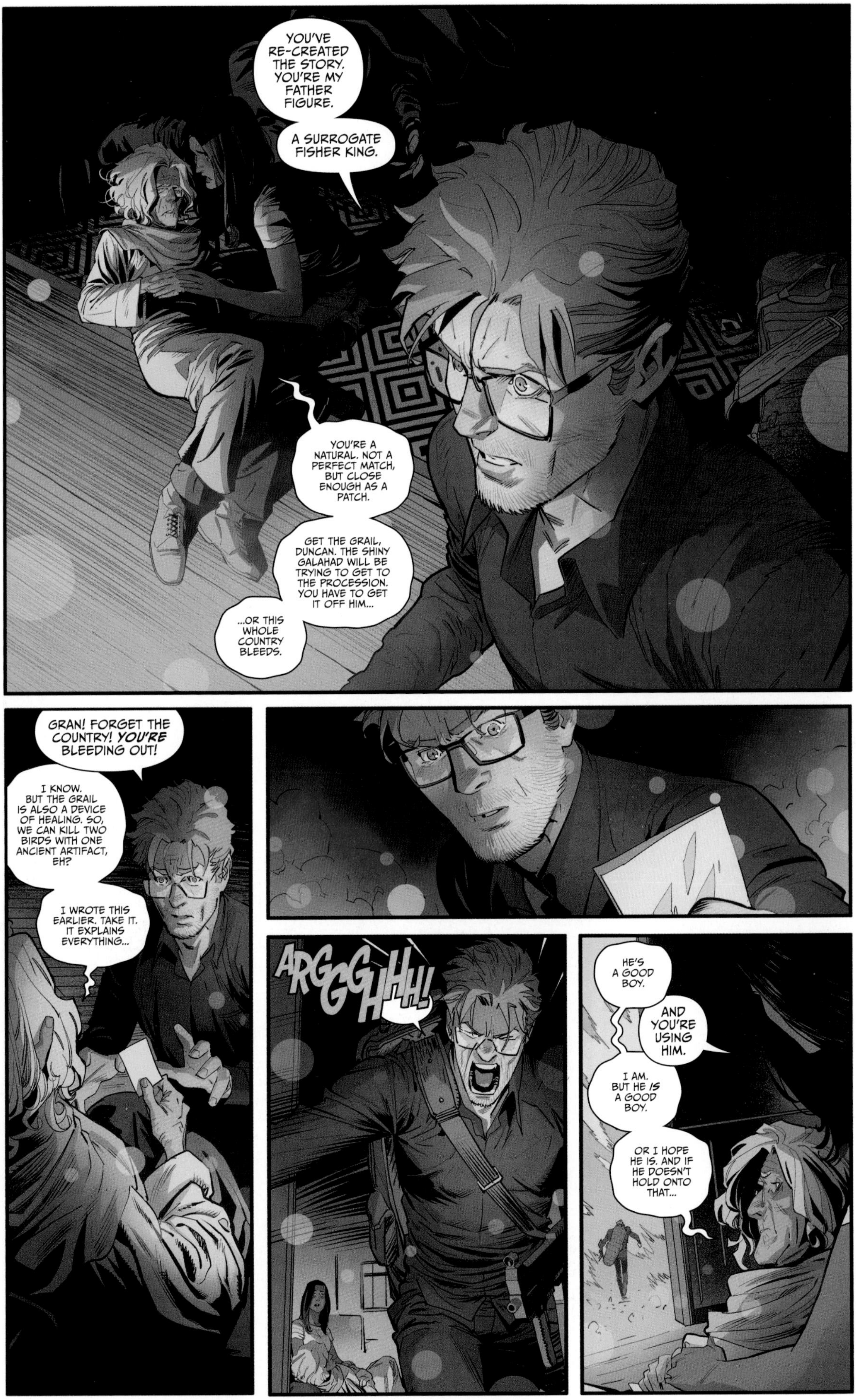
YOU'VE RE-CREATED THE STORY. YOU'RE MY FATHER FIGURE.
A SURROGATE FISHER KING.
YOU'RE A NATURAL. NOT A PERFECT MATCH, BUT CLOSE ENOUGH AS A PATCH.
GET THE GRAIL, DUNCAN. THE SHINY GALAHAD WILL BE TRYING TO GET TO THE PROCESSION. YOU HAVE TO GET IT OFF HIM...
...OR THIS WHOLE COUNTRY BLEEDS.
GRAN! FORGET THE COUNTRY! *YOU'RE* BLEEDING OUT!
I KNOW. BUT THE GRAIL IS ALSO A DEVICE OF HEALING. SO, WE CAN KILL TWO BIRDS WITH ONE ANCIENT ARTIFACT, EH?
I WROTE THIS EARLIER. TAKE IT. IT EXPLAINS EVERYTHING...
ARGGGHHH!
HE'S A GOOD BOY.
AND YOU'RE USING HIM.
I AM. BUT HE *IS* A GOOD BOY.
OR I HOPE HE IS. AND IF HE DOESN'T HOLD ONTO THAT...

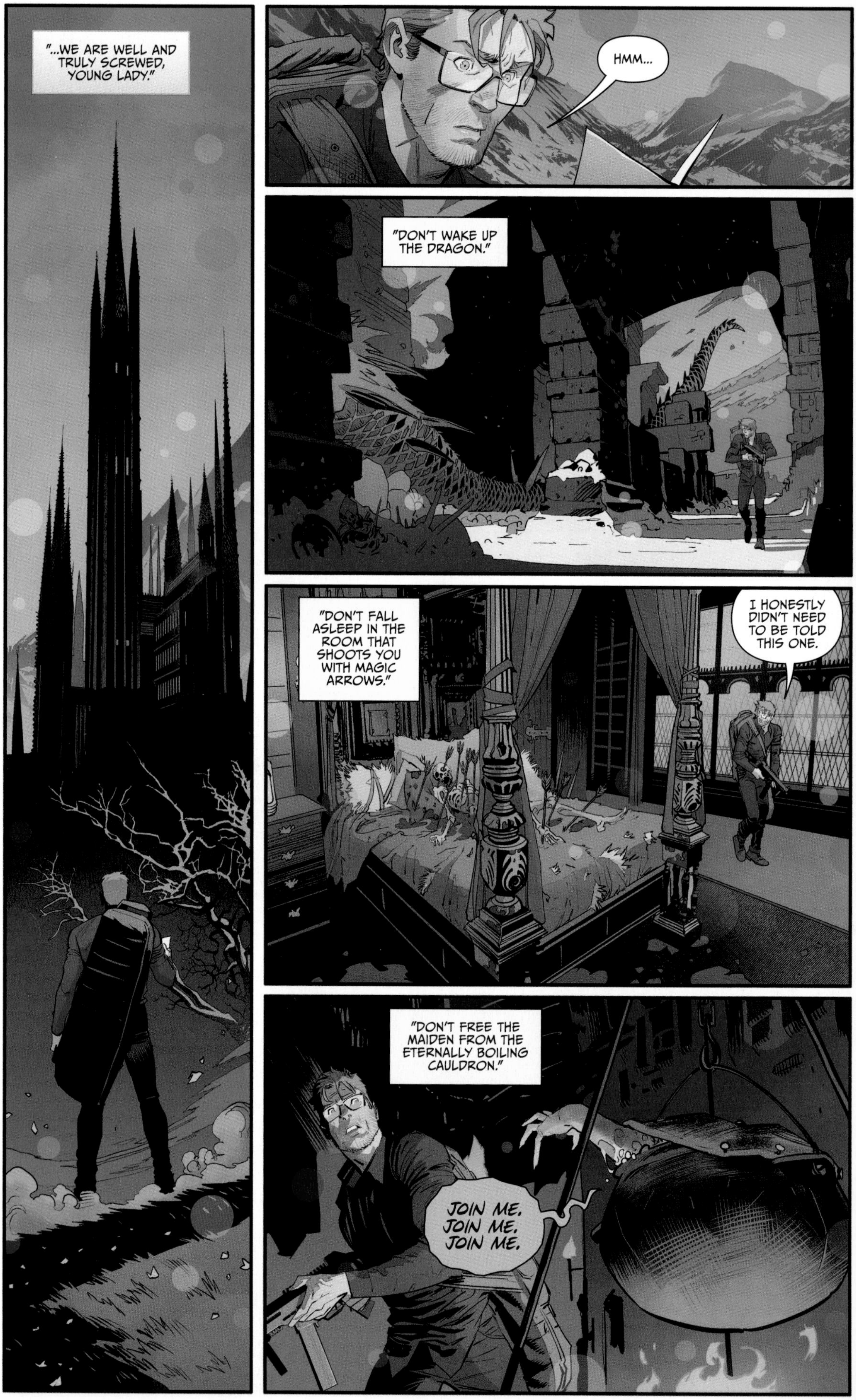
"...WE ARE WELL AND TRULY SCREWED, YOUNG LADY."
HMM...
"DON'T WAKE UP THE DRAGON."
"DON'T FALL ASLEEP IN THE ROOM THAT SHOOTS YOU WITH MAGIC ARROWS."
I HONESTLY DIDN'T NEED TO BE TOLD THIS ONE.
"DON'T FREE THE MAIDEN FROM THE ETERNALLY BOILING CAULDRON."
JOIN ME. JOIN ME. JOIN ME.

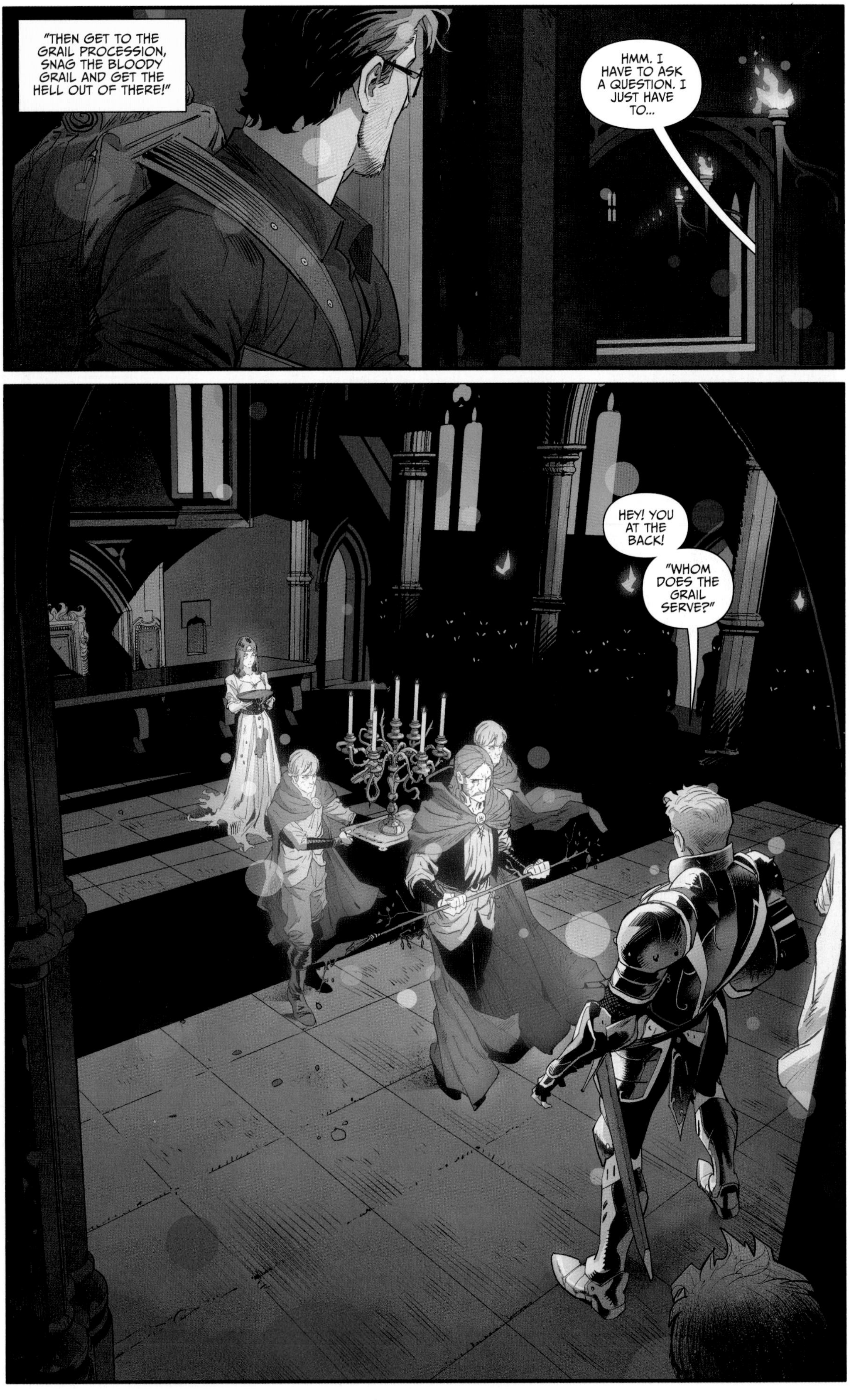
"THEN GET TO THE GRAIL PROCESSION, SNAG THE BLOODY GRAIL AND GET THE HELL OUT OF THERE!"
HMM. I HAVE TO ASK A QUESTION. I JUST HAVE TO...
HEY! YOU AT THE BACK!
"WHOM DOES THE GRAIL SERVE?"

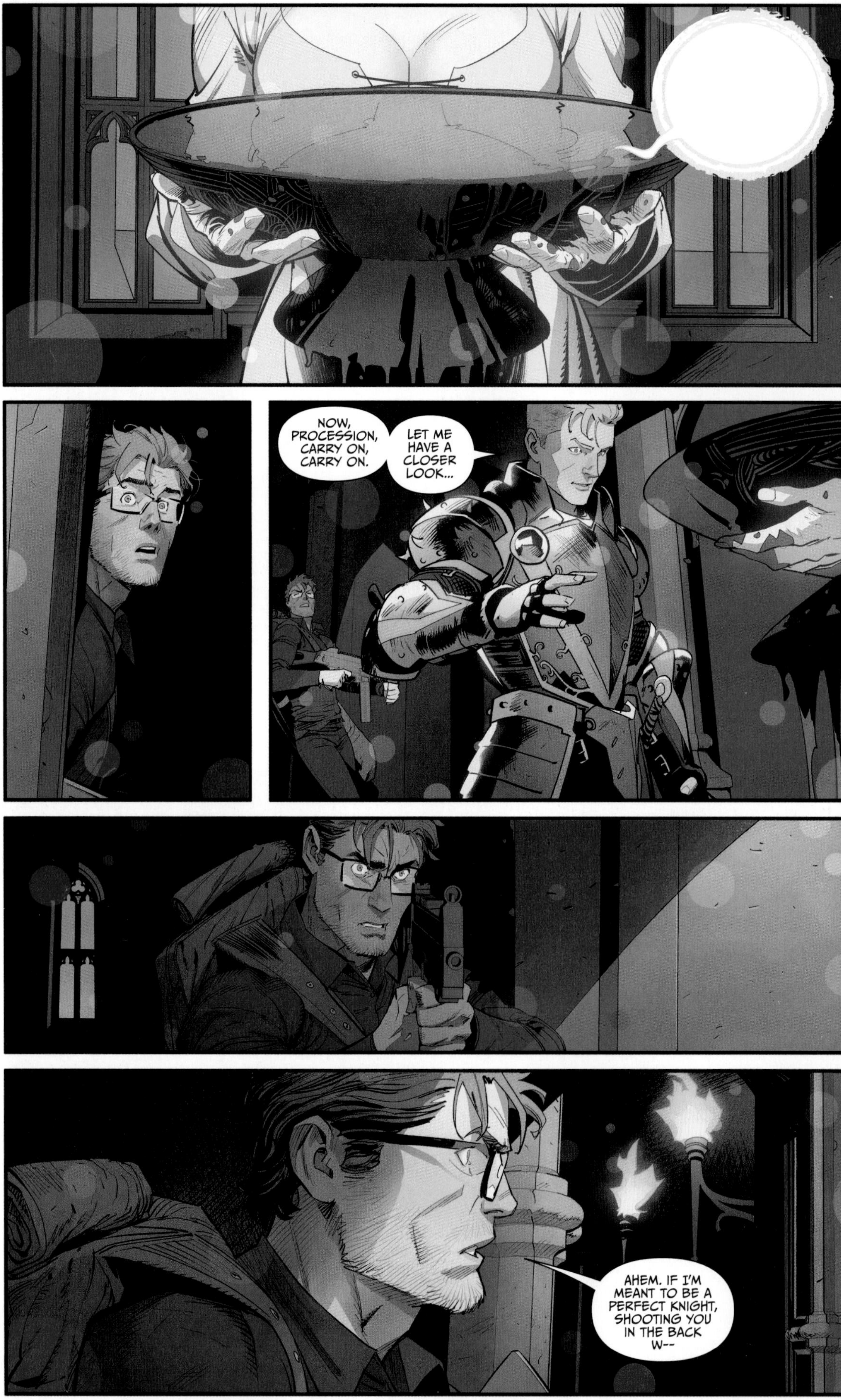
NOW, PROCESSION, CARRY ON, CARRY ON.
LET ME HAVE A CLOSER LOOK...
AHEM. IF I'M MEANT TO BE A PERFECT KNIGHT, SHOOTING YOU IN THE BACK W--

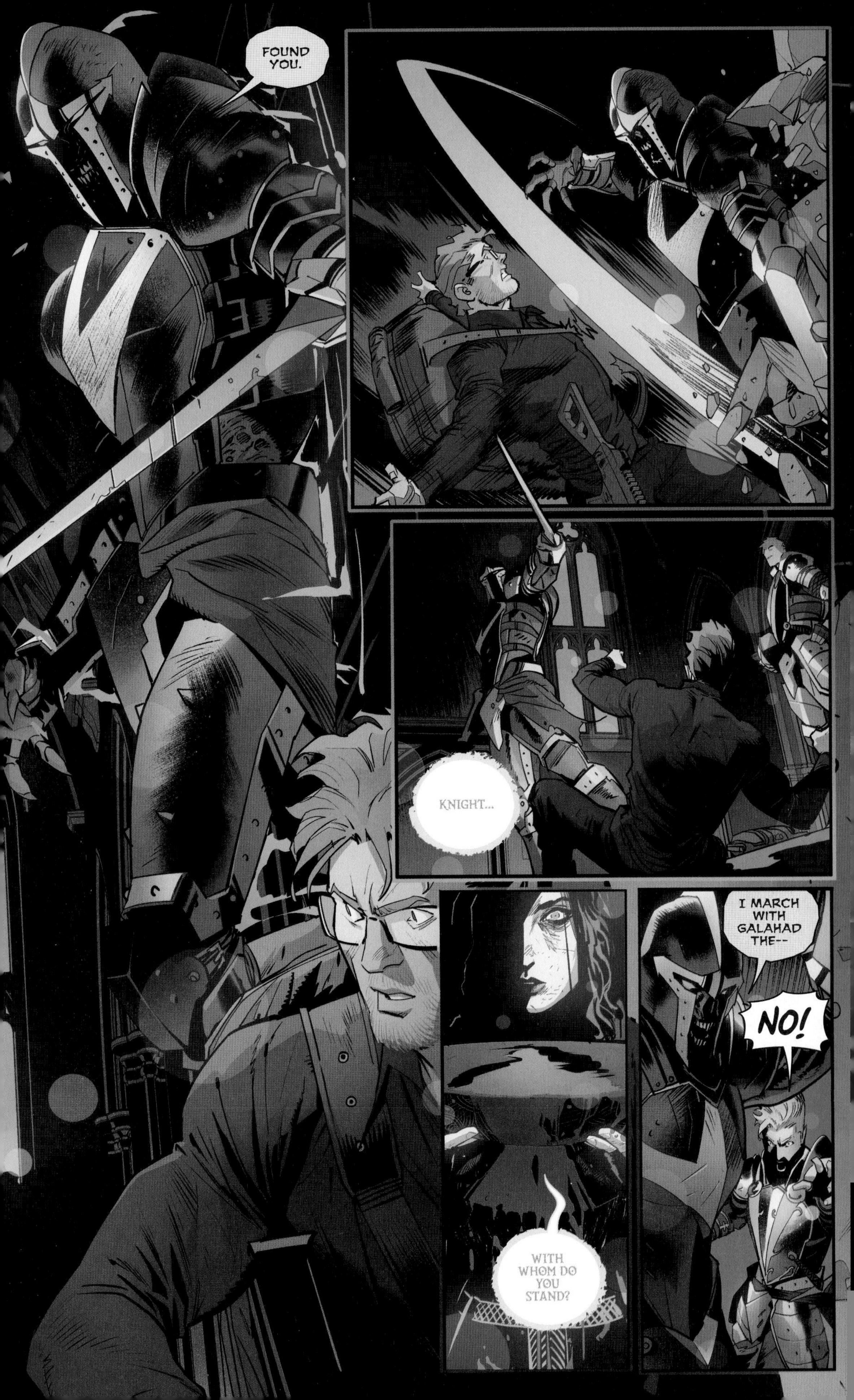
FOUND YOU.
KNIGHT...
WITH WHOM DO YOU STAND?
I MARCH WITH GALAHAD THE--
NO!

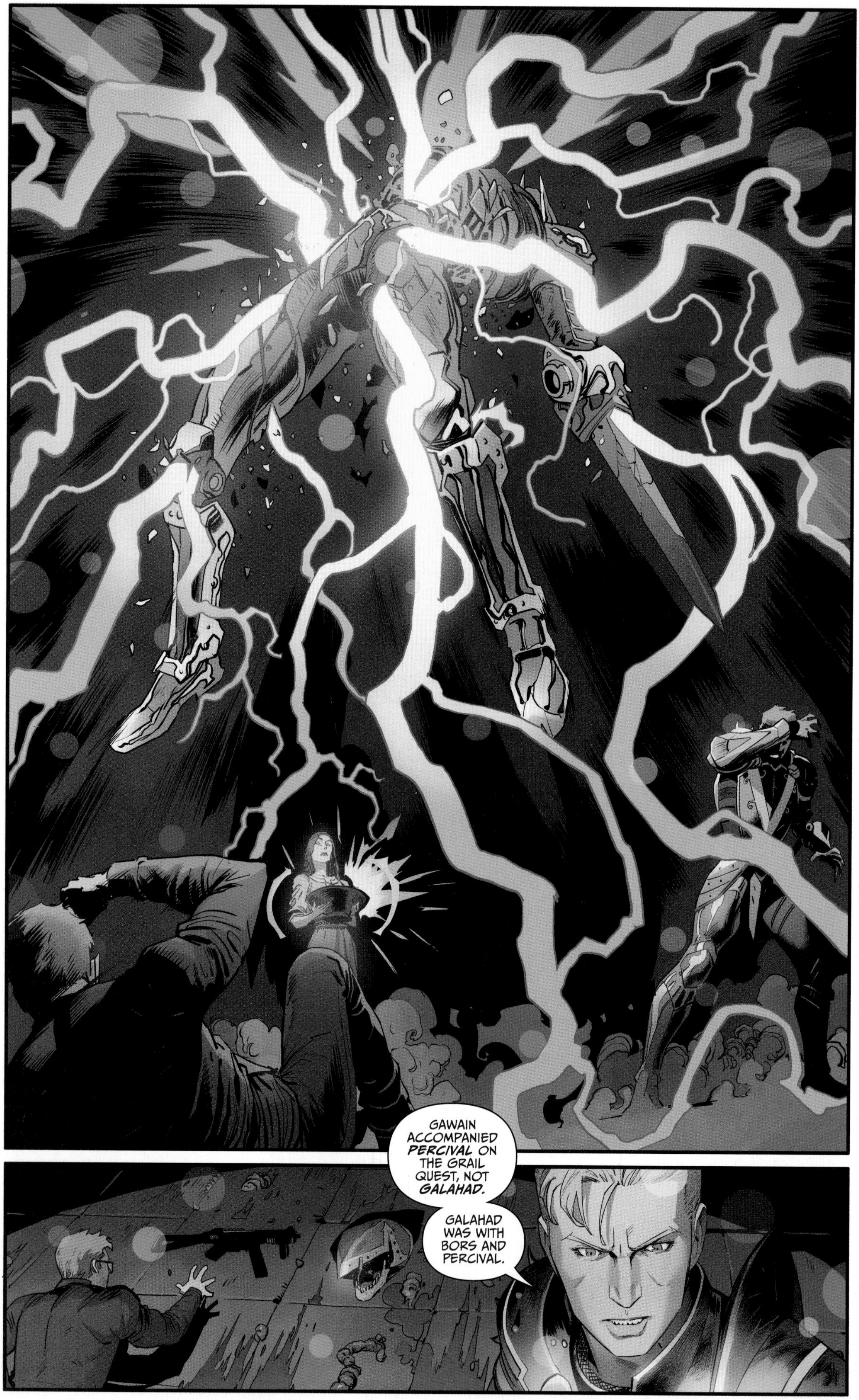
GAWAIN ACCOMPANIED PERCIVAL ON THE GRAIL QUEST, NOT GALAHAD.
GALAHAD WAS WITH BORS AND PERCIVAL.

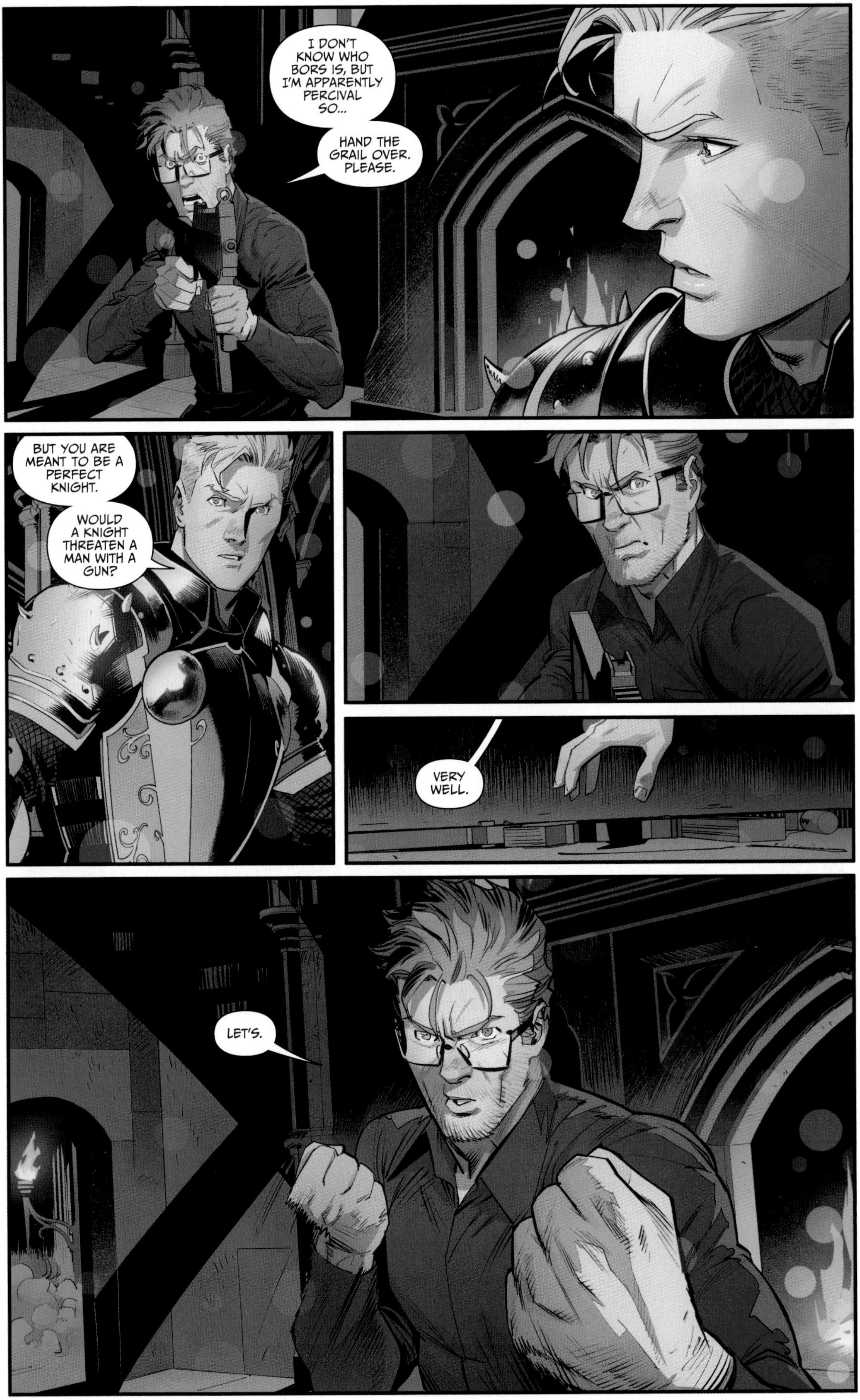
I DON'T KNOW WHO BORS IS, BUT I'M APPARENTLY PERCIVAL SO...
HAND THE GRAIL OVER. PLEASE.
BUT YOU ARE MEANT TO BE A PERFECT KNIGHT.
WOULD A KNIGHT THREATEN A MAN WITH A GUN?
VERY WELL.
LET'S.

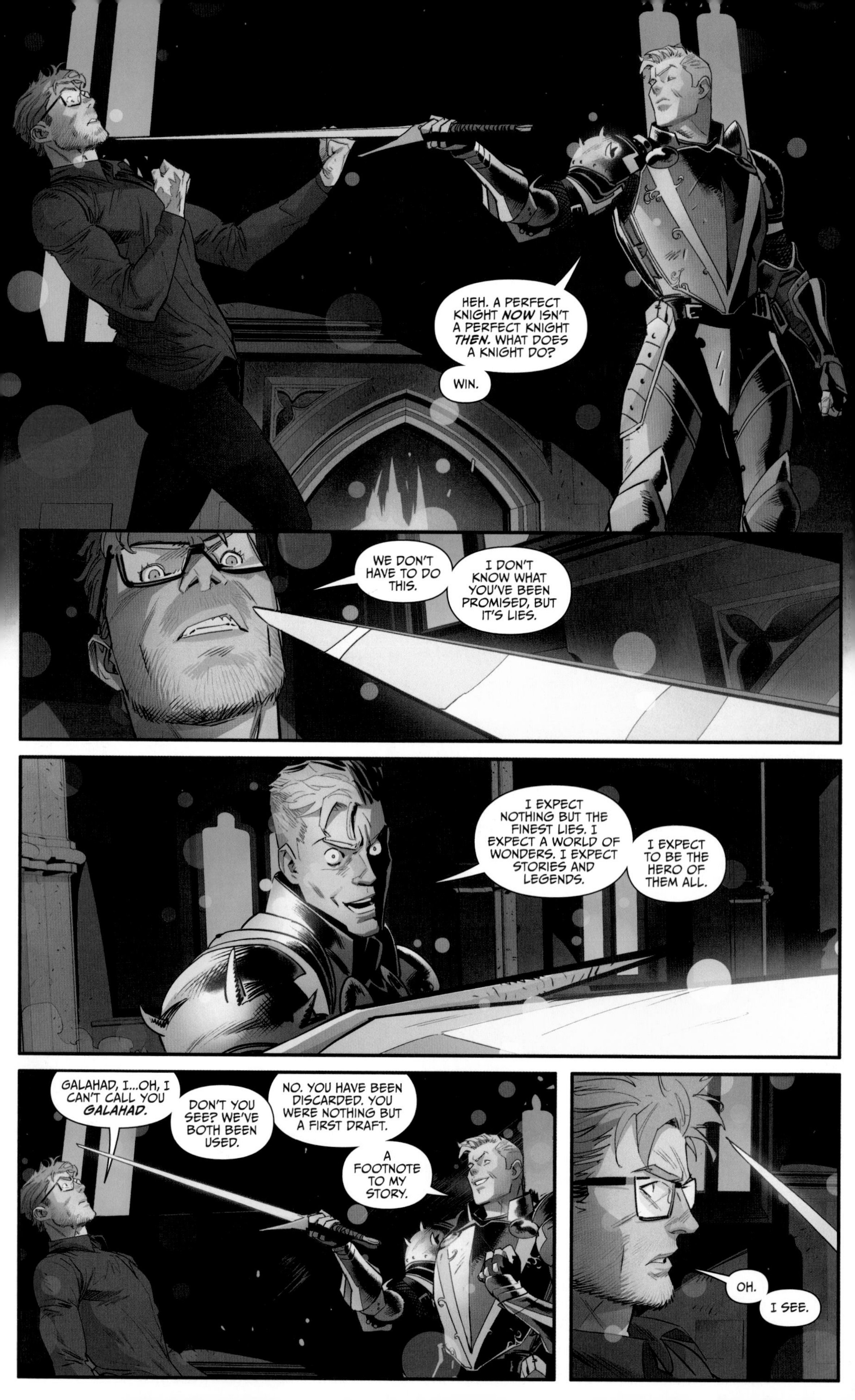
HEH. A PERFECT KNIGHT *NOW* ISN'T A PERFECT KNIGHT *THEN*. WHAT DOES A KNIGHT DO?
WIN.
WE DON'T HAVE TO DO THIS.
I DON'T KNOW WHAT YOU'VE BEEN PROMISED, BUT IT'S LIES.
I EXPECT NOTHING BUT THE FINEST LIES. I EXPECT A WORLD OF WONDERS. I EXPECT STORIES AND LEGENDS.
I EXPECT TO BE THE HERO OF THEM ALL.
GALAHAD, I...OH, I CAN'T CALL YOU *GALAHAD*.
DON'T YOU SEE? WE'VE BOTH BEEN USED.
NO. YOU HAVE BEEN DISCARDED. YOU WERE NOTHING BUT A FIRST DRAFT.
A FOOTNOTE TO MY STORY.
OH.
I SEE.

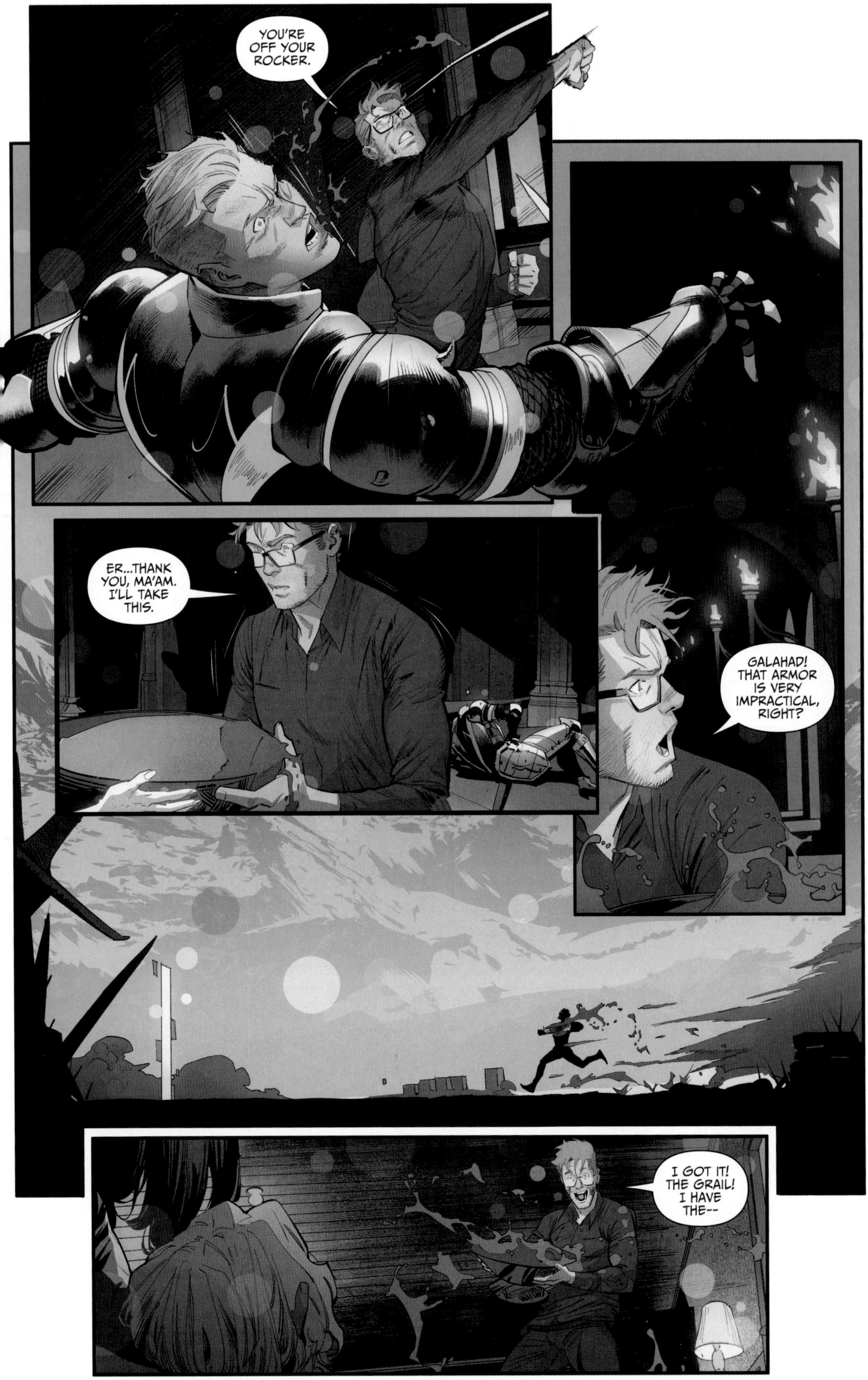
YOU'RE OFF YOUR ROCKER.
ER...THANK YOU, MA'AM. I'LL TAKE THIS.
GALAHAD! THAT ARMOR IS VERY IMPRACTICAL, RIGHT?
I GOT IT! THE GRAIL! I HAVE THE--

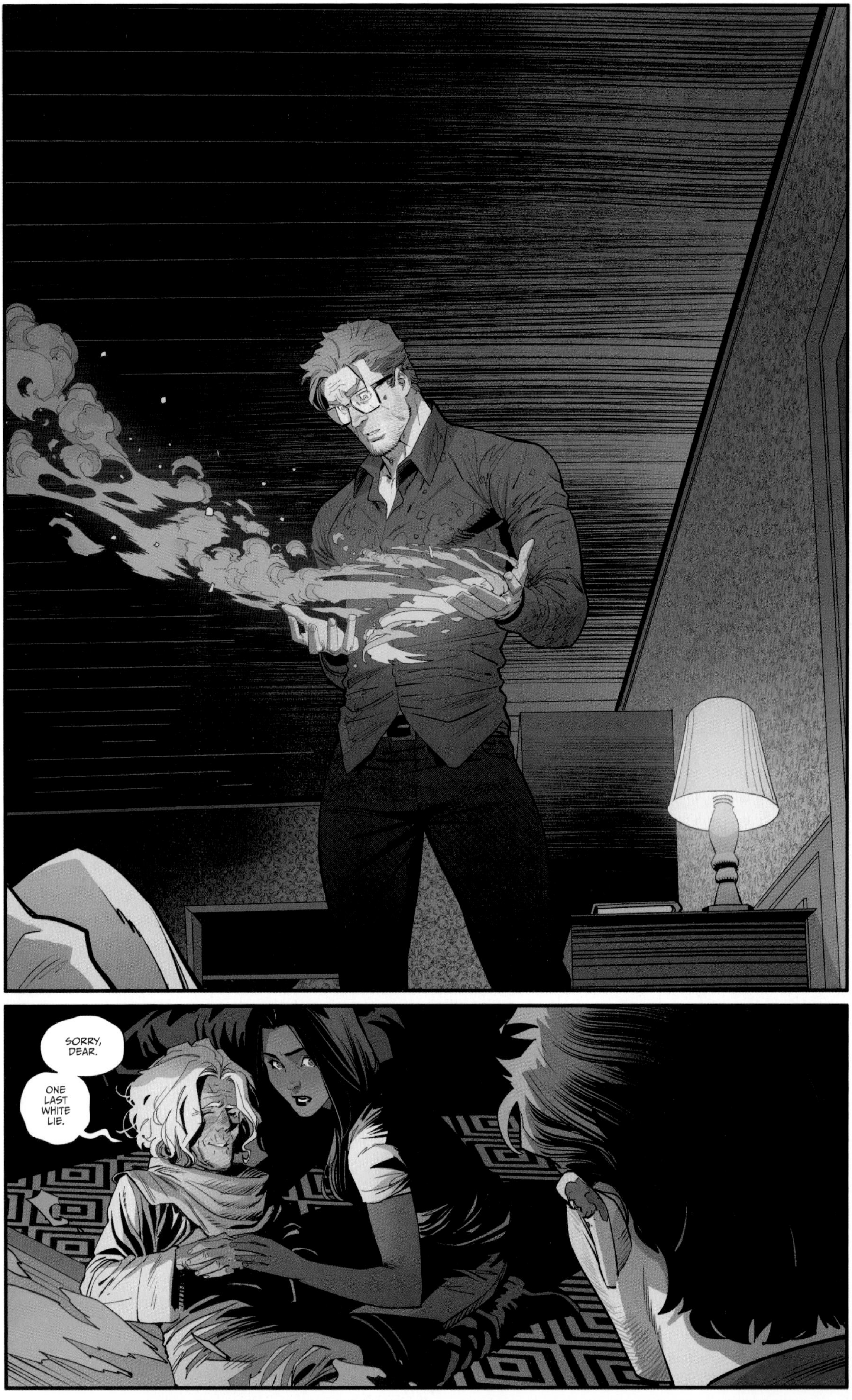
SORRY, DEAR.
ONE LAST WHITE LIE.

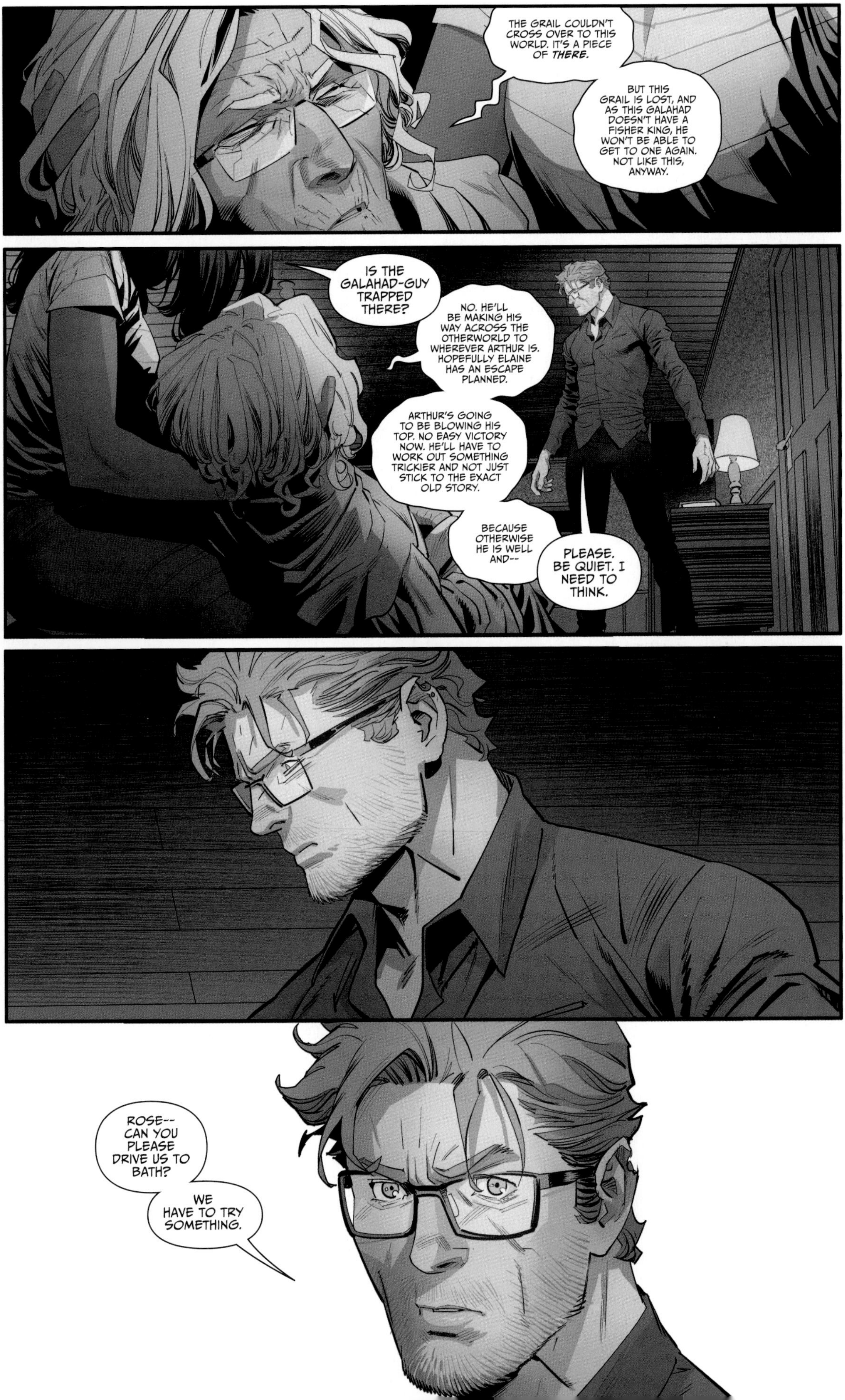

THE GRAIL COULDN'T CROSS OVER TO THIS WORLD. IT'S A PIECE OF *THERE.*
BUT THIS GRAIL IS LOST, AND AS THIS GALAHAD DOESN'T HAVE A FISHER KING, HE WON'T BE ABLE TO GET TO ONE AGAIN. NOT LIKE THIS, ANYWAY.
IS THE GALAHAD-GUY TRAPPED THERE?
NO. HE'LL BE MAKING HIS WAY ACROSS THE OTHERWORLD TO WHEREVER ARTHUR IS. HOPEFULLY ELAINE HAS AN ESCAPE PLANNED.
ARTHUR'S GOING TO BE BLOWING HIS TOP. NO EASY VICTORY NOW. HE'LL HAVE TO WORK OUT SOMETHING TRICKIER AND NOT JUST STICK TO THE EXACT OLD STORY.
BECAUSE OTHERWISE HE IS WELL AND--
PLEASE. BE QUIET. I NEED TO THINK.
ROSE-- CAN YOU PLEASE DRIVE US TO BATH?
WE HAVE TO TRY SOMETHING.

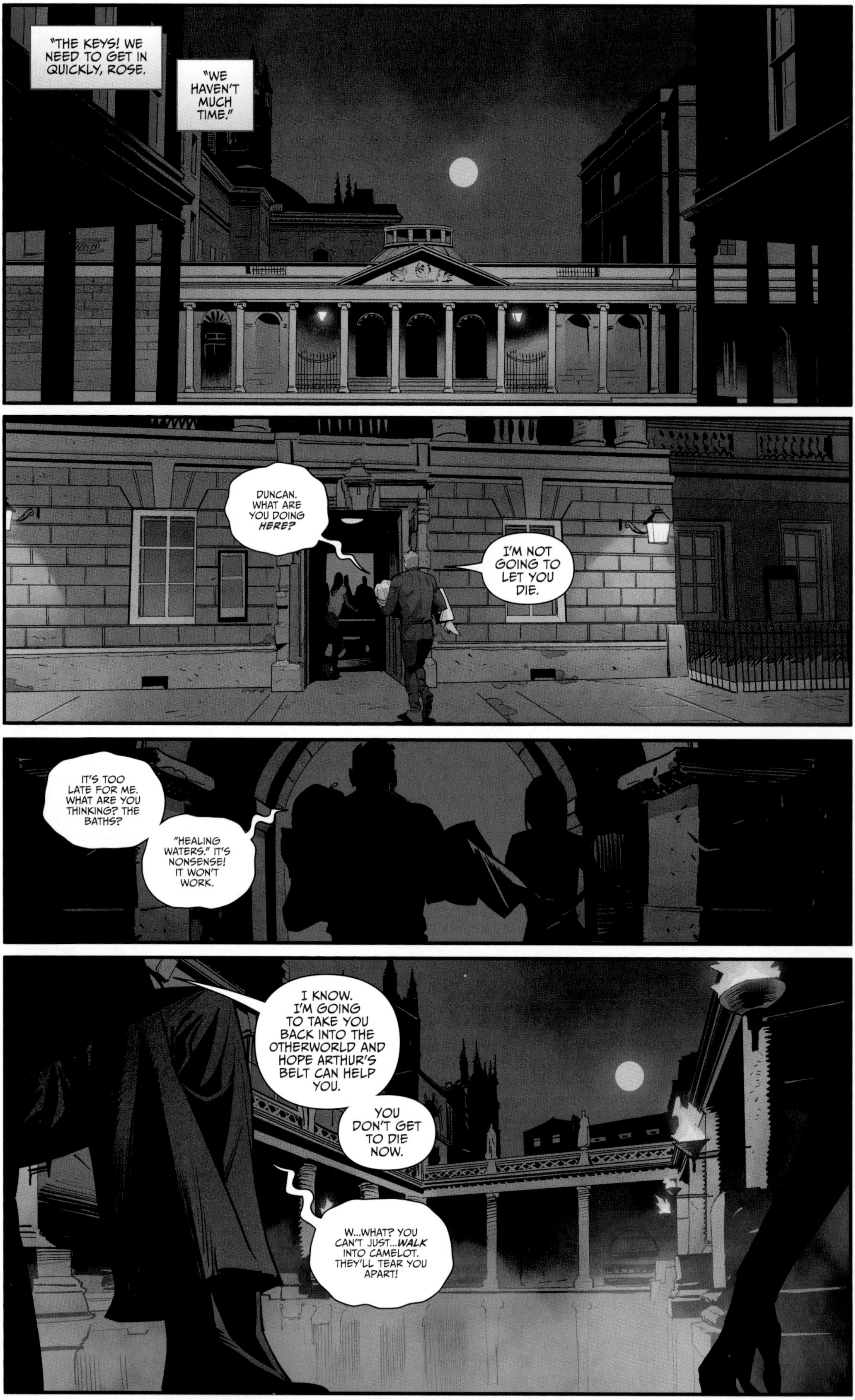
"THE KEYS! WE NEED TO GET IN QUICKLY, ROSE.
"WE HAVEN'T MUCH TIME."
DUNCAN. WHAT ARE YOU DOING HERE?
I'M NOT GOING TO LET YOU DIE.
IT'S TOO LATE FOR ME. WHAT ARE YOU THINKING? THE BATHS?
"HEALING WATERS." IT'S NONSENSE! IT WON'T WORK.
I KNOW. I'M GOING TO TAKE YOU BACK INTO THE OTHERWORLD AND HOPE ARTHUR'S BELT CAN HELP YOU.
YOU DON'T GET TO DIE NOW.
W...WHAT? YOU CAN'T JUST...WALK INTO CAMELOT. THEY'LL TEAR YOU APART!

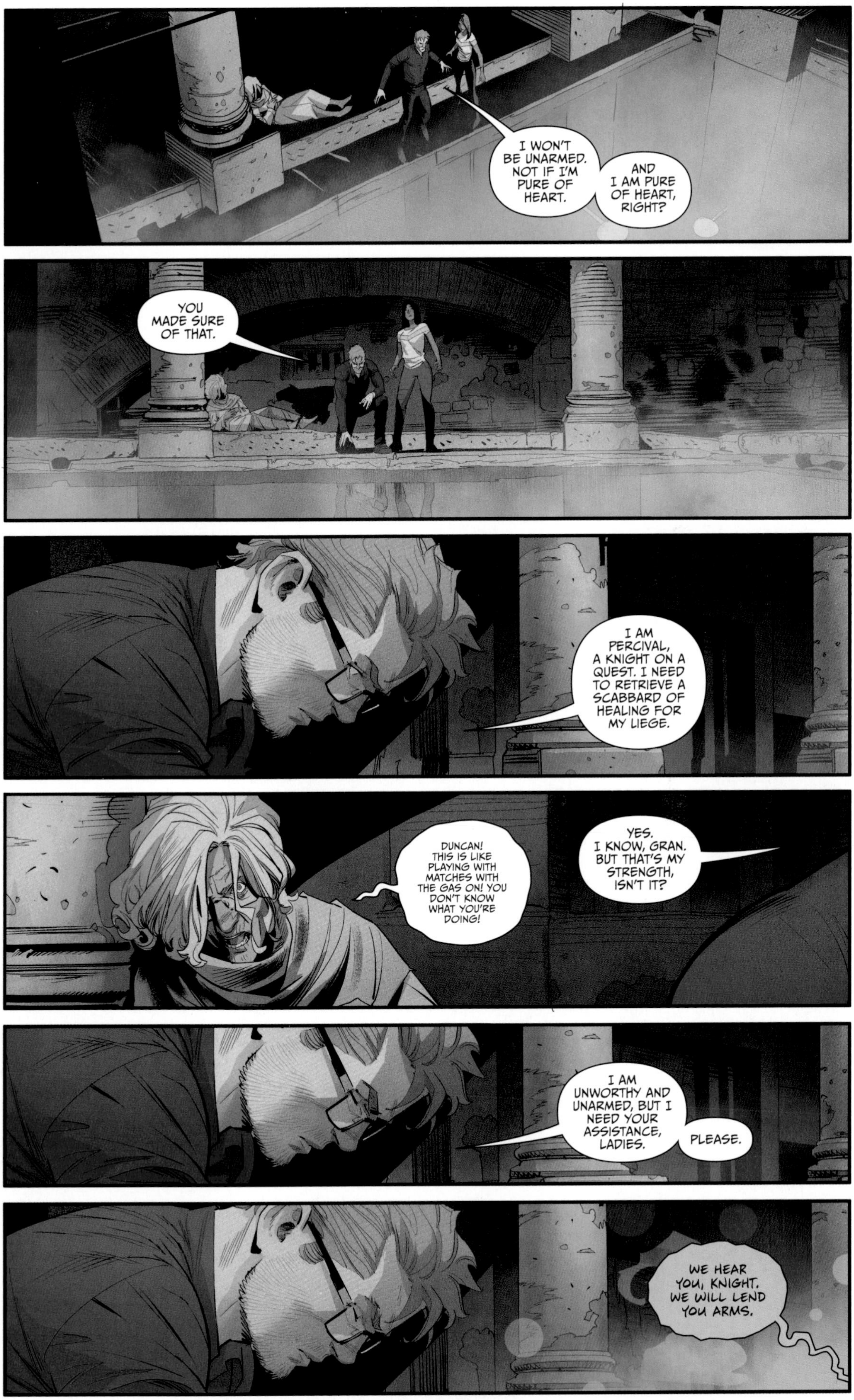
I WON'T BE UNARMED. NOT IF I'M PURE OF HEART.
AND I AM PURE OF HEART, RIGHT?
YOU MADE SURE OF THAT.
I AM PERCIVAL, A KNIGHT ON A QUEST. I NEED TO RETRIEVE A SCABBARD OF HEALING FOR MY LIEGE.
DUNCAN! THIS IS LIKE PLAYING WITH MATCHES WITH THE GAS ON! YOU DON'T KNOW WHAT YOU'RE DOING!
YES. I KNOW, GRAN. BUT THAT'S MY STRENGTH, ISN'T IT?
I AM UNWORTHY AND UNARMED, BUT I NEED YOUR ASSISTANCE, LADIES.
PLEASE.
WE HEAR YOU, KNIGHT. WE WILL LEND YOU ARMS.

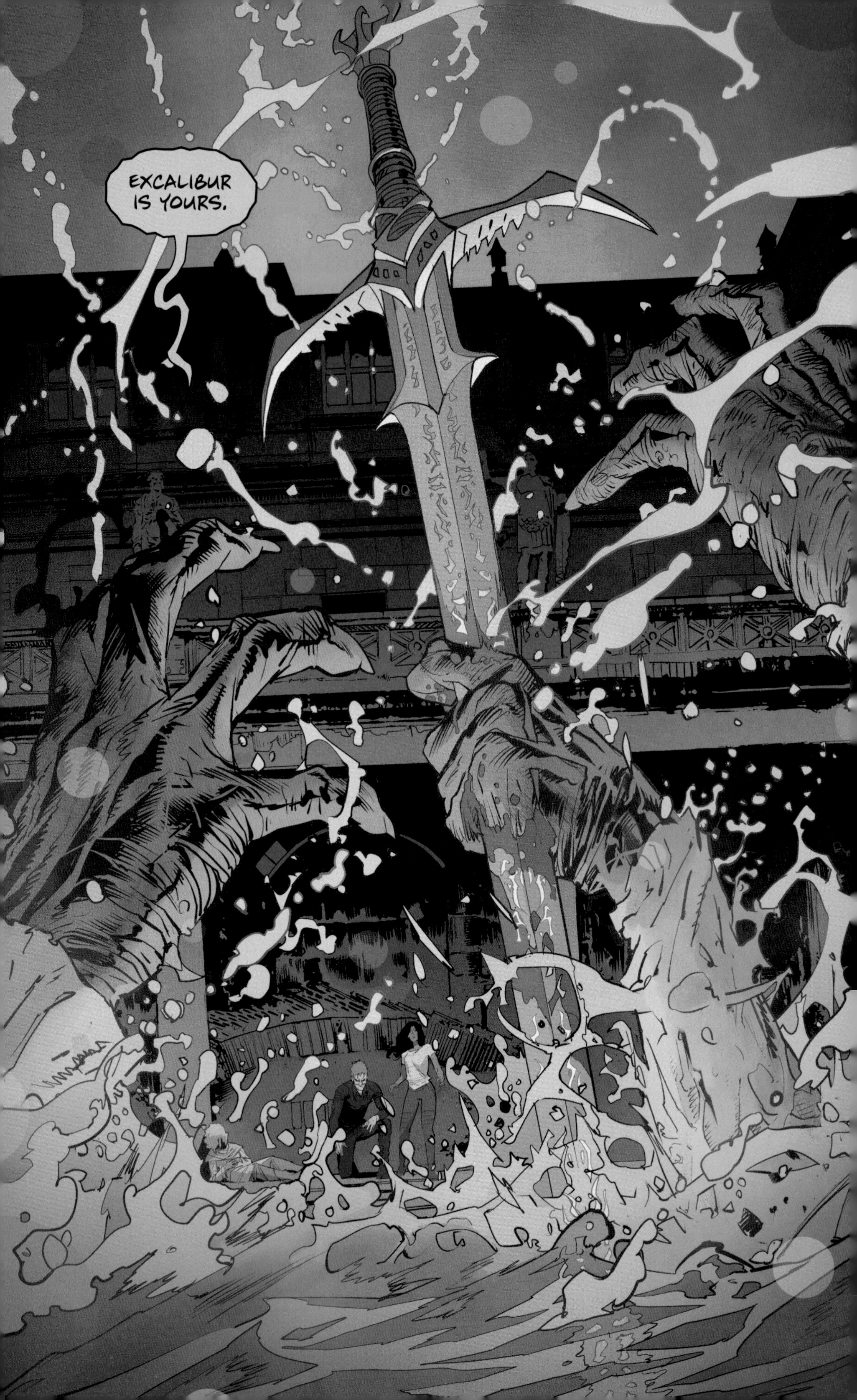
EXCALIBUR IS YOURS.

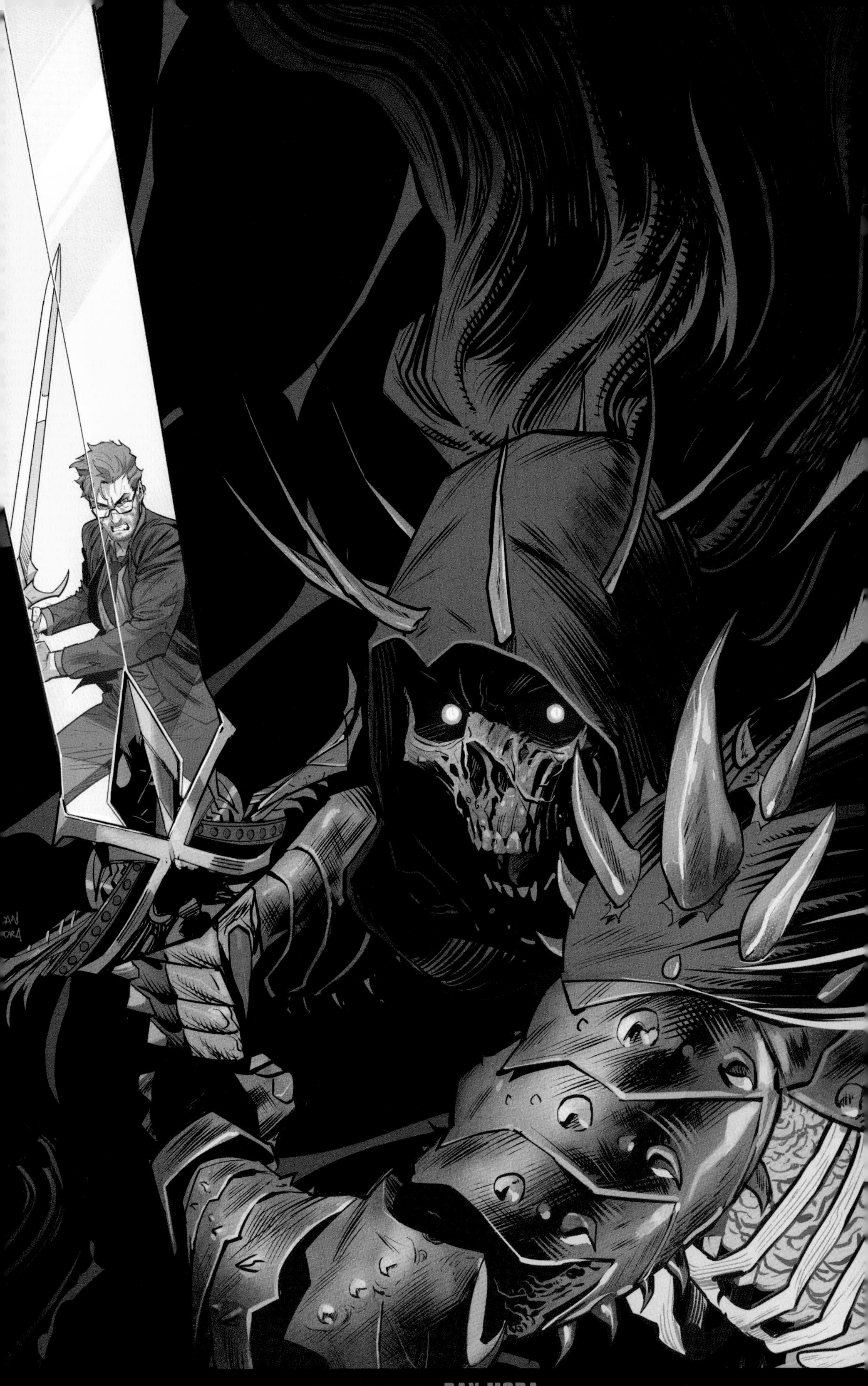

ISSUE SIX COVER BY **DAN MORA**

CHAPTER SIX

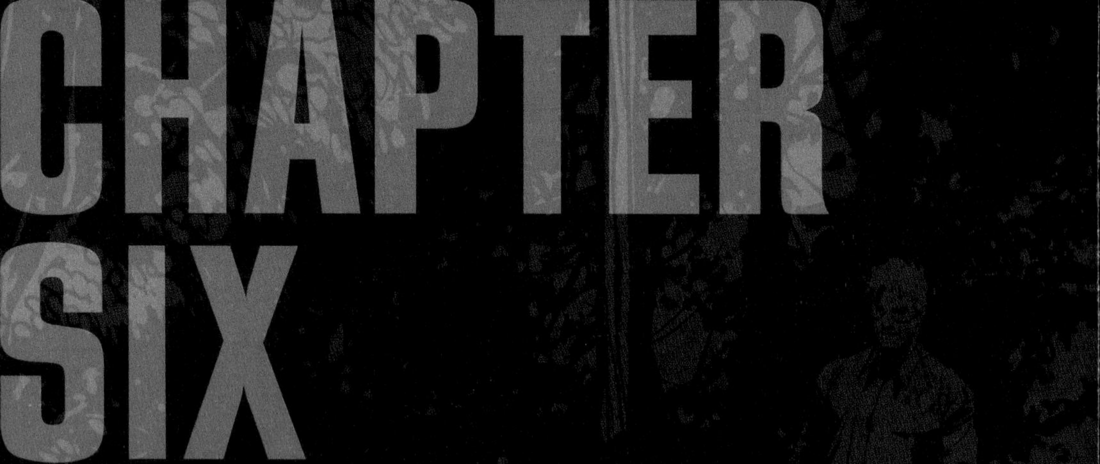

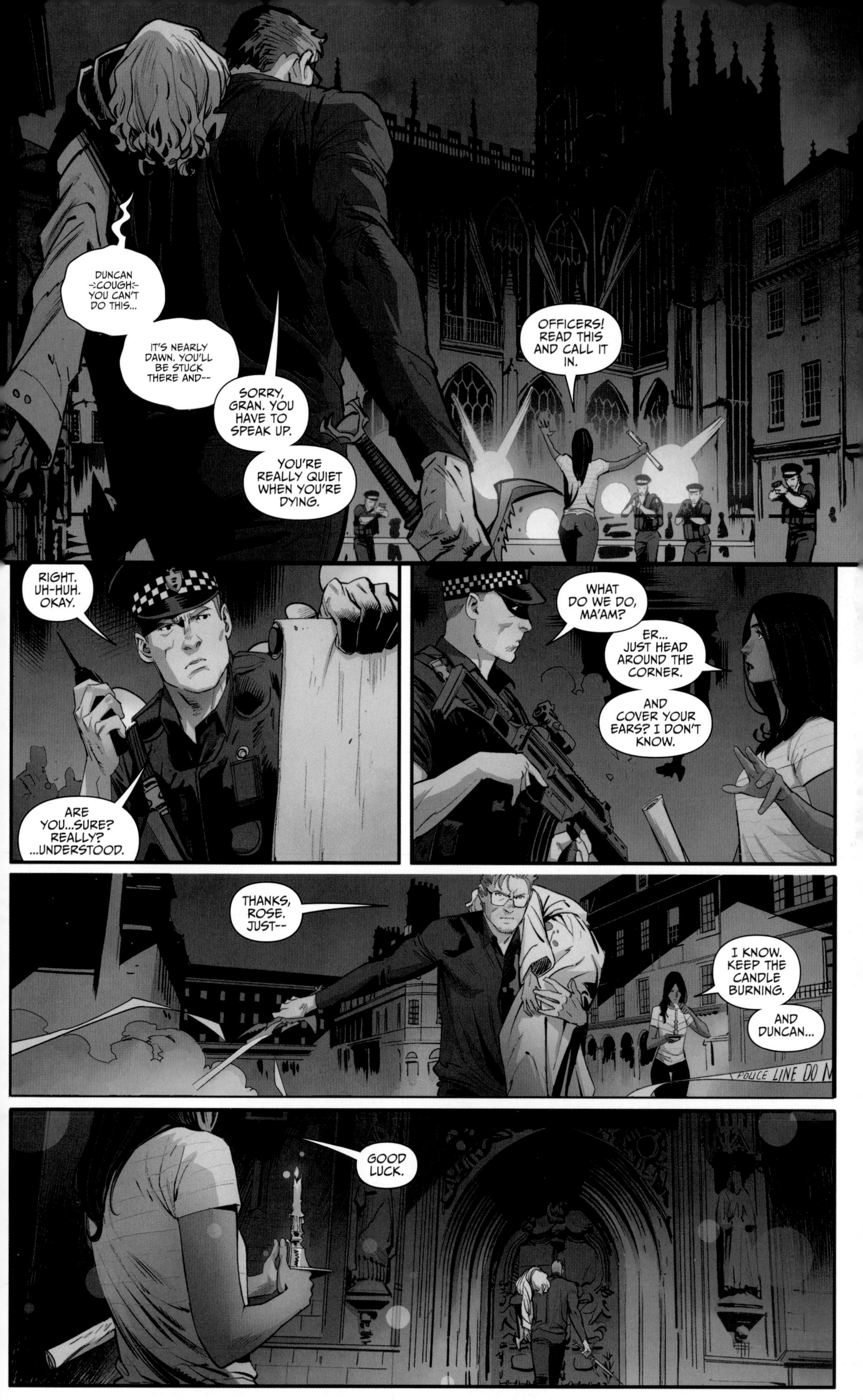
DUNCAN -:COUGH:- YOU CAN'T DO THIS...
IT'S NEARLY DAWN. YOU'LL BE STUCK THERE AND--
SORRY, GRAN. YOU HAVE TO SPEAK UP.
YOU'RE REALLY QUIET WHEN YOU'RE DYING.
OFFICERS! READ THIS AND CALL IT IN.
RIGHT. UH-HUH. OKAY.
ARE YOU...SURE? REALLY? ...UNDERSTOOD.
WHAT DO WE DO, MA'AM?
ER... JUST HEAD AROUND THE CORNER.
AND COVER YOUR EARS? I DON'T KNOW.
THANKS, ROSE. JUST--
I KNOW. KEEP THE CANDLE BURNING.
AND DUNCAN...
POLICE LINE DO N
GOOD LUCK.

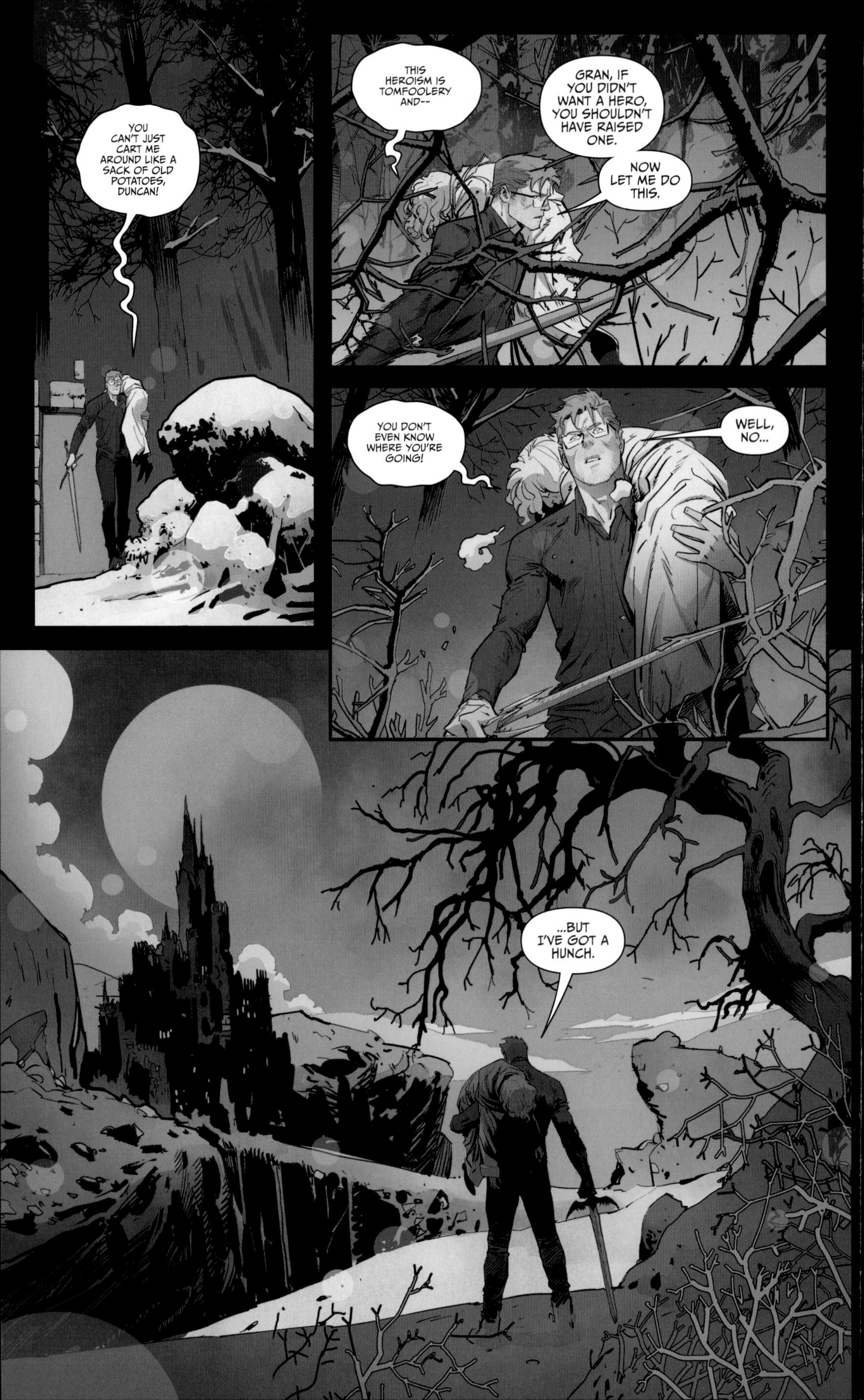
YOU CAN'T JUST CART ME AROUND LIKE A SACK OF OLD POTATOES, DUNCAN!
THIS HEROISM IS TOMFOOLERY AND--
GRAN, IF YOU DIDN'T WANT A HERO, YOU SHOULDN'T HAVE RAISED ONE.
NOW LET ME DO THIS.
YOU DON'T EVEN KNOW WHERE YOU'RE GOING!
WELL, NO...
...BUT I'VE GOT A HUNCH.

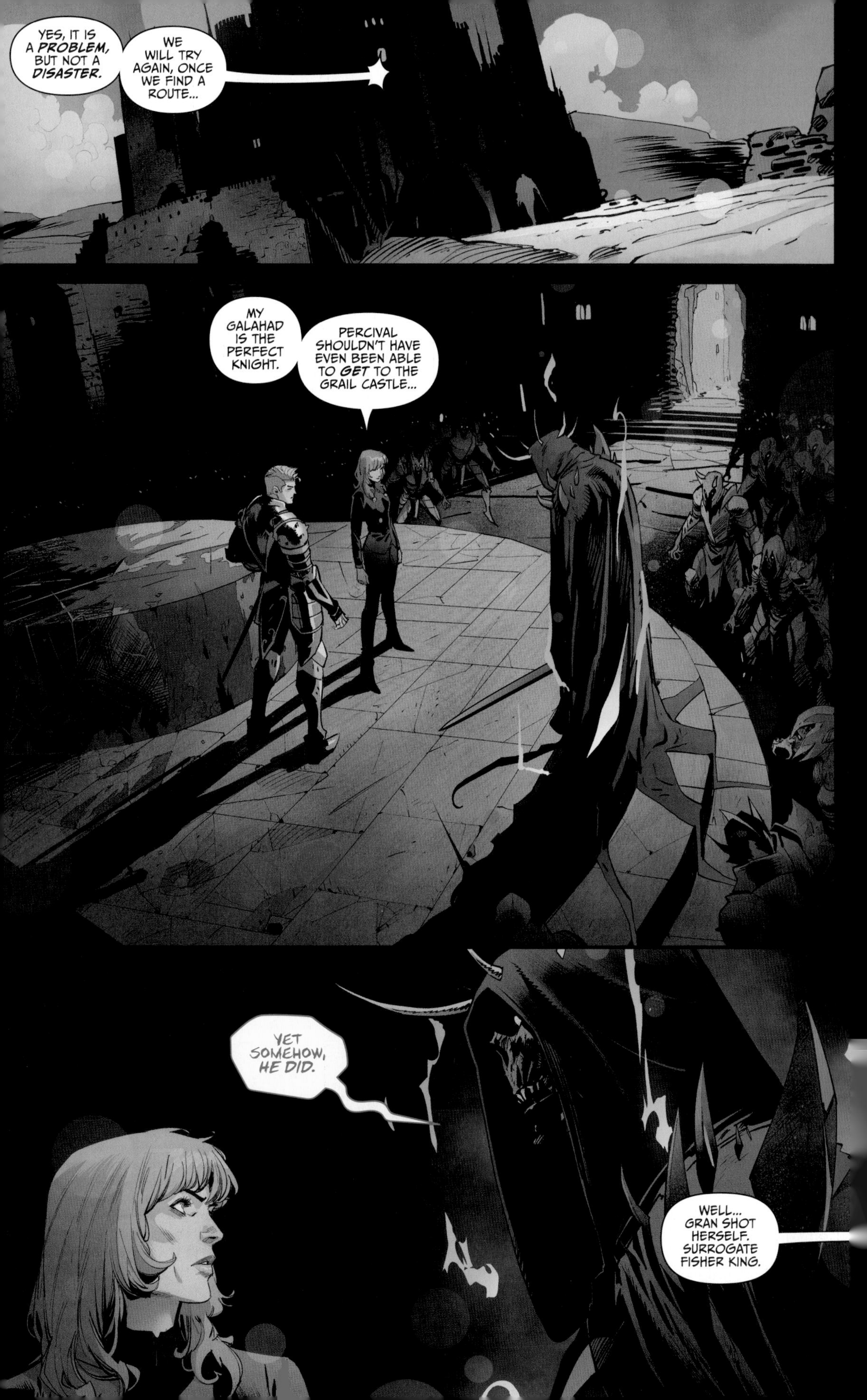
YES, IT IS A PROBLEM, BUT NOT A DISASTER.
WE WILL TRY AGAIN, ONCE WE FIND A ROUTE...
MY GALAHAD IS THE PERFECT KNIGHT.
PERCIVAL SHOULDN'T HAVE EVEN BEEN ABLE TO GET TO THE GRAIL CASTLE...
YET SOMEHOW, HE DID.
WELL... GRAN SHOT HERSELF. SURROGATE FISHER KING.

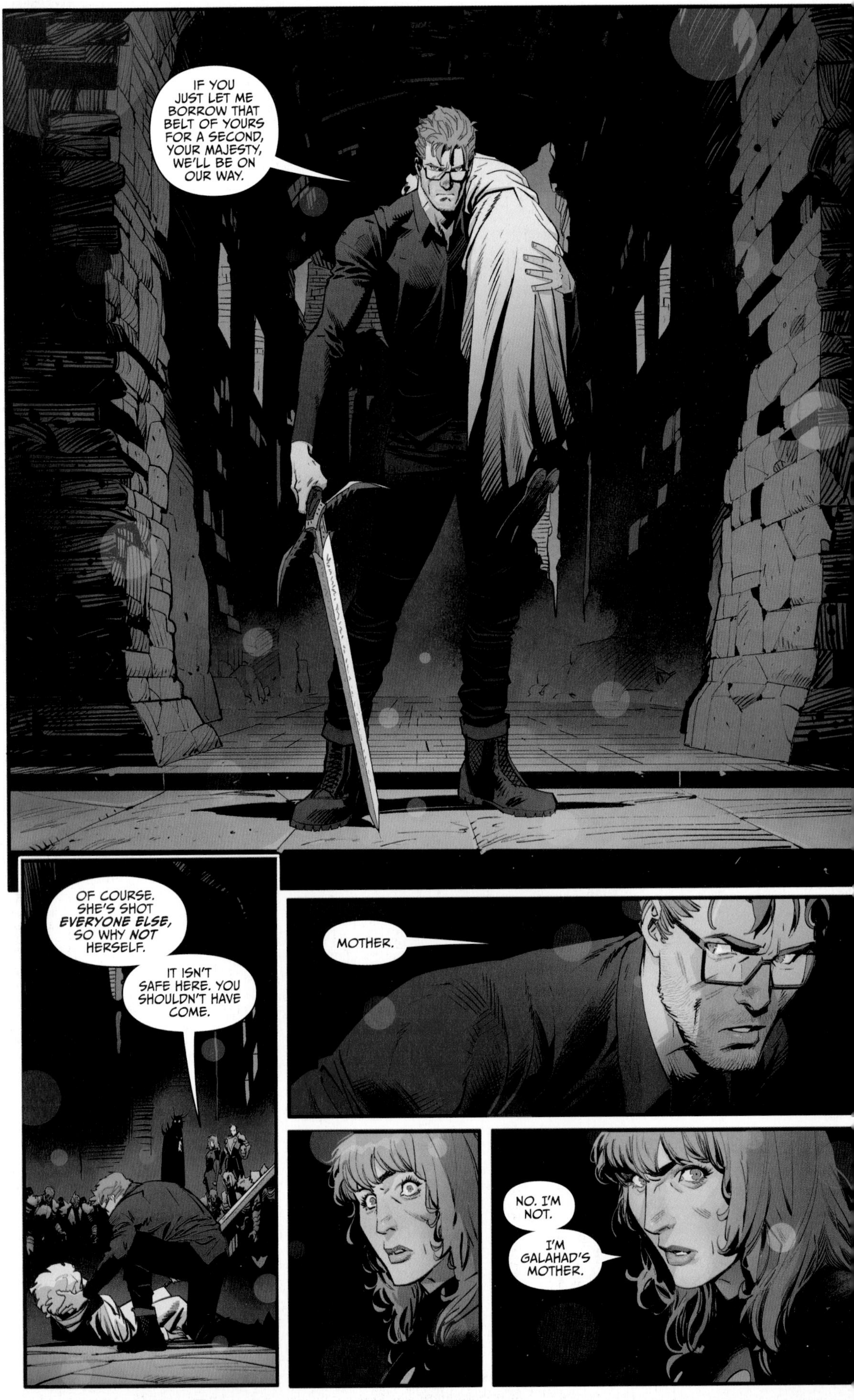
IF YOU JUST LET ME BORROW THAT BELT OF YOURS FOR A SECOND, YOUR MAJESTY, WE'LL BE ON OUR WAY.
OF COURSE. SHE'S SHOT *EVERYONE ELSE*, SO WHY *NOT* HERSELF.
IT ISN'T SAFE HERE. YOU SHOULDN'T HAVE COME.
MOTHER.
NO. I'M NOT.
I'M GALAHAD'S MOTHER.

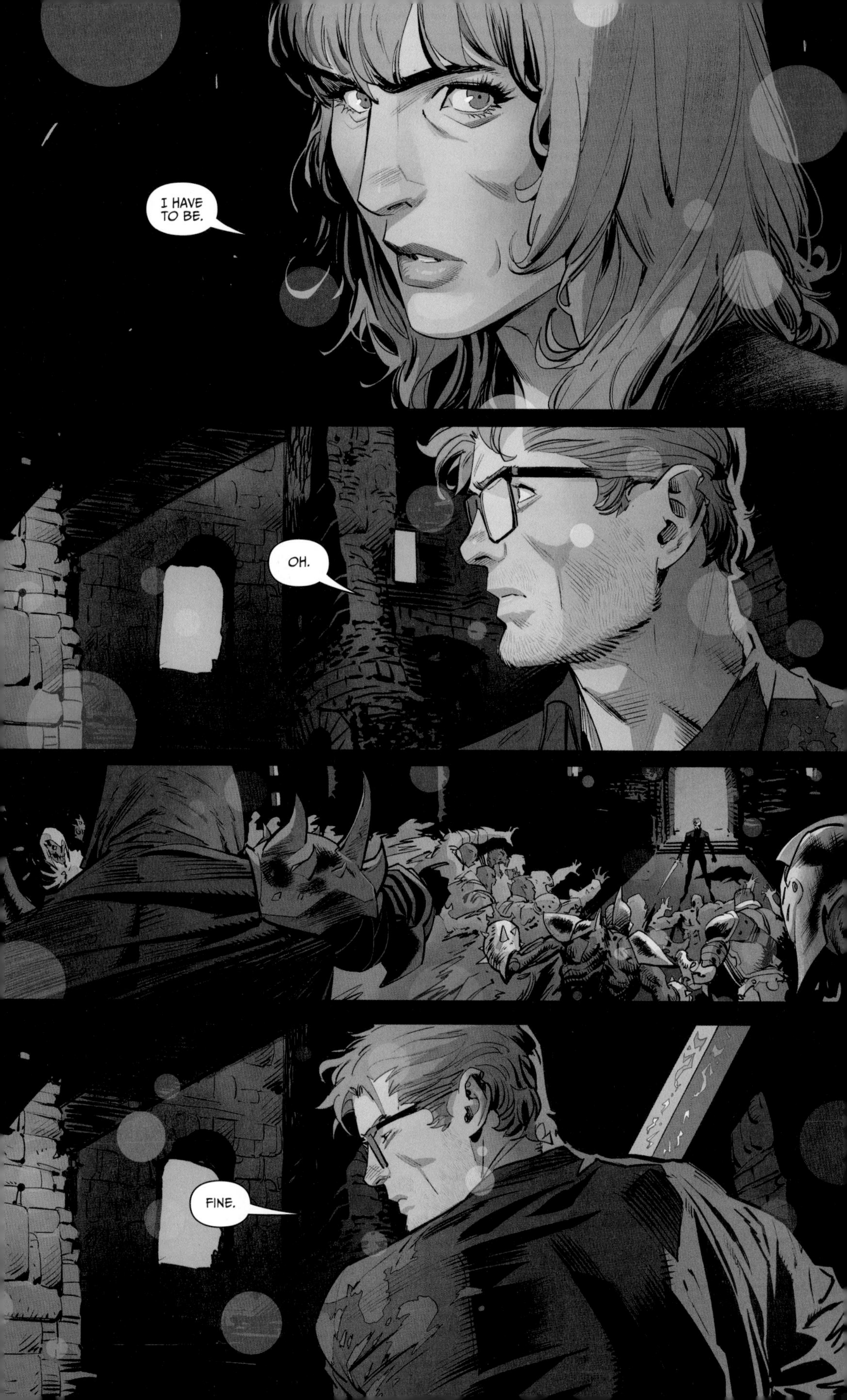
I HAVE TO BE.
OH.
FINE.

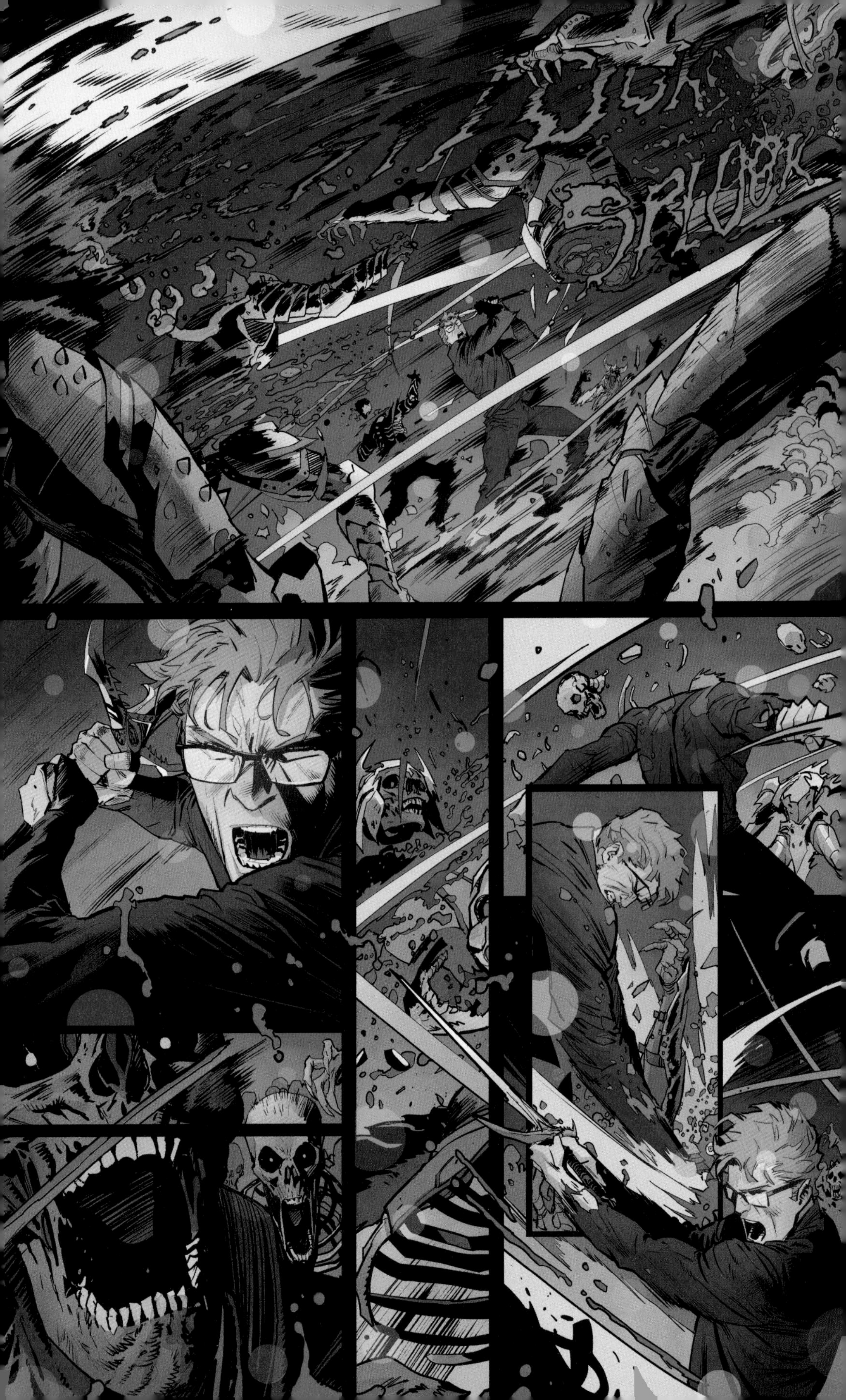
SPLOOK

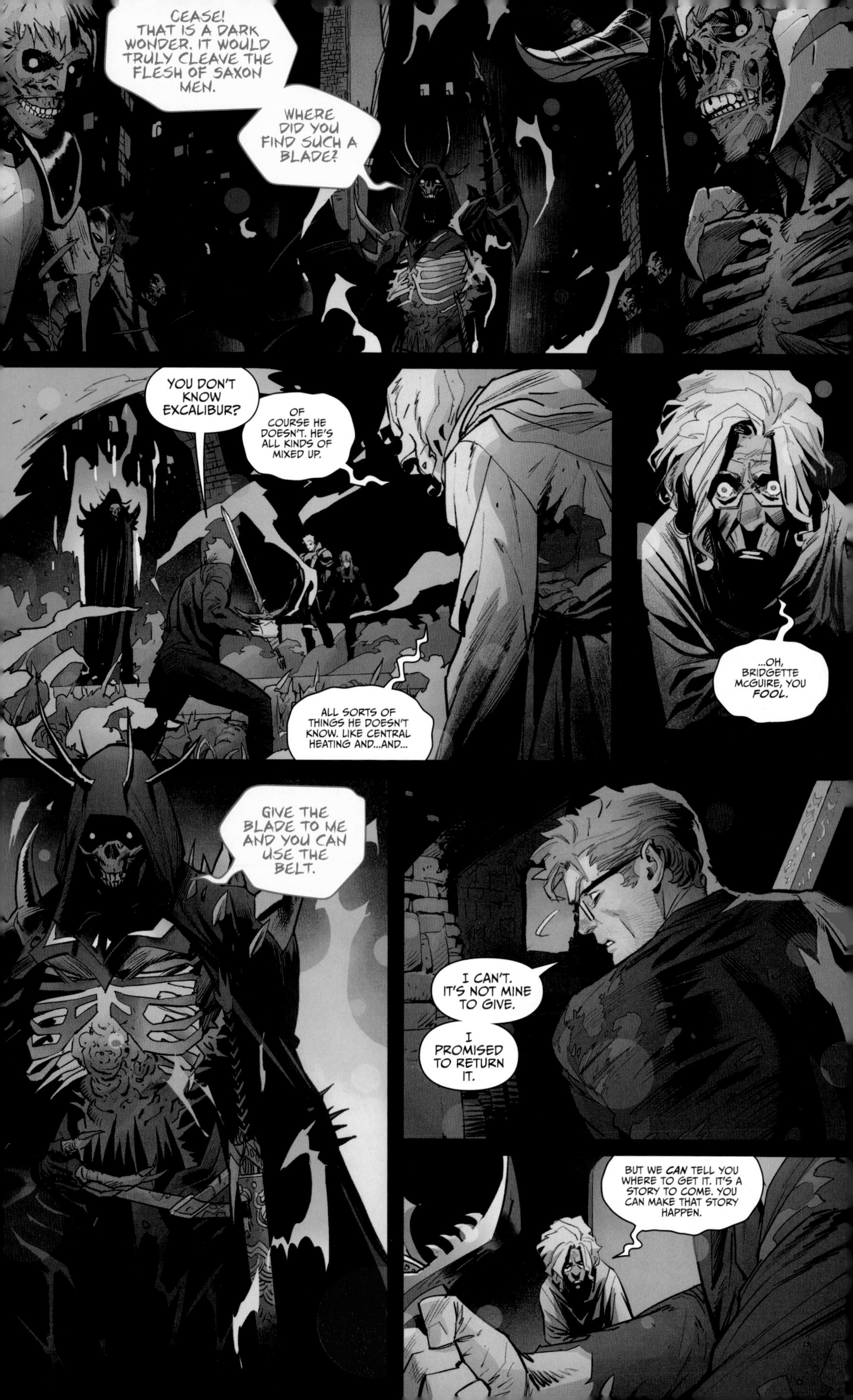
CEASE! THAT IS A DARK WONDER. IT WOULD TRULY CLEAVE THE FLESH OF SAXON MEN.
WHERE DID YOU FIND SUCH A BLADE?
YOU DON'T KNOW EXCALIBUR?
OF COURSE HE DOESN'T. HE'S ALL KINDS OF MIXED UP.
ALL SORTS OF THINGS HE DOESN'T KNOW. LIKE CENTRAL HEATING AND...AND...
...OH, BRIDGETTE MCGUIRE, YOU *FOOL*.
GIVE THE BLADE TO ME AND YOU CAN USE THE BELT.
I CAN'T. IT'S NOT MINE TO GIVE.
I PROMISED TO RETURN IT.
BUT WE *CAN* TELL YOU WHERE TO GET IT. IT'S A STORY TO COME. YOU CAN MAKE THAT STORY HAPPEN.

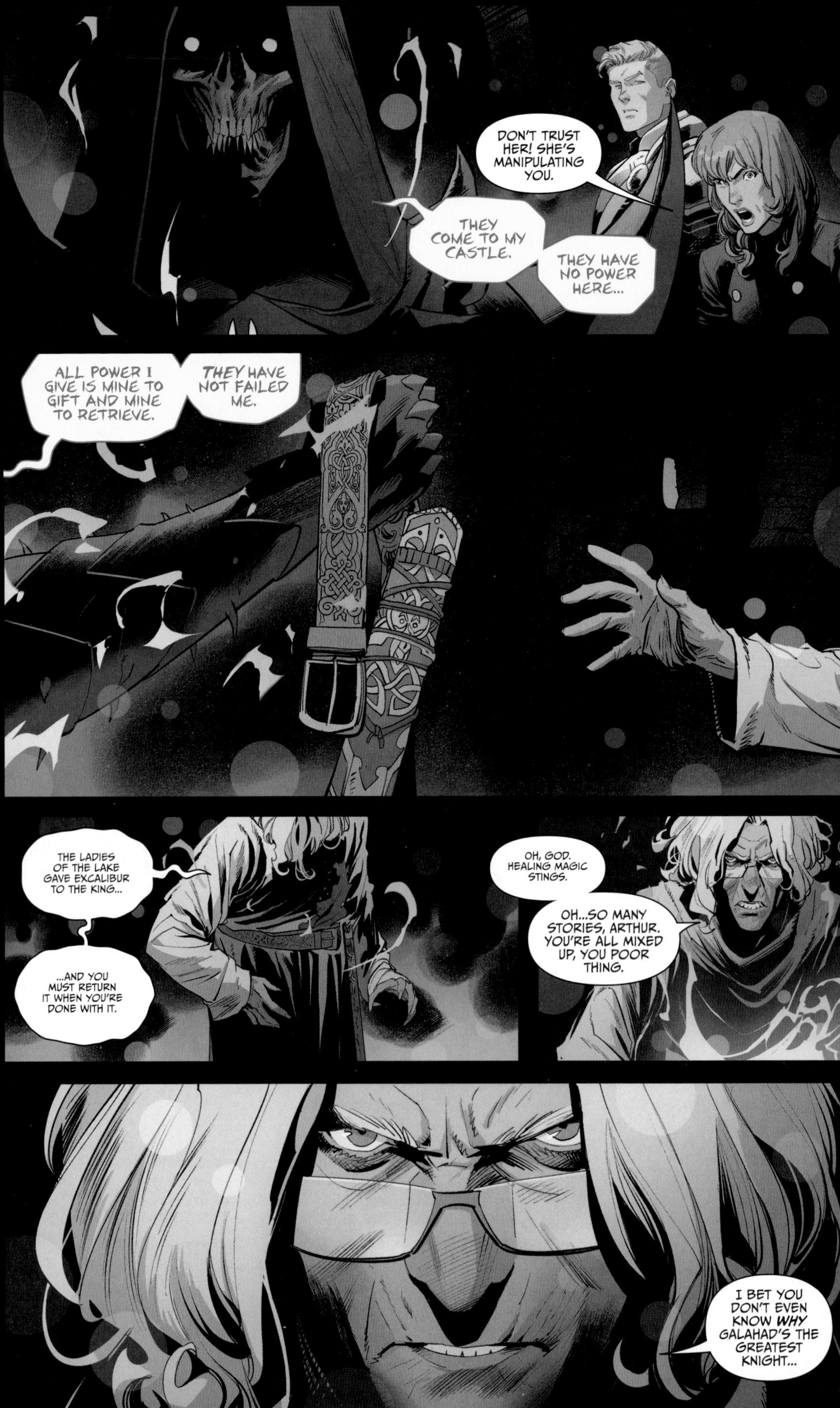
DON'T TRUST HER! SHE'S MANIPULATING YOU.
THEY COME TO MY CASTLE.
THEY HAVE NO POWER HERE...
ALL POWER I GIVE IS MINE TO GIFT AND MINE TO RETRIEVE.
THEY HAVE NOT FAILED ME.
THE LADIES OF THE LAKE GAVE EXCALIBUR TO THE KING...
...AND YOU MUST RETURN IT WHEN YOU'RE DONE WITH IT.
OH, GOD. HEALING MAGIC STINGS.
OH...SO MANY STORIES, ARTHUR. YOU'RE ALL MIXED UP, YOU POOR THING.
I BET YOU DON'T EVEN KNOW WHY GALAHAD'S THE GREATEST KNIGHT...

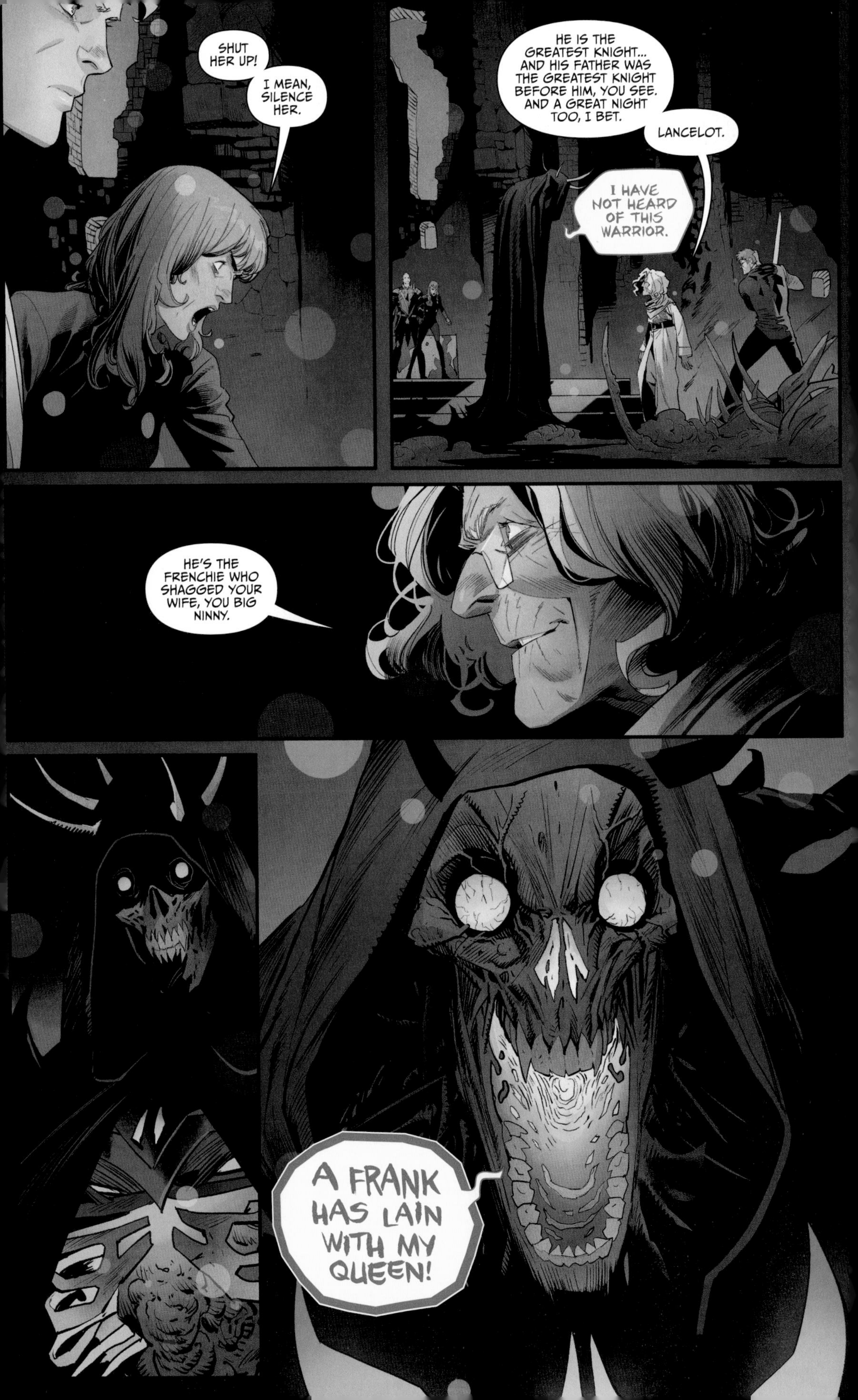
SHUT HER UP!
I MEAN, SILENCE HER.
HE IS THE GREATEST KNIGHT... AND HIS FATHER WAS THE GREATEST KNIGHT BEFORE HIM, YOU SEE. AND A GREAT NIGHT TOO, I BET.
LANCELOT.
I HAVE NOT HEARD OF THIS WARRIOR.
HE'S THE FRENCHIE WHO SHAGGED YOUR WIFE, YOU BIG NINNY.
A FRANK HAS LAIN WITH MY QUEEN!

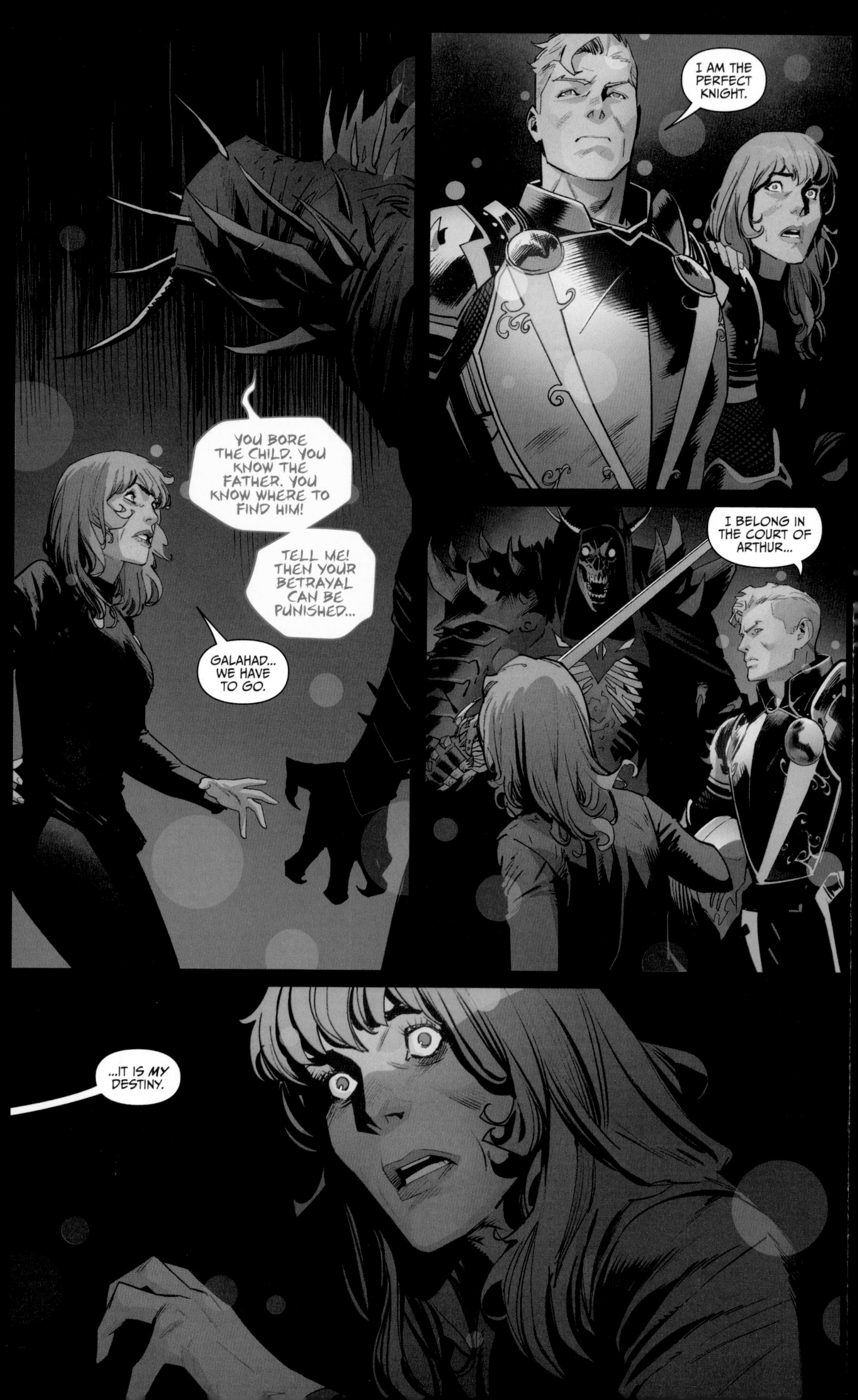
YOU BORE THE CHILD. YOU KNOW THE FATHER. YOU KNOW WHERE TO FIND HIM!
TELL ME! THEN YOUR BETRAYAL CAN BE PUNISHED...
GALAHAD... WE HAVE TO GO.
I AM THE PERFECT KNIGHT.
I BELONG IN THE COURT OF ARTHUR...
...IT IS MY DESTINY.

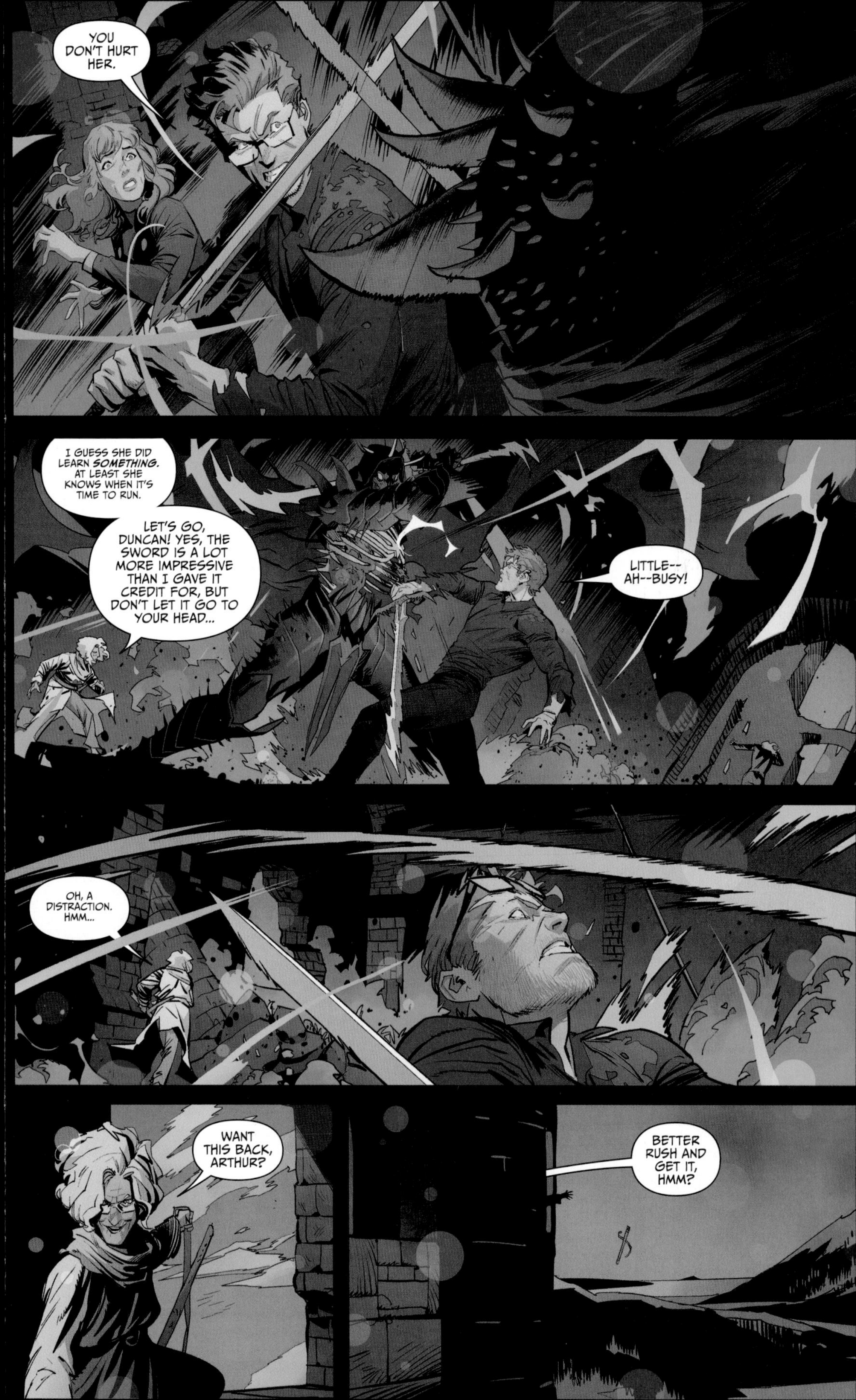
YOU DON'T HURT HER.
I GUESS SHE DID LEARN SOMETHING. AT LEAST SHE KNOWS WHEN IT'S TIME TO RUN.
LET'S GO, DUNCAN! YES, THE SWORD IS A LOT MORE IMPRESSIVE THAN I GAVE IT CREDIT FOR, BUT DON'T LET IT GO TO YOUR HEAD...
LITTLE--AH--BUSY!
OH, A DISTRACTION. HMM...
WANT THIS BACK, ARTHUR?
BETTER RUSH AND GET IT, HMM?

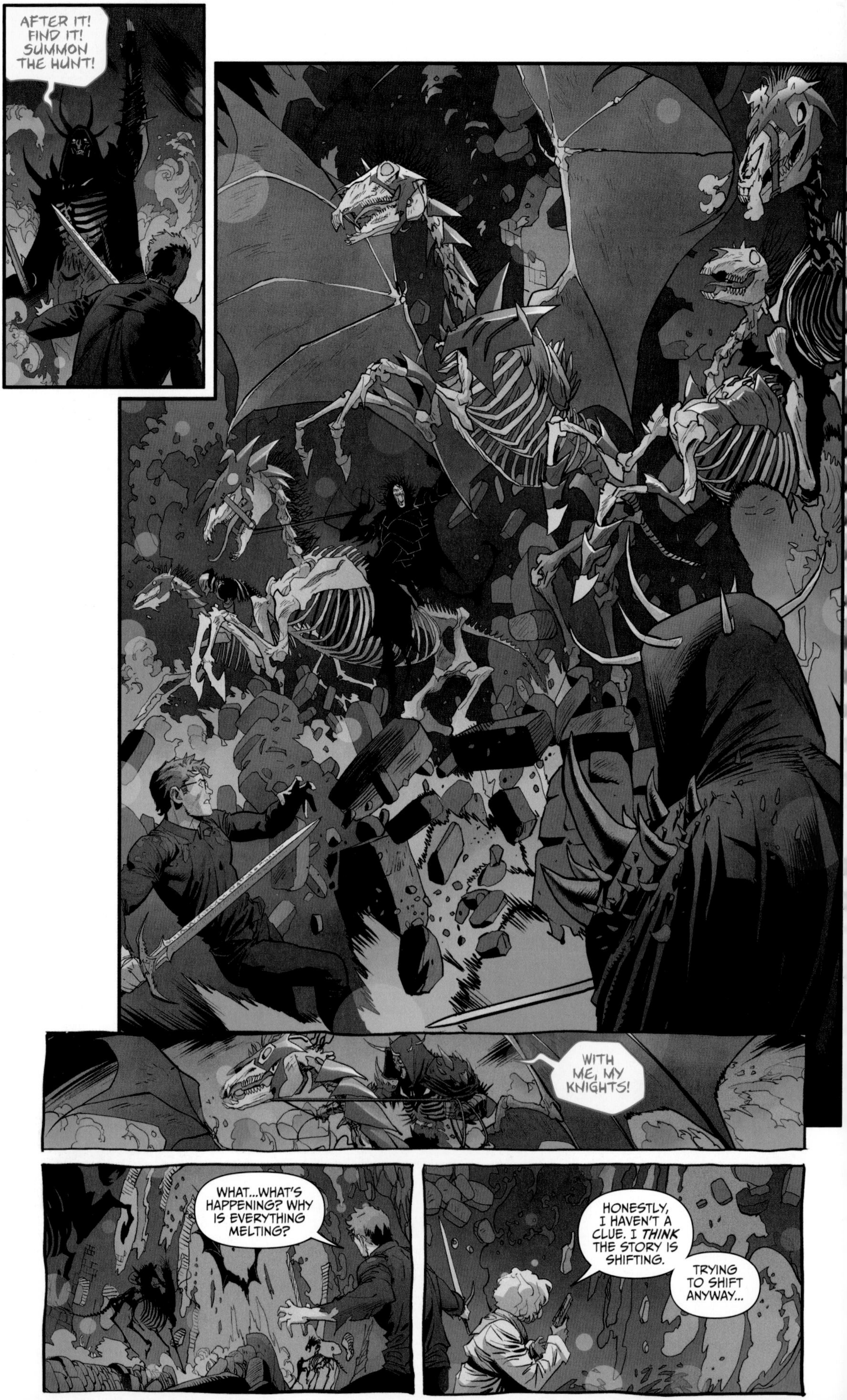
AFTER IT! FIND IT! SUMMON THE HUNT!
WITH ME, MY KNIGHTS!
WHAT...WHAT'S HAPPENING? WHY IS EVERYTHING MELTING?
HONESTLY, I HAVEN'T A CLUE. I THINK THE STORY IS SHIFTING.
TRYING TO SHIFT ANYWAY...

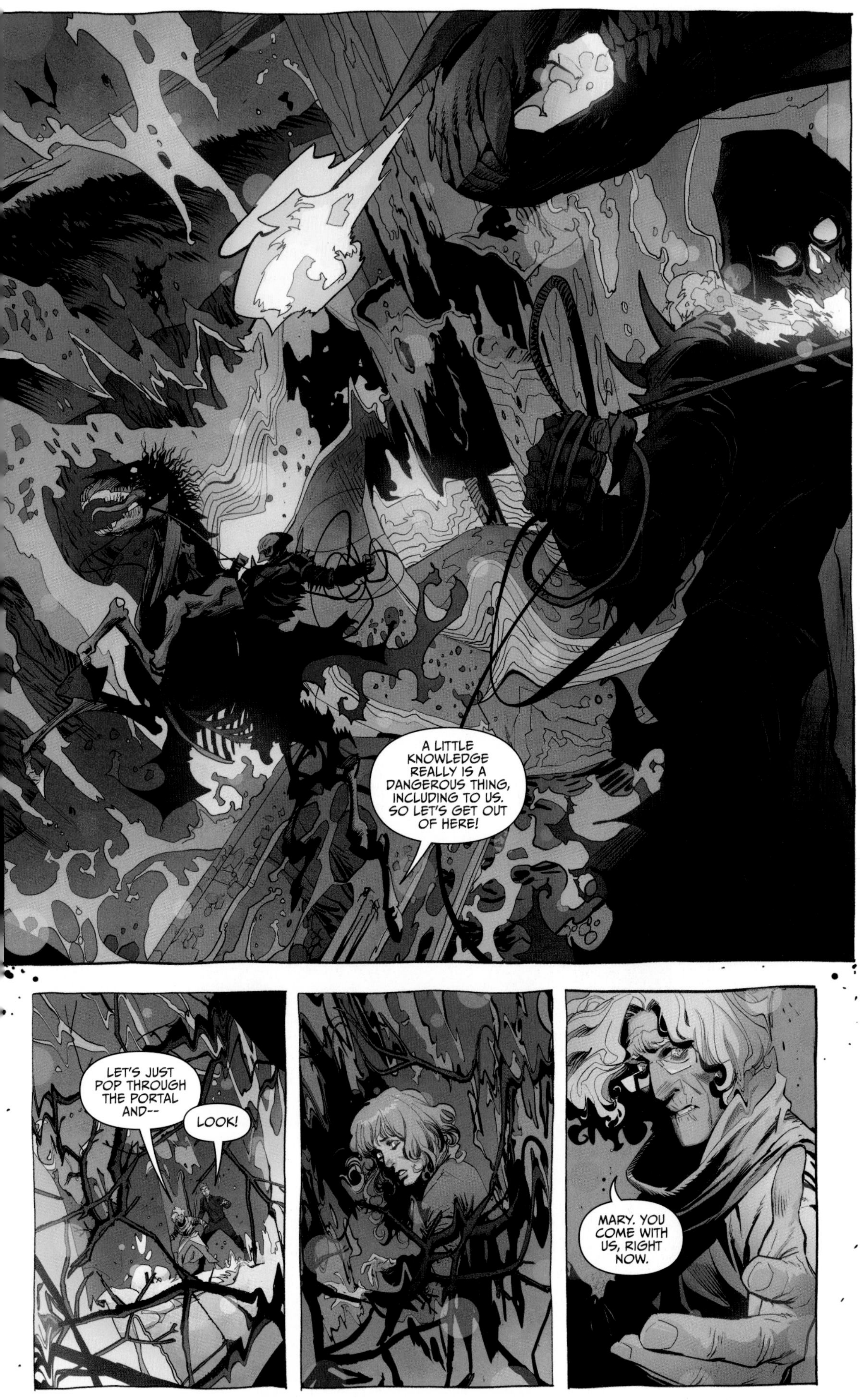
A LITTLE KNOWLEDGE REALLY IS A DANGEROUS THING, INCLUDING TO US. SO LET'S GET OUT OF HERE!
LET'S JUST POP THROUGH THE PORTAL AND--
LOOK!
MARY. YOU COME WITH US, RIGHT NOW.

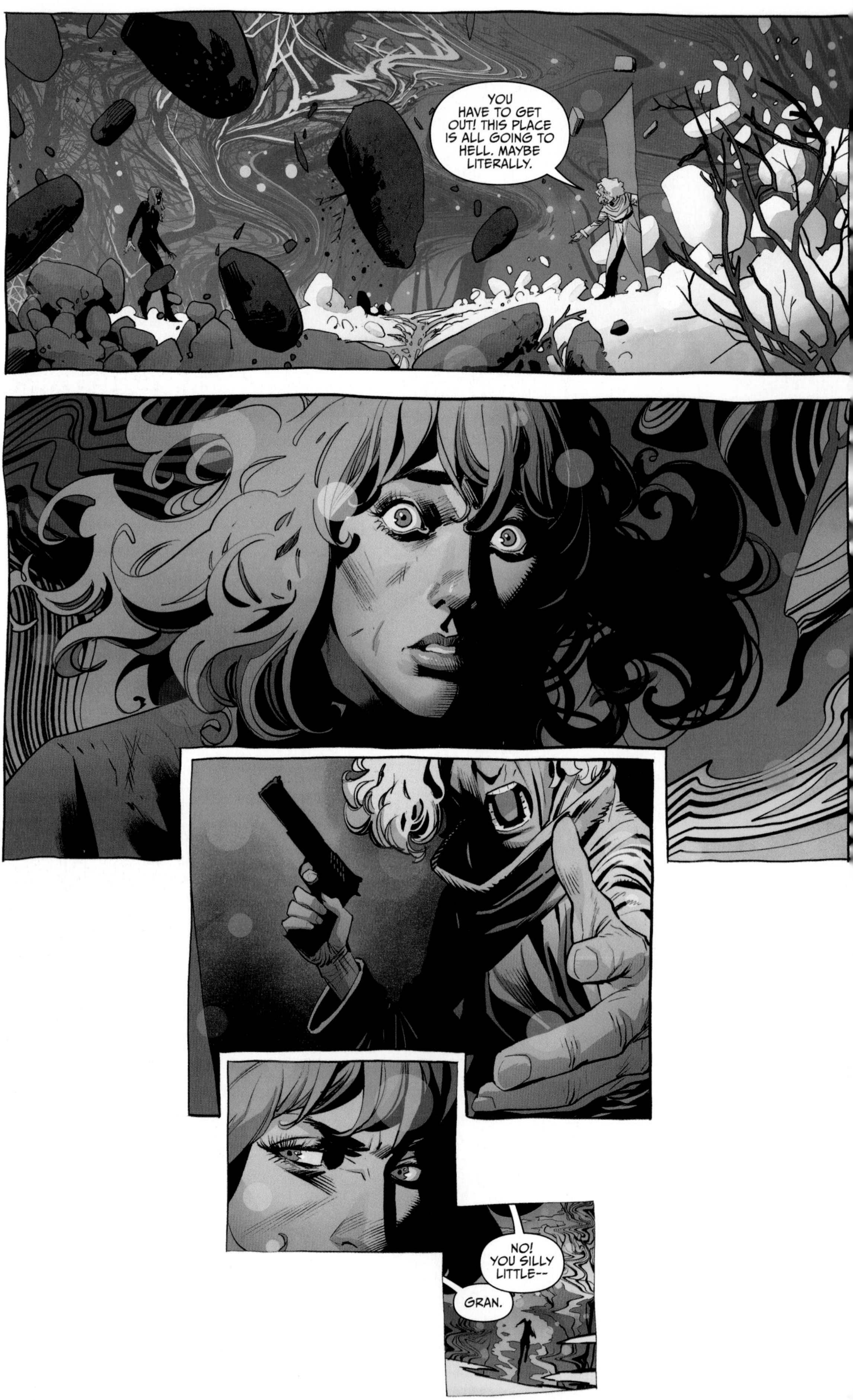
YOU HAVE TO GET OUT! THIS PLACE IS ALL GOING TO HELL. MAYBE LITERALLY.
NO! YOU SILLY LITTLE--
GRAN.

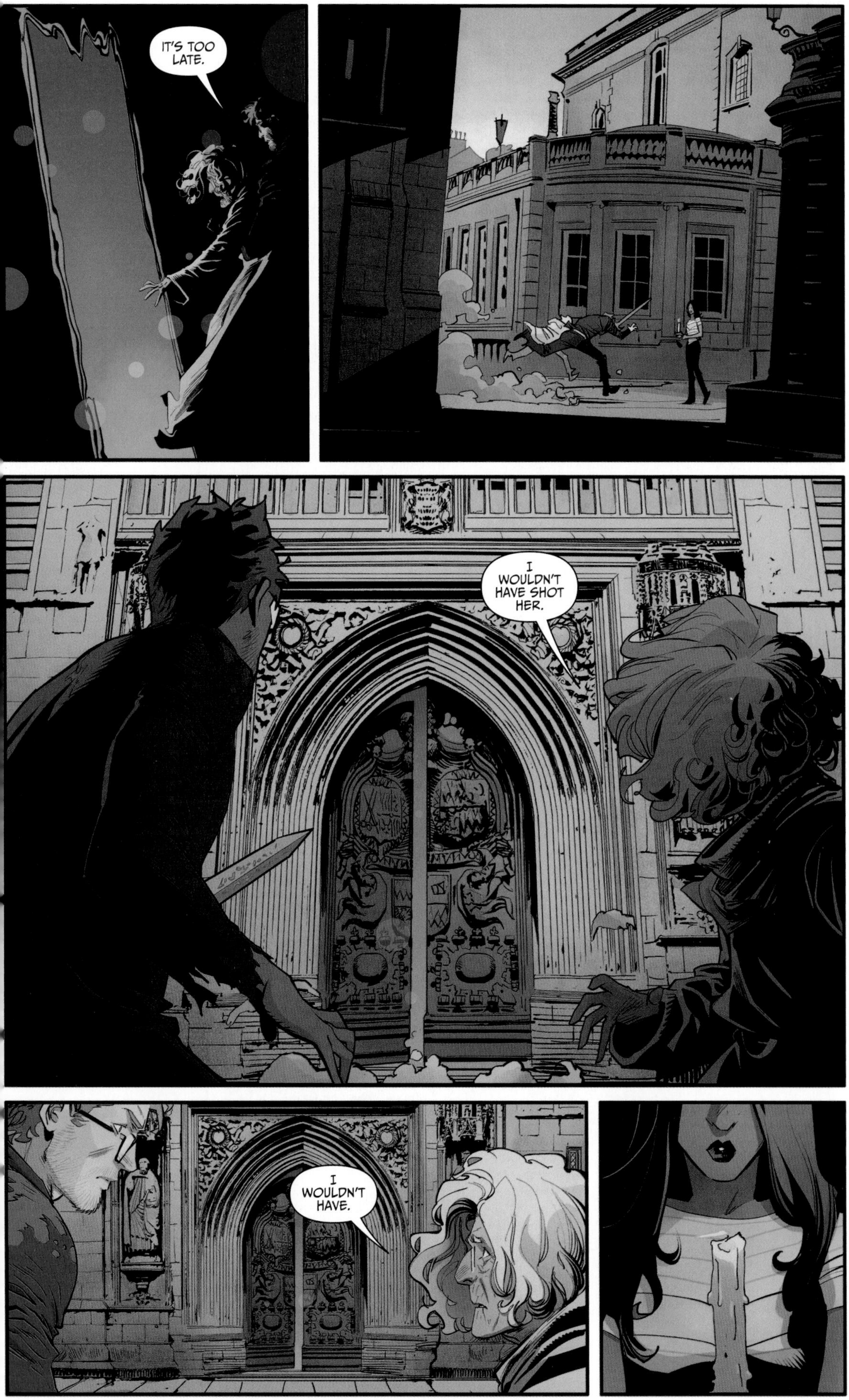
IT'S TOO LATE.
I WOULDN'T HAVE SHOT HER.
I WOULDN'T HAVE.

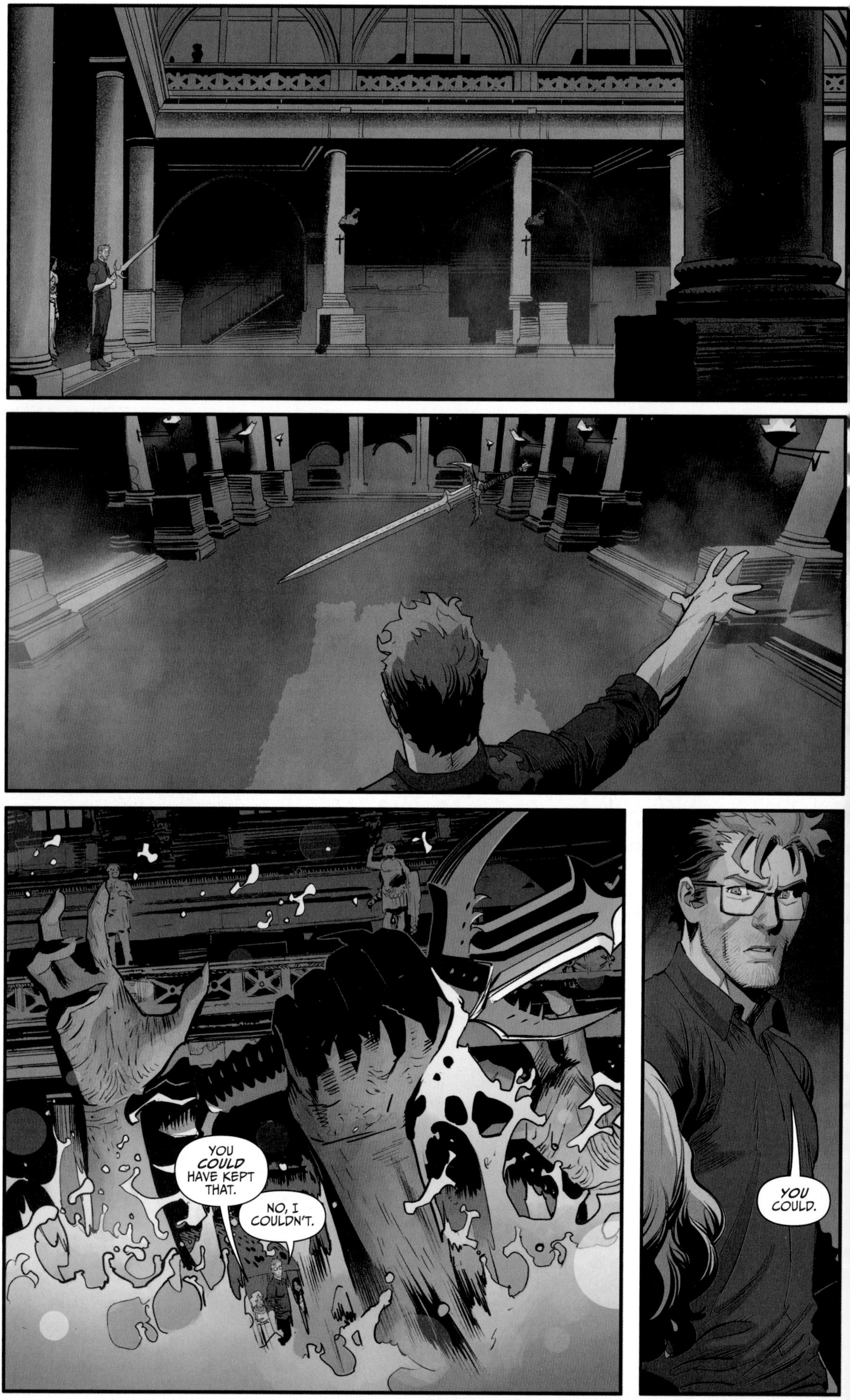
YOU COULD HAVE KEPT THAT.
NO, I COULDN'T.
YOU COULD.

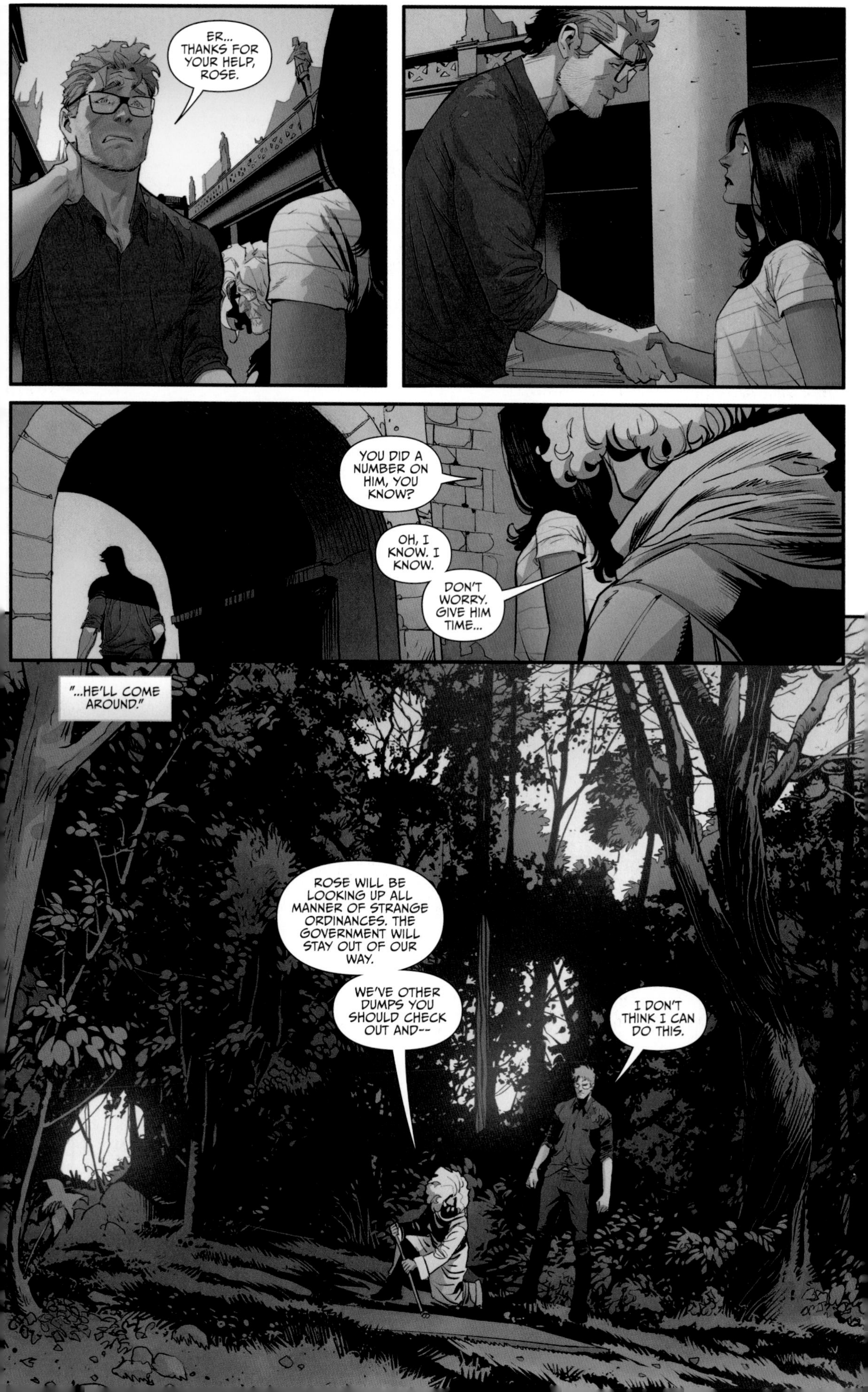
ER... THANKS FOR YOUR HELP, ROSE.
YOU DID A NUMBER ON HIM, YOU KNOW?
OH, I KNOW. I KNOW.
DON'T WORRY. GIVE HIM TIME...
"...HE'LL COME AROUND."
ROSE WILL BE LOOKING UP ALL MANNER OF STRANGE ORDINANCES. THE GOVERNMENT WILL STAY OUT OF OUR WAY.
WE'VE OTHER DUMPS YOU SHOULD CHECK OUT AND--
I DON'T THINK I CAN DO THIS.

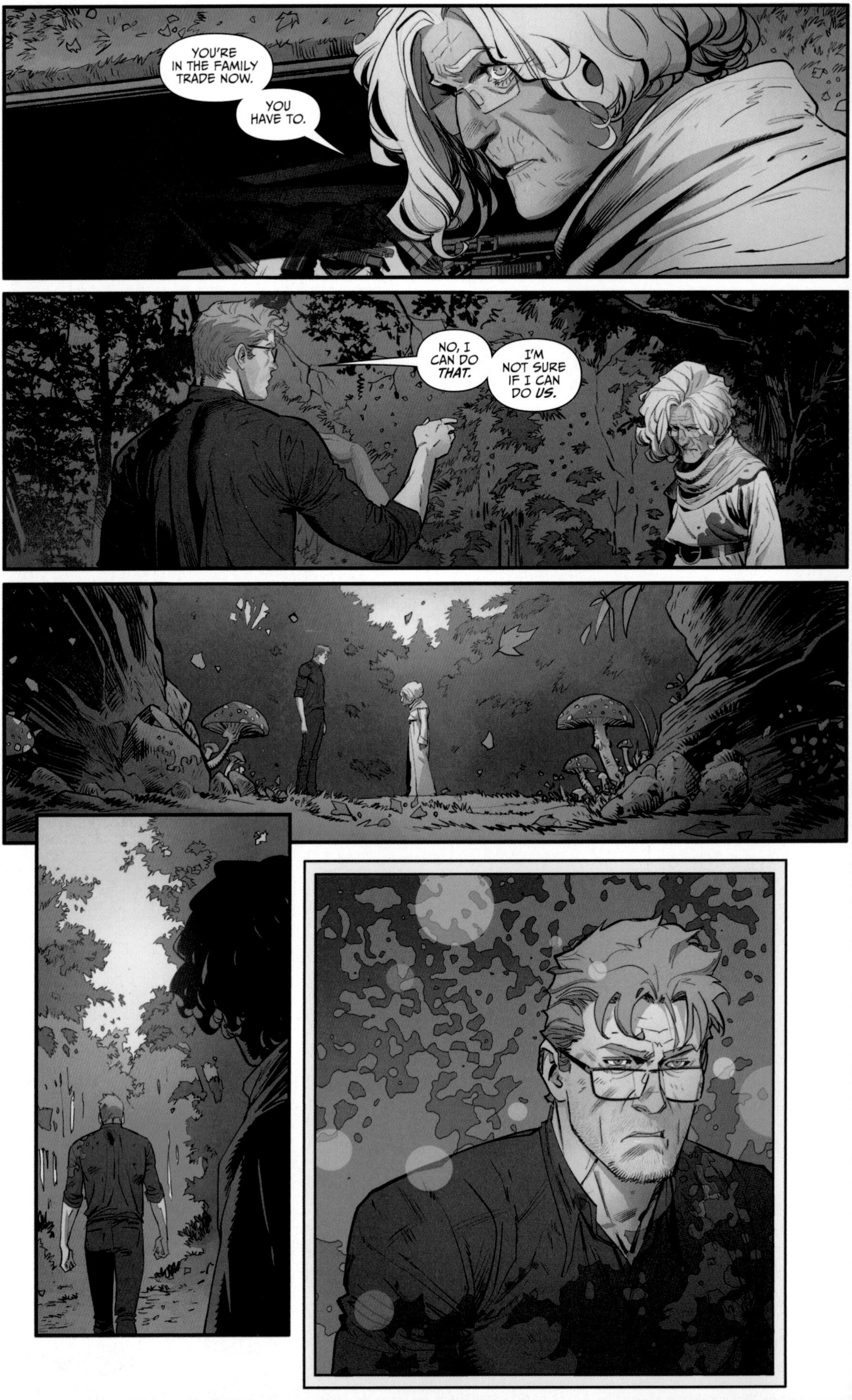
YOU'RE IN THE FAMILY TRADE NOW.
YOU HAVE TO.
NO, I CAN DO *THAT.*
I'M NOT SURE IF I CAN DO *US.*

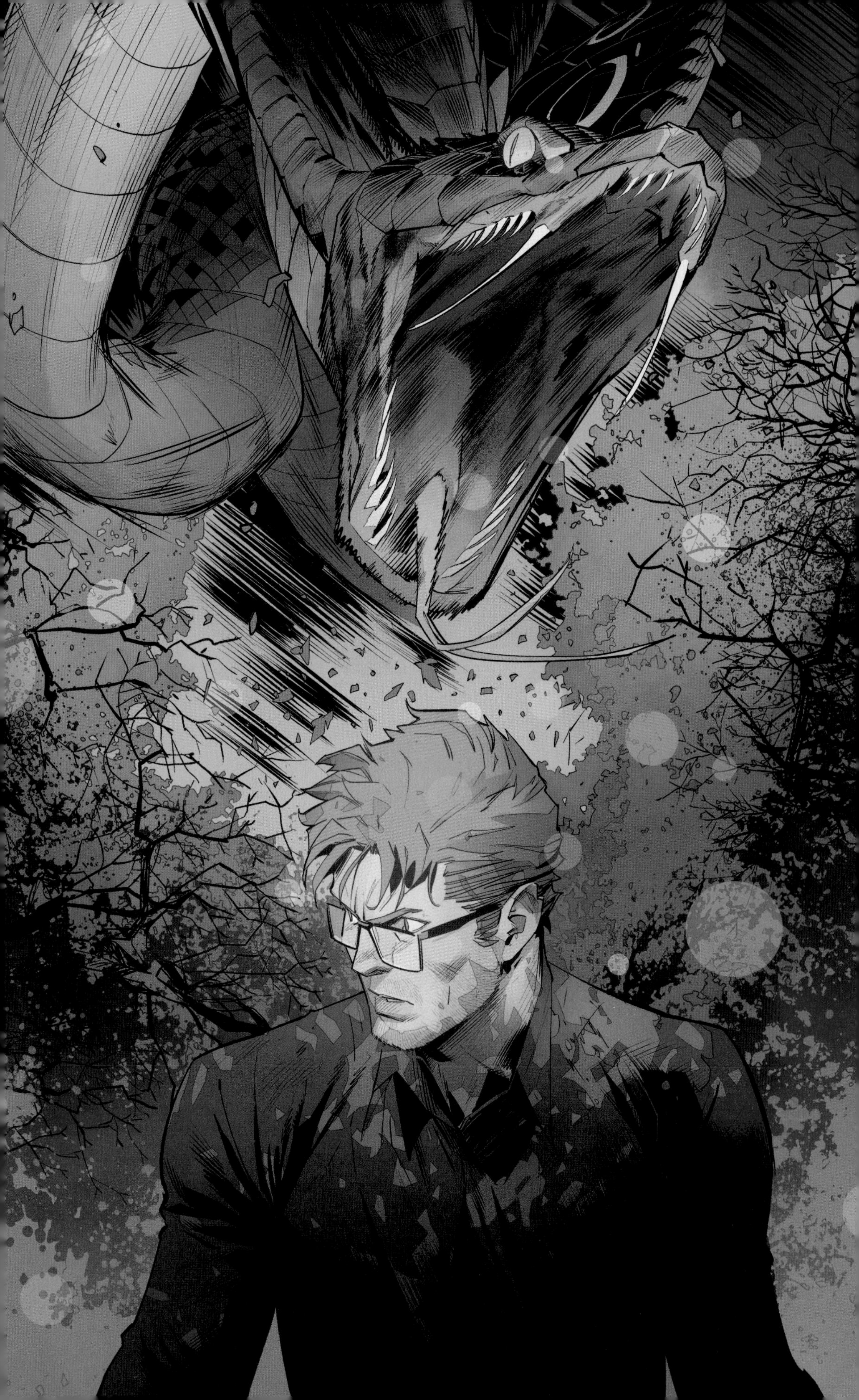

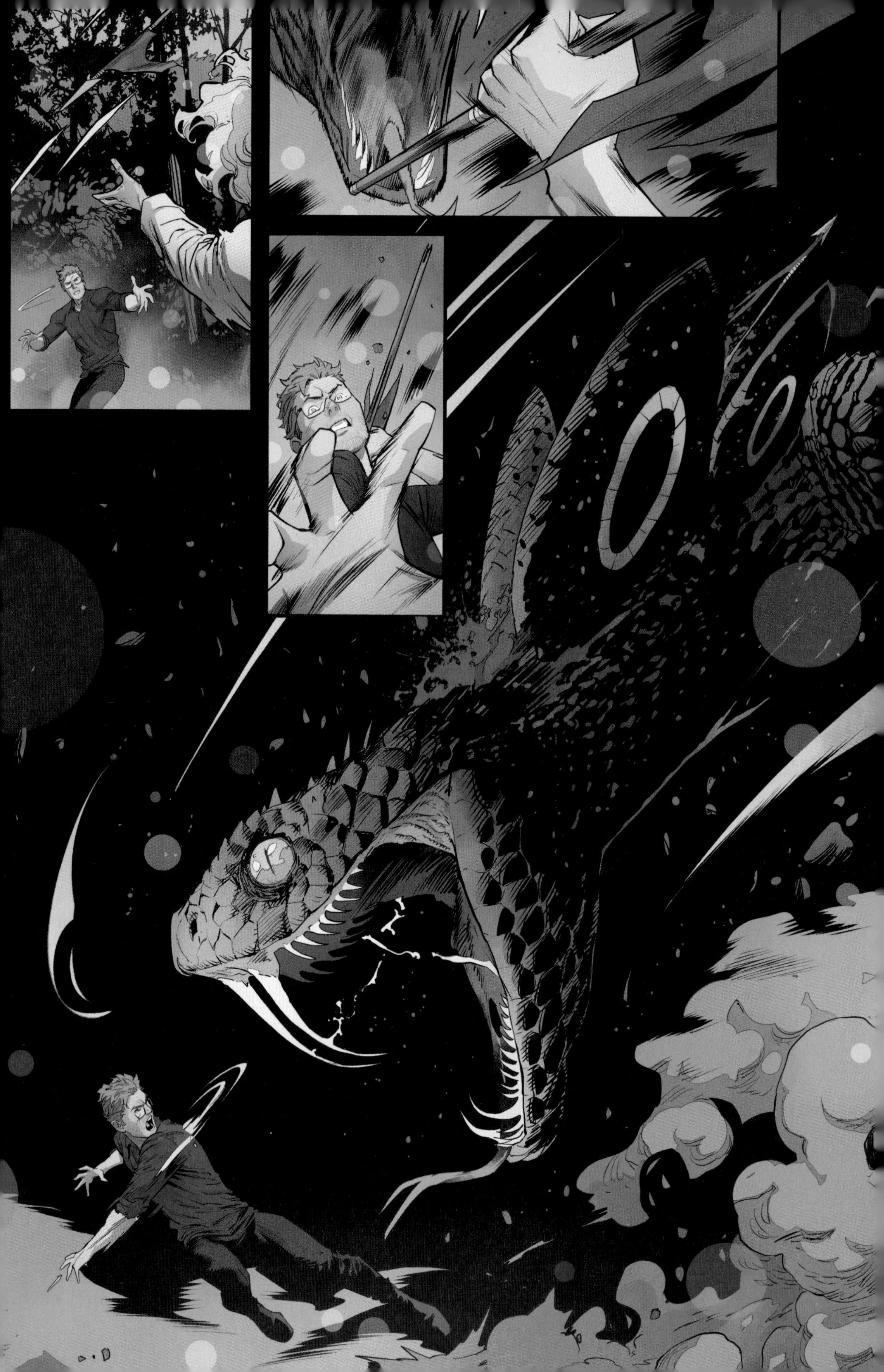

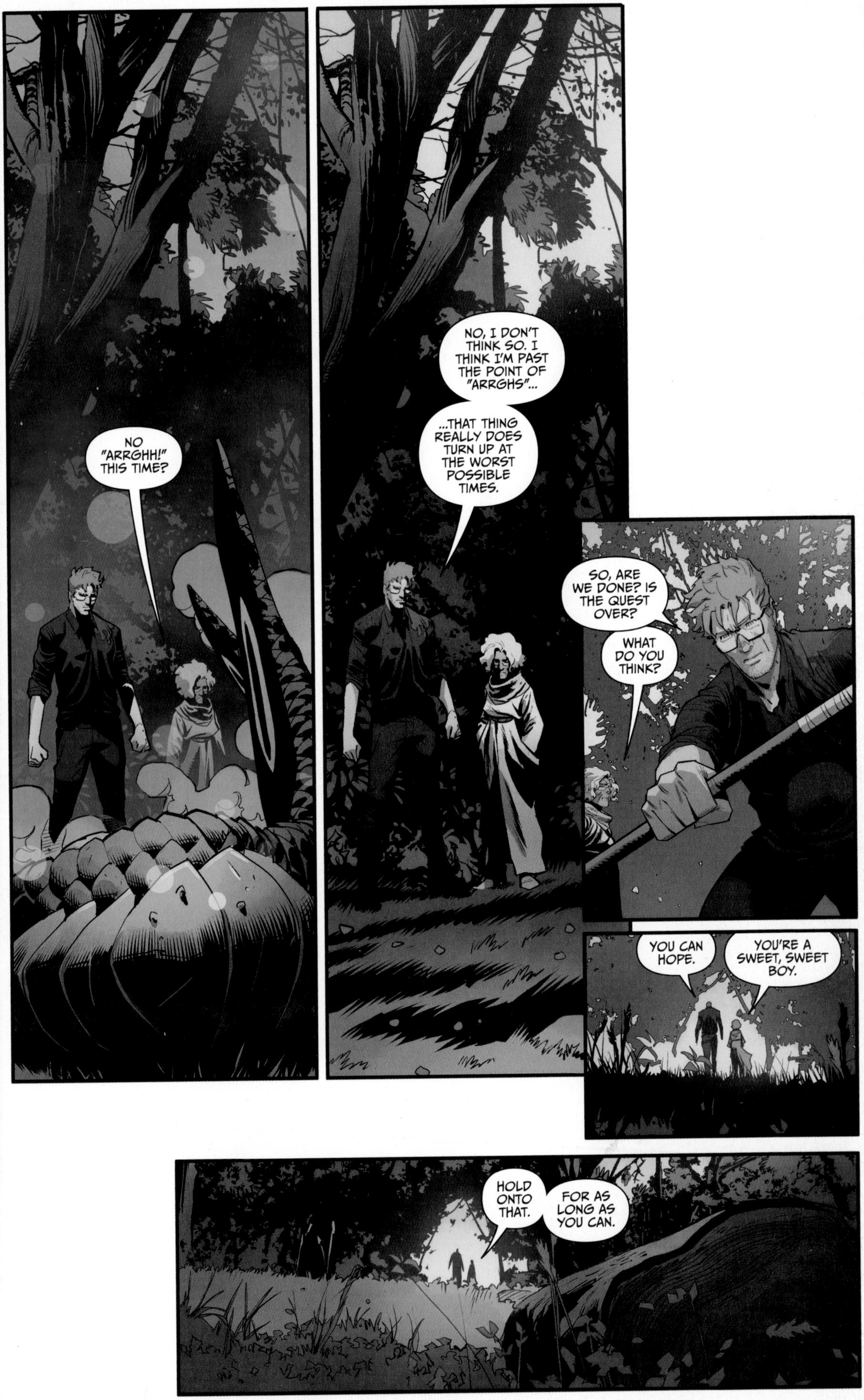
NO "ARRGHH!" THIS TIME?
NO, I DON'T THINK SO. I THINK I'M PAST THE POINT OF "ARRGHS"...
...THAT THING REALLY DOES TURN UP AT THE WORST POSSIBLE TIMES.
SO, ARE WE DONE? IS THE QUEST OVER?
WHAT DO YOU THINK?
YOU CAN HOPE.
YOU'RE A SWEET, SWEET BOY.
HOLD ONTO THAT.
FOR AS LONG AS YOU CAN.

ONCE & FUTURE ™

THE KING IS UNDEAD

GILLEN

MORA

BONVILLAIN

DUKESHIRE

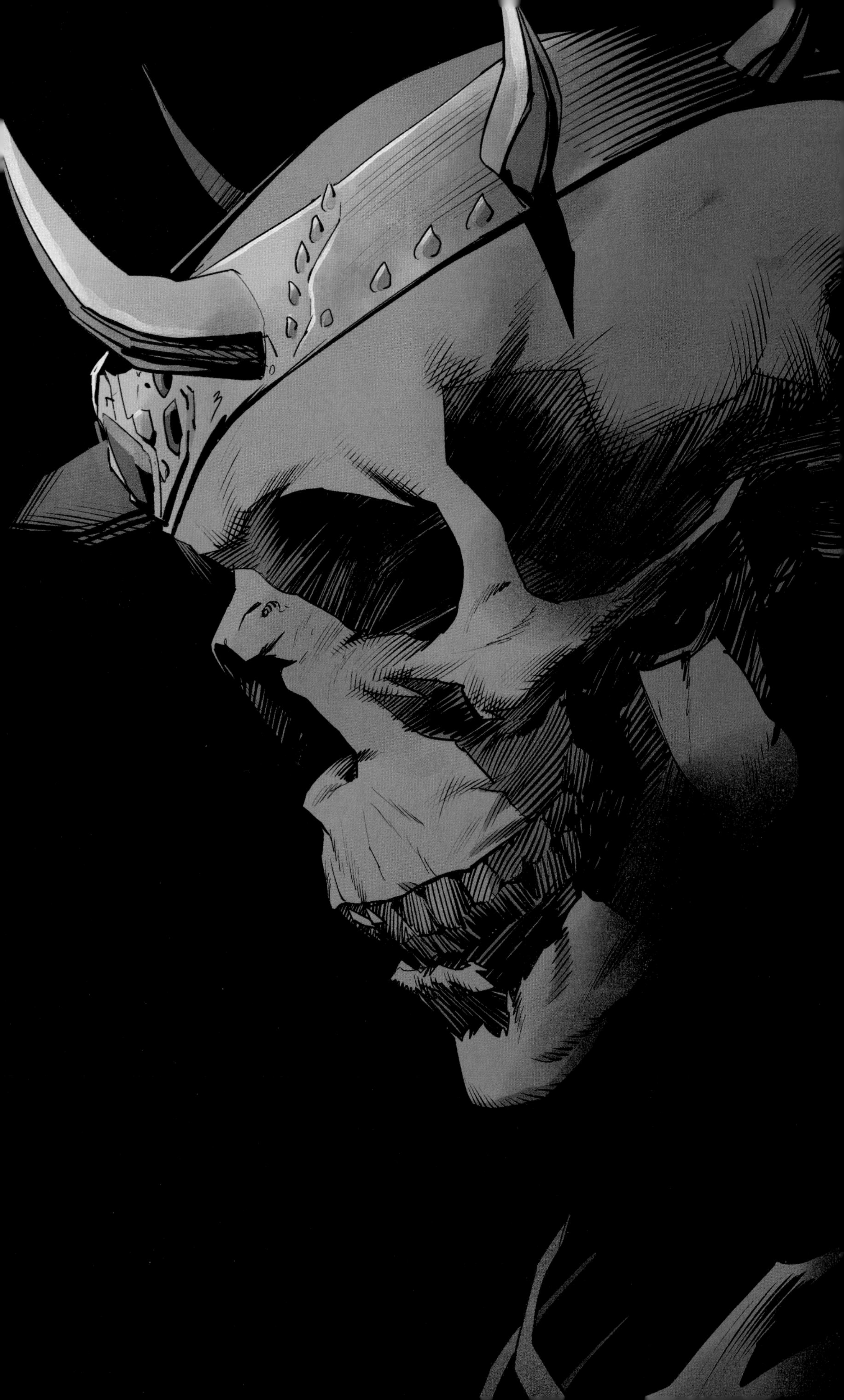

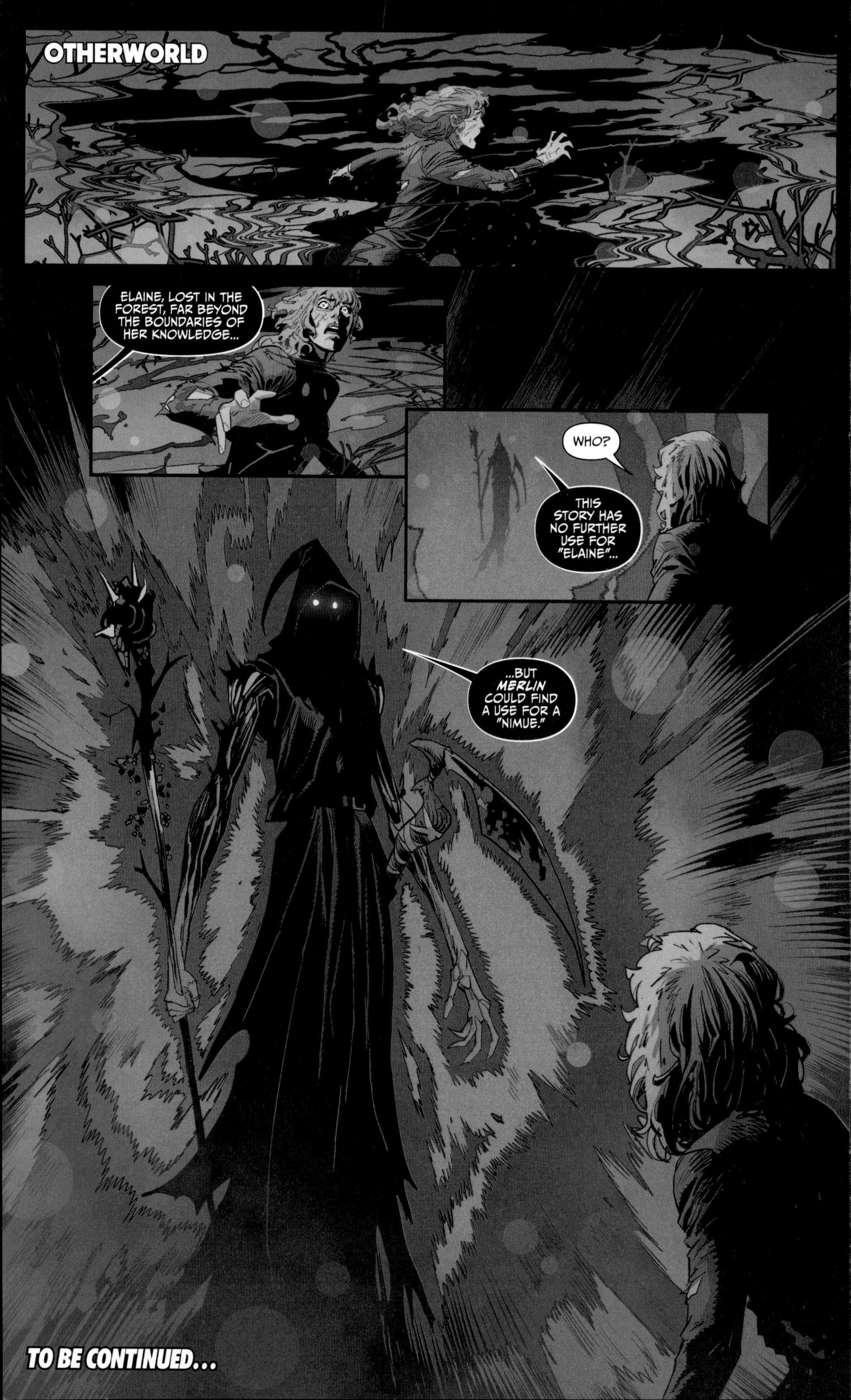
OTHERWORLD
ELAINE, LOST IN THE FOREST, FAR BEYOND THE BOUNDARIES OF HER KNOWLEDGE...
WHO?
THIS STORY HAS NO FURTHER USE FOR "ELAINE"...
...BUT MERLIN COULD FIND A USE FOR A "NIMUE."
TO BE CONTINUED...

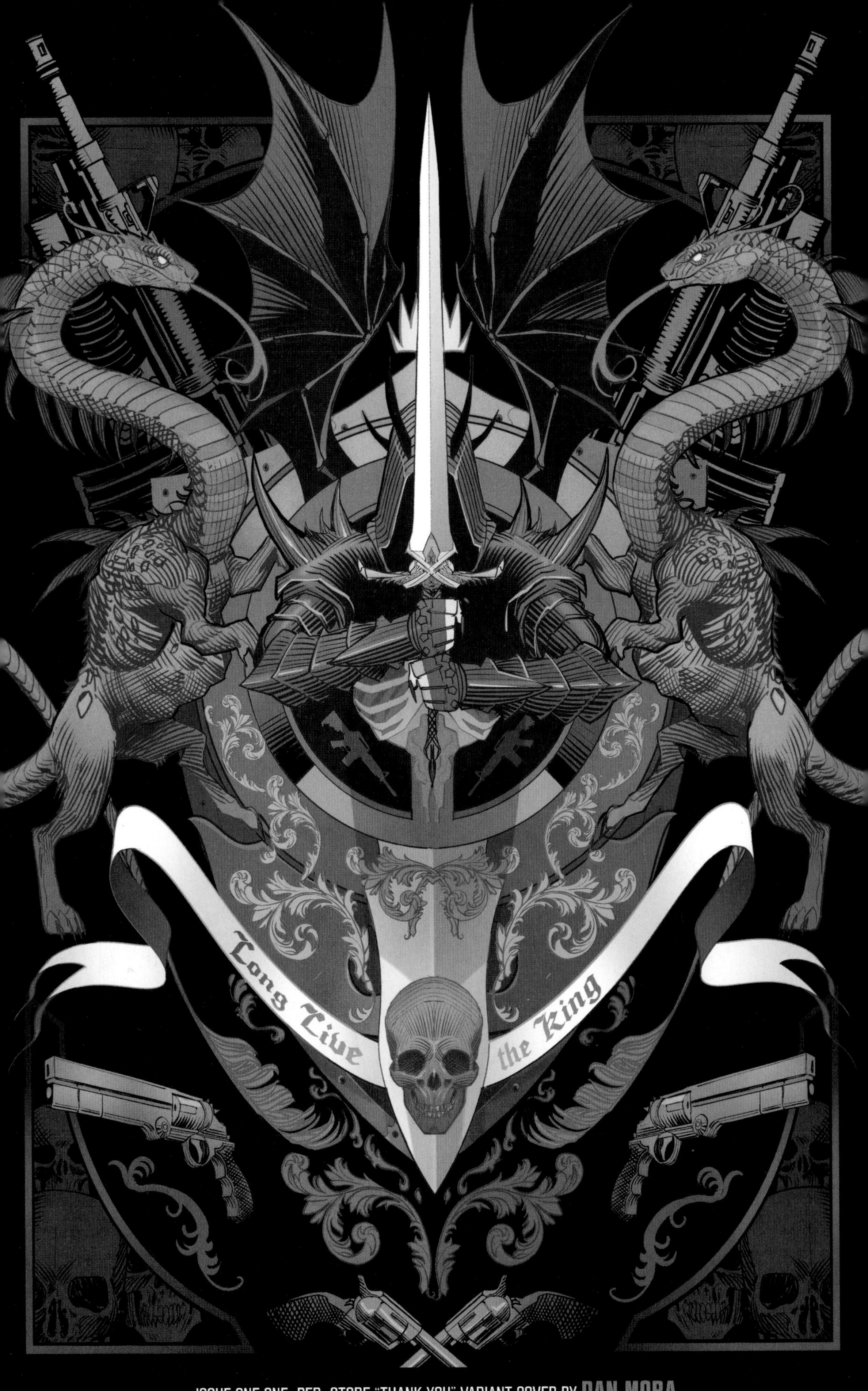
Long Live the King

ISSUE ONE ONE-PER-STORE "THANK YOU" VARIANT COVER BY **DAN MORA**

COVER GALLERY

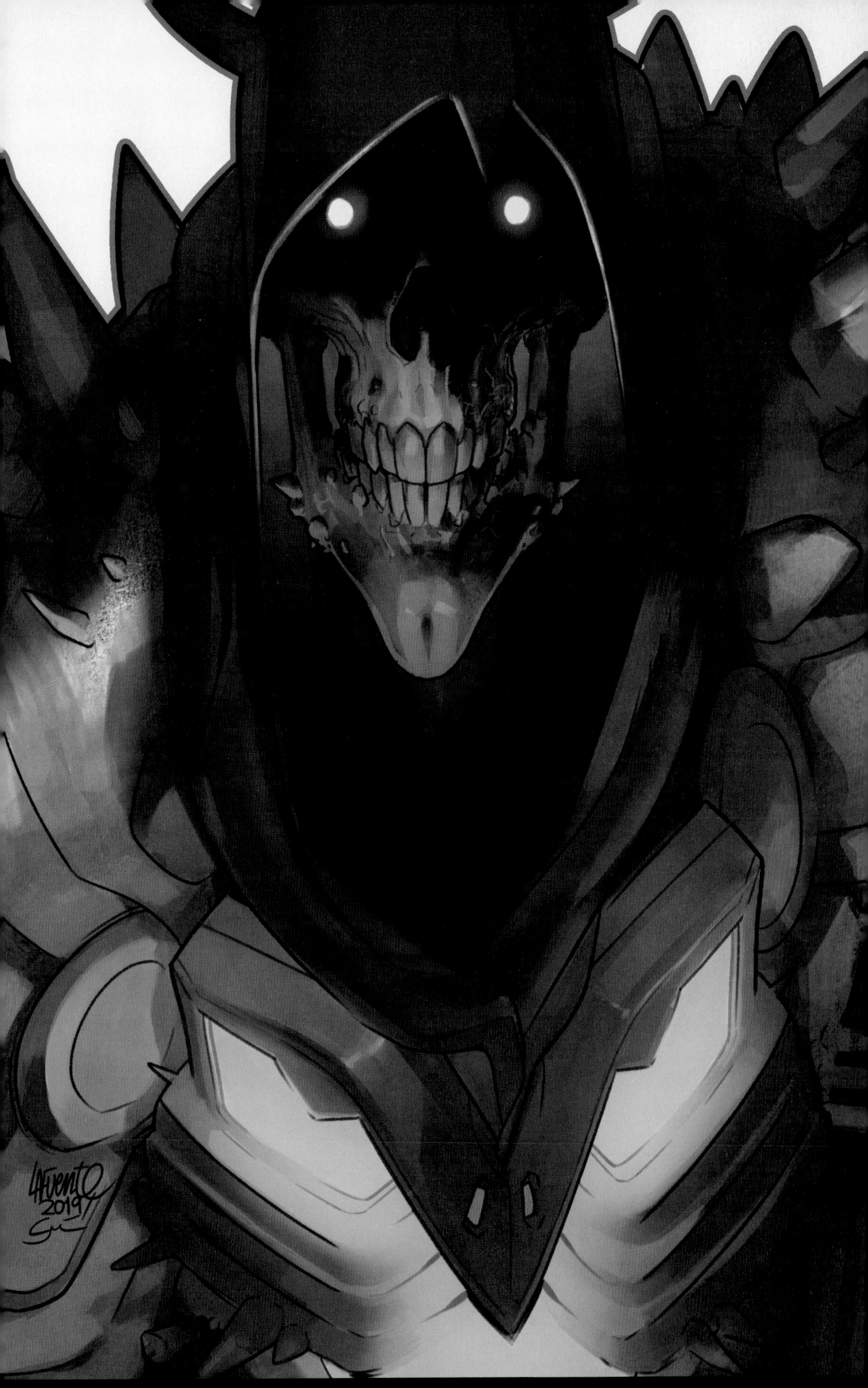
LAFUENTE
2019

ISSUE ONE FORBIDDEN PLANET AND JETPACK COMICS EXCLUSIVE VARIANT COVER BY DAVID LAFUENTE WITH COLORS BY GERMÁN GARCÍA

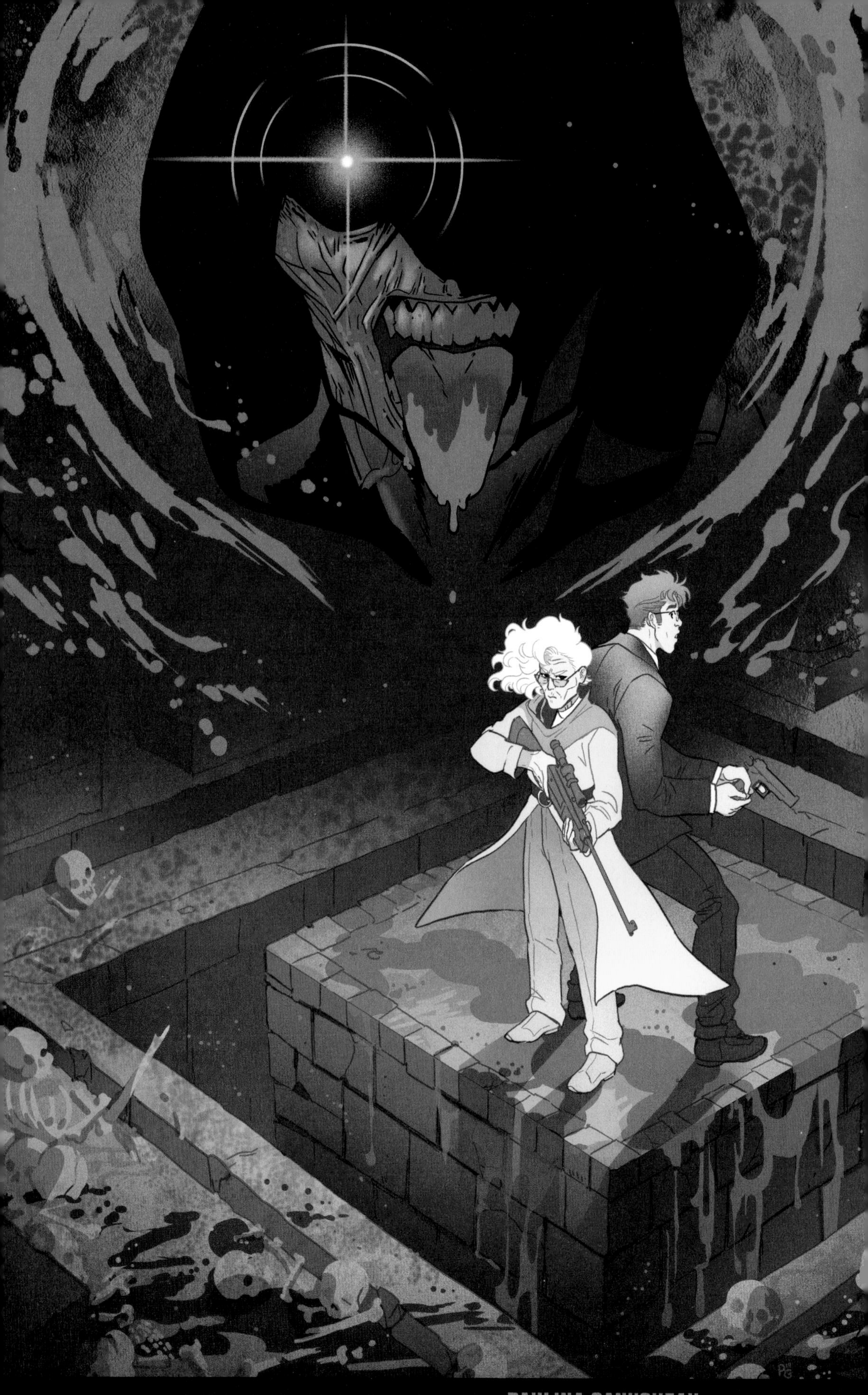

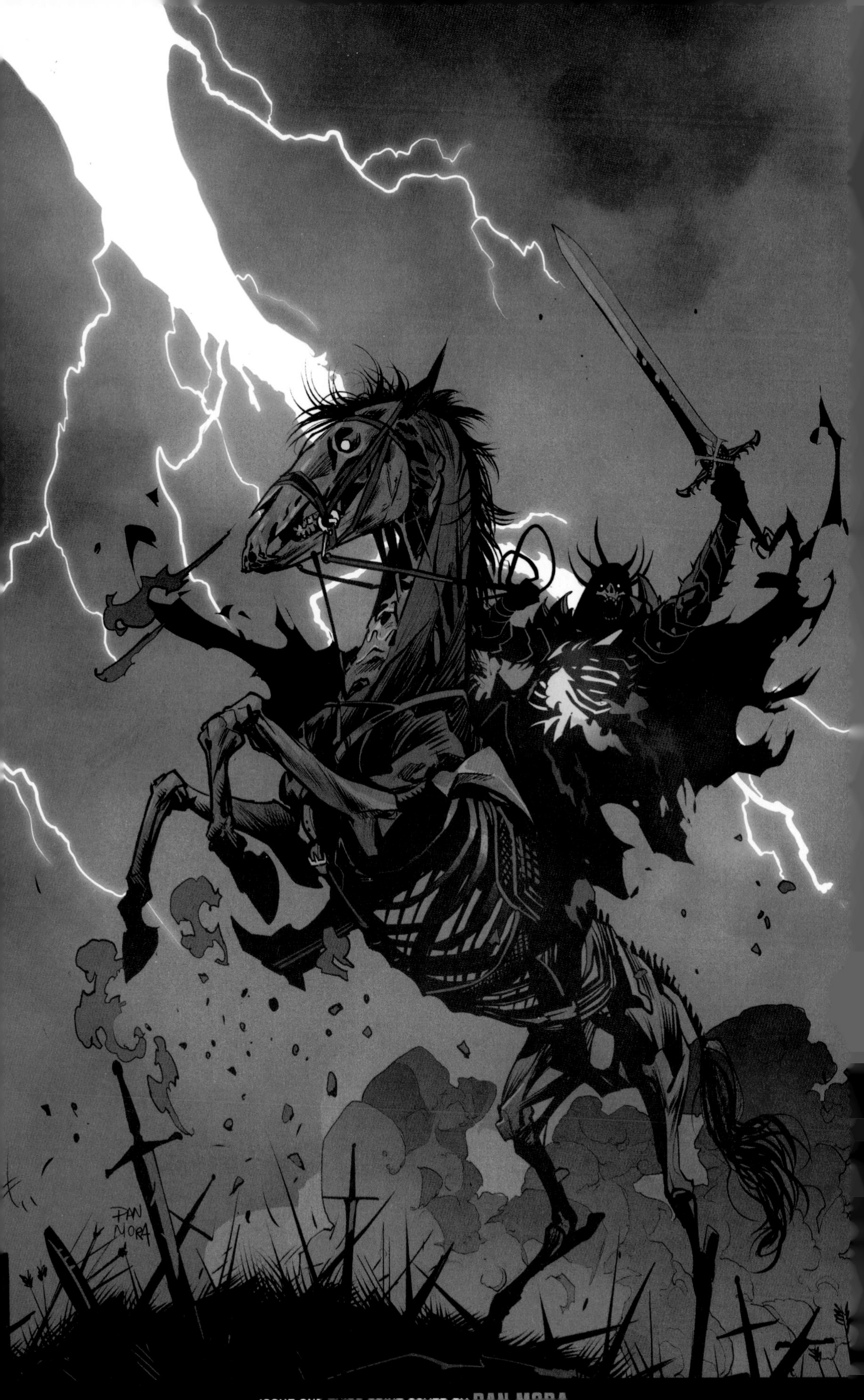
DAN MORA

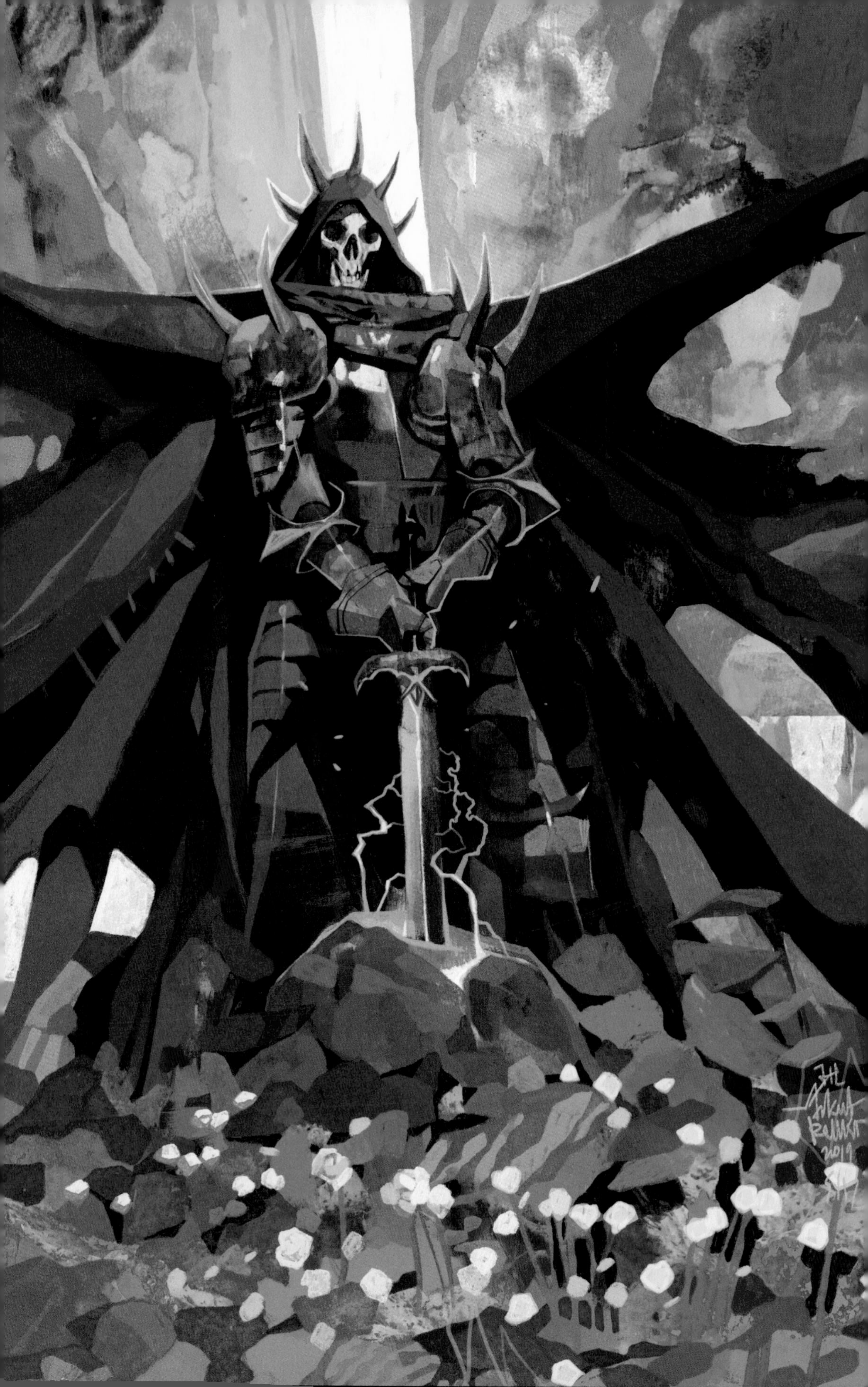

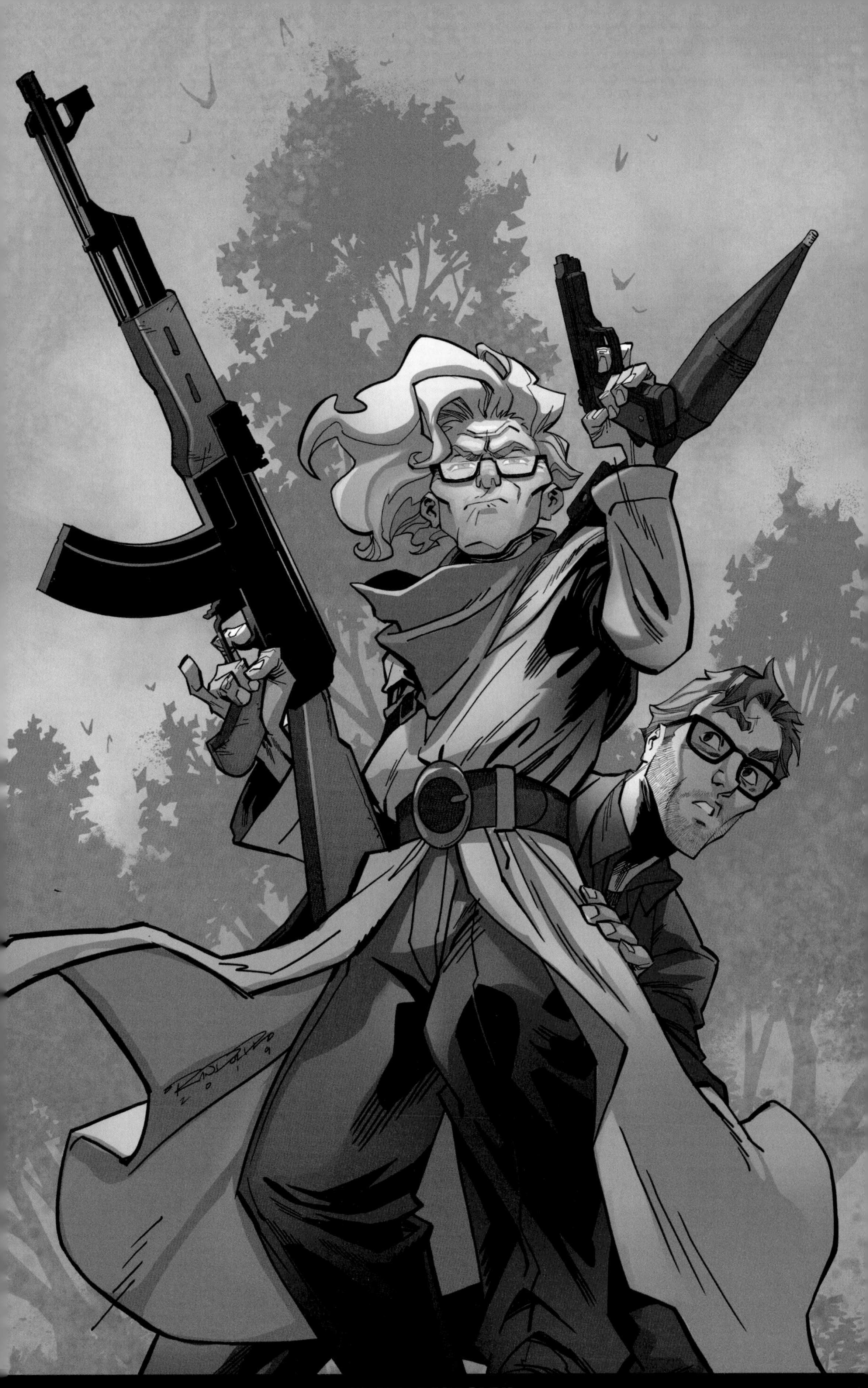

ISSUE ONE FIFTH PRINT COVER BY **KHARY RANDOLPH** WITH COLORS BY **RAÚL ANGULO**

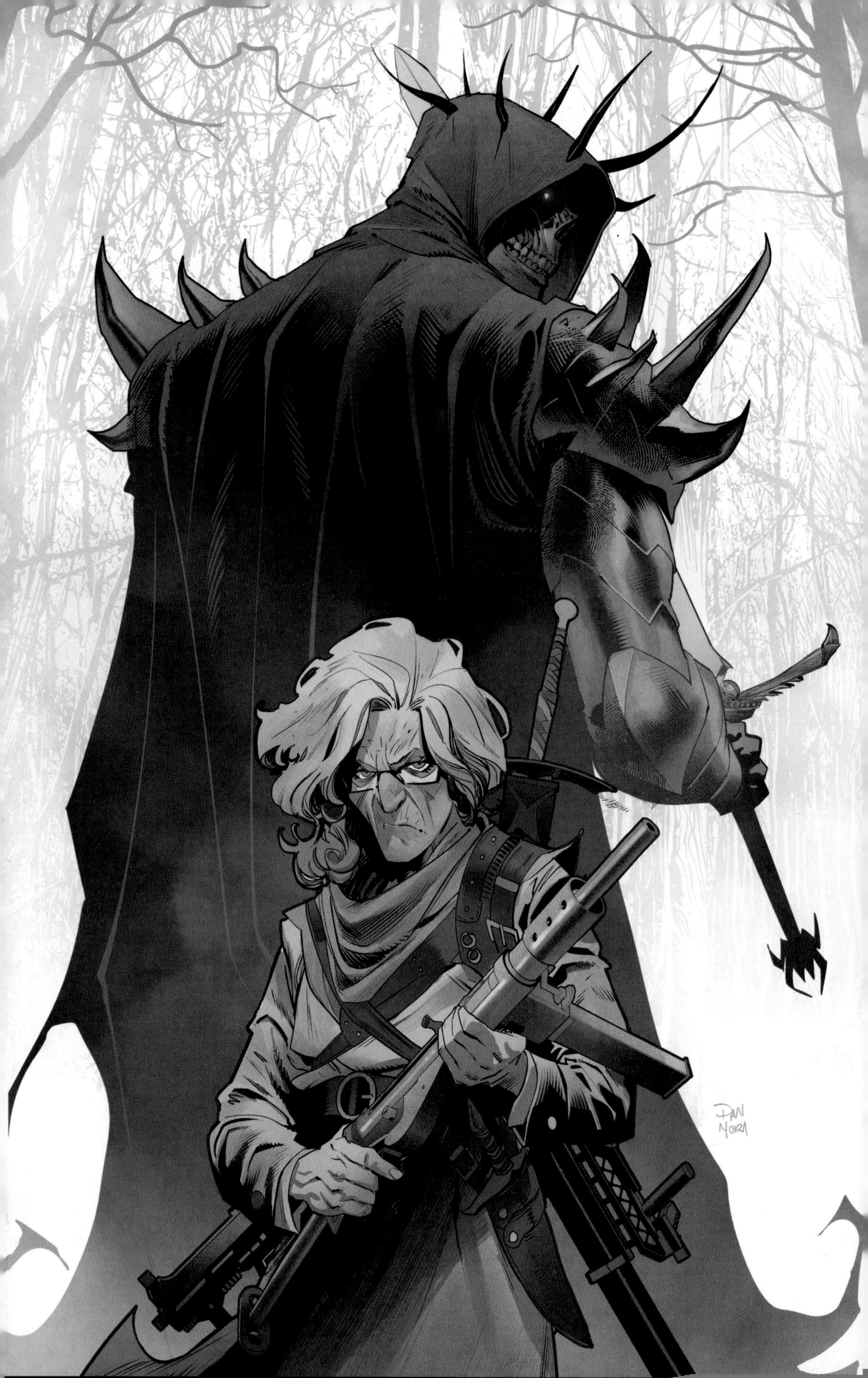
DAN
MORA

BAYLISS

AFTER
STEVE
BISSETTE

DANIEL BAYLISS

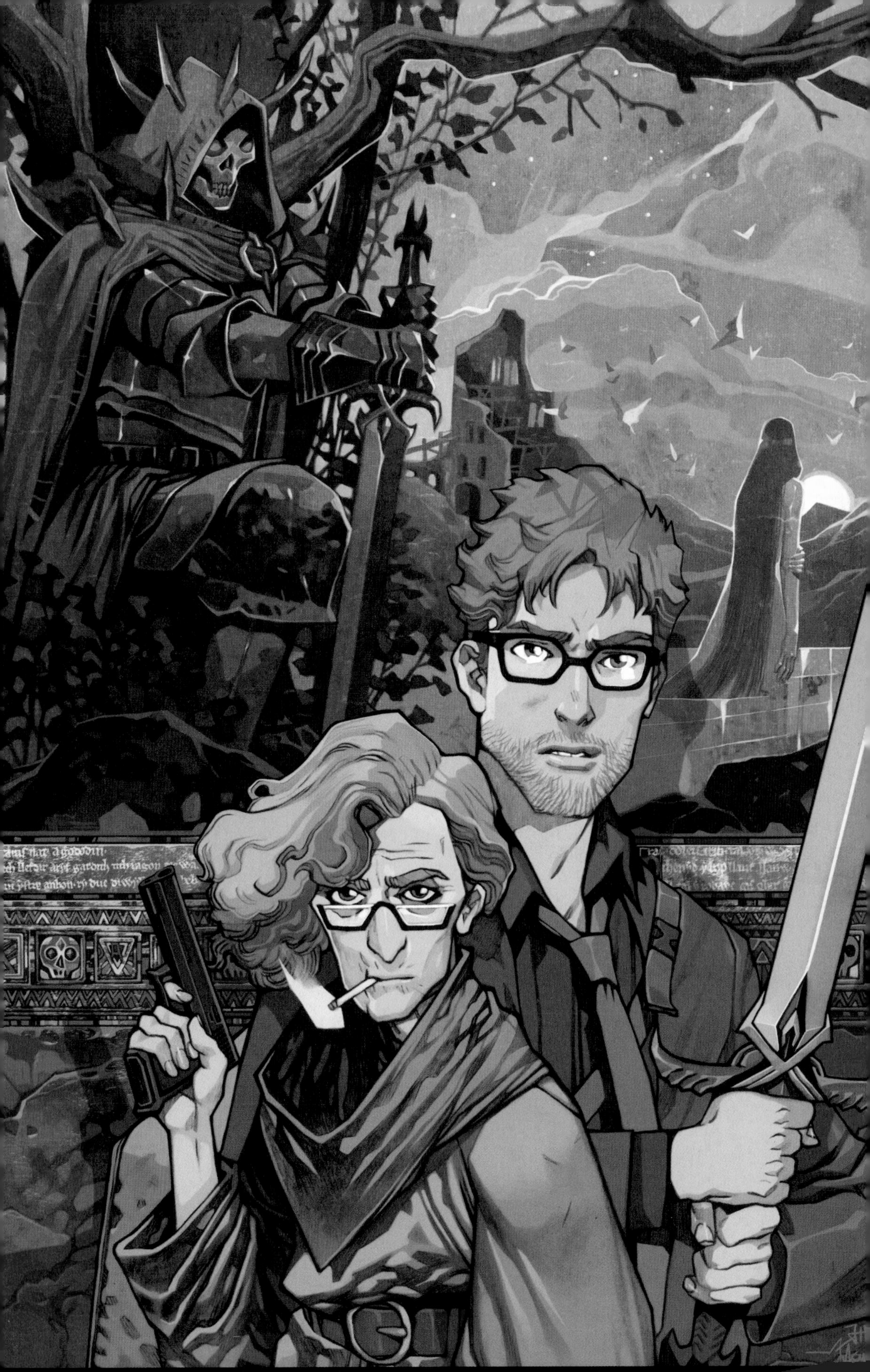

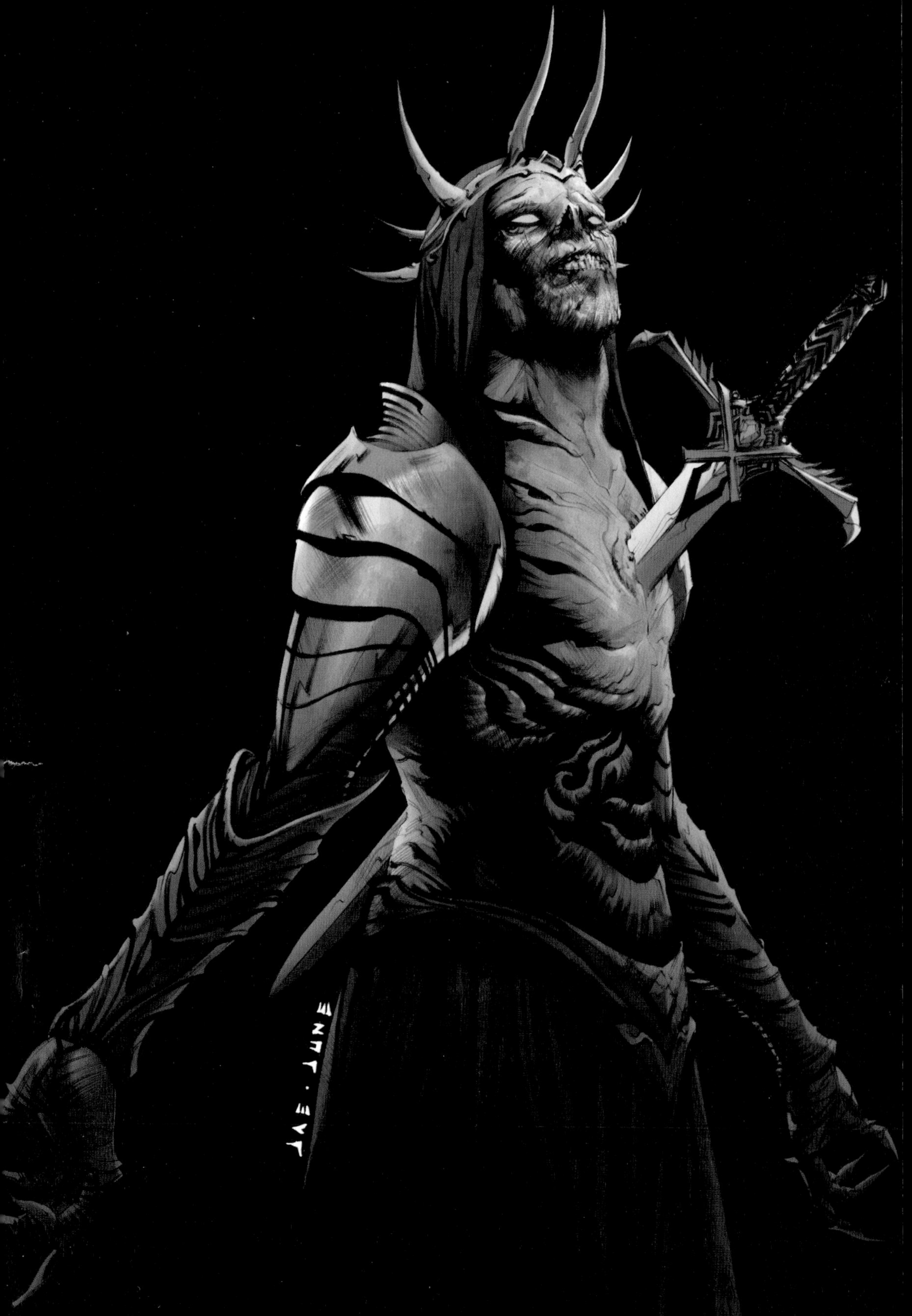

ISSUE TWO THIRD PRINT COVER BY **JAE LEE** AND **JUNE CHUNG**

DISCOVER
VISIONARY CREATORS

THE WOODS
JAMES TYNION IV • MICHAEL DIALYNAS
VOL 1
THE ARROW

"The Spire is fantastic! My kind of genre free-for-all."
—BRIAN K. VAUGHAN (Saga)
THE SPIRE
SIMON SPURRIER
JEFF STOKELY
ANDRÉ MAY

MARK WAID • PETER KRAUSE
IRREDEEMABLE
AFTERWORD BY GRANT MORRISON

MARK WAID • JEAN DIAZ
INCORRUPTIBLE

MICHAEL ALAN NELSON
DAN MORA
GABRIEL CASSATA
HEXED
THE HARLOT & THE THIEF VOLUME ONE

ABNETT & CULBARD
WILD'S END
FIRST LIGHT
"IT'S REALLY GREAT!"
JEFF LEMIRE

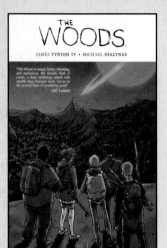

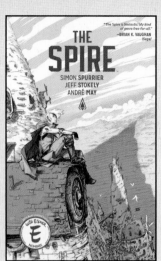

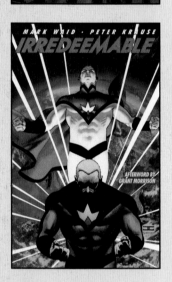

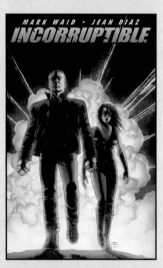

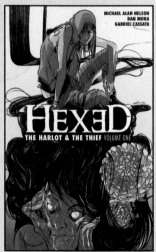

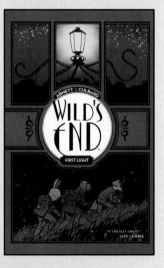

James Tynion IV
The Woods
Volume 1
ISBN: 978-1-60886-454-6 | $9.99 US
Volume 2
ISBN: 978-1-60886-495-9 | $14.99 US
Volume 3
ISBN: 978-1-60886-773-8 | $14.99 US

The Backstagers
Volume 1
ISBN: 978-1-60886-993-0 | $14.99 US

Simon Spurrier
Six-Gun Gorilla
ISBN: 978-1-60886-390-7 | $19.99 US

The Spire
ISBN: 978-1-60886-913-8 | $29.99 US

Weavers
ISBN: 978-1-60886-963-3 | $19.99 US

Mark Waid
Irredeemable
Volume 1
ISBN: 978-1-93450-690-5 | $16.99 US
Volume 2
ISBN: 978-1-60886-000-5 | $16.99 US

Incorruptible
Volume 1
ISBN: 978-1-60886-015-9 | $16.99 US
Volume 2
ISBN: 978-1-60886-028-9 | $16.99 US

Michael Alan Nelson
Hexed The Harlot & The Thief
Volume 1
ISBN: 978-1-60886-718-9 | $14.99 US
Volume 2
ISBN: 978-1-60886-816-2 | $14.99 US

Day Men
Volume 1
ISBN: 978-1-60886-393-8 | $9.99 US
Volume 2
ISBN: 978-1-60886-852-0 | $9.99 US

Dan Abnett
Wild's End
Volume 1: First Light
ISBN: 978-1-60886-735-6 | $19.99 US
Volume 2: The Enemy Within
ISBN: 978-1-60886-877-3 | $19.99 US

Hypernaturals
Volume 1
ISBN: 978-1-60886-298-6 | $16.99 US
Volume 2
ISBN: 978-1-60886-319-8 | $19.99 US

BOOM! STUDIOS™

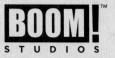

AVAILABLE AT YOUR LOCAL COMICS SHOP AND BOOKSTORE
To find a comics shop in your area, visit www.comicshoplocator.com
WWW.**BOOM-STUDIOS**.COM